I0124783

Samuel Taylor Coleridge, Ernest Hartley Coleridge

Letters of Ernest Hartley Coleridge

Edited by Ernest Hartley Coleridge. Vol. 1

Samuel Taylor Coleridge, Ernest Hartley Coleridge

Letters of Ernest Hartley Coleridge
Edited by Ernest Hartley Coleridge. Vol. 1

ISBN/EAN: 9783744688413

Printed in Europe, USA, Canada, Australia, Japan

Cover: Foto ©Thomas Meinert / pixelio.de

More available books at **www.hansebooks.com**

LETTERS

OF

SAMUEL TAYLOR COLERIDGE

EDITED BY

ERNEST HARTLEY COLERIDGE

IN TWO VOLUMES
VOL. I

LONDON
WILLIAM HEINEMANN
1895

[*All rights reserved.*]

The Riverside Press, Cambridge, Mass., U. S. A.
Printed by H. O. Houghton and Company.

INTRODUCTION

HITHERTO no attempt has been made to publish a collection of Coleridge's Letters. A few specimens were published in his lifetime, both in his own works and in magazines, and, shortly after his death in 1834, a large number appeared in print. Allsop's "Letters, Conversations, and Recollections of S. T. Coleridge," which was issued in 1836, contains forty-five letters or parts of letters; Cottle in his "Early Recollections" (1837) prints, for the most part incorrectly, and in piecemeal, some sixty in all, and Gillman, in his "Life of Coleridge" (1838), contributes, among others, some letters addressed to himself, and one, of the greatest interest, to Charles Lamb. In 1847, a series of early letters to Thomas Poole appeared for the first time in the Biographical Supplement to the "Biographia Literaria," and in 1848, when Cottle reprinted his "Early Recollections," under the title of "Reminiscences of Coleridge and Southey," he included sixteen letters to Thomas and Josiah Wedgwood. In Southey's posthumous "Life of Dr. Bell," five letters of Coleridge lie imbedded, and in "Southey's Life and Correspondence" (1849-50), four of his letters find an appropriate place. An interesting series was published in 1858 in the "Fragmentary Remains of Sir H. Davy," edited by his brother, Dr. Davy; and in the "Diary of H. C. Robinson," published in 1869, a few letters from Coleridge are interspersed. In 1870, the late Mr. W. Mark W. Call printed in the "Westminster Review" eleven letters from Coleridge to Dr. Brabant of Devizes,

dated 1815 and 1816; and a series of early letters to
Godwin, 1800–1811 (some of which had appeared in
"Macmillan's Magazine" in 1864), was included by Mr.
Kegan Paul in his "William Godwin" (1876). In 1874,
a correspondence between Coleridge (1816–1818) and his
publishers, Gale & Curtis, was contributed to "Lippin-
cott's Magazine," and in 1878, a few letters to Matilda
Betham were published in "Fraser's Magazine." During
the last six years the vast store which still remained unpublished has been drawn upon for various memoirs and
biographies. The following works containing new letters
are given in order of publication: Herr Brandl's "Samuel
T. Coleridge and the English Romantic School," 1887;
"Memorials of Coleorton," edited by Professor Knight,
1887; "Thomas Poole and his Friends," by Mrs. H. Sandford, 1888; "Life of Wordsworth," by Professor Knight,
1889; "Memoirs of John Murray," by Samuel Smiles,
LL. D., 1891; "De Quincey Memorials," by Alex. Japp,
LL. D., 1891; "Life of Washington Allston," 1893.

Notwithstanding these heavy draughts, more than half
of the letters which have come under my notice remain
unpublished. Of more than forty which Coleridge wrote
to his wife, only one has been published. Of ninety letters
to Southey which are extant, barely a tenth have seen the
light. Of nineteen addressed to W. Sotheby, poet and
patron of poets, fourteen to Lamb's friend John Rickman, and four to Coleridge's old ·college friend, Archdeacon Wrangham, none have been published. Of more
than forty letters addressed to the Morgan family, which
belong for the most part to the least known period of
Coleridge's life, — the years which intervened between his
residence in Grasmere and his final settlement at Highgate, — only two or three, preserved in the MSS. Depart-
ment of the British Museum, have been published. Of
numerous letters written in later life to his friend and
amanuensis, Joseph Henry Green; to Charles Augustus

Tulk, M. P. for Sudbury; to his friends and hosts, the
Gillmans; to Cary, the translator of Dante, only a few
have found their way into print. Of more than forty to
his brother, the Rev. George Coleridge, which were accidentally discovered in 1876, only five have been printed.
Of some fourscore letters addressed to his nephews, William Hart Coleridge, John Taylor Coleridge, Henry Nelson Coleridge, Edward Coleridge, and to his son Derwent,
all but two, or at most three, remain in manuscript. Of
the youthful letters to the Evans family, one letter has
recently appeared in the " Illustrated London News," and
of the many addressed to John Thelwall, but one was
printed in the same series.

The letters to Poole, of which more than a hundred
have been preserved, those addressed to his Bristol friend,
Josiah Wade, and the letters to Wordsworth, which, though
few in number, are of great length, have been largely used
for biographical purposes, but much, of the highest interest, remains unpublished. Of smaller groups of letters,
published and unpublished, I make no detailed mention,
but in the latter category are two to Charles Lamb, one
to John Sterling, five to George Cattermole, one to John
Kenyon, and many others to more obscure correspondents.
Some important letters to Lord Jeffrey, to John Murray,
to De Quincey, to Hugh James Rose, and to J. H. B.
Williams, have, in the last few years, been placed in my
hands for transcription.

A series of letters written between the years 1796 and
1814 to the Rev. John Prior Estlin, minister of the
Unitarian Chapel at Lewin's Mead, Bristol, was printed
some years ago for the Philobiblon Society, with an introduction by Mr. Henry A. Bright. One other series of
letters has also been printed for private circulation. In
1889, the late Miss Stuart placed in my hands transcrip-
tions of eighty-seven letters addressed by Coleridge to her
father, Daniel Stuart, editor of " The Morning Post " and

" Courier," and these, together with letters from Wordsworth and Southey, were printed in a single volume bearing the title, " Letters from the Lake Poets." Miss
Stuart contributed a short account of her father's life,
and also a reminiscence of Coleridge, headed " A Farewell."

Coleridge's biographers, both of the past and present
generations, have met with a generous response to their
appeal for letters to be placed in their hands for reference
and for publication, but it is probable that many are in
existence which have been withheld, sometimes no doubt
intentionally, but more often from inadvertence. From
his boyhood the poet was a voluminous if an irregular
correspondent, and many letters which he is known to
have addressed to his earliest friends — to Middleton, to
Robert Allen, to Valentine and Sam Le Grice, to Charles
Lloyd, to his Stowey neighbour, John Cruikshank, to Dr.
Beddoes, and others — may yet be forthcoming. It is
certain that he corresponded with Mrs. Clarkson, but if
any letters have been preserved they have not come under
my notice. It is strange, too, that among the letters of
the Highgate period, which were sent to Henry Nelson
Coleridge for transcription, none to John Hookham Frere,
to Blanco White, or to Edward Irving appear to have
been forthcoming.

The foregoing summary of published and unpublished
letters, though necessarily imperfect, will enable the
reader to form some idea of the mass of material from
which the present selection has been made. A complete
edition of Coleridge's Letters must await the " coming
of the milder day," a renewed long-suffering on the part
of his old enemy, the " literary public." In the mean-
while, a selection from some of the more important is
here offered in the belief that many, if not all, will find
a place in permanent literature. The letters are arranged
in chronological order, and are intended rather to illus-

trate the story of the writer's life than to embody his
critical opinions, or to record the development of his philosophical and theological speculations. But letters of
a purely literary character have not been excluded, and
in selecting or rejecting a letter, the sole criterion has
been, Is it interesting? is it readable?

In letter-writing perfection of style is its own recommendation, and long after the substance of a letter has
lost its savour, the form retains its original or, it may be,
an added charm. Or if the author be the founder of a
sect or a school, his writings, in whatever form, are received by the initiated with unquestioning and insatiable
delight. But Coleridge's letters lack style. The fastidious critic who touched and retouched his exquisite lyrics,
and always for the better, was at no pains to polish his
letters. He writes to his friends as if he were talking to
them, and he lets his periods take care of themselves.
Nor is there any longer a school of reverent disciples to
receive what the master gives and because he gives it.
His influence as a teacher has passed into other channels,
and he is no longer regarded as the oracular sage "ques-
tionable" concerning all mysteries. But as a poet, as a
great literary critic, and as a "master of sentences," he
holds his own and appeals to the general ear; and though,
since his death, in 1834, a second generation has all but
passed away, an unwonted interest in the man himself
survives and must always survive. For not only, as
Wordsworth declared, was he "a wonderful man," but
the story of his life was a strange one, and as he tells it,
we "cannot choose but hear." Coleridge, often to his
own detriment, "wore his heart on his sleeve," and, now
to one friend, now to another, sometimes to two or three
friends on the same day, he would seek to unburthen
himself of his hopes and fears, his thoughts and fancies,
his bodily sufferings, and the keener pangs of the soul.
It is, to quote his own words, these "profound touches of

the human heart " which command our interest in Coleridge's Letters, and invest them with their peculiar
charm.

At what period after death, and to what extent the private letters of a celebrated person should be given to the
world, must always remain an open question both of taste
and of morals. So far as Coleridge is concerned, the
question was decided long ago. Within a few years of
his death, letters of the most private and even painful
character were published without the sanction and in spite
of the repeated remonstrances of his literary executor, and
of all who had a right to be heard on the subject. Thence-
forth, as the published writings of his immediate descend-
ants testify, a fuller and therefore a fairer revelation was
steadily contemplated. Letters collected for this purpose
find a place in the present volume, but the selection has
been made without reference to previous works or to any
final presentation of the material at the editor's disposal.

My acknowledgments are due to many still living, and
to others who have passed away, for their generous permission to print unpublished letters, which remained in
their possession or had passed into their hands.

For the continued use of the long series of letters which
Poole entrusted to Coleridge's literary executor in 1836,
I have to thank Mrs. Henry Sandford and the Bishop of
Gibraltar. For those addressed to the Evans family I am
indebted to Mr. Alfred Morrison of Fonthill. The letters to Thelwall were placed in my hands by the late Mr.
F. W. Cosens, who afforded me every facility for their
transcription. For those to Wordsworth my thanks are
due to the poet's grandsons, Mr. William and Mr. Gor-
don Wordsworth. Those addressed to the Gillmans I
owe to the great kindness of their granddaughter, Mrs.
Henry Watson, who placed in my hands all the materials
at her disposal. For the right to publish the letters to
H. F. Cary I am indebted to my friend the Rev. Offley

Cary, the grandson of the translator of Dante. My acknowledgments are further due to the late Mr. John Murray for the right to republish letters which appeared in the "Memoirs of John Murray," and two others which were not included in that work ; and to Mrs. Watt, the daughter of John Hunter of Craigcrook, for letters addressed to Lord Jeffrey. From the late Lord Houghton I received permission to publish the letters to the Rev. J. P. Estlin, which were privately printed for the Philobiblon Society. I have already mentioned my obligations to the late Miss Stuart of Harley Street.

For the use of letters addressed to his father and grandfather, and for constant and unwearying advice and assistance in this work I am indebted, more than I can well express, to the late Lord Coleridge. Alas! I can only record my gratitude.

To Mr. William Rennell Coleridge of Salston, Ottery St. Mary, my especial thanks are due for the interesting collection of unpublished letters, many of them relating to the "Army Episode," which the poet wrote to his brother, the Rev. George Coleridge.

I have also to thank Miss Edith Coleridge for the use of letters addressed to her father, Henry Nelson Coleridge; my cousin, Mrs. Thomas W. Martyn of Torquay, for Coleridge's letter to his mother, the earliest known to exist; and Mr. Arthur Duke Coleridge for one of the latest he ever wrote, that to Mrs. Aders.

During the preparation of this work I have received valuable assistance from men of letters and others. I trust that I may be permitted to mention the names of Mr. Leslie Stephen, Professor Knight, Mrs. Henry Sandford, Dr. Garnett of the British Museum, Professor Emile Legouis of Lyons, Mrs. Henry Watson, the Librarians of the Oxford and Cambridge Club, and of the Kensington Public Library, and Mrs. George Boyce of Chertsey.

Of my friend, Mr. Dykes Campbell, I can only say that

he has spared neither time nor trouble in my behalf. Not
only during the progress of the work has he been ready
to give me the benefit of his unrivalled knowledge of the
correspondence and history of Coleridge and of his contemporaries, but he has largely assisted me in seeing the
work through the press. For the selection of the letters,
or for the composition or accuracy of the notes, he must
not be held in any way responsible; but without his aid,
and without his counsel, much, which I hope has been accomplished, could never have been attempted at all. Of
the invaluable assistance which I have received from his
published works, the numerous references to his edition
of Coleridge's " Poetical Works" (Macmillan, 1893), and
his "Samuel Taylor Coleridge, A Narrative " (1894), are
sufficient evidence. Of my gratitude he needs no assurance.

ERNEST HARTLEY COLERIDGE.

PRINCIPAL EVENTS IN THE LIFE OF S. T. COLERIDGE

Born, October 21, 1772.

Death of his father, October 4, 1781.

Entered at Christ's Hospital, July 18, 1782.

Elected a "Grecian," 1788.

Discharged from Christ's Hospital, September 7, 1791.

Went into residence at Jesus College, Cambridge, October, 1791.

Enlisted in King's Regiment of Light Dragoons, December 2, 1793.

Discharged from the army, April 10, 1794.

Visit to Oxford and introduction to Southey, June, 1794.

Proposal to emigrate to America — Pantisocracy — Autumn, 1794.

Final departure from Cambridge, December, 1794.

Settled at Bristol as public lecturer, January, 1795.

Married to Sarah Fricker, October 4, 1795.

Publication of "Conciones ad Populum," Clevedon, November 16, 1795.

Pantisocrats dissolve — Rupture with Southey — November, 1795.

Publication of first edition of Poems, April, 1796.

Issue of "The Watchman," March 1–May 13, 1796.

Birth of Hartley Coleridge, September 19, 1796.

Settled at Nether-Stowey, December 31, 1796.

Publication of second edition of Poems, June, 1797.

Settlement of Wordsworth at Alfoxden, July 14, 1797.

The "Ancient Mariner" begun, November 13, 1797.

First part of "Christabel," begun, 1797.

Acceptance of annuity of £150 from J. and T. Wedgwood, January, 1798.

Went to Germany, September 16, 1798.

Returned from Germany, July, 1799.

First visit to Lake Country, October–November, 1799.

Began to write for "Morning Post," December, 1799.

Translation of Schiller's "Wallenstein," Spring, 1800.

Settled at Greta Hall, Keswick, July 24, 1800.

Birth of Derwent Coleridge, September 14, 1800.

Wrote second part of "Christabel," Autumn, 1800.

Began study of German metaphysics, 1801.

Birth of Sara Coleridge, December 23, 1802.

Publication of third edition of Poems, Summer, 1803.

Set out on Scotch tour, August 14, 1803.

Settlement of Southey at Greta Hall, September, 1803.

Sailed for Malta in the Speedwell, April 9, 1804.

Arrived at Malta, May 18, 1804.

First tour in Sicily, August–November, 1804.

Left Malta for Syracuse, September 21, 1805.

Residence in Rome, January–May, 1806.

Returned to England, August, 1806.

Visit to Wordsworth at Coleorton, December 21, 1806.

Met De Quincey at Bridgwater, July, 1807.

First lecture at Royal Institution, January 12, 1808.

Settled at Allan Bank, Grasmere, September, 1808.

First number of "The Friend," June 1, 1809.

Last number of "The Friend," March 15, 1810.

Left Greta Hall for London, October 10, 1810.

Settled at Hammersmith with the Morgans, November 3, 1810.

First lecture at London Philosophical Society, November 18, 1811.

Last visit to Greta Hall, February–March, 1812.

First lecture at Willis's Rooms, May 12, 1812.

First lecture at Surrey Institution, November 3, 1812.

Production of "Remorse" at Drury Lane, January 23, 1813.

Left London for Bristol, October, 1813.

First course of Bristol lectures, October–November, 1813.

Second course of Bristol lectures, December 30, 1813.

Third course of Bristol lectures, April, 1814.

Residence with Josiah Wade at Bristol, Summer, 1814.

Rejoined the Morgans at Ashley, September, 1814.

Accompanied the Morgans to Calne, November, 1814.

Settles with Mr. Gillman at Highgate, April 16, 1816.

Publication of "Christabel," June, 1816.

Publication of the "Statesman's Manual," December, 1816.

Publication of second "Lay Sermon," 1817.

Publication of "Biographia Literaria" and "Sibylline Leaves," 1817.

First acquaintance with Joseph Henry Green, 1817.

Publication of "Zapolya," Autumn, 1817.

First lecture at "Flower-de-Luce Court," January 27, 1818.

Publication of "Essay on Method," January, 1818.

Revised edition of "The Friend," Spring, 1818.

Introduction to Thomas Allsop, 1818.

First lecture on "History of Philosophy," December 14, 1818.

First lecture on "Shakespeare" (last course), December 17, 1818.

Last public lecture, "History of Philosophy," March 29, 1819.

Nominated "Royal Associate" of Royal Society of Literature, May, 1824.

Read paper to Royal Society on "Prometheus of Æschylus," May 15, 1825.

Publication of "Aids to Reflection," May–June, 1825.

Publication of "Poetical Works," in three volumes, 1828.

Tour on the Rhine with Wordsworth, June–July, 1828.

Revised issue of "Poetical Works," in three volumes, 1829.

Marriage of Sara Coleridge to Henry Nelson Coleridge, September 3, 1829.

Publication of "Church and State," 1830.

Visit to Cambridge, June, 1833.

Death, July 25, 1834.

PRINCIPAL AUTHORITIES REFERRED TO IN THESE VOLUMES

1. The Complete Works of Samuel Taylor Coleridge. New York: Harper and Brothers. 7 vols. 1853.

2. Biographia Literaria [etc.]. By S. T. Coleridge. Second edition, prepared for publication in part by the late H. N. Coleridge: completed and published by his widow. 2 vols. 1847.

3. Essays on His Own Times. By Samuel Taylor Coleridge. Edited by his daughter. London: William Pickering. 3 vols. 1850.

4. The Table Talk and Omniana of Samuel Taylor Coleridge. Edited by T. Ashe. George Bell and Sons. 1884.

5. Letters, Conversations, and Recollections of S. T. Coleridge. [Edited by Thomas Allsop. First edition published anonymously.] Moxon. 2 vols. 1836.

6. The Life of S. T. Coleridge, by James Gillman. In 2 vols. (Vol. I. only was published.) 1838.

7. Memorials of Coleorton: being Letters from Coleridge, Wordsworth and his sister, Southey, and Sir Walter Scott, to Sir George and Lady Beaumont of Coleorton, Leicestershire, 1803-1834. Edited by William Knight, University of St. Andrews. 2 vols. Edinburgh. 1887.

8. Unpublished Letters from S. T. Coleridge to the Rev. John Prior Estlin. Communicated by Henry A. Bright (to the Philobiblon Society). n. d.

9. Letters from the Lake Poets — S. T. Coleridge, William Wordsworth, Robert Southey — to Daniel Stuart, editor of *The Morning Post* and *The Courier*. 1800-1838. *Printed for private circulation*. 1889. [Edited by Mr. Ernest Hartley Coleridge, in whom the copyright of the letters of S. T. Coleridge is vested.]

10. The Poetical Works of Samuel Taylor Coleridge. Edited, with a Biographical Introduction, by James Dykes Campbell. London and New York: Macmillan and Co. 1893.

11. Samuel Taylor Coleridge. A Narrative of the Events of His Life. By James Dykes Campbell. London and New York: Macmillan and Co. 1894.

12. Early Recollections: chiefly relating to the late S. T. Coleridge, during his long residence in Bristol. 2 vols. By Joseph Cottle. 1837.

13. Reminiscences of S. T. Coleridge and R. Southey. By Joseph Cottle. 1847.

14. Fragmentary Remains, literary and scientific, of Sir Humphry Davy, Bart. Edited by his brother, John Davy, M. D. 1858.

15. The Autobiography of Leigh Hunt. London. 1860.

16. Diary, Reminiscences, and Correspondence of Henry Crabb Robinson. Selected and Edited by Thomas Sadler, Ph. D. London. 1869.

17. A Group of Englishmen (1795–1815) : being records of the younger Wedgwoods and their Friends. By Eliza Meteyard. 1871.

18. Memoir and Letters of Sara Coleridge [Mrs. H. N. Coleridge]. Edited by her daughter. 2 vols. 1873.

19. Samuel Taylor Coleridge and the English Romantic School. By Alois Brandl. English Edition by Lady Eastlake. London. 1887.

20. The Letters of Charles Lamb. Edited by Alfred Ainger. 2 vols. 1888.

21. Thomas Poole and his Friends. By Mrs. Henry Sandford. 2 vols. 1888.

22. The Life and Correspondence of R. Southey. Edited by his son, the Rev. Charles Cuthbert Southey. 6 vols. 1849–50.

23. Selections from the Letters of R. Southey. Edited by his son-in-law, John Wood Warter, B. D. 4 vols. 1856.

24. The Poetical Works of Robert Southey, Esq., LL. D. 9 vols. London. 1837.

25. Memoirs of William Wordsworth. By Christopher Wordsworth, D. D., Canon of Westminster [afterwards Bishop of Lincoln]. 2 vols. 1851.

26. The Life of William Wordsworth. By William Knight, LL. D. 3 vols. 1889.

27. The Complete Poetical Works of William Wordsworth. With an Introduction by John Morley. London and New York : Macmillan and Co. 1889.

CONTENTS OF VOLUME I

NOTE. Where a letter has been printed previously to its appearance in this work, the name of the book or periodical containing it is added in parenthesis.

CHAPTER I. STUDENT LIFE, 1785-1794.

CONTENTS

CHAPTER VI. A LAKE POET, 1800–1803.

CX. THOMAS POOLE, August 14, 1800. (Illustrated London News, May 27, 1893) 335

CXI. SIR H. DAVY, October 9, 1800. (Fragmentary Remains, 1858, p. 80) 336

CXII. SIR H. DAVY, October 18, 1800. (Fragmentary Remains, 1858, p. 79) 339

CXIII. SIR H. DAVY, December 2, 1800. (Fragmentary Remains, 1858, p. 83) 341

CXIV. THOMAS POOLE, December 5, 1800. (Eight lines published, Thomas Poole and his Friends, 1887, ii. 21) . 343

CXV. SIR H. DAVY, February 3, 1801. (Fragmentary Remains, 1858, p. 86) 345

CXVI. THOMAS POOLE, March 16, 1801 348

CXVII. THOMAS POOLE, March 23, 1801 350

CXVIII. ROBERT SOUTHEY [May 6, 1801] . . . 354

CXIX. ROBERT SOUTHEY, July 22, 1801 . . . 356

CXX. ROBERT SOUTHEY, July 25, 1801 . . . 359

CXXI. ROBERT SOUTHEY, August 1, 1801 . . . 361

CXXII. THOMAS POOLE, September 19, 1801. (Thomas Poole and his Friends, 1887, ii. 65) 364

CXXIII. ROBERT SOUTHEY, December 31, 1801 . . 365

CXXIV. MRS. S. T. COLERIDGE [February 24, 1802] . . 367

CXXV. W. SOTHEBY, July 13, 1802 369

CXXVI. W. SOTHEBY, July 19, 1802 376

CXXVII. ROBERT SOUTHEY, July 29, 1802 . . . 384

CXXVIII. ROBERT SOUTHEY, August 9, 1802 . . . 393

CXXIX. W. SOTHEBY, August 26, 1802 . . . 396

CXXX. W. SOTHEBY, September 10, 1802 . . . 401

CXXXI. W. SOTHEBY, September 27, 1802 . . . 408

CXXXII. MRS. S. T. COLERIDGE, November 16, 1802 . . 410

CXXXIII. REV. J. P. ESTLIN, December 7, 1802. (Privately printed, Philobiblon Society) 414

CXXXIV. ROBERT SOUTHEY, December 25, 1802 . . 415

CXXXV. THOMAS WEDGWOOD, January 9, 1803 . . 417

CXXXVI. MRS. S. T. COLERIDGE, April 4, 1803 . . 420

CXXXVII. ROBERT SOUTHEY, July 2, 1803 . . . 422

CXXXVIII. ROBERT SOUTHEY, July, 1803 . . . 425

CXXXIX. ROBERT SOUTHEY, August 7, 1803 . . . 427

CXL. MRS. S. T. COLERIDGE, September 1, 1803 . . 431

CXLI. ROBERT SOUTHEY, September 10, 1803 . . 434

CXLII. ROBERT SOUTHEY, September 13, 1803 . . 437

CXLIII. MATTHEW COATES, December 5, 1803 . . 441

LIST OF ILLUSTRATIONS

CHAPTER I

STUDENT LIFE

1785–1794

LETTERS

OF

SAMUEL TAYLOR COLERIDGE

CHAPTER I

STUDENT LIFE

1785–1794

THE five autobiographical letters addressed to Thomas Poole were written at Nether Stowey, at irregular intervals during the years 1797–98. They are included in the first chapter of the "Biographical Supplement" to the "Biographia Literaria." The larger portion of this so-called Biographical Supplement was prepared for the press by Henry Nelson Coleridge, and consists of the opening chapters of a proposed "biographical sketch," and a selection from the correspondence of S. T. Coleridge. His widow, Sara Coleridge, when she brought out the second edition of the "Biographia Literaria" in 1847, published this fragment and added some matter of her own. This edition has never been reprinted in England, but is included in the American edition of Coleridge's Works, which was issued by Harper & Brothers in 1853.

The letters may be compared with an autobiographical note dated March 9, 1832, which was written at Gillman's request, and forms part of the first chapter of his "Life of Coleridge."[1] The text of the present issue of the autobiographical letters is taken from the original MSS., and differs in many important particulars from that of 1847.

[1] Pickering, 1838.

I. TO THOMAS POOLE.

Monday, February, 1797.

MY DEAR POOLE, — I could inform the dullest author how he might write an interesting book. Let him relate the events of his own life with honesty, not disguising the feelings that accompanied them. I never yet read even a Methodist's Experience in the "Gospel Magazine" without receiving instruction and amusement; and I should almost despair of that man who could peruse the Life of John Woolman [1] without an amelioration of heart. As to my Life, it has all the charms of variety, — high life and low life, vices and virtues, great folly and some wisdom. However, what I am depends on what I have been ; and you, *my best Friend !* have a right to the narration. To me the task will be a useful one. It will renew and deepen my reflections on the past ; and it will perhaps make you behold with no unforgiving or impatient eye those weaknesses and defects in my character, which so many untoward circumstances have concurred to plant there.

My family on my mother's side can be traced up, I know not how far. The Bowdons inherited a small farm in the Exmoor country, in the reign of Elizabeth, as I have been told, and, to my own knowledge, they have inherited nothing better since that time. On my father's side I can rise no higher than my grandfather, who was born in the Hundred of Coleridge [2] in the county of Devon,

---

[1] The Journal of John Woolman, the Quaker abolitionist, was published in Philadelphia in 1774, and in London in 1775. From a letter of Charles Lamb, dated January 5, 1797, we may conclude that Charles Lloyd had, in the first instance, drawn Coleridge's attention to the writings of John Woolman. Compare, too, *Essays of Elia*, "A Quakers' Meeting." "Get the writings of John Woolman by heart; and love the early Quakers." *Letters of Charles Lamb*, 1888, i. 61 ; *Prose Works*, 1836, ii. 106.

[2] I have been unable to trace any connection between the family of Coleridge and the Parish or Hun-

christened, educated, and apprenticed to the parish. He afterwards became a respectable woollen-draper in the town of South Molton.[1] (I have mentioned these particulars, as the time may come in which it will be useful to be able to prove myself a genuine *sans-culotte*, my veins uncontaminated with one drop of gentility.) My father received a better education than the others of his family, in consequence of his own exertions, not of his superior advantages. When he was not quite sixteen years old, my grandfather became bankrupt, and by a series of misfortunes was reduced to extreme poverty. My father received the half of his last crown and his blessing, and walked off to seek his fortune. After he had proceeded a few miles, he sat him down on the side of the road, so overwhelmed with painful thoughts that he wept audibly. A gentleman passed by, who knew him, and, inquiring into his distresses, took my father with him, and settled him in a neighbouring town as a schoolmaster. His school increased and he got money and knowledge: for he commenced a severe and ardent student. Here, too, he married his first wife, by whom he had three daughters, all now alive. While his first wife lived, having scraped up money enough at the age of twenty[2] he

dred of Coleridge in North Devon. Coldridges or Coleridges have been settled for more than two hundred years in Doddiscombsleigh, Ashton, and other villages of the Upper Teign, and to the southwest of Exeter the name is not uncommon. It is probable that at some period before the days of parish registers, strangers from Coleridge who had settled farther south were named after their birthplace.

[1] Probably a mistake for Crediton. It was at Crediton that John Coleridge, the poet's father, was born (Feb. 21, 1718) and educated; and here, if anywhere, it must have been that the elder John Coleridge "became a respectable woollen-draper."

[2] John Coleridge, the younger, was in his thirty-first year when he was matriculated as sizar at Sidney Sussex College, Cambridge, March 18, 1748. He is entered in the college books as *filius Johannis textoris.* On the 13th of June, 1749, he was appointed to the mastership of Squire's Endowed Grammar School at South Molton. It is strange that Coleridge forgot or failed to record this incident in his father's life. His mother came from the neighbour-

walked to Cambridge, entered at Sidney College, distinguished himself for Hebrew and Mathematics, and might
have had a fellowship if he had not been married. He
returned — his wife died. Judge Buller's father gave
him the living of Ottery St. Mary, and put the present
judge to school with him. He married my mother, by
whom he had ten children, of whom I am the youngest,
born October 20, 1772.

These sketches I received from my mother and aunt,
but I am utterly unable to fill them up by any particu-
larity of times, or places, or names. Here I shall conclude my first letter, because I cannot pledge myself for
the accuracy of the accounts, and I will not therefore
mingle them with those for the accuracy of which in the
minutest parts I shall hold myself amenable to the Tri-
bunal of Truth. You must regard this letter as the first
chapter of an history which is devoted to dim traditions
of times too remote to be pierced by the eye of investigation.   Yours affectionately,

                                    S. T. COLERIDGE.

II. TO THE SAME.

Sunday, March, 1797.

MY DEAR POOLE, — My father (Vicar of, and Schoolmaster at, Ottery St. Mary, Devon) was a profound
mathematician, and well versed in the Latin, Greek, and
Oriental Languages. He published, or rather attempted
to publish, several works ; 1st, Miscellaneous Disserta-
tions arising from the 17th and 18th Chapters of the
Book of Judges ; 2d, *Sententiæ excerptæ*, for the use of
his own school ; and 3d, his best work, a Critical Latin
Grammar ; in the preface to which he proposes a bold
innovation in the names of the cases. My father's new

hood, and several of his father's judge, followed him from South
scholars, among them Francis Bul- Molton to Ottery St. Mary.
ler, afterwards the well-known

nomenclature was not likely to become popular, although it must be allowed to be both sonorous and expressive. *Exempli gratiâ*, he calls the ablative the *quippe-quare-quale-quia-quidditive case!* My father made the world his confidant with respect to his learning and ingenuity, and the world seems to have kept the secret very faithfully. His various works, uncut, unthumbed, have been preserved free from all pollution. This piece of good luck promises to be hereditary; for all *my* compositions have the same amiable *home-studying* propensity. The truth is, my father was not a first-rate genius; he was, however, a first-rate Christian. I need not detain you with his character. In learning, good-heartedness, absentness of mind, and excessive ignorance of the world, he was a perfect Parson Adams.

My mother was an admirable economist, and managed exclusively. My eldest brother's name was John. He went over to the East Indies in the Company's service; he was a successful officer and a brave one, I have heard. He died of a consumption there about eight years ago. My second brother was called William. He went to Pembroke College, Oxford, and afterwards was assistant to Mr. Newcome's School, at Hackney. He died of a putrid fever the year before my father's death, and just as he was on the eve of marriage with Miss Jane Hart, the eldest daughter of a very wealthy citizen of Exeter. My third brother, James, has been in the army since the age of sixteen, has married a woman of fortune, and now lives at Ottery St. Mary, a respectable man. My brother Edward, the wit of the family, went to Pembroke College, and afterwards to Salisbury, as assistant to Dr. Skinner. He married a woman twenty years older than his mother. She is dead, and he now lives at Ottery St. Mary. My fifth brother, George, was educated at Pembroke College, Oxford, and from there went to Mr. Newcome's, Hackney, on the death of William. He stayed there fourteen years, when the living of Ottery St. Mary[1] was given him. There he has now a fine school, and has lately married Miss Jane Hart, who with beauty and wealth had remained a faithful widow to the memory of William for sixteen years. My brother George is a man of reflective mind and elegant genius. He possesses learning in a greater degree than any of the family, excepting myself. His manners are grave and hued over with a tender sadness. In his moral character he approaches every way nearer to perfection than any man I ever yet knew; indeed, he is worth the whole family in a lump. My sixth brother, Luke (indeed, the seventh, for one brother, the second, died in his infancy, and I had forgot to mention him), was bred as a medical man. He married Miss Sara Hart, and died at the age of twenty-two, leaving one child, a lovely boy, still alive. My brother Luke was a man of uncommon genius, a severe student, and a good man. The eighth child was a sister, Anne.[2] She died a little after my brother Luke, aged twenty-one;

> Rest, gentle Shade! and wait thy Maker's will;
> Then rise *unchang'd*, and be an Angel still!

The ninth child was called Francis. He went out as a midshipman, under Admiral Graves. His ship lay on the Bengal coast, and he accidentally met his brother John, who took him to land, and procured him a commission in the Army. He died from the effects of a delirious fever brought on by his excessive exertions at the siege of Seringapatam, at which his conduct had been so gallant, that Lord Cornwallis paid him a high compliment in the presence of the army, and presented him with a val-

---

[1] George Coleridge was Chaplain Priest, and Master of the King's School, but never Vicar of Ottery St. Mary.

[2] Anne ("Nancy") Coleridge died in her twenty-fifth year. Her illness and early death form the subject of two of Coleridge's early sonnets. *Poetical Works of Samuel Taylor Coleridge*, Macmillan, 1893, p. 13. See, also, "Lines to a Friend," p. 37, and "Frost at Midnight," p. 127.

uable gold watch, which my mother now has. All my brothers are remarkably handsome ; but they were as inferior to Francis as I am to them. He went by the name of " the handsome Coleridge." The tenth and last child was S. T. Coleridge, the subject of these epistles, born (as I told you in my last) October 20,[1] 1772.

From October 20, 1772, to October 20, 1773. Christened Samuel Taylor Coleridge — my godfather's name being Samuel Taylor, Esq. I had another godfather (his name was Evans), and two godmothers, both called " Monday."[2] From October 20, 1773, to October 20, 1774. In this year I was carelessly left by my nurse, ran to the fire, and pulled out a live coal — burnt myself dreadfully. While my hand was being dressed by a Mr. Young, I spoke for the first time (so my mother informs me) and said, "nasty Doctor Young!" The snatching at fire, and the circumstance of my first words expressing hatred to professional men — are they at all ominous? This year I went to school. My schoolmistress,

---

[1] A mistake for October 21st.

[2] Compare some doggerel verses " On Mrs. Monday's Beard " which Coleridge wrote on a copy of Southey's *Omniana*, under the heading of " Beards " (*Omniana*, 1812, ii. 54). Southey records the legend of a female saint, St. Vuilgefortis, who in answer to her prayers was rewarded with a beard as a mark of divine favour. The story is told in some Latin elegiacs from the *Annus Sacer Poeticus* of the Jesuit Sautel which Southey quotes at length. Coleridge comments thus, " *Pereant qui ante nos nostra dixere!* What! can nothing be one's own ? This is the more vexatious, for at the age of eighteen I lost a legacy of Fifty pounds for the following Epigram on my Godmother's Beard, which

she had the *barbarity* to revenge by striking me out of her Will."

The epigram is not worth quoting, but it is curious to observe that, even when scribbling for his own amusement, and without any view to publication, Coleridge could not resist the temptation of devising an " apologetic preface."

The verses, etc., are printed in *Table Talk and Omniana*, Bell, 1888, p. 391. The editor, the late Thomas Ashe, transcribed them from Gillman's copy of the *Omniana*, now in the British Museum. I have followed a transcript of the marginal note made by Mrs. H. N. Coleridge before the volume was cut in binding. Her version supplies one or two omissions.

the very image of Shenstone's, was named Old Dame Key.
She was nearly related to Sir Joshua Reynolds.

From October 20, 1774, to October 20, 1775. I was
inoculated ; which I mention because I distinctly remember it, and that my eyes were bound ; at which I manifested so much obstinate indignation, that at last they
removed the bandage, and unaffrighted I looked at the
lancet, and suffered the scratch. At the close of the year
I could read a chapter in the Bible.

Here I shall end, because the remaining years of my
life *all* assisted to form *my particular mind ;* — the three
first years had nothing in them that seems to relate to it.

(Signature cut out.)

III. TO THE SAME.

October 9, 1797.

MY DEAREST POOLE, — From March to October — a
long silence ! But [as] it is possible that I may have been
preparing materials for future letters,[1] the time cannot
be considered as altogether subtracted from you.

From October, 1775, to October, 1778. These three
years I continued at the Reading School, because I was
too little to be trusted among my father's schoolboys.
After breakfast I had a halfpenny given me, with which
I bought three cakes at the baker's close by the school
of my old mistress ; and these were my dinner on every
day except Saturday and Sunday, when I used to dine at
home, and wallowed in a beef and pudding dinner. I am
remarkably fond of beans and bacon ; and this fondness
I attribute to my father having given me a penny for

---

[1] The meaning is that the events
which had taken place between
March and October, 1797, the composition, for instance, of his tragedy,
Osorio, the visit of Charles Lamb to
the cottage at Nether Stowey, the
settling of Wordsworth and his sister
Dorothy at Alfoxden, would hereafter be recorded in his autobiography.
He had failed to complete the record of the past, only because he had
been too much occupied with the
present.

having eat a large quantity of beans on Saturday. For the other boys did not like them, and as it was an economic food, my father thought that my attachment and penchant for it ought to be encouraged. My father was very fond of me, and I was my mother's darling : in consequence I was very miserable. For Molly, who had nursed my brother Francis, and was immoderately fond of him, hated me because my mother took more notice of me than of Frank, and Frank hated me because my mother gave me now and then a bit of cake, when he had none, — quite forgetting that for one bit of cake which I had and he had not, he had twenty sops in the pan, and pieces of bread and butter with sugar on them from Molly, from whom I received only thumps and ill names.

So I became fretful and timorous, and a tell-tale ; and the schoolboys drove me from play, and were always tormenting me, and hence I took no pleasure in boyish sports, but read incessantly. My father's sister kept an *everything* shop at Crediton, and there I read through all the gilt-cover little books[1] that could be had at that time, and likewise all the uncovered tales of Tom Hickathrift, Jack the Giant-killer, etc., etc., etc., etc. And I

---

[1] He records his timorous passion for fairy stories in a note to *The Friend* (ed. 1850, i. 192). Another version of the same story is to be found in some MS. notes (taken by J. Tomalin) of the Lectures of 1811, the only record of this and other lectures : —

Lecture 5th, 1811. " Give me," cried Coleridge, with enthusiasm, " the works which delighted my youth ! Give me the *History of St. George*, and the *Seven Champions of Christendom*, which at every leisure moment I used to hide myself in a corner to read ! Give me the *Arabian Nights' Entertainments*, which I used to watch, till the sun shining on the bookcase approached, and, glowing full upon it, gave me the courage to take it from the shelf. I heard of no little Billies, and sought no praise for giving to beggars, and I trust that my heart is not the worse, or the less inclined to feel sympathy for all men, because I first learnt the powers of my nature, and to reverence that nature — for who can feel and reverence the nature of man and not feel deeply for the affliction of others possessing like powers and like nature ? " Tomalin's *Shorthand Report of Lecture V*.

used to lie by the wall and *mope*, and my spirits used to
come upon me suddenly; and in a flood of them I was
accustomed to race up and down the churchyard, and act
over all I had been reading, on the docks, the nettles, and
the rank grass. At six years old I remember to have read
Belisarius, Robinson Crusoe, and Philip Quarles; and then
I found the Arabian Nights' Entertainments, one tale of
which (the tale of a man who was compelled to seek for
a pure virgin) made so deep an impression on me (I had
read it in the evening while my mother was mending
stockings), that I was haunted by spectres, whenever I
was in the dark: and I distinctly remember the anxious
and fearful eagerness with which I used to watch the
window in which the books lay, and whenever the sun lay
upon them, I would seize it, carry it by the wall, and bask
and read. My father found out the effect which these
books had produced, and burnt them.

So I became a *dreamer*, and acquired an indisposition
to all bodily activity; and I was fretful, and inordinately
passionate, and as I could not play at anything, and was
slothful, I was despised and hated by the boys; and because I could read and spell and had, I may truly say, a
memory and understanding forced into almost an unnatural ripeness, I was flattered and wondered at by all the
old women. And so I became very vain, and despised
most of the boys that were at all near my own age, and
before I was eight years old I was a *character*. Sensibility, imagination, vanity, sloth, and feelings of deep and
bitter contempt for all who traversed the orbit of my understanding, were even then prominent and manifest.

From October, 1778, to 1779. That which I began to
be from three to six I continued from six to nine. In this
year [1778] I was admitted into the Grammar School, and
soon outstripped all of my age. I had a dangerous putrid
fever this year. My brother George lay ill of the same
fever in the next room. My poor brother Francis, I

remember, stole up in spite of orders to the contrary, and
sat by my bedside and read Pope's Homer to me. Frank
had a violent love of beating me; but whenever that
was superseded by any humour or circumstances, he was
always very fond of me, and used to regard me with a
strange mixture of admiration and contempt. Strange
it was not, for he hated books, and loved climbing,
fighting, playing and robbing orchards, to distraction.

My mother relates a story of me, which I repeat here,
because it must be regarded as my first piece of wit.
During my fever, I asked why Lady Northcote (our
neighbour) did not come and see me. My mother said
she was afraid of catching the fever. I was piqued, and
answered, " Ah, Mamma! the four Angels round my bed
an't afraid of catching it!" I suppose you know the
prayer : —

> " Matthew! Mark! Luke and John!
> God bless the bed which I lie on.
> Four angels round me spread,
> Two at my foot, and two at my head."

This prayer I said nightly, and most firmly believed the
truth of it. Frequently have I (half-awake and half-
asleep, my body diseased and fevered by my imagination),
seen armies of ugly things bursting in upon me, and these
four angels keeping them off. In my next I shall carry
on my life to my father's death.

God bless you, my dear Poole, and your affectionate
S. T. COLERIDGE.

IV. TO THE SAME.

October 16, 1797.

DEAR POOLE,— From October, 1779, to October, 1781.
I had asked my mother one evening to cut my cheese
entire, so that I might toast it. This was no easy matter,
it being a *crumbly* cheese. My mother, however, did it.
I went into the garden for something or other, and in

the mean time my brother Frank *minced* my cheese "to disappoint the favorite." I returned, saw the exploit, and in an agony of passion flew at Frank. He pretended to have been seriously hurt by my blow, flung himself on the ground, and there lay with outstretched limbs. I hung over him moaning, and in a great fright ; he leaped up, and with a horse-laugh gave me a severe blow in the face. I seized a knife, and was running at him, when my mother came in and took me by the arm. I expected a flogging, and struggling from her I ran away to a hill at the bottom of which the Otter flows, about one mile from Ottery. There I stayed ; my rage died away, but my obstinacy vanquished my fears, and taking out a little shilling book which had, at the end, morning and evening prayers, I very devoutly repeated them — thinking at the *same time* with inward and gloomy satisfaction how miserable my mother must be ! I distinctly remember my feelings when I saw a Mr. Vaughan pass over the bridge, at about a furlong's distance, and how I watched the calves in the fields [1] beyond the river. It grew dark and I fell asleep. It was towards the latter end of October, and it proved a dreadful stormy night. I felt the cold in my sleep, and dreamt that I was pulling the blanket over me, and actually pulled over me a dry thorn bush which lay on the hill. In my sleep I had rolled from the top of the hill to within three yards of the river, which flowed by the unfenced edge at the bottom. I awoke several times, and finding myself wet and stiff and cold, closed my eyes again that I might forget it.

In the mean time my mother waited about half an hour,

---

[1] Compare a MS. note dated July 19, 1803. "Intensely hot day, left off a waistcoat, and for yarn wore silk stockings. Before nine o'clock had unpleasant chillness, heard a noise which I thought Derwent's in sleep ; listened and found it was a calf bellowing. Instantly came on my mind that night I slept out at Ottery, and the calf in the field across the river whose lowing so deeply impressed me. Chill and child and calf lowing."

expecting my return when the *sulks* had evaporated. I
not returning, she sent into the churchyard and round
the town. Not found! Several men and all the boys
were sent to ramble about and seek me. In vain! My
mother was almost distracted; and at ten o'clock at night
I was *cried* by the crier in Ottery, and in two villages
near it, with a reward offered for me. No one went to
bed; indeed, I believe half the town were up all the
night. To return to myself. About five in the morning,
or a little after, I was broad awake, and attempted to get
up and walk; but I could not move. I saw the shepherds
and workmen at a distance, and cried, but so faintly that
it was impossible to hear me thirty yards off. And there
I might have lain and died; for I was now almost given
over, the ponds and even the river, near where I was
lying, having been dragged. But by good luck, Sir
Stafford Northcote,[1] who had been out all night, resolved
to make one other trial, and came so near that he heard
me crying. He carried me in his arms for near a quarter
of a mile, when we met my father and Sir Stafford's
servants. I remember and never shall forget my father's
face as he looked upon me while I lay in the servant's
arms — so calm, and the tears stealing down his face; for
I was the child of his old age. My mother, as you may
suppose, was outrageous with joy. [Meantime] in rushed
a *young lady*, crying out, "I hope you'll whip him,
Mrs. Coleridge!" This woman still lives in Ottery; and
neither philosophy or religion have been able to conquer
the antipathy which I *feel* towards her whenever I see
her. I was put to bed and recovered in a day or so, but
I was certainly injured. For I was weakly and subject to
the ague for many years after.

---

[1] Sir Stafford, the seventh baro-
net, grandfather of the first Lord
Iddesleigh, was at that time a youth
of eighteen. His name occurs among
the list of scholars who were subscribers to the second edition of the
Critical Latin Grammar.

My father (who had so little of parental ambition in him, that he had destined his children to be blacksmiths, etc., and had accomplished his intention but for my mother's pride and spirit of aggrandizing her family) — my father had, however, resolved that I should be a parson. I read every book that came in my way without distinction; and my father was fond of me, and used to take me on his knee and hold long conversations with me. I remember that at eight years old I walked with him one winter evening from a farmer's house, a mile from Ottery, and he told me the names of the stars and how Jupiter was a thousand times larger than our world, and that the other twinkling stars were suns that had worlds rolling round them; and when I came home he shewed me how they rolled round. I heard him with a profound delight and admiration: but without the least mixture of wonder or incredulity. For from my early reading of fairy tales and genii, etc., etc., my mind had been habituated *to the Vast*, and I never regarded *my senses* in any way as the criteria of my belief. I regulated all my creeds by my conceptions, not by my *sight*, even at that age. Should children be permitted to read romances, and relations of giants and magicians and genii? I know all that has been said against it; but I have formed my faith in the affirmative. I know no other way of giving the mind a love of the Great and the Whole. Those who have been led to the same truths step by step, through the constant testimony of their senses, seem to me to want a sense which I possess. They contemplate nothing but *parts*, and all *parts* are necessarily little. And the universe to them is but a mass of *little things*. It is true, that the mind *may* become credulous and prone to superstition by the former method; but are not the experimentalists credulous even to madness in believing any absurdity, rather than believe the grandest truths, if they have not the testimony of their own senses in their favour? I have known some who have been *rationally* educated, as it is styled. They were marked by a microscopic acuteness, but when they looked at great things, all became a blank and they saw nothing, and denied (very illogically) that anything could be seen, and uniformly put the negation of a power for the possession of a power, and called the want of imagination judgment and the never being moved to rapture philosophy!

Towards the latter end of September, 1781, my father went to Plymouth with my brother Francis, who was to go as midshipman under Admiral Graves, who was a friend of my father's. My father settled my brother, and returned October 4, 1781. He arrived at Exeter about six o'clock, and was pressed to take a bed there at the Harts', but he refused, and, to avoid their entreaties, he told them, that he had never been superstitious, but that the night before he had had a dream which had made a deep impression. He dreamt that Death had appeared to him as he is commonly painted, and touched him with his dart. Well, he returned home, and all his family, I excepted, were up. He told my mother his dream;[1] but he was in high health and good spirits, and there was a bowl of punch made, and my father gave a long and particular account of his travel, and that he had placed Frank under a religious captain, etc. At length he went to bed, very well and in high spirits. A short time after he had lain down he complained of a pain in his bowels. My mother got him some peppermint water, and, after a pause, he said, "I am much better now, my dear!" and lay down again. In a minute my mother heard a noise in his throat, and spoke to him, but he did not answer; and she spoke repeatedly in vain. Her *shriek* awaked me, and I said, "Papa is dead!" I did not know of my father's return,

---

[1] Compare a MS. note dated March 5, 1818. "Memory counterfeited by present impressions. One great cause of the coincidence of dreams with the event — ἡ μήτηρ ἐμή."

but I knew that he was expected. How I came to think of his death I cannot tell; but so it was. Dead he was. Some said it was the gout in the heart;— probably it was a fit of apoplexy. He was an Israelite without guile, simple, generous, and taking some Scripture texts in their literal sense, he was conscientiously indifferent to the good and the evil of this world.

God love you and   S. T. COLERIDGE.

V. TO THE SAME.

February 19, 1798.

From October, 1781, to October, 1782.

After the death of my father, we of course changed houses, and I remained with my mother till the spring of 1782, and was a day-scholar to Parson Warren, my father's successor. He was not very deep, I believe; and I used to delight my mother by relating little instances of his deficiency in grammar knowledge,— every detraction from his merits seemed an oblation to the memory of my father, especially as Parson Warren did certainly *pulpitize* much better. Somewhere I think about April, 1782, Judge Buller, who had been educated by my father, sent for me, having procured a Christ's Hospital Presentation. I accordingly went to London, and was received by my mother's brother, Mr. Bowdon, a tobacconist and (at the same time) clerk to an underwriter. My uncle lived at the corner of the Stock Exchange and carried on his shop by means of a confidential servant, who, I suppose, fleeced him most unmercifully. He was a widower and had one daughter who lived with a Miss Cabriere, an old maid of great sensibilities and a taste for literature. Betsy Bowdon had obtained an unlimited influence over her mind, which she still retains. Mrs. Holt (for this is her name now) was not the kindest of daughters — but, indeed, my poor uncle would have wearied the patience and affection of an Euphrasia. He received me with great affection, and I stayed ten weeks at his house, during which time I went occasionally to Judge Buller's. My uncle was very proud of me, and used to carry me from coffee-house to coffee-house and tavern to tavern, where I drank and talked and disputed, as if I had been a man. Nothing was more common than for a large party to exclaim in my hearing that I was a *prodigy*, etc., etc., etc., so that while I remained at my uncle's I was most completely spoiled and pampered, both mind and body.

At length the time came, and I donned the *blue* coat [1] and yellow stockings and was sent down into Hertford, a town twenty miles from London, where there are about three hundred of the younger Blue-Coat boys. At Hertford I was very happy, on the whole, for I had plenty to eat and drink, and pudding and vegetables almost every day. I stayed there six weeks, and then was drafted up to the great school at London, where I arrived in September, 1782, and was placed in the second ward, then called Jefferies' Ward, and in the under Grammar School. There are twelve wards or dormitories of unequal sizes, beside the sick ward, in the great school, and they contained all together seven hundred boys, of whom I think nearly one third were the sons of clergymen. There are five schools, — a mathematical, a grammar, a drawing, a reading and a writing school, — all very large buildings. When a boy is admitted, if he reads very badly, he is either sent to Hertford or the reading school. (N. B. Boys are admissible from seven to twelve years old.) If he learns to read tolerably well before nine, he is drafted into the Lower Grammar School; if not, into the Writing School, as having given proof of unfitness for classical attainments. If before he is eleven he climbs up to the first form of the Lower Grammar School, he is drafted into the head Grammar School; if not, at eleven years old, he is sent

---

[1] The date of admission to Hertford was July 18, 1782. Eight weeks later, September 12, he was sent up to London to the great school.

into the Writing School, where he continues till fourteen
or fifteen, and is then either apprenticed and articled as
clerk, or whatever else his turn of mind or of fortune shall
have provided for him. Two or three times a year the
Mathematical Master beats up for recruits for the King's
boys, as they are called; and all who like the Navy are
drafted into the Mathematical and Drawing Schools, where
they continue till sixteen or seventeen, and go out as mid-
shipmen and schoolmasters in the Navy. The boys, who
are drafted into the Head Grammar School remain there
till thirteen, and then, if not chosen for the University, go
into the Writing School.

Each dormitory has a nurse, or matron, and there is a
head matron to superintend all these nurses. The boys
were, when I was admitted, under excessive subordination
to each other, according to rank in school; and every ward
was governed by four Monitors (appointed by the *Steward*,
who was the supreme Governor out of school, — our tem-
poral lord), and by four *Markers*, who wore silver medals
and were appointed by the Head Grammar Master, who
was our supreme spiritual lord. The same boys were commonly both monitors and markers. We read in classes on
Sundays to our *Markers*, and were catechized by them,
and under their sole authority during prayers, etc. All
other authority was in the monitors; but, as I said, the
same boys were ordinarily both the one and the other.
Our diet was very scanty.[1] Every morning, a bit of dry

[1] Compare the autobiographical
note of 1832. "I was in a continual
low fever. My whole being was,
with eyes closed to every object of
present sense, to crumple myself up
in a sunny corner and read, read,
read; fixing myself on Robinson
Crusoe's Island, finding a mountain
of plumb cake, and eating a room
for myself, and then eating it into
the shapes of tables and chairs —
hunger and fancy." Lamb in his
*Christ's Hospital Five and Thirty
Years Ago*, and Leigh Hunt in his
Autobiography, are in the same tale
as to the insufficient and ill-cooked
meals of their Bluecoat days. *Life
of Coleridge*, by James Gillman,
1838, p. 20; Lamb's *Prose Works*,
1836, ii. 27; *Autobiography of Leigh
Hunt*, 1860, p. 60.

bread and some bad small beer. Every evening, a larger
piece of bread and cheese or butter, whichever we liked.
For dinner, — on Sunday, boiled beef and broth ; Monday,
bread and butter, and milk and water ; on Tuesday, roast
mutton ; Wednesday, bread and butter, and rice milk ;
Thursday, boiled beef and broth ; Saturday, bread and
butter, and pease-porritch. Our food was portioned ; and,
excepting on Wednesdays, I never had a belly full. Our
appetites were *damped*, never satisfied ; and we had no
vegetables.

S. T. COLERIDGE.

VI. TO HIS MOTHER.

February 4, 1785 [London, Christ's Hospital].

DEAR MOTHER,[1] — I received your letter with pleasure
on the second instant, and should have had it sooner, but
that we had not a holiday before last Tuesday, when my
brother delivered it me. I also with gratitude received
the two handkerchiefs and the half-a-crown from Mr. Badcock, to whom I would be glad if you would give my thanks.
I shall be more careful of the somme, as I now consider
that were it not for my kind friends I should be as destitute
of many little necessaries as some of my schoolfellows are ;
and Thank God and my relations for them ! My brother
Luke saw Mr. James Sorrel, who gave my brother a half-
a-crown from Mrs. Smerdon, but mentioned not a word
of the plumb cake, and said he would call again. Return
my most respectful thanks to Mrs. Smerdon for her kind
favour. My aunt was so kind as to accommodate me with
a box. I suppose my sister Anna's beauty has many ad-

---

[1] Coleridge's " letters home " were
almost invariably addressed to his
brother George. It may be gathered from his correspondence that at
rare intervals he wrote to his mother
as well, but, contrary to her usual
practice, she did not, with this one
exception, preserve his letters. It
was, indeed, a sorrowful consequence
of his " long exile " at Christ's Hospital, that he seems to have passed
out of his mother's ken, that absence
led to something like indifference on
both sides.

mirers. My brother Luke says that Burke's Art of Speaking would be of great use to me. If Master Sam and
Harry Badcock are not gone out of (Ottery), give my
kindest love to them. Give my compliments to Mr. Blake
and Miss Atkinson, Mr. and Mrs. Smerdon, Mr. and Mrs.
Clapp, and all other friends in the country. My uncle,
aunt, and cousins join with myself and Brother in love to
my sisters, and hope they are well, as I, your dutiful son,
                    S. COLERIDGE, am at present.

P. S.   Give my kind love to Molly.

VII. TO THE REV. GEORGE COLERIDGE.

Undated, from Christ's Hospital, before 1790.

DEAR BROTHER, — You will excuse me for reminding
you that, as our holidays commence next week, and I
shall go out a good deal, a good pair of breeches will be no
inconsiderable accession to my appearance. For though
my present pair are excellent for the purposes of drawing mathematical figures on them, and though a walking
thought, sonnet, or epigram would appear on them in
very *splendid* type, yet they are not altogether so well
adapted for a female eye — not to mention that I should
have the charge of vanity brought against me for wearing
a looking-glass. I hope you have got rid of your cold —
and I am your affectionate brother,
                    SAMUEL TAYLOR COLERIDGE.

P. S.   Can you let me have them time enough for re-
adaptation before Whitsunday? I mean that they may
be made up for me before that time.

VIII. TO THE SAME.

October 16, 1791.

DEAR BROTHER, — Here I am, videlicet, Jesus College.
I had a tolerable journey, went by a night coach packed

up with five more, one of whom had a long, broad, red-hot face, four feet by three. I very luckily found Middleton at Pembroke College, who (after breakfast, etc.) conducted me to Jesus. Dr. Pearce is in Cornwall and not expected to return to Cambridge till the summer, and what is still more extraordinary (and, n. b., rather shameful) neither of the tutors are here. I *keep* (as the phrase is) in an absent member's rooms till one of the aforesaid duetto return to appoint me my own. Neither Lectures, Chapel, or anything is begun. The College is very thin, and Middleton has not the least acquaintance with any of Jesus except a very blackguardly fellow whose physiog. I did not like. So I sit down to dinner in the Hall in silence, except the noise of suction which accompanies my eating, and rise up ditto. I then walk to Pembroke and sit with my friend Middleton. Pray let me hear from you. Le Grice will send a parcel in two or three days.

Believe me, with sincere affection and gratitude, yours ever,

S. T. COLERIDGE.

IX. TO THE SAME.

January 24, 1792.

DEAR BROTHER, — Happy am I, that the country air and exercise have operated with due effect on your health and spirits — and happy, too, that I can inform you, that my own corporealities are in a state of better health, than I ever recollect them to be. This indeed I owe in great measure to the care of Mrs. Evans,[1] with whom I spent a fortnight at Christmas: the relaxation from study coöperating with the cheerfulness and attention, which I met

[1] Compare the autobiographical note of 1832 as quoted by Gillman. About this time he became acquainted with a widow lady, " whose son," says he, " I, as upper boy, had protected, and who therefore looked up to me, and taught me what it was to have a mother. I loved her as such. She had three daughters, and of course I fell in love with the eldest." *Life of Coleridge*, p. 28.

there, proved very potently medicinal. I have indeed experienced from her a tenderness scarcely inferior to the solicitude of maternal affection. I wish, my dear brother, that some time, when you walk into town, you would call at Villiers Street, and take a dinner or dish of tea there. Mrs. Evans has repeatedly expressed her wish, and I too have made a half promise that you would. I assure you, you will find them not only a very amiable, but a very sensible family.

I send a parcel to Le Grice on Friday morning, which (*you may depend on it as a certainty*) will contain your sermon. I hope you will like it.

I am sincerely concerned at the state of Mr. Sparrow's health. Are his complaints consumptive? Present my respects to him and Mrs. Sparrow.

When the Scholarship falls, I do not know. It *must be* in the course of two or three months. I do not relax in my exertions, neither do I find it any impediment to my mental acquirements that prudence has obliged me to relinquish the *mediæ pallescere nocti*. We are examined as Rustats,[1] on the Thursday in Easter Week. The examination for my year is "the last book of Homer and Horace's *De Arte Poetica*." The Master (*i. e.* Dr. Pearce) told me that he would do me a service by pushing my examination as deep as he possibly could. If ever hogslard is pleasing, it is when our superiors trowel it on. Mr. Frend's company[2] is by no means invidious. On the contrary, Pearce himself is very intimate with him. No!

---

[1] Scholarship of Jesus College, Cambridge, for sons of clergymen.

[2] At this time Frend was still a Fellow of Jesus College. Five years had elapsed since he had resigned from conscientious motives the living of Madingley in Cambridgeshire, but it was not until after the publication of his pamphlet *Peace and Union*, in 1793, that the authorities took alarm. He was deprived of his Fellowship, April 17, and banished from the University, May 30, 1793. Coleridge's demeanour in the Senate House on the occasion of Frend's trial before the Vice-Chancellor forms the subject of various contradictory anecdotes. See *Life of Coleridge*, 1838, p. 55; *Reminiscences of Cambridge*, Henry Gunning, 1855, i. 272-275.

Though I am not an *Alderman*, I have yet *prudence* enough to respect that *gluttony of faith* waggishly yclept orthodoxy.

Philanthropy generally keeps pace with health — my acquaintance becomes more general.   I am intimate with an undergraduate of our College, his name Caldwell,[1] who is pursuing the same line of study (nearly) as myself. Though a man of fortune, he is prudent ; nor does he lay claim to that right, which wealth confers on its possessor, of being a fool.   Middleton is fourth senior optimate — an honourable place, but by no means so high as the whole University expected, or (I believe) his merits deserved. He desires his love to Stevens:[2] to which you will add mine.

At what time am I to receive my pecuniary assistance? Quarterly or half yearly?   The Hospital issue their money half yearly, and we receive the products of our scholarship at once, a little after Easter.   Whatever additional supply you and my brother may have thought necessary would be therefore more conducive to my comfort, if I received it quarterly — as there are a number of little things which require us to have some ready money in our pockets — particularly if we happen to be unwell.   But this as well as everything of the pecuniary kind I leave entirely *ad arbitrium tuum*.

I have written my mother, of whose health I am rejoiced to hear.   God send that she may long continue to recede

[1] The Rev. George Caldwell was afterwards Fellow and Tutor of Jesus College. His name occurs among the list of subscribers to the original issue of *The Friend. Letters of the Lake Poets*, 1889, p. 452.

[2] " First Grecian of my time was Launcelot Pepys Stevens [Stephens], kindest of boys and men, since the Co - Grammar Master, and inseparable companion of Dr. T[rollop]e." *Lamb's Prose Works*, 1835, ii. 45.

He was at this time Senior-Assistant Master at Newcome's Academy at Clapton near Hackney, and a colleague of George Coleridge. The school, which belonged to three generations of Newcomes, was of high repute as a private academy, and commanded the services of clever young schoolmasters as assistants or ushers. Mr. Sparrow, whose name is mentioned in the letter, was headmaster.

from old age, while she advances towards it! Pray write me very soon.

Yours with gratitude and affection,

S. T. COLERIDGE.

X. TO MRS. EVANS.

February 13, 1792.

MY VERY DEAR, — What word shall I add sufficiently expressive of the warmth which I feel? You covet to be near my heart. Believe me, that you and my sister have the very first row in the front box of my heart's little theatre — and — God knows! *you are not crowded.* There, my dear spectators! you shall see what you shall see — Farce, Comedy, and Tragedy — my laughter, my cheerfulness, and my melancholy. A thousand figures pass before you, shifting in perpetual succession; these are my joys and my sorrows, my hopes and my fears, my good tempers and my peevishness: you will, however, observe two that remain unalterably fixed, and these are love and gratitude. In short, my dear Mrs. Evans, my whole heart shall be laid open like any sheep's heart; my virtues, if I have any, shall not be more exposed to your view than my weaknesses. Indeed, I am of opinion that foibles are the cement of affection, and that, however we may *admire* a perfect character, we are seldom inclined to love and praise those whom we cannot sometimes blame. Come, ladies! will you take your seats in this play-house? Fool that I am! Are you not already there? Believe me, you are!

I am extremely anxious to be informed concerning your health. Have you not felt the kindly influence of this more than vernal weather, as well as the good effects of your own recommenced regularity? I would I could transmit you a little of my superfluous good health! I am indeed at present most wonderfully well, and if I continue so, I may soon be mistaken for one of your *very* children:

at least, in clearness of complexion and rosiness of cheek
I am no contemptible likeness of them, though that
ugly arrangement of features with which nature has distinguished me will, I fear, long stand in the way of such
honorable assimilation. You accuse me of evading the
bet, and imagine that my silence proceeded from a consciousness of the charge. But you are mistaken. I not
only read *your* letter first, but, on my sincerity! I felt
no inclination to do otherwise; and I am confident, that
if Mary had happened to have stood by me and had seen
me take up *her* letter in preference to her *mother's*, with
all that ease and energy which she can so gracefully exert
upon proper occasions, she would have lifted up her beautiful little leg, and kicked me round the room. Had Anne
indeed favoured me with a few lines, I confess I should
have seized hold of them before either of your letters;
but then this would have arisen from my love of *novelty*,
and not from any deficiency in filial respect. So much
for your bet!

You can scarcely conceive what uneasiness poor Tom's
accident has occasioned me; in everything that relates
to him I feel solicitude truly fraternal. Be particular
concerning him in your next. I was going to write him
an half angry letter for the long intermission of his correspondence; but I must change it to a consolatory one.
You mention not a word of Bessy. Think you I do not
love her?

And so, my dear Mrs. Evans, you are to take your
Welsh journey in May? Now may the Goddess of
Health, the rosy-cheeked goddess that blows the breeze
from the Cambrian mountains, renovate that dear old
lady, and make her young again! I always loved that
old lady's looks. Yet do not flatter yourselves, that you
shall take this journey *tête-à-tête*. You will have an unseen companion at your side, one who will attend you in
your jaunt, who will be present at your arrival; one whose

heart will melt with unutterable tenderness at your maternal transports, who will climb the Welsh hills with you,
who will feel himself happy in knowing you to be so.   In
short, as St. Paul says, though absent in body, I shall be
present in mind.   Disappointment?   You must not, you
shall not be disappointed ; and if a poetical invocation can
help you to drive off that ugly foe to happiness here it is
for you.

TO DISAPPOINTMENT.

Hence ! thou fiend of gloomy sway,
Thou lov'st on withering blast to ride
O'er fond Illusion's air-built pride.
  Sullen Spirit ! Hence ! Away !

Where Avarice lurks in sordid cell,
Or mad Ambition builds the dream,
Or Pleasure plots th' unholy scheme
  There with Guilt and Folly dwell !

But oh ! when Hope on Wisdom's wing
Prophetic whispers pure delight,
Be distant far thy cank'rous blight,
  Demon of envenom'd sting.

Then haste thee, Nymph of balmy gales !
Thy poet's prayer, sweet May ! attend !
Oh ! place my parent and my friend
  'Mid her lovely native vales.

Peace, that lists the woodlark's strains,
Health, that breathes divinest treasures,
Laughing Hours, and Social Pleasures
  Wait my friend in Cambria's plains.

Affection there with mingled ray
Shall pour at once the raptures high

Of filial and maternal Joy;
Haste thee then, delightful May!

And oh! may Spring's fair flowerets fade,
May Summer cease her limbs to lave
In cooling stream, may Autumn grave
Yellow o'er the corn-cloath'd glade;

Ere, from sweet retirement torn,
She seek again the crowded mart:
Nor thou, my selfish, selfish heart
Dare her slow return to mourn!

In what part of the country is my dear Anne to be?
Mary must and shall be with you. I want to know all
your summer residences, that I may be on that very spot
with all of you. It is not improbable that I may steal
down from Cambridge about the beginning of April just
to look at you, that when I see you again in autumn I
may know how many years younger the Welsh air has
made you. I shall go into Devonshire on the 21st of
May, unless my good fortune in a particular affair should
detain me till the 4th of June.

I lately received the thanks of the College for a declamation[1] I spoke in public; indeed, I meet with the most
pointed marks of respect, which, as I neither flatter nor
fiddle, I suppose to be sincere. I write these things not
from vanity, but because I know they will please you.

I intend to leave off suppers, and two or three other
little unnecessaries, and in conjunction with Caldwell hire
a garden for the summer. It will be nice exercise — your
advice. La! it will be so charming to walk out in one's
own *garding*, and sit and drink tea in an arbour, and

[1] A Latin essay on *Posthumous Fame*, described as a declamation and stated to have been composed by S. T. Coleridge, March, 1792, is pre- served at Jesus College, Cambridge. Some extracts were printed in the College magazine, *The Chanticleer*, Lent Term, 1886.

pick pretty nosegays. To plant and transplant, and be dirty and amused! Then to look with contempt on your Londoners with your mock gardens and your smoky windows, making a beggarly show of withered flowers stuck in pint pots, and quart pots, menacing the heads of the passengers below.

Now suppose I conclude something in the manner with which Mary concludes all her letters to me, " *Believe me your sincere friend,*" and dutiful humble servant to command!

Now I do hate that way of concluding a letter. 'T is as dry as a stick, as stiff as a poker, and as cold as a cucumber. It is not half so good as my old

God bless you

and

Your affectionately grateful

S. T. COLERIDGE.

XI. TO MARY EVANS.

February 13, 11 o'clock.

Ten of the most talkative young ladies now in London!

Now by the most accurate calculation of the specific quantities of sounds, a female tongue, *when it exerts itself to the utmost,* equals the noise of eighteen sign-posts, which the wind swings backwards and forwards in full creak. If then one equals eighteen, ten must equal one hundred and eighty; consequently, the circle at Jermyn Street unitedly must have produced a noise equal to that of one hundred and eighty old crazy sign-posts, inharmoniously agitated as aforesaid. Well! to be sure, there are few disagreeables for which the pleasure of Mary and Anne Evans' company would not amply compensate; but faith! I feel myself half inclined to thank God that I was fifty-two miles off during this *clattering clapperation* of tongues. Do you keep ale at Jermyn Street? If so, I hope it is not *soured.*

Such, my dear Mary, were the reflections that instantly
suggested themselves to me on reading the former part
of your letter. Believe me, however, that my gratitude
keeps pace with my sense of your exertions, as I can most
feelingly conceive the difficulty of writing amid that
second edition of Babel with additions. That your health
is restored gives me sincere delight. May the giver of
all pleasure and pain preserve it so! I am likewise glad
to hear that your hand is re-whiten'd, though I cannot
help smiling at a certain young lady's *effrontery* in having
boxed a young gentleman's ears till her own hand became
black and blue, and attributing those unseemly marks to
the poor unfortunate object of her resentment. *You are
at liberty, certainly, to say what you please.*

It has been confidently affirmed by most excellent
judges (tho' the best may be mistaken) that I have grown
very handsome lately. Pray that I may have grace not
to be vain. Yet, ah! who can read the stories of Pamela,
or Joseph Andrews, or Susannah and the three Elders,
and not perceive what a dangerous snare beauty is?
Beauty is like the grass, that groweth up in the morning
and is withered before night. Mary! Anne! Do not be
vain of your beauty!!!!!

I keep a cat. Amid the strange collection of strange
animals with which I am surrounded, I think it necessary
to have some meek well-looking being, that I may keep
my social affections alive. Puss, like her master, is a
very gentle brute, and I behave to her with all possible
politeness. Indeed, a cat is a very worthy animal. To
be sure, I have known some very malicious cats in my
lifetime, but then they were old — and besides, they had
not nearly so many legs as you, my sweet Puss. I wish,
Puss! I could break you of that indecorous habit of
turning your back front to the fire. It is not frosty
weather now.

N. B. — If ever, Mary, you should feel yourself inclined

to visit me at Cambridge, pray do not suffer the consideration of my having a cat to deter you. *Indeed*, I will keep her *chained up* all the while you stay.

I was in company the other day with a very dashing literary lady. After my departure, a friend of mine asked her her opinion of me. She answered: " The best I can say of him is, that he is a very gentle bear." What think you of this character?

What a lovely anticipation of spring the last three or four days have afforded! Nature has not been very profuse of her ornaments to the country about Cambridge; yet the clear rivulet that runs through the grove adjacent to our College, and the numberless little birds (particularly robins) that are singing away, and above all, the little lambs, each by the side of its mother, recall the most pleasing ideas of pastoral simplicity, and almost soothe one's soul into congenial innocence. Amid these delightful scenes, of which the uncommon flow of health I at present possess permits me the full enjoyment, I should not deign to think of London, were it not for a little family, whom I trust I need not name. What bird of the air whispers me that you too will soon enjoy the same and more delightful pleasures in a much more delightful country? What we strongly wish we are very apt to believe. At present, my presentiments on that head amount to confidence.

Last Sunday, Middleton and I set off at one o'clock on a ramble. We sauntered on, chatting and contemplating, till to our great surprise we came to a village seven miles from Cambridge. And here at a farmhouse we drank tea. The rusticity of the habitation and the inhabitants was charming; we had cream to our tea, which though not brought in a *lordly dish*, Sisera would have jumped at. Being here informed that we could return to Cambridge another way, over a common, for the sake of diversifying our walk, we chose this road, " if road it might be called,

where road was none," though we were not unapprized of
its difficulties. The fine weather deceived us. We forgot
that it was a summer day in warmth only, and not in
length ; but we were soon reminded of it. For on the
pathless solitude of this common, the night overtook us —
we must have been four miles distant from Cambridge —
the night, though calm, was as dark as the place was
dreary: here steering our course by our imperfect conceptions of the point in which *we conjectured Cambridge*
to lie, we wandered on " with cautious steps and slow."
We feared the bog, the stump, and the fen : we feared
the ghosts of the night — at least, those material and
knock-me-down ghosts, the apprehension of which causes
you, Mary (valorous girl that you are!), always to peep
under your bed of a night. As we were thus creeping
forward like the two children in the wood, we spy'd
something white moving across the common. This we
made up to, though contrary to our *supposed* destination.
It proved to be a man with a white bundle. We enquired
our way, and luckily he was going to Cambridge. He
informed us that we had gone half a mile out of our way,
and that in five minutes more we must have arrived at a
deep quagmire grassed over. What an escape! The man
was as glad of our company as we of his — for, it seemed,
the poor fellow was afraid of Jack o' Lanthorns — the
superstition of this county attributing a kind of fascina-
tion to those wandering vapours, so that whoever fixes his
eyes on them is forced by some irresistible impulse to
follow them. He entertained us with many a dreadful
tale. By nine o'clock we arrived at Cambridge, betired
and bemudded. I never recollect to have been so much
fatigued.

Do you spell the word *scarsely?* When Momus, the
fault-finding God, endeavoured to discover some imperfection in Venus, he could only censure the creaking of
her slipper. I, too, Momuslike, can only fall foul on a

single *s*. Yet will not my dear Mary be angry with me, or think the remark trivial, when she considers that half a grain is of consequence in the weight of a diamond.

I had entertained hopes that you would *really* have *sent* me a piece of sticking plaister, which would have been very convenient at that time, I having cut my finger. I had to buy sticking plaister, etc. What is the use of a man's knowing you girls, if he cannot *chouse* you out of such little things as that? Do not your fingers, Mary, feel an odd kind of titillation to be about my ears for my impudence?

On Saturday night, as I was sitting by myself all alone, I heard a creaking sound, something like the noise which a crazy chair would make, if pressed by the tremendous weight of Mr. Barlow's extremities. I cast my eyes around, and what should I behold but a *Ghost* rising out of the floor! A deadly paleness instantly overspread my body, which retained no other symptom of life *but* its violent trembling. My hair (as is usual in frights of this nature) stood upright by many degrees stiffer than the oaks of the mountains, yea, stiffer than Mr. ——; yet was it rendered oily-pliant by the profuse perspiration that burst from every pore. This spirit advanced with a book in his hand, and having first dissipated my terrors, said as follows: " I am the Ghost of *Gray*. There lives a young lady " (then he mentioned *your* name), " of whose judgment I entertain so high an opinion, that *her* approbation of my works would make the turf lie lighter on me ; present her with this book, and transmit it to her as soon as possible, adding my love to her. And, as for you, O young man ! " (now he addressed himself to me) " write no more verses. In the first place your poetry is vile stuff ; and secondly " (here he sighed almost to bursting), " all poets go to —ll ; we are so intolerably addicted to the vice of lying ! " He vanished, and convinced me of the truth of his last dismal account by the sulphurous stink which he left behind him.

His first mandate I have obeyed, and, I hope you will
receive *safe* your ghostly admirer's present.   But so far
have I been from obeying his second injunction, that I
never had the scribble-mania stronger on me than for these
last three or four days : nay, not content with suffering it
myself, I must pester those I love best with the blessed
effects of my disorder.

Besides two *things*, which you will find in the next
sheet, I cannot forbear filling the remainder of this
sheet with an Odeling, though I know and approve your
aversion to *mere prettiness*, and though my tiny love
ode possesses no other property in the world.   Let then
its shortness recommend it to your perusal — *by the by*,
the *only* thing in which it resembles you, for wit, sense,
elegance, or beauty it has none.

AN ODE IN THE MANNER OF ANACREON.[1]

As late in wreaths gay flowers I bound,
Beneath some roses Love I found,
And by his little frolic pinion
As quick as thought I seiz'd the minion,
Then in my cup the prisoner threw,
And drank him in its sparkling dew :
And sure I feel my angry guest
Flutt'ring *his wings* within my breast !

Are you quite asleep, dear Mary ?   Sleep on ; but when
you awake, read the following productions, and then, I 'll
be bound, you will sleep again sounder than ever.

A WISH WRITTEN IN JESUS WOOD, FEBRUARY 10, 1792.[2]

Lo ! through the dusky silence of the groves,
Thro' vales irriguous, and thro' green retreats,
With languid murmur creeps the placid stream
And works its secret way.

[1] *Poetical Works*, p. 19.   [2] *Ibid.* p. 19.

Awhile meand'ring round its native fields,
It rolls the playful wave and winds its flight:
Then downward flowing with awaken'd speed
    Embosoms in the Deep!

Thus thro' its silent tenor may my Life
Smooth its meek stream by sordid wealth unclogg'd,
Alike unconscious of forensic storms,
    And Glory's blood-stain'd palm!

And when dark Age shall close Life's little day,
Satiate of sport, and weary of its toils,
E'en thus may slumb'rous Death my decent limbs
    Compose with icy hand!

A LOVER'S COMPLAINT TO HIS MISTRESS

WHO DESERTED HIM IN QUEST OF A MORE WEALTHY HUSBAND IN
THE EAST INDIES.[1]

The dubious light sad glimmers o'er the sky:
'T is silence all.   By lonely anguish torn.
With wandering feet to gloomy groves I fly,
And wakeful Love still tracks my course forlorn.

And will you, cruel Julia? will you go?
And trust you to the Ocean's dark dismay?
Shall the wide, wat'ry world between us flow?
And winds unpitying snatch my Hopes away?

Thus could you sport with my too easy heart?
Yet tremble, lest not unaveng'd I grieve!
The winds may learn your own delusive art,
And faithless Ocean smile — but to deceive!

I have written too long a letter.   Give me a hint, and
I will avoid a repetition of the offence.

It's a compensation for the above-written rhymes

---

[1] *Poetical Works*, p. 20.

(which if you ever condescend to read a second time, pray
let it be by the light of their own flames) in my next letter I will send some delicious poetry lately published by
the exquisite Bowles.

To-morrow morning I fill the rest of this sheet with a
letter to Anne. And now, good-night, dear sister! and
peaceful slumbers await us both!

S. T. COLERIDGE.

XII. TO ANNE EVANS.

February 19, 1792.

DEAR ANNE, — To be sure I felt myself rather disappointed at my not receiving a few lines from you; but I
am nevertheless greatly rejoiced at your amicable dispo-
sitions towards me. Please to accept two kisses, as the
seals of reconciliation — you will find them on the word
" Anne " at the beginning of the letter — at least, there I
left them. I must, however, give you warning, that the
next time you are affronted with Brother Coly, and show
your resentment by that most cruel of all punishments,
silence, I shall address a letter to you as long and as sorrowful as Jeremiah's Lamentations, and somewhat in the
style of your sister's favourite lover, beginning with, —

TO THE IRASCIBLE MISS.

DEAR MISS, &c.

My dear Anne, you are my Valentine. I dreamt of
you this morning, and I have seen no female in the whole
course of the day, except an old bedmaker belonging to
the College, and I don't count her one, as the bristle of
her beard makes me suspect her to be of the masculine
gender. Some one of the genii must have conveyed your
image to me so opportunely, nor will you think this impossible, if you will read the little volumes which contain
their exploits, and crave the honour of your acceptance.

If I could draw, I would have sent a pretty heart stuck
through with arrows, with some such sweet posy under-
neath it as this : —

> " The rose is red, the violet blue ;
> The pink is sweet, and so are you."

But as the Gods have not made me a drawer (of anything
but corks), you must accept the will for the deed.

You never wrote or desired your sister to write concerning the bodily health of the Barlowites, though you know
my affection for that family. Do not forget this in your
next.

Is Mr. Caleb Barlow recovered of the rheumatism?
The quiet ugliness of Cambridge supplies me with very
few communicables in the news way. The most important
is, that Mr. Tim Grubskin, of this town, citizen, is dead.
Poor man ! he loved fish too well. A violent commotion
in his bowels carried him off. They say he made a very
good end. There is his epitaph : —

> " A loving friend and tender parent dear,
> Just in all actions, and he the Lord did fear,
> Hoping, that, when the day of Resurrection come,
> He shall arise in glory like the Sun."

It was composed by a Mr. Thistlewait, the town crier,
and is much admired. We are all mortal ! !

His wife carries on the business. It is whispered about
the town that a match between her and Mr. Coe, the shoemaker, is not improbable. He certainly seems very assid-
uous in consoling her, but as to anything matrimonial I
do not write it as a well authenticated fact.

I went the other evening to the concert, and spent the
time there much to my heart's content in cursing Mr.
Hague, who played on the violin most piggishly, and a
Miss (I forget her name) — Miss Humstrum, who sung
most sowishly. O the Billington ! That I should be absent during the oratorios ! The prince unable to conceal
his pain ! Oh ! oh ! oh ! oh ! oh ! oh ! oh ! oh ! oh !

To which house is Mrs. B. engaged this season?

The mutton and winter cabbage are confoundedly tough here, though very venerable for their old age. Were you ever at Cambridge, Anne? The river Cam is a handsome stream of a muddy complexion, somewhat like Miss Yates, to whom you will present my love (if you like).

In Cambridge there are sixteen colleges, that look like workhouses, and fourteen churches that look like little houses. The town is very fertile in alleys, and mud, and cats, and dogs, besides men, women, ravens, clergy, proctors, tutors, owls, and other two-legged cattle. It likewise — but here I must interrupt my description to hurry to Mr. Costobadie's lectures on Euclid, who is as mathematical an author, my dear Anne, as you would wish to read on a long summer's day. Addio! God bless you, ma chère soeur, and your affectionate frère,

                                    S. T. COLERIDGE.

P. S. I add a postscript on purpose to communicate a joke to you. A party of us had been drinking wine together, and three or four freshmen were most deplorably intoxicated. (I have too great a respect for delicacy to say drunk.) As we were returning homewards, two of them fell into the gutter (or kennel). We ran to assist one of them, who very generously stuttered out, as he lay sprawling in the mud: "N-n-n-no — n-n-no! — save my f-fr-fr-friend there; n-never mind me, I can swim."

Won't you write me a long letter now, Anne?

P. S. Give my respectful compliments to Betty, and say that I enquired after her health with the most emphatic energy of impassioned avidity.

XIII. TO MRS. EVANS.

February 22 [? 1792].

DEAR MADAM, — The incongruity of the dates in these letters you will immediately perceive. The truth is that

I had written the foregoing heap of nothingness six or seven days ago, but I was prevented from sending it by a variety of disagreeable little impediments.

Mr. Massy must be arrived in Cambridge by this time; but to call on an utter stranger just arrived with so trivial a message as yours and his uncle's love to him, when I myself had been in Cambridge five or six weeks, would appear rather awkward, not to say ludicrous. If, however, I meet him at any wine party (which is by no means improbable) I shall take the opportunity of mentioning it *en passant.* As to Mr. M.'s debts, the most intimate friends in college are perfect strangers to each other's affairs; consequently it is little likely that I should procure any information of this kind.

I hope and trust that neither yourself nor my sisters have experienced any ill effects from this wonderful change of weather. A very slight cold is the only favour with which it has honoured *me.* I feel myself apprehensive for all of you, but more particularly for Anne, whose frame I think most susceptible of cold.

Yesterday a Frenchman came dancing into my room, of which he made but three steps, and presented me with a card. I had scarcely collected, by glancing my eye over it, that he was a tooth-monger, before he seized hold of my muzzle, and, baring my teeth (as they do a horse's, in order to know his age), he exclaimed, as if in violent agitation: "Mon Dieu! Monsieur, all your teeth will fall out in a day or two, unless you permit me the honour of *scaling* them!" This ineffable piece of assurance discovered such a genius for impudence, that I could not suffer it to go unrewarded. So, after a hearty laugh, I sat down, and let the rascal *chouse* me out of half a guinea by scraping my grinders — the more readily, indeed, as I recollected the great penchant which all your family have for delicate teeth.

So (I hear) Allen[1] will be most precipitately emancipated. Good luck have thou of thy emancipation, Bobbee! Tell him from me that if he does not kick Richards'[2] fame out of doors by the superiority of his own, I will never forgive him.

If you will send me a box of Mr. Stringer's tooth powder, mamma! we will accept of it.

And now, Right Reverend Mother in God, let me claim your permission to subscribe myself with all observance and gratitude, your most obedient humble servant, and lowly slave,

SAMUEL TAYLOR COLERIDGE,

Reverend in the future tense, and scholar of Jesus College in the present time.

XIV. TO MARY EVANS.

JESUS COLLEGE, CAMBRIDGE, February 22 [1792].

DEAR MARY, — *Writing long letters* is not the fault into which I am most apt to fall, but whenever I do, by

[1] Robert Allen, Coleridge's earliest friend, and almost his exact contemporary (born October 18, 1772), was admitted to University College, Oxford, as an exhibitioner, in the spring of 1792. He entertained Coleridge and his *compagnon de voyage*, Joseph Hucks, on the occasion of the memorable visit to Oxford in June, 1794, and introduced them to his friend, Robert Southey of Balliol. He is mentioned in letters of Lamb to Coleridge, June 10, 1796, and October 11, 1802. In both instances his name is connected with that of Stoddart, and it is probable that it was through Allen that Coleridge and Stoddart became acquainted. For anecdotes concerning Allen, see Lamb's Essay, "Christ's Hospital," etc., *Prose Works*, 1836,

ii. 47, and *Leigh Hunt's Autobiography*, 1860, p. 74. See, also, *Letters to Allsop*, 1864, p. 170.

[2] George Richards, a contemporary of Stephens, and, though somewhat senior, of Middleton, was a University prize-man and Fellow of Oriel. He was "author," says Lamb, "of the 'Aboriginal Britons,' the most spirited of Oxford prize poems." In after life he made his mark as a clergyman, as Bampton Lecturer (in 1800), and as Vicar of St. Martin-in-the-Fields. He was appointed Governor of Christ's Hospital in 1822, and founded an annual prize, the "Richards' Gold Medal," for the best copy of Latin hexameters. *Christ's Hospital. List of Exhibitioners, from 1566–1885*, compiled by A. M. Lockhart.

some inexplicable ill luck, my prolixity is always directed to those whom I would yet least of all wish to torment. You think, and think rightly, that I had no occasion to *increase* the preceding accumulations of wearisomeness, but I wished to inform you that I have sent the poem of Bowles, which I mentioned in a former sheet; though I dare say you would have discovered this without my information. If the pleasure which you receive from the perusal of it prove equal to that which I have received, it will make you some small return for the exertions of friendship, which you must have found necessary in order to travel through my long, long, long letter.

Though it may be a little effrontery to point out beauties, which would be obvious to a far less sensible heart than yours, yet I cannot forbear the self-indulgence of remarking to you the exquisite description of Hope in the third page and of Fortitude in the sixth; but the poem "On leaving a place of residence" appears to me to be almost superior to any of Bowles's compositions.

I hope that the Jermyn Street ledgers are well. How can they be otherwise in such lovely keeping?

Your Jessamine Pomatum, I trust, is as strong and as odorous as ever, and the roasted turkeys at Villiers Street honoured, as usual, with a thick crust of your Mille (what do you call it?) powder.

I had a variety of other interesting inquiries to make, but time and memory fail me.

Without a swanskin waistcoat, what is man? I have got a swanskin waistcoat, — a most attractive external.

Yours with sincerity of friendship,
SAMUEL TAYLOR C.

XV. TO THE REV. GEORGE COLERIDGE.

Monday night, April [1792].

DEAR BROTHER, — You would have heard from me long since had I not been entangled in such various businesses as have occupied my whole time. Besides my ordinary business, which, as I look forward to a smart contest some time this year, is not an indolent one, I have been writing for *all* the prizes, namely, the Greek Ode, the Latin Ode, and the Epigrams. I have little or no expectation of success, as a Mr. Smith,[1] a man of immense genius, author of some papers in the " Microcosm," is among my numerous competitors. The prize medals will be adjudged about the beginning of June. If you can think of a good thought for the beginning of the Latin Ode upon the miseries of the W. India slaves, communicate. My Greek Ode [2] is, I think, my *chef d'œuvre* in poetical composition. I have sent you a sermon metamorphosed from an obscure publication by vamping, transposition, etc. If you like it, I can send you two more of the same kidney. Our examination as Rustats comes [off] on the Thursday

[1] Robert Percy (Bobus) Smith, 1770-1845, the younger brother of Sydney Smith, was Browne Medalist in 1791. His Eton and Cambridge prize poems, in Lucretian metre, are among the most finished specimens of modern Latinity. The principal contributors to the *Microcosm* were George Canning, John and Robert Smith, Hookham Frere, and Charles Ellis. *Gentleman's Magazine*, N. S., xxiii. 440.

[2] For complete text of the Greek Sapphic Ode, " On the Slave Trade," which obtained the Browne gold medal for 1792, see Appendix B, p. 476, to Coleridge's *Poetical Works*, Macmillan, 1893. See, also, Mr. Dykes Campbell's note on the style and composition of the ode, p. 653. I possess a transcript of the Ode, taken, I believe, by Sara Coleridge in 1823, on the occasion of her visit to Ottery St. Mary. The following note is appended : —

" Upon the receipt of the above poem, Mr. George Coleridge, being vastly pleased by the composition, thinking it would be a sort of compliment to the superior genius of his brother the author, composed the following lines : —

IBI HÆC INCONDITA SOLUS.

Say *Holy Genius* — Heaven - descended Beam,
Why interdicted is the sacred Fire
That flows spontaneous from thy golden Lyre?
Why *Genius* like the emanative Ray
That issuing from the dazzling Fount of Light
Wakes all creative Nature into Day,
Art thou not all-diffusive, all benign?
Thy *partial* hand I blame. For *Pity* oft
In Supplication's Vest — a weeping child
That meets me pensive on the barren wild,
And pours into my soul Compassion soft,
The never-dying strain commands to flow —
Man sure is vain, nor sacred Genius hears,
Now speak in melody — now weep in Tears.
                                          G. C."

in Easter week.   After it a man of our college has offered
to take me to town in his gig, and, if he can bring me
back, I think I shall accept his offer, as the expense, at all
events, will not be more than 12 shillings, and my very
commons, and tea, etc., would amount to more than that
in the week which I intend to stay in town.   Almost all
the men are out of college, and I am most villainously
vapoured.   I wrote the following the other day under the
title of " A Fragment found in a Lecture-Room : " —

> Where deep in mud Cam rolls his slumbrous stream,
> And bog and desolation reign supreme ;
> Where all Bœotia clouds the misty brain,
> The owl Mathesis pipes her loathsome strain.
> Far, far aloof the frighted Muses fly,
> Indignant Genius scowls and passes by :
> The frolic Pleasures start amid their dance,
> And Wit congealed stands fix'd in wintry trance.
> But to the sounds with duteous haste repair
> Cold Industry, and wary-footed Care ;
> And Dulness, dosing on a couch of lead,
> Pleas'd with the song uplifts her heavy head,
> The sympathetic numbers lists awhile,
> Then yawns propitiously a frosty smile. . . .
> [Cætera desunt.]

This morning I went for the first time with a party on
the river.   The clumsy dog to whom we had entrusted the
sail was fool enough to fasten it.   A gust of wind embraced the opportunity of turning over the boat, and bap-
tizing all that were in it.   We swam to shore, and walked
dripping home, like so many river gods.   Thank God !
I do not feel as if I should be the worse for it.

I was matriculated on Saturday.[1]   Oath-taking is very
healthy in spring, I should suppose.   I am grown very
fat.   We have two men at our college, great cronies,

[1] He was matriculated as pen-   been in residence since September,
sioner March 31, 1792.   He had   1791.

their names Head and Bones; the first an unlicked cub of a Yorkshireman, the second a very fierce buck. I call them *Raw Head* and *Bloody Bones*.

As soon as you can make it convenient I should feel thankful if you could transmit me ten or five pounds, as I am at present cashless.

Pray, was the bible clerk's place accounted a disreputable one at Oxford in your time? Poor Allen, who is just settled there, complains of the great distance with which the men treat him. 'Tis a childish University! Thank God! I am at Cambridge. Pray let me hear from you soon, and whether your health has held out this long campaign. I hope, however, soon to see you, till when believe me, with gratitude and affection, yours ever,

S. T. COLERIDGE.

XVI. TO MRS. EVANS.

February 5, 1793.

MY DEAR MRS. EVANS, — This is the third day of my resurrection from the couch, or rather, the sofa of sickness. About a fortnight ago, a quantity of matter took it into its head to form in my left gum, and was attended with such violent pain, inflammation, and swelling, that it threw me into a fever. However, God be praised, my gum has at last been opened, a villainous tooth extracted, and all is well. I am still very weak, as well I may, since for seven days together I was incapable of swallowing anything but spoon meat, so that in point of spirits I am but the dregs of my former self — a decaying flame agonizing in the snuff of a tallow candle — a kind of hobgoblin, clouted and bagged up in the most contemptible shreds, rags, and yellow relics of threadbare mortality. The event of our examination [1] was such as surpassed

[1] For the Craven Scholarship. In an article contributed to the *Gentleman's Magazine* of December, 1834, portions of which are printed in Gillman's *Life of Coleridge*, C. V. Le Grice, a co-Grecian with Coleridge

my expectations, and perfectly accorded with my wishes.
After a very severe trial of six days' continuance, the
number of the competitors was reduced from seventeen
to four, and after a further process of ordeal we, the sur-
vivors, were declared equal each to the other, and the
Scholarship, according to the will of its founder, awarded
to the youngest of us, who was found to be a Mr. Butler
of St. John's College. I am just two months older than
he is, and though I would doubtless have rather had it
myself, I am yet not at all sorry at his success; for he is
sensible and unassuming, and besides, from his circumstances, such an accession to his annual income must have
been very acceptable to him. So much for myself.

I am greatly rejoiced at your brother's recovery; in
proportion, indeed, to the anxiety and fears I felt on your
account during his illness. I recollected, my most dear
Mrs. Evans, that you are frequently troubled with a
strange forgetfulness of yourself, and too apt to go far
beyond your strength, if by any means you may alle-
viate the sufferings of others. Ah! how different from
the majority of others whom we courteously dignify with
the name of human — a vile herd, who sit still in the
severest distresses of their *friends*, and cry out, There
is a lion in the way! animals, who walk with leaden
sandals in the paths of charity, yet to gratify their own
inclinations will run a mile in a breath. Oh! I do know
a set of little, dirty, pimping, petty-fogging, ambidextrous
fellows, who would set your house on fire, though it were
but to roast an egg for themselves! Yet surely, considering it were a selfish view, the pleasures that arise from
whispering peace to those who are in trouble, and healing
the broken in heart, are far superior to all the unfeeling
can enjoy.

and Allen, gives the names of the
four competitors. The successful
candidate was Samuel Butler, afterwards Head Master of Shrewsbury
and Bishop of Lichfield. *Life of
Coleridge*, 1838, p. 50.

I have inclosed a little work of that great and good man
Archdeacon Paley; it is entitled *Motives of Contentment*,
addressed to the poorer part of our fellow men. The
twelfth page I particularly admire, and the twentieth. The
reasoning has been of some service to *me*, who am of the
race of the Grumbletonians. My dear friend Allen has a
resource against most misfortunes in the natural gaiety of
his temper, whereas my hypochondriac, gloomy spirit *amid
blessings* too frequently warbles out the hoarse gruntings
of discontent! Nor have all the lectures that divines and
philosophers have given us for these three thousand years
past, on the vanity of riches, and the cares of greatness,
etc., prevented me from sincerely regretting that Nature
had not put it into the head of some *rich* man to beget
me for his *first*-born, whereas now I am likely to get bread
just when I shall have no teeth left to chew it. Cheer
up, my little one (thus I answer I)! *better late than
never.* Hath literature been thy choice, and hast thou
food and raiment? Be thankful, be *amazed* at thy good
fortune! Art thou dissatisfied and desirous of other
things? Go, and make twelve votes at an election; it
shall do thee more service and procure thee greater pre-
ferment than to have made twelve commentaries on the
twelve prophets. My dear Mrs. Evans! excuse the wan-
derings of my castle building imagination. I have not a
thought which I conceal from you. I *write* to others, but
my pen talks to you. Convey my softest affections to
Betty, and believe me,

Your grateful and affectionate boy,
S. T. COLERIDGE.

XVII. TO MARY EVANS.

JESUS COLLEGE, CAMBRIDGE, February 7, 1793.

I would to Heaven, my dear Miss Evans, that the god of
wit, or news, or politics would whisper in my ear something
that might be worth sending fifty-four miles — but alas! I

am so closely blocked by an army of misfortunes that really
there is no passage left open for mirth or anything else.
Now, just to give you a few articles in the large inventory
of my calamities.   Imprimis, a gloomy, uncomfortable
morning.   Item, my head aches.   Item, the Dean has set
me a swinging imposition for missing morning chapel.
Item, of the two only coats which I am worth in the world,
both have holes in the elbows.   Item, Mr. Newton, our
mathematical lecturer, has recovered from an illness.   But
the story is rather a laughable one, so I must tell it you.
Mr. Newton (a tall, thin man with a little, tiny, blushing
face) is a great botanist.   Last Sunday, as he was stroll-
ing out with a friend of his, some curious plant suddenly
caught his eye.   He turned round his head with great
eagerness to call his companion to a participation of discovery, and unfortunately continuing to walk forward he
fell into a pool, deep, muddy, and full of chickweed.   I
was lucky enough to meet him as he was entering the college gates on his return (a sight I would not have lost for
the Indies), his best black clothes all green with duck-
weed, he shivering and dripping, in short a perfect river
god.   I went up to him (you must understand we hate
each other most cordially) and sympathized with him in
all the tenderness of condolence.   The consequence of his
misadventure was a violent cold attended with fever, which
confined him to his room, prevented him from giving lectures, and freed me from the necessity of attending them;
but this misfortune I supported with truly Christian fortitude.   However, I constantly asked after his health with
filial anxiety, and this morning, making my usual inquiries, I was informed, to my infinite astonishment and vexation, that he was perfectly recovered and intended to give
lectures this very day!!!   Verily, I swear that six of his
duteous pupils — myself as their general — sallied forth
to the apothecary's house with a fixed determination to
thrash him for having performed so speedy a cure, but,

luckily for himself, the rascal was not at home.   But here
comes my fiddling master, for (but this is a secret) I am
learning to play on the violin.   Twit, twat, twat, twit!
"Pray, M. de la Penche, do you think I shall ever make
anything of this violin?   Do you think I have an ear for
music?"   "Un magnifique!   Un superbe!   Par honneur,
sir, you be a ver great genius in de music.   Good morning, monsieur!"   This M. de la Penche is a better judge
than I thought for.

This new whim of mine is partly a scheme of self-
defence.   Three neighbours have run music-mad lately —
two of them fiddle-scrapers, the third a flute-tooter — and
are perpetually annoying me with their vile performances,
compared with which the gruntings of a whole herd of
sows would be seraphic melody.   Now I hope, by frequently playing myself, to render my ear callous.   Besides, the evils of life are crowding upon me, and music
is "the sweetest assuager of cares."   It helps to relieve
and soothe the mind, and is a sort of refuge from calamity,
from slights and neglects and censures and insults and dis-
appointments; from the warmth of real enemies and the
coldness of pretended friends; from your *well wishers*
(as they are justly called, in opposition, I suppose, to *well
doers*), men whose inclinations to serve you always de-
crease in a most mathematical proportion as their opportunities to do it increase; from the

> "Proud man's contumely, and the spurns
> Which patient merit of th' unworthy takes;"

from grievances that are the growth of all times and
places and not peculiar to *this age*, which authors call this
critical age, and divines this *sinful age*, and politicians
this age of revolutions.   An acquaintance of mine calls
it this *learned age* in due reverence to his own abilities,
and like Monsieur Whatd'yecallhim, who used to pull off
his hat when he spoke of himself.   The poet laureate calls
it "*this golden age*," and with good reason, —

> For *him* the fountains with Canary flow,
> And, best of fruit, spontaneous guineas grow.

Pope, in his "Dunciad," makes it *this leaden age*, but I choose to call it without an epithet, *this* age. Many things we must expect to meet with which it would be hard to bear, if a compensation were not found in honest endeavours to do well, in virtuous affections and connections, and in harmless and reasonable amusements. And why should *not* a man amuse himself sometimes? *Vive la bagatelle!*

I received a letter this morning from my friend Allen. He is up to his ears in business, and I sincerely congratulate him upon it — occupation, I am convinced, being the great secret of happiness. "Nothing makes the temper so fretful as indolence," said a young lady who, beneath the soft surface of feminine delicacy, possesses a mind acute by nature, and strengthened by habits of reflection. 'Pon my word, Miss Evans, I beg your pardon a thousand times for bepraising you to your face, but, really, I have written so long that I had forgot to whom I was writing.

Have you read Mr. Fox's letter to the Westminster electors? It is quite the political *go* at Cambridge, and has converted many souls to the Foxite faith.

Have you seen the Siddons this season? or the Jordan? An acquaintance of mine has a tragedy coming out early in the next season, the principal character of which Mrs. Siddons will act. He has importuned me to write the prologue and epilogue, but, conscious of my inability, I have excused myself with a jest, and told him I was too good a Christian to be accessory to the damnation of anything.

There is an old proverb of a river of words and a spoonful of sense, and I think this letter has been a pretty good proof of it. But as nonsense is better than blank paper, I will fill this side with a song I wrote lately. My friend, Charles Hague [1] the composer, will set it to wild music.

[1] Musical glee composer, 1769–1821. *Biographical Dictionary.*

I shall sing it, and accompany myself on the violin. *Ça
ira !*

Cathloma, who reigned in the Highlands of Scotland
about two hundred years after the birth of our Saviour,
was defeated and killed in a war with a neighbouring
prince, and Nina Thoma his daughter (according to the
custom of those times and that country) was imprisoned
in a cave by the seaside.   This is supposed to be her complaint : —

> How long will ye round me be swelling,
>   O ye blue-tumbling waves of the sea ?
> Not always in caves was my dwelling,
>   Nor beneath the cold blast of the Tree ;
>
> Thro' the high sounding Hall of Cathloma
>   In the steps of my beauty I strayed,
> The warriors beheld Nina Thoma,
>   And they blessed the dark-tressed Maid !
>
> By my Friends, by my Lovers discarded,
>   Like the Flower of the Rock now I waste,
> That lifts its fair head unregarded,
>   And scatters its leaves on the blast.
>
> A Ghost ! by my cavern it darted !
>   In moonbeams the spirit was drest —
> For lovely appear the Departed,
>   When they visit the dreams of my rest !
>
> But dispersed by the tempest's commotion,
>   Fleet the shadowy forms of Delight ;
> Ah ! cease, thou shrill blast of the Ocean !
>   To howl thro' my Cavern by night.[1]

Are you asleep, my dear Mary?   I have administered
rather a strong dose of opium; however, if in the course

[1] *Poetical Works*, p. 20.

of your nap you should chance to dream that I am, with
ardor of eternal friendship, your affectionate

S. T. COLERIDGE,

you will never have dreamt a truer dream in all your days.

XVIII. TO ANNE EVANS.

JESUS COLLEGE, CAMBRIDGE, February 10, 1793.

MY DEAR ANNE, — A little before I had received your
mamma's letter, a bird of the air had informed me of
your illness — and sure never did owl or night-raven
(" those mournful messengers of heavy things ") pipe a
more loathsome song.   But I flatter myself that ere you
have received this scrawl of mine, by care and attention
you will have lured back the rosy-lipped fugitive, Health.
I know of no misfortune so little susceptible of consolation
as sickness : it is indeed easy to offer comfort, when we
ourselves are well ; *then* we can be full of grave saws
upon the duty of resignation, etc. ; but alas ! when the
sore visitations of pain come *home*, all our philosophy
vanishes, and nothing remains to be seen.   I speak of
myself, but a mere sensitive animal, with little wisdom
and no patience.   Yet if anything can throw a melancholy
smile over the pale, wan face of illness, it must be the
sight and attentions of those we love.   There are one or
two beings, in this planet of ours, whom God has formed
in so kindly a mould that I could almost consent to be ill
in order to be nursed by them.

O turtle-eyed affection !
If thou be present — who can be distrest ?
Pain seems to smile, and sorrow is at rest :
No more the thoughts in wild repinings roll,
And tender murmurs hush the soften'd soul.

But I will not proceed at this rate, for I am writing
and thinking myself fast into the spleen, and feel very
obligingly disposed to communicate the same doleful fit
to you, my dear sister.   Yet permit me to say, it is almost

your own fault. You were half angry at my writing *laughing nonsense* to you, and see what you have got in exchange — pale-faced, solemn, stiff-starched stupidity. I must confess, indeed, that the latter is rather more in unison with my present feelings, which from one untoward freak of fortune or other are not of the most comfortable kind. Within this last month I have lost a brother[1] and a friend ! But I struggle for cheerfulness — and sometimes, when the sun shines out, I succeed in the effort. This at least I endeavour, not to infect the cheerfulness of others, and not to write my vexations upon my forehead. I read a story lately of an old Greek philosopher, who once harangued so movingly on the miseries of life, that his audience went home and hanged themselves ; but he himself (my author adds) lived many years afterwards in very sleek condition.

God love you, my dear Anne ! and receive as from a brother the warmest affections of your

S. T. COLERIDGE.

XIX. TO THE REV. GEORGE COLERIDGE.

Wednesday morning, July 28, 1793.

MY DEAR BROTHER, — I left Salisbury on Tuesday morning — should have stayed there longer, but that Ned, ignorant of my coming, had preëngaged himself on a journey to Portsmouth with Skinner. I left Ned well and merry, as likewise his wife, who, by all the Cupids, is a very worthy old lady.[2]

Monday afternoon, Ned, Tatum, and myself sat from four till ten drinking ! and then arose as cool as three undressed cucumbers. Edward and I (O ! the wonders

---

[1] Francis Syndercombe Coleridge, who died shortly after the fall of Seringapatam, February 6, 1792.

[2] Edward Coleridge, the Vicar of Ottery's fourth son, was then assistant master in Dr. Skinner's school at Salisbury. His marriage with an elderly widow who was supposed to have a large income was a source of perennial amusement to his family. Some years after her death he married his first cousin, Anne Bowdon.

of this life) disputed with great coolness and forbearance
the whole time. We neither of us were *convinced*,
though now and then Ned was *convicted*. Tatum umpire
sat,
　　　　And by decision more embroiled the fray.

I found all well in Exeter, to which place I proceeded
directly, as my mother might have been unprepared from
the supposition I meant to stay longer in Salisbury. I
shall dine with James to-day at brother Phillips'.[1]

My ideas are so discomposed by the jolting of the
coach that I can write no more at present.

A piece of gallantry!

I presented a moss rose to a lady. Dick Hart[2] asked
her if she was not afraid to put it in her bosom, as perhaps there might be love in it. I immediately wrote the
following little ode or song or what you please to call it.[3]
It is of the namby-pamby genus.

THE ROSE.

As late each flower that sweetest blows
I plucked, the Garden's pride!
Within the petals of a Rose
A sleeping Love I spied.

Around his brows a beaming wreath
Of many a lucent hue;
All purple glowed his cheek beneath,
Inebriate with dew.

[1] The husband of Coleridge's half sister Elizabeth, the youngest of the vicar's first family, "who alone was bred up with us after my birth, and who alone of the three I was wont to think of as a sister." See Autobiographical Notes of 1832. *Life of Coleridge*, 1838, p. 9.

[2] The brother of Mrs. Luke and of Mrs. George Coleridge.

[3] A note to the *Poems of Samuel Taylor Coleridge*, Moxon, 1852, gives a somewhat different version of the origin of this poem, first printed in the edition of 1796 as Effusion 27, and of the lines included in Letter XX., there headed "Cupid turned Chymist," but afterwards known as "Kisses."

I softly seized the unguarded Power,
Nor scared his balmy rest ;
And placed him, caged within the flower,
On Angelina's breast.

But when unweeting of the guile
Awoke the prisoner sweet,
He struggled to escape awhile
And stamped his faery feet.

Ah ! soon the soul-entrancing sight
Subdued the impatient boy !
He gazed ! he thrilled with deep delight !
Then clapped his wings for joy.

" And O ! " he cried, " of magic kind
What charms this Throne endear !
Some other Love let Venus find —
I 'll fix *my* empire here."

An extempore! Ned during the dispute, thinking he
had got me down, said, " Ah! Sam! you *blush!* " " Sir,"
answered I,

Ten thousand Blushes
Flutter round me drest like little Loves,
And veil my visage with their crimson wings.

There is no meaning in the lines, but we both agreed they
were very pretty. If you see Mr. Hussy, you will not
forget to present my respects to him, and to his accomplished daughter, who certes is a very sweet young lady.

God bless you and your grateful and affectionate

S. T. COLERIDGE.

XX. TO THE SAME.

[Postmark, August 5, 1793.]

MY DEAR BROTHER, — Since my arrival in the country
I have been anxiously expecting a letter from you, nor
can I divine the reason of your silence. From the letter

to my brother James, a few lines of which he read to me,
I am fearful that your silence proceeds from displeasure.
If so, what is left for me to do but to grieve? The past
is not in my power. For the follies of which I may have
been guilty, I have been greatly disgusted; and I trust
the memory of them will operate to future consistency of
conduct.

My mother is very well, — indeed, better for her illness.
Her complexion and eye, the truest indications of health,
are much clearer. Little William and his mother are
well. My brother James is at Sidmouth. I was there
yesterday. He, his wife, and children are well. Frederick is a charming child. Little James had a most provi-
dential escape the day before yesterday. As my brother
was in the field contiguous to his place he heard two men
scream, and turning round saw a horse leap over little
James, and then kick at him. He ran up; found him unhurt. The men said that the horse was feeding with his
tail toward the child, and looking round ran at him open-
mouthed, pushed him down and leaped over him, and then
kicked back at him. Their screaming, my brother sup-
poses, prevented the horse from repeating the blow.
Brother was greatly agitated, as you may suppose. I
stayed at Tiverton about ten days, and got no small kudos
among the young belles by complimentary effusions in the
poetic way.

A specimen : —

CUPID TURNED CHYMIST.

Cupid, if storying Legends tell aright,
Once framed a rich Elixir of Delight.
A chalice o'er love-kindled flames he fix'd,
And in it Nectar and Ambrosia mix'd :
With these the magic dews which Evening brings,
Brush'd from the Idalian star by faery wings :
Each tender pledge of sacred Faith he join'd,
Each gentler Pleasure of th' unspotted mind —

Day-dreams, whose tints with sportive brightness glow,
And Hope, the blameless parasite of Woe.
The eyeless Chymist heard the process rise,
The steamy chalice bubbled up in sighs;
Sweet sounds transpired, as when the enamor'd dove
Pours the soft murmuring of responsive Love.
The finished work might Envy vainly blame,
And " Kisses " was the precious Compound's name.
With half the God his Cyprian Mother blest,
And breath'd on Nesbitt's lovelier lips the rest.

Do you know Fanny Nesbitt? She was my fellow-traveler in the Tiverton diligence from Exeter. [She is], I think, a very pretty girl. The orders for tea are: Imprimis, five pounds of ten shillings green; Item, four pounds of eight shillings green; in all nine pounds of tea.

God bless you and your obliged

S. T. COLERIDGE.

XXI. TO G. L. TUCKETT.[1]

HENLEY, Thursday night, February 6 [1794].

DEAR TUCKETT, — I have this moment received your long letter! The Tuesday before last, an accident of the Reading Fair, our regiment was disposed of for the week in and about the towns within ten miles of Reading, and, as it was not known before we set off to what places we

[1] G. L. Tuckett, to whom this letter was addressed, was the first to disclose to Coleridge's family the unwelcome fact that he had enlisted in the army. He seems to have guessed that the runaway would take his old schoolfellows into his confidence, and that they might be induced to reveal the secret. He was, I presume, a college acquaintance, — possibly an old Blue, who had left the University and was reading for the bar. In an unpublished letter from Robert Allen to Coleridge, dated February, 1796, there is an amusing reference to this kindly Deus ex Machina. " I called upon Tuckett, who thus prophesied : ' You know how subject Coleridge is to fits of idleness. Now, I 'll lay any wager, Allen, that after three or four numbers (of the Watchman) the sheets will contain nothing but parliamentary debates, and Coleridge will add a note at the bottom of the page : " I should think myself deficient in my duty to the Public if I did not give these interesting debates at full length." ' "

would go, my letters were kept at the Reading post-office
till our return. I was conveyed to Henley-upon-Thames,
which place our regiment left last Tuesday; but I am
ordered to remain on account of these dreadfully trouble-
some eruptions, and that I might nurse my comrade, who
last Friday sickened of the confluent smallpox. So here
I am, *videlicet* the Henley workhouse.[1] It is a little house
of one apartment situated in the midst of a large garden,
about a hundred yards from the house. It is four strides
in length and three in breadth; has four windows, which
look to all the winds. The almost total want of sleep, the
putrid smell, and the fatiguing struggles with my poor
comrade during his delirium are nearly too much for me
in my present state. In return I enjoy external peace,
and kind and respectful behaviour from the people of the
workhouse. Tuckett, your motives must have been excellent ones; how could they be otherwise! As an *agent*,
therefore, you are blameless, but your efforts in my behalf
demand my gratitude — *that* my heart will pay you, into
whatever depth of horror your mistaken activity may
eventually have precipitated me. As an *agent*, you stand
acquitted, but the action was *morally* base. In an hour of
extreme anguish, under the most solemn imposition of
secrecy, I entrusted my place and residence to the young
men at Christ's Hospital; the intelligence which you ex-
torted from their imbecility should have remained sacred
with you. It lost not the obligation of secrecy by the
transfer. But your *motives* justify you? To the eye of
your friendship the divulging might have appeared *necessary*, but what shadow of *necessity* is there to excuse you in
showing my letters — to stab the very heart of confidence.

[1] It would seem that there were alleviations to the misery and dis-comfort of this direful experience. In a MS. note dated January, 1805, he recalls as a suitable incident for a projected work, *The Soother in Ab-sence*, the "*Domus quadrata horten-sis*, at Henley-on-Thames," and "the beautiful girl" who, it would seem, soothed the captivity of the forlorn trooper.

You have acted, Tuckett, so uniformly well that reproof
must be new to you. I doubtless shall have offended you.
I would to God that I, too, possessed the tender irritable-
ness of unhandled sensibility. Mine is a sensibility gangrened with inward corruption and the keen searching of
the air from without. Your gossip with the commanding
officer seems so totally useless and unmotived that I almost find a difficulty in believing it.

A letter from my brother George! I feel a kind of
pleasure that it is not directed — it lies unopened — am I
not already sufficiently miserable? The anguish of those
who love me, of him beneath the shadow of whose protection I grew up — does it not plant the pillow with thorns
and make my dreams full of terrors? Yet I dare not burn
the letter — it seems as if there were a horror in the action. One pang, however acute, is better than long-continued solicitude. My brother George possessed the cheering consolation of conscience — but I am talking I know
not what — yet there is a pleasure, doubtless an exquisite
pleasure, mingled up in the most painful of our virtuous
emotions. Alas! my poor mother! What an intolerable
weight of guilt is suspended over my head by a hair on
one hand; and if I endure to live — the look ever downward — insult, pity, hell! God or Chaos, preserve me!
What but infinite Wisdom or infinite Confusion can do
it?

XXII. TO THE REV. GEORGE COLERIDGE.

February 8, 1794.

My more than brother! What shall I say? What
shall I write to you? Shall I profess an abhorrence of my
past conduct? Ah me! too well do I know its iniquity!
But to abhor! this feeble and exhausted heart supplies
not so strong an emotion. O my wayward soul! I have
been a fool even to madness. What shall I dare to promise? My mind is illegible to myself. I am lost in the

labyrinth, the trackless wilderness of my own bosom. Truly may I say, "I am wearied of being saved." My frame is chill and torpid. The ebb and flow of my hopes and fears has stagnated into recklessness. One wish only can I read distinctly in my heart, that it were possible for me to be forgotten as though I had never been! The shame and sorrow of those who loved me! The anguish of him who protected me from my childhood upwards, the sore travail of her who bore me! Intolerable images of horror! They haunt my sleep, they enfever my dreams! O that the shadow of Death were on my eyelids, that I were like the loathsome form by which I now sit! O that without guilt I might ask of my Maker annihilation! My brother, my brother! pray for me, comfort me, my brother! I am very wretched, and, though my complaint be bitter, my stroke is heavier than my groaning.

S. T. COLERIDGE.

XXIII. TO THE SAME.

Tuesday night, February 11, 1794.

I am indeed oppressed, oppressed with the greatness of your love! Mine eyes gush out with tears, my heart is sick and languid with the weight of unmerited kindness. I had intended to have given you a minute history of my thoughts and actions for the last two years of my life. A most severe and faithful history of the heart would it have been — the Omniscient knows it. But I am so universally unwell, and the hour so late, that I must defer it till to-morrow. To-night I shall have a bed in a separate room from my comrade, and, I trust, shall have repaired my strength by sleep ere the morning. For eight days and nights I have not had my clothes off. My comrade is not dead; there is every hope of his escaping death. Closely has he been pursued by the mighty hunter! Undoubtedly, my brother, I could wish to return to College; I know what I *must suffer* there, but deeply do I feel

Colonel James Coleridge

what I *ought* to suffer. Is my brother James still at
Salisbury? I will write to him, to all.

Concerning my emancipation, it appears to me that my
discharge can be easily procured by *interest*, with great
difficulty by *negotiation ;* but of this is not my brother
James a more competent judge?

What my future life may produce I dare not anticipate.
Pray for me, my brother. I will pray nightly to the
Almighty dispenser of good and evil, that his chastise-
ment may not have harrowed my heart in vain. Scepticism has mildewed my hope in the Saviour. I was far
from disbelieving the truth of revealed religion, but still
far from a steady faith — the " Comforter that should
have relieved my soul " was far from me.

Farewell! to-morrow I will resume my pen. Mr.
Boyer! indeed, indeed, my heart thanks him; how often
in the petulance of satire, how ungratefully have I injured
that man!

S. T. COLERIDGE.

XXIV. TO CAPTAIN JAMES COLERIDGE.

February 20, 1794.

In a mind which vice has not utterly divested of sensibility, few occurrences can inflict a more acute pang than
the receiving proofs of tenderness and love where only resentment and reproach were expected and deserved. The
gentle voice of conscience which had incessantly murmured
within the soul then raises its tone and speaks with a
tongue of thunder. My conduct towards you, and towards
my other brothers, has displayed a strange combination
of madness, ingratitude, and dishonesty. But you forgive
me. May my Maker forgive me! May the time arrive
when I shall have forgiven myself!

With regard to my emancipation, every inquiry I have
made, every piece of intelligence I could collect, alike
tend to assure me that it may be done by *interest*, but

not by negotiation without an expense which I should tremble to write. Forty guineas were offered for a discharge the day after a young man was sworn in, and were refused. His friends made interest, and his discharge came down from the War Office. If, however, negotiation *must* be first attempted, it will be expedient to write to our colonel — his name is Gwynne — he holds the rank of general in the army. His address is General Gwynne, K. L. D., King's Mews, London.

My assumed name is Silas Tomkyn Comberbacke, 15th, or King's Regiment of Light Dragoons, G Troop. My *number* I do not know. It is of no import. The bounty I received was six guineas and a half; but a light horseman's bounty is a mere lure; it is expended for him in things which he must have had without a bounty — gaiters, a pair of leather breeches, stable jacket, and shell; horse cloth, surcingle, watering bridle, brushes, and the long etc. of military accoutrement. I *enlisted* the 2d of December, 1793, was attested and sworn the 4th. I am at present nurse to a sick man, and shall, I believe, stay at Henley another week. There will be a large draught from our regiment to complete our troops abroad. The men were picked out to-day. I suppose I am not one, being a very indocile equestrian. Farewell.

S. T. COLERIDGE.

Our regiment is at Reading, and Hounslow, and Maidenhead, and Kensington; our headquarters, Reading, Berks. The commanding officer there, Lieutenant Hopkinson, our adjutant.

To CAPTAIN JAMES COLERIDGE, Tiverton, Devonshire.

XXV. TO THE REV. GEORGE COLERIDGE.

THE COMPASSES, HIGH WYCOMBE, March 12, 1794.

MY DEAR BROTHER, — Accept my poor thanks for the day's enclosed, which I received safely. I explained the

whole matter to the adjutant, who laughed and said I
had been used scurvily ; he deferred settling the bill till
Thursday morning. A Captain Ogle,[1] of our regiment,
who is returned from abroad, has taken great notice of
me. When he visits the stables at night he always enters
into conversation with me, and to-day, finding from the
corporal's report that I was unwell, he sent me a couple of
bottles of wine. These things demand my gratitude. I
wrote last week — *currente calamo* — a declamation for
my friend Allen on the comparative good and evil of
novels. The credit which he got for it I should almost
blush to tell you. All the fellows have got copies, and
they meditate having it printed, and dispersing it through
the University. The best part of it I built on a sentence
in a last letter of yours, and indeed, I wrote most part of
it *feelingly*.

I met yesterday, smoking in the recess, a chimney
corner of the pot-house [2] at which I am quartered, a man
of the greatest information and most original genius I
ever lit upon. His philosophical theories of heaven and
hell would have both amused you and given you hints for
much speculation. He solemnly assured me that he believed himself divinely inspired. He slept in the same
room with me, and kept me awake till three in the morning with his ontological disquisitions. Some of the ideas

[1] In the various and varying reminiscences of his soldier days, which
fell " from Coleridge's own mouth,"
and were repeated by his delighted
and credulous hearers, this officer
plays an important part. Whatever
foundation of fact there may be
for the touching anecdote that the
Latin sentence, " *Eheu ! quam infor-
tunii miserrimum est fuisse felicem,*"
scribbled on the walls of the stable
at Reading, caught the attention of
Captain Ogle, " himself a scholar,"
and led to Comberbacke's detection,

he was not, as the poet Bowles and
Miss Mitford maintained, the sole
instrument in procuring the discharge. He may have exerted himself privately, but his name does not
occur in the formal correspondence
which passed between Coleridge's
brothers and the military authorities.

[2] The Compasses, now The
Chequers, High Wycombe, where
Coleridge was billeted just a hundred years ago, appears to have preserved its original aspect.

would have made you shudder from their daring impiety, others would have astounded with their sublimity. My memory, tenacious and systematizing, would enable [me] to write an octavo from his conversation. "I find [says he] from the intellectual atmosphere that emanes from, and envelops you, that you are in a state of recipiency." He was deceived. I have little faith, yet am wonderfully fond of speculating on mystical schemes. Wisdom may be gathered from the maddest flights of imagination, as medicines were stumbled upon in the wild processes of alchemy. God bless you. Your ever grateful

S. T. COLERIDGE.

Tuesday evening. — I leave this place [High Wycombe] on Thursday, 10 o'clock, for Reading. A letter will arrive in time before I go.

XXVI. TO THE SAME.

Sunday night, March 21, 1794.

I have endeavoured to feel what I ought to feel. Affiliated to you from my childhood, what must be my present situation? But I know you, my dear brother; and I entertain a humble confidence that my efforts in well-doing shall in some measure repay you. There is a *vis inertiæ* in the human mind — I am convinced that a man once corrupted will ever remain so, unless some sudden revolution, some unexpected change of place or station, shall have utterly altered his connection. When these shocks of adversity have electrified his moral frame, he feels a convalescence of soul, and becomes like a being recently formed from the hands of nature.

The last letter I received from you at High Wycombe was that almost blank letter which enclosed the guinea. I have written to the postmaster. I have breeches and waistcoats at Cambridge, three or four shirts, and some neckcloths, and a few pairs of stockings; the clothes, which, rather from the order of the regiment than the impulse of my necessities, I parted with in Reading on my first arrival at the regiment, I disposed of for a mere trifle, comparatively, and at a small expense can recover them all but my coat and hat. They are gone irrevocably. My shirts, which I have with me, are, all but one, worn to rags — mere rags; their texture was ill-adapted to the labour of the stables.

Shall I confess to you my weakness, my more than brother? I am afraid to meet you. When I call to mind the toil and wearisomeness of your avocations, and think how you sacrifice your amusements and your health; when I recollect your habitual and self-forgetting economy, how generously severe, my soul sickens at its own guilt. A thousand reflections crowd in my mind; they are almost too much for me. Yet you, my brother, would comfort me, not reproach me, and extend the hand of forgiveness to one whose purposes were virtuous, though infirm, and whose energies vigorous, though desultory. Indeed, I long to see you, although I cannot help dreading it.

I mean to write to Dr. Pearce. The letter I will enclose to you. Perhaps it may not be proper to write, perhaps it may be necessary. You will best judge. The discharge should, I think, be sent down to the adjutant — yet I don't know; it would be more comfortable to me to receive my dismission in London, were it not for the appearing in these clothes.

By to-morrow I shall be enabled to tell the exact expenses of equipping, etc.

I must conclude abruptly. God bless you, and your ever grateful

S. T. COLERIDGE.

XXVII. TO THE SAME.

End of March, 1794.

MY DEAR BROTHER, — I have been rather uneasy, that I have not heard from you since my departure from High Wycombe. Your letters are a comfort to me in the comfortless hour — they are manna in the wilderness. I should have written you long ere this, but in truth I have been blockaded by a whole army of petty vexations, bad quarters, etc., and within this week I have been thrown three times from my horse and run away with to the no small perturbation of my nervous system almost every day. I ride a horse, young, and as undisciplined as myself. After tumult and agitation of any kind the mind and all its affections seem to *doze* for a while, and we sit shivering with chilly feverishness wrapped up in the ragged and threadbare cloak of mere animal enjoyment.

On Sunday last I was surprised, or rather confounded, with a visit from Mr. Cornish, so confounded that for more than a minute I could not speak to him. He behaved with great delicacy and much apparent solicitude of friendship. He passed through Reading with his sister Lady Shore. I have received several letters from my friends at Cambridge, of most soothing contents. They write me, that with "undiminished esteem and increased affection, the *Jesuites* look forward to my return as to that of a lost brother!"

My present address is the White Hart, Reading, Berks. Adieu, most dear brother!

S. T. COLERIDGE.

XXVIII. TO THE SAME.

March 27, 1794.

MY DEAR BROTHER, — I find that I was too sanguine in my expectations of recovering all my clothes. My coat, which I had supposed gone, and all the stockings, viz.,

four pairs of almost new silk stockings, and two pairs of
new silk and cotton, I can get again for twenty-three shillings. I have ordered, therefore, a pair of breeches, which
will be nineteen shillings, a waistcoat at twelve shillings,
a pair of shoes at seven shillings and four pence. Besides
these I must have a hat, which will be eighteen shillings,
and two neckcloths, which will be five or six shillings.
These things I have ordered. My travelling expenses will
be about half a guinea. Have I done wrong in ordering
these things ? Or did you mean me to do it by desiring me
to arrange what was necessary for my personal appearance at Cambridge ? I have so seldom acted right, that
in every step I take of my own accord I tremble lest I
should be wrong. I forgot in the above account to mention a flannel waistcoat ; it will be six shillings. The
military dress is almost oppressively warm, and so very ill
as I am at present I think it imprudent to hazard cold.
I will see you at London, or rather at Hackney. There
will be two or three trifling expenses on my leaving the
army ; I know not their exact amount. The adjutant dis-
missed me from all duty yesterday. My head throbs so,
and I am so sick at stomach that it is with difficulty I can
write. One thing more I wished to mention. There are
three books, which I parted with at Reading. The bookseller, whom I have occasionally obliged by composing
advertisements for his newspaper, has offered them me at
the same price he bought them. They are a very valuable
edition of Casimir [1] by Barbou,[2] a Synesius [3] by Canterus

---

[1] See Notes to *Poetical Works of Coleridge* (1893), p. 568. The " intended translation " was advertised
in the *Cambridge Intelligencer* for
June 14 and June 16, 1794 : " Proposals for publishing by subscription *Imitations from the Modern
Latin Poets, with a Critical and Biographical Essay on the Restoration
of Literature.* By S. T. Coleridge,
of Jesus College, Cambridge. . . .

" In the course of the Work will
be introduced a copious selection
from the Lyrics of Casimir, and a
new Translation of the Basia of Se-
cundus."

One ode, "Ad Lyram," was printed in *The Watchman*, No. 11, March
9, 1796, p. 49.

[2] *The Barbou Casimir*, published
at Paris in 1759.

[3] Compare the note to chapter

and Bentley's Quarto Edition. They are worth thirty shillings, at least, and I sold them for fourteen. The two first I mean to translate. I have finished two or three Odes of Casimir, and shall on my return to College send them to Dodsley as a specimen of an intended translation. Barbou's edition is the only one that contains all the works of Casimir. God bless you. Your grateful

S. T. C.

XXIX. TO THE SAME.

Sunday night, March 30, 1794.

My dear Brother, — I received your enclosed. I am fearful, that as you advise me to go immediately to Cambridge after my discharge, that the utmost contrivances of economy will not enable [me] to make it adequate to all the expenses of my clothes and travelling. I shall go across the country on many accounts. The expense (I have examined) will be as nearly equal as well can be. The *fare* from Reading to High Wycombe on the outside is four shillings, from High Wycombe to Cambridge (for *there is* a coach that passes through Cambridge from Wycombe) I suppose about twelve shillings, perhaps a trifle more. I shall be two days and a half on the road, *two nights*. Can I calculate the expense at less than half a guinea, including all things? An additional guinea would perhaps be sufficient. Surely, my brother, I am not so utterly abandoned as not to feel the *meaning* and *duty* of *economy*. Oh me! I wish to God I were happy; but it would be strange indeed if I were so.

I long ago theoretically and in a less degree experimentally knew the necessity of faith in order to regulate

xii. of the *Biographia Literaria:* "In the Biographical Sketch of my Literary Life I may be excused if I mention here that I had translated the eight Hymns of Synesius from the Greek into English Anacreontics before my fifteenth year." The edition referred to may be that published at Basle in 1567. *Interprete G. Cantero.* Bentley's Quarto Edition was probably the Quarto Edition of Horace, published in 1711.

virtue, nor did I even seriously disbelieve the existence of
a future state. In short, my religious creed bore and,
perhaps, bears a correspondence with my mind and heart.
I had too much vanity to be altogether a Christian, too
much tenderness of nature to be utterly an infidel. Fond
of the dazzle of wit, fond of subtlety of argument, I could
not read without some degree of pleasure the levities of
Voltaire or the reasonings of Helvetius; but, tremblingly
alive to the feelings of humanity, and susceptible to the
charms of truth, my heart forced me to admire the " beauty
of holiness " in the Gospel, forced me to *love* the Jesus,
whom my reason (or perhaps my reasonings) would not
permit me to worship, — my faith, therefore, was made up
of the Evangelists and the deistic philosophy — a kind of
religious twilight. I said, "*perhaps bears*," — yes! my
brother, for who can say, "*Now* I'll be a Christian"?
Faith is neither altogether voluntary; we cannot believe
what we choose, but we can certainly cultivate such habits
of thinking and acting as will give force and effective
energy to the arguments on either side.

If I receive my discharge by Thursday, I will be, God
pleased, in Cambridge on Sunday. Farewell, my brother!
Believe me your severities only wound me as they awake
the *voice* within to speak, ah! how more harshly! I feel
gratitude and love towards you, even when I shrink and
shiver.   Your affectionate

                                    S. T. COLERIDGE.

XXX. TO THE SAME.

April 7, 1794.

MY DEAR BROTHER, — The last three days I have
spent at Bray, near Maidenhead, at the house of a gentleman who has behaved with particular attention to me.
I accepted his invitation as it was in my power in some
measure to repay his kindness by the revisal of a performance he is about to publish, and by writing him a

dedication and preface. At my return I found two letters from you, the one containing the two guineas, which will be perfectly adequate to my expenses, and, my brother, what some part of your letter made me feel, I am ill able to express; but of this at another time. I have signed the certificate of my expenses, but not my discharge. The moment I receive it I shall set off for Cambridge immediately, most probably through London, as the gentleman, whose house I was at at Bray, has pressed me to take his horse, and accompany him on Wednesday morning, as he himself intends to ride to town that day. If my discharge comes down on Tuesday morning I shall embrace his offer, particularly as I shall be introduced to his bookseller, a thing of some consequence to my present views.

Clagget[1] has set four songs of mine most divinely, for two violins and a pianoforte. I have done him some services, and he wishes me to write a serious opera, which he will set, and have introduced. It is to be a joint work. I think of it. The rules for *adaptable* composition which he has given me are excellent, and I feel my powers greatly strengthened, owing, I believe, to my having read little or nothing for these last four months.

XXXI. TO THE SAME.

May 1, 1794.

MY DEAR BROTHER, — I have been convened before the fellows.[2] Dr. Pearce behaved with great asperity, Mr. Plampin[3] with exceeding and most delicate kindness. My

---

[1] Charles Clagget, a musical composer and inventor of musical instruments, flourished towards the close of the eighteenth century. I have been unable to ascertain whether the songs in question were ever published. *Dictionary of Music and Musicians*, edited by George Grove, D. C. L., 1879, article "Clagget," i. 359.

[2] The entry in the College Register of Jesus College is brief and to the point: " 1794 Apr.: *Coleridge admonitus est per magistrum in præsentiâ sociorum.*"

[3] A letter to George Coleridge dated April 16, 1794, and signed J. Plampin, has been preserved. The pains and penalties to which Coleridge had subjected himself are

sentence is a reprimand (not a public one, but *implied* in the sentence), a month's confinement to the precincts of the College, and to translate the works of Demetrius Phalareus into English. It is a thin quarto of about ninety Greek pages. All the fellows tried to persuade the Master to greater leniency, but in vain. Without the least affectation I applaud his conduct, and think nothing of it. The confinement is nothing. I have the fields and grove of the College to walk in, and what can I wish more? What do I wish more? Nothing. The Demetrius is dry, and utterly untransferable to *modern* use, and yet from the Doctor's words I suspect that he wishes it to be a publication, as he has more than once sent to know how I go on, and pressed me to exert erudition in some notes, and to write a preface. Besides this, I have had a declamation to write in the routine of college business, and the Rustat examination, at which I got credit. I get up every morning at five o'clock.

Every one of my acquaintance I have dropped solemnly and forever, except those of my College with whom before my departure I had been least of all connected — who had always remonstrated against my imprudences, yet have treated me with almost fraternal affection, Mr. Caldwell particularly. I thought the most *decent* way of dropping acquaintances was to express my intention, openly and irrevocably.

I find I must either go out at a by-term or degrade to the Christmas after next; but more of this to-morrow. I have been engaged in finishing a Greek ode. I mean to write for all the prizes. I have had no time upon my hands. I shall aim at correctness and perspicuity, not *genius*. My last ode was so *sublime* that nobody could

stated in full, but the kindly nature of the writer is shown in the concluding sentence: "I am happy in adding that I thought your brother's conduct on his return extremely proper; and I beg to assure you that it will give me much pleasure to see him take such an advantage of his experience as his own good sense will dictate."

understand it. *If* I should be so *very lucky* as to win one of the prizes, I could *comfortably* ask the Doctor advice concerning the *time* of my degree. I will write to-morrow.

God bless you, my brother! my father!

S. T. COLERIDGE.

XXXII. TO ROBERT SOUTHEY.

GLOUCESTER, Sunday morning, July 6, 1794.

S. T. Coleridge to R. Southey, Health and Republicanism to be! When you write, direct to me, "To be kept at the Post Office, Wrexham, Denbighshire, N. Wales." I mention this circumstance *now*, lest carried away by a flood of confluent ideas I should forget it. You are averse to gratitudinarian flourishes, else would I talk about hospitality, attentions, etc. However, as I must not thank you, I will thank my stars. Verily, Southey, I like not Oxford nor the inhabitants of it. I would say, thou art a nightingale among owls, but thou art so songless and heavy towards night that I will rather liken thee to the matin lark. Thy *nest* is in a blighted cornfield, where the sleepy poppy nods its red-cowled head, and the weak-eyed mole plies his dark work; but thy soaring is even unto heaven. Or let me add (for my appetite for similes is truly canine at this moment) that as the Italian nobles their new-fashioned doors, so thou dost make the adamantine gate of democracy turn on its golden hinges to most sweet music. Our journeying has been intolerably fatiguing from the heat and whiteness of the roads, and the *unhedged* country presents nothing but *stone* fences, dreary to the eye and scorching to the touch. But we shall soon be in Wales.

Gloucester is a nothing-to-be-said-about town. The women have almost all of them sharp noses.

. . . .

It is *wrong*, Southey! for a little girl with a half-

famished sickly baby in her arms to put her head in at
the window of an inn — "Pray give me a bit of bread
and meat!" from a party dining on lamb, green peas,
and salad. Why? Because it is *impertinent* and *obtrusive!* "I am a gentleman! and wherefore the clamorous
voice of woe intrude upon mine ear?" My companion is
a man of cultivated, though not vigorous understanding;
his feelings are all on the side of humanity; yet such are
the unfeeling remarks, which the lingering remains of
aristocracy occasionally prompt. When the pure system
of pantisocracy shall have *aspheterized* — from ἀ, non,
and σφέτερος, proprius (we really *wanted* such a word), instead of travelling along the circuitous, dusty, beaten
highroad of diction, you thus cut across the soft, green,
pathless field of novelty! Similes for ever! Hurrah! I
have bought a little blank book, and portable ink horn;
[and] as I journey onward, I ever and anon pluck the
wild flowers of poesy, "inhale their odours awhile," then
throw them away and think no more of them. I will not
do so! Two lines of mine: —

> And o'er the sky's unclouded blue
> The sultry heat *suffus'd* a *brassy* hue.

The cockatrice is a foul dragon with a *crown* on its head.
The Eastern nations believe it to be hatched by a viper
on a cock's egg. Southey, dost thou not see wisdom
in her *Coan* vest of allegory? The cockatrice is emblematic of monarchy, a *monster* generated by *ingratitude*
or *absurdity.* When serpents *sting*, the only remedy is
to kill the *serpent*, and *besmear* the *wound* with the *fat.*
Would you desire better sympathy?

Description of heat from a poem I am manufacturing,
the title: "Perspiration. A Travelling Eclogue."

> The dust flies smothering, as on clatt'ring wheel
> Loath'd aristocracy careers along;

The distant track quick vibrates to the eye,
And white and dazzling undulates with heat,
Where scorching to the unwary travellers' touch,
The stone fence flings its narrow slip of shade ;
Or, where the worn sides of the chalky road
Yield their scant excavations (sultry grots !),
Emblem of languid patience, we behold
The fleecy files faint-ruminating lie.

Farewell, sturdy Republican ! Write me concerning Burnett and thyself, and concerning etc., etc. My next shall be a more sober and chastened epistle ; but, you see, I was in the humour for metaphors, and, to tell thee the truth, I have so often serious reasons to quarrel with my inclination, that I do not choose to contradict it for trifles. To Lovell, fraternity and civic remembrances ! Hucks' compliments.

S. T. COLERIDGE.

Addressed to " Robert Southey.   Miss Tyler's, Bristol."

XXXIII. TO THE SAME.

WREXHAM, Sunday, July 15, 1794.[1]

Your letter, Southey ! made me melancholy. Man is a bundle of habits, but of all habits the habit of despondence is the most pernicious to virtue and happiness. I once shipwrecked my frail bark on that rock ; a friendly plank was vouchsafed me. Be you wise by my experience,

---

[1] A week later, July 22, in a letter addressed to H. Martin, of Jesus College, to whom, in the following September, he dedicated "The Fall of Robespierre," Coleridge repeated almost verbatim large portions of this *lettre de voyage.* The incident of the sentiment and the Welsh clergyman takes a somewhat different shape, and both versions differ from the report of the same occurrence contained in Hucks' account of the tour, which was published in the following year. Coleridge's letters from foreign parts were written with a view to literary effect, and often with the half-formed intention of sending them to the "booksellers." They are to be compared with "letters from our own correspondent," and in respect of picturesque adventure, dramatic dialogue, and so forth, must be judged solely by a literary standard. *Biographia Literaria,* 1847, ii. 338-343 ; J. Hucks' *Tour in North Wales,* 1795, p. 25.

and receive unhurt the flower, which I have climbed precipices to pluck.   Consider the high advantages which you
possess in so eminent a degree — health, strength of mind,
and confirmed habits of strict morality.   Beyond all doubt,
by the creative powers of your genius, you might supply
whatever the stern simplicity of republican wants could
require.   Is there no possibility of procuring the office of
clerk in a compting-house ?   A month's application would
qualify you for it.   For God's sake, Southey! enter not
into the church.   Concerning Allen I say little, but I feel
anguish at times.   This earnestness of remonstrance! I
will not offend you by asking your pardon for it.   The
following is a *fact*.   A friend of Hucks' after long struggles between principle and *interest*, as it is improperly
called, accepted a place under government.   He took the
oaths, shuddered, went home and threw himself in an
agony out of a two-pair of stairs window!   These dreams
of despair are most soothing to the imagination.   I well
know it.   We shroud ourselves in the mantle of distress,
and tell our poor hearts, "This is *happiness!*"   There
is a *dignity* in all these solitary emotions that flatters the
pride of our nature.   Enough of sermonizing.   As I was
meditating on the capability of pleasure in a mind like
yours, I unwarily fell into poetry : [1] —

> 'T is thine with fairy forms to talk,
> And thine the philosophic walk ;
> And what to thee the sweetest are —
> The setting sun, the Evening Star —
> The tints, that live along the sky,
> The Moon, that meets thy raptured eye,
> Where grateful oft the big drops start,
> Dear silent pleasures of the Heart !
> But if thou pour one votive lay,
> For humble independence pray ;

[1] The lines are from " Happiness," See *Poetical Works*, p. 17. See, too,
an early poem first published in 1834. Editor's Note, p. 564.

Whom (sages say) in days of yore
Meek Competence to Wisdom bore.
So shall thy little vessel glide
With a fair breeze adown the tide,
Till Death shall close thy tranquil eye
While Faith exclaims : " Thou shalt not die ! "

> " The heart-smile glowing on his aged cheek
> Mild as decaying light of summer's eve,"

are lines eminently beautiful. The whole is pleasing.
For a motto ! Surely my memory has suffered an epileptic
fit. A Greek motto would be pedantic. These lines will
perhaps do : —

All mournful to the pensive sages' eye,[1]
The monuments of human glory lie ;
Fall'n palaces crush'd by the ruthless haste
Of Time, and many an empire's silent waste —

. . . .
But where a sight shall shuddering sorrow find
Sad as the ruins of the human mind, —

BOWLES.

A better will soon occur to me. Poor Poland ! They
go on sadly there. Warmth of particular friendship does
not imply absorption. The nearer you approach the sun,
the more intense are his rays. Yet what distant corner of
the system do they not cheer and vivify ? The ardour of
private attachments makes philanthropy a necessary *habit*
of the soul. I love my friend. Such as *he* is, all mankind
are or might be. The deduction is evident. Philanthropy
(and indeed every other virtue) is a thing of *concretion*.
Some home-born feeling is the centre of the ball, that
rolling on through life collects and assimilates every congenial affection. What did you mean by *II.* has " my

---

[1] Quoted from a poem by Bowles entitled, " Verses inscribed to His Grace the Duke of Leeds, and other Promoters of the Philanthropic Society." Southey adopted the last two lines of the quotation as a motto for his " Botany Bay Eclogues." *Poetical Works of Milman, Bowles, etc.,* Paris, 1829, p. 117 ; Southey's *Poetical Works,* 1837, ii. 71.

understanding"? I have puzzled myself in vain to discover the import of the sentence. The only sense it *seemed* to bear was so like *mock-humility*, that I scolded myself for the momentary supposition.[1] My heart is so heavy at present, that I will defer the finishing of this letter till to-morrow.

I saw a face in Wrexham Church this morning, which recalled " Thoughts full of bitterness and images " too dearly loved! now past and but " Remembered like sweet sounds of yesterday ! " At Ross (sixteen miles from Gloucester) we took up our quarters at the King's Arms, once the house of Kyrle, the Man of Ross. I gave the window-shutter the following effusion :[2] —

> Richer than Misers o'er their countless hoards,
> Nobler than Kings, or king-polluted Lords,
> Here dwelt the Man of Ross ! O Traveller, hear!
> Departed Merit claims the glistening tear.
> Friend to the friendless, to the sick man health,
> With generous joy he viewed his modest wealth ;
> He heard the widow's heaven-breathed prayer of praise,
> He mark'd the sheltered orphan's tearful gaze ;
> And o'er the dowried maiden's glowing cheek
> Bade bridal love suffuse its blushes meek.
> If 'neath this roof thy wine-cheer'd moments pass,
> Fill to the good man's name one grateful glass !
> To higher zest shall Memory wake thy soul,
> And Virtue mingle in the sparkling bowl.
> But if, like me, thro' life's distressful scene,
> Lonely and sad thy pilgrimage hath been,
> And if thy breast with heart-sick anguish fraught,
> Thou journeyest onward tempest-tost in thought,
> Here cheat thy cares, — in generous visions melt,
> And *dream* of Goodness thou hast never felt !

I will resume the pen to-morrow.

[1] Southey, we may suppose, had contrasted Hucks with Coleridge. " H. is on my level, not yours."

[2] *Poetical Works*, p. 33. See, too, Editor's Note, p. 570.

Monday, 11 o'clock. Well, praised be God! here I am. Videlicet, Ruthin, sixteen miles from Wrexham. At Wrexham Church I glanced upon the face of a Miss E. Evans, a young lady with [whom] I had been in habits of fraternal correspondence. She turned excessively pale; she thought it my ghost, I suppose. I retreated with all possible speed to our inn. There, as I was standing at the window, passed by Eliza Evans, and with her to my utter surprise her sister, Mary Evans, *quam efflictim et perdite amabam.* I apprehend she is come from London on a visit to her grandmother, with whom Eliza lives. I turned sick, and all but fainted away! The two sisters, as H. informs me, passed by the window anxiously several times afterwards; but I had retired.

> *Vivit, sed mihi non vivit — nova forte marita,*
> *Ah dolor! alterius carâ a cervice pependit.*
> *Vos, malefida valete accensæ insomnia mentis,*
> *Littora amata valete! Vale, ah! formosa Maria!*

My fortitude would not have supported me, had I *recognized* her — I mean *appeared* to do it! I neither ate nor slept yesterday. But love is a local anguish; I am sixteen miles distant, and am not half so miserable. I must endeavour to forget it amid the terrible graces of the wild wood scenery that surround me. I never durst even in a whisper avow my passion, though I knew she loved me. Where were my fortunes? and why should I make her miserable! Almighty God bless her! Her image is in the sanctuary of my heart, and never can it be torn away but with the strings that grapple it to life. Southey! there are few men of whose delicacy I think so highly as to have written all this. I am glad I have so deemed of you. We are soothed by communications.

Denbigh (eight miles from Ruthin).

And now to give you some little account of our journey. From Oxford to Gloucester, to Ross, to Hereford, to

Leominster, to Bishop's Castle, to Welsh Pool, to Llanfyllin, nothing occurred worthy notice except that at the last place I preached pantisocracy and aspheterism with so much success that two great huge fellows of butcher-like appearance danced about the room in enthusiastic agitation. And one of them of his own accord called for a large glass of brandy, and drank it off to this his own toast, " God save the King ! And may he be the last." Southey ! Such men may be of use. They would kill the golden calf *secundum artem*. From Llanfyllin we penetrated into the interior of the country to Llangunnog, a village most romantically situated. We dined there on hashed mutton, cucumber, bread and cheese, and beer, and had two pots of ale — the sum total of the expense being sixteen pence for both of us ! From Llangunnog we walked over the mountains to Bala — most sublimely terrible ! It was scorchingly hot. I applied my mouth ever and anon to the side of the rocks and sucked in draughts of water cold as ice, and clear as infant diamonds in their embryo dew ! The rugged and stony clefts are stupendous, and in winter must form cataracts most astonishing. At this time of the year there is just water enough dashed down over them to " soothe, not disturb the pensive traveller's ear." I slept by the side of one an hour or more. As we descended the mountain, the sun was reflected in the river, that winded through the valley with insufferable brightness ; it rivalled the sky. At Bala is nothing remarkable except a lake of eleven miles in circumference. At the inn I was sore afraid that I had caught the itch from a Welsh democrat, who was charmed with my sentiments : he grasped my hand with flesh-bruising ardor, and I trembled lest some disappointed citizens of the *animalcular* republic should have emigrated.

Shortly after, into the same room, came a well-dressed clergyman and four others, among whom (the landlady whispers me) was a justice of the peace and the doctor of the parish. I was asked for a gentleman. I gave General Washington. The parson said in a low voice, "Republicans!" After which, the medical man said, "Damn toasts! I gives a sentiment: May all republicans be guillotined!" Up starts the Welsh democrat. "May all fools be gulloteen'd — and then you will be the first." Thereon rogue, villain, traitor flew thick in each other's faces as a hailstorm. This is nothing in Wales. They *make calling one another liars*, etc., necessary vent-holes to the superfluous fumes of the temper. At last I endeavoured to articulate by observing that, whatever might be our opinions in politics, the appearance of a clergyman in the company assured me we were all Christians; "though," continued I, "it is rather difficult to reconcile the last sentiment with the spirit of Christianity." "Pho!" quoth the parson, "Christianity! Why, we are not at church now, are we? The gemman's sentiment was a very good one; it showed he was *sincere* in his principles." Welsh politics could not prevail over Welsh hospitality. They all, except the parson, shook me by the hand, and said I was an open-hearted, honest-speaking fellow, though I was a bit of a democrat.

From Bala we travelled onward to Llangollen, a most beautiful village in a most beautiful situation. On the road we met two Cantabs of my college, Brookes and Berdmore. These rival *pedestrians* — perfect *Powells* — were vigorously pursuing their tour in a *post-chaise!* We laughed famously. Their only excuse was that Berdmore had been ill. From Llangollen to Wrexham, from Wrexham to Ruthin, to Denbigh. At Denbigh is a ruined castle; it surpasses everything I could have conceived. I wandered there an hour and a half last evening (this is Tuesday morning). Two well-dressed young men were walking there. "Come," says one, "I'll play my flute; 't will be romantic." "Bless thee for the thought, man of genius and sensibility!" I exclaimed, and preattuned my heartstring to tremulous emotion. He sat adown (the moon just peering) amid the awful part of the ruins, and the romantic youth struck up the affecting tune of " Mrs. Carey." [1] 'T is fact, upon my honour.

God bless you, Southey! We shall be at Aberystwith [2] this day week. When will you come out to meet us? There you must direct your letter. Hucks' compliments. I anticipate much accession of republicanism from Lovell. I have positively done nothing but dream of the system of no property every step of the way since I left you, till last Sunday. Heigho!

ROBERT SOUTHEY, No. 8 Westcott Buildings, Bath.

XXXIV. TO THE SAME.

10 o'clock, Thursday morning, September 18, 1794.

Well, my dear Southey! I am at last arrived at Jesus. My God! how tumultuous are the movements of my heart. Since I quitted this room what and how important events have been evolved! America! Southey! Miss Fricker! Yes, Southey, you are right. Even Love is the creature of strong motive. I certainly love her. I *think* of her incessantly and with unspeakable tenderness, — with that inward melting away of soul that symptomatizes it.

Pantisocracy! Oh, I shall have such a scheme of it! My head, my heart, are all alive. I have drawn up my arguments in battle array; they shall have the *tacti-*

---

[1] Hucks records the incident in much the same words, but gives the name of the tune as " Corporal Casey."

[2] The letter to Martin gives further particulars of the tour, including the ascent of Penmaen Mawr in company with Brookes and Berdmore. Compare *Table Talk* for May 31, 1830 : " I took the thought of *grinning for joy* in that poem (*The Ancient Mariner*) from my companion's remark to me, when we had climbed to the top of Plinlimmon, and were nearly dead with thirst. We could not speak from the constriction till we found a little puddle under a stone. He said to me, ' You grinned like an idiot.' He had done the same." The parching thirst of the pedestrians, and their excessive joy at the discovery of a spring of water, are recorded by Hucks. *Tour in North Wales*, 1795, p. 62.

cian excellence of the mathematician with the enthusiasm
of the poet. The head shall be the mass; the heart the
fiery spirit that fills, informs, and agitates the whole. Har-
wood — pish! I say nothing of him.

SHAD GOES WITH US. HE IS MY BROTHER!
I am longing to be with you. Make Edith my sister.
Surely, Southey, we shall be *frendotatoi meta frendous* —
most friendly where all are friends. She must, therefore,
be more emphatically my sister.

Brookes and Berdmore, as I suspected, have spread my
opinions in mangled forms at Cambridge. Caldwell, the
most pantisocratic of aristocrats, has been laughing at
me. Up I arose, terrible in reasoning. He fled from me,
because "he could not answer for his own sanity, sitting
so near a madman of genius." He told me that the
strength of my imagination had intoxicated my reason,
and that the acuteness of my reason had given a directing
influence to my imagination. Four months ago the remark would not have been more elegant than just. Now
it is nothing.

I like your sonnets exceedingly — the best of any I
have yet seen.[1] "Though to the eye fair is the extended
vale" should be "to the eye though fair the extended vale."
I by no means disapprove of discord introduced to produce
effect, nor is my ear so fastidious as to be angry with it
where it could not have been avoided without weakening
the sense. But discord for discord's sake is rather too
licentious.

"Wild wind" has no other but alliterative beauty; it
applies to a storm, not to the autumnal breeze that makes
the trees rustle mournfully. Alter it to "That rustle to
the sad wind moaningly."

"'T was a long way and tedious," and the three last
lines are marked beauties — unlaboured strains poured
soothingly along from the feeling simplicity of heart. The

[1] Southey's *Poetical Works*, 1837, ii. 93.

next sonnet is altogether exquisite, — the circumstance
common yet new to poetry, the moral accurate and full of
soul.[1] " I never saw," etc., is most exquisite. I am almost
ashamed to write the following, it is so inferior. Ashamed?
No, Southey! God knows my heart! I am *delighted* to
feel you superior to me in genius as in virtue.

> No more my visionary soul shall dwell
> On joys that were ; no more endure to weigh
> The shame and anguish of the evil day.
> Wisely forgetful !   O'er the ocean swell
> Sublime of Hope, I seek the cottag'd dell
> Where Virtue calm with careless step may stray,
> And, dancing to the moonlight roundelay,
> The wizard Passions weave an holy spell.
> Eyes that have ach'd with sorrow ! ye shall weep
> Tears of doubt-mingled joy, like theirs who start
> From precipices of distemper'd sleep,
> On which the fierce-eyed fiends their revels keep,
> And see the rising sun, and feel it dart
> New rays of pleasance trembling to the heart.[2]

I have heard from Allen, and write the third letter to
him. Yours is the second. Perhaps you would like two
sonnets I have written to my Sally. When I have received an answer from Allen I will tell you the contents
of his first letter.

My compliments to Heath.

I will write you a huge, big letter next week. At present I have to transact the tragedy business, to wait on the
Master, to write to Mrs. Southey, Lovell, etc., etc.

God love you, and

                              S. T. COLERIDGE.

[1] Southey's *Poetical Works*, 1837,   [2] See Letter XLI. p. 110, note 1.
ii. 94.

XXXV. TO THE SAME.

Friday morning, September 19, 1794.

My fire was blazing cheerfully — the tea-kettle even now boiled over on it. Now sudden sad it looks. But, see, it blazes up again as cheerily as ever. Such, dear Southey, was the effect of your this morning's letter on my heart. Angry, no! I esteem and confide in you the more; but it *did* make me sorrowful. I was blameless; it was therefore only a passing cloud empictured on the breast. Surely had I written to you the *first* letter you directed to *me* at Cambridge, I *would* not have believed that you *could* have received it without answering it. Still less that you could have given a momentary pain to her that loved you. If I could have imagined no *rational* excuse for you, I would have peopled the vacancy with events of impossibility!

On Wednesday, September 17, I arrived at Cambridge. Perhaps the very hour you were writing in the severity of offended friendship, was I pouring forth the heart to Sarah Fricker. I did not call on Caldwell; I saw no one. On the moment of my arrival I shut my door, and wrote to her. But why not before?

In the first place Miss F. did not authorize me to direct immediately to her. It was *settled* that through *you* in our weekly *parcels* were the letters to be conveyed. The moment I arrived at Cambridge, and all yesterday, was I writing letters to you, to your mother, to Lovell, etc., to complete a parcel.

In London I wrote twice to you, intending daily to go to Cambridge; of course I deferred the parcel till then. I was taken ill, very ill. I exhausted my finances, and ill as I was, I sat down and scrawled a few guineas' worth of nonsense for the booksellers, which Dyer disposed of for me. Languid, sick at heart, in the back room of an inn! Lofty conjunction of circumstances for me to write

to Miss F. Besides, I told her I should write the moment
I arrived at Cambridge. I have fulfilled the promise.
Recollect, Southey, that when you mean to go to a place
to-morrow, and to-morrow, and to-morrow, the time that
intervenes is lost. Had I meant at first to stay in London, a fortnight should not have elapsed without my
writing to her. If you are satisfied, tell Miss F. that
you are *so*, but assign no reasons — I ought not to have
been suspected.

The tragedy [1] will be printed in less than a week. I
shall put my name, because it will sell at least a hundred
copies in Cambridge. It would appear ridiculous to put
two names to *such* a work. But, if you choose it, mention
it and it shall be done. To every man who *praises* it, of
course I give the *true* biography of it; to those who
laugh at it, I laugh again, and I am too well known at
Cambridge to be thought the less of, even though I had
published James Jennings' Satire.

. . . .

Southey! Precipitance is wrong. There may be too
high a state of health, perhaps even *virtue* is liable to a
plethora. I have been the slave of impulse, the child
of imbecility. But my inconsistencies have given me a
tarditude and reluctance to think ill of any one. Having
been often suspected of wrong when I was altogether
right, from *fellow-feeling* I judge not too hastily, and
from appearances. Your undeviating simplicity of rectitude has made you rapid in decision. Having never
erred, you feel more *indignation* at error than *pity* for it.
There is *phlogiston* in your heart. Yet am I grateful
for it. You would not have written so angrily but for
the greatness of your esteem and affection. The more
highly we have been wont to think of a character, the

---

[1] " A tragedy, of which the first act was written by S. T. Coleridge." See footnote to quotation from " The Fall of Robespierre," which occurs in the text of " An Address on the Present War." *Conciones ad Populum*, 1795, p. 66.

more pain and irritation we suffer from the discovery of its imperfections. My heart is very heavy, much more so than when I began to write.

Yours most fraternally.

S. T. COLERIDGE.

XXXVI. TO THE SAME.

Friday night, September 26, 1794.

MY DEAR, DEAR SOUTHEY, — I am beyond measure distressed and agitated by your letter to Favell. On the evening of the Wednesday before last, I arrived in Cambridge; that night and the next day I dedicated to writing to you, to Miss F., etc. On the Friday I received your letter of phlogistic rebuke. I answered it immediately, wrote a second letter to Miss F., inclosed them in the aforesaid parcel, and sent them off by the mail directed to Mrs. Southey, No. 8 Westcott Buildings, Bath. They should have arrived on Sunday morning. Perhaps you have not heard from Bath; perhaps — damn perhapses! My God, my God! what a deal of pain you must have suffered before you wrote that letter to Favell. It is an Ipswich Fair time, and the Norwich company are theatricalizing. They are the first provincial actors in the kingdom. Much against my will, I am engaged to drink tea and go to the play with Miss Brunton [1] (Mrs. Merry's

---

[1] One of six sisters, daughters of John Brunton of Norwich. Elizabeth, the eldest of the family, was married in 1791 to Robert Merry the dramatist, the founder of the so-called Della Cruscan school of poetry. Louisa Brunton, the youngest sister, afterwards Countess of Craven, made her first appearance at Covent Garden Theatre on October 5, 1803, and at most could not have been more than twelve or thirteen years of age in the autumn of 1794.

Coleridge's Miss Brunton, to whom he sent a poem on the French Revolution, that is, "The Fall of Robespierre," must have been an intermediate sister less known to fame. It is curious to note that "The Right Hon. Lady Craven" was a subscriber to the original issue of *The Friend* in 1809. *National Dictionary of Biography*, articles "Craven" and "Merry." *Letters of the Lake Poets*, 1885, p. 455.

sister). The young lady, and indeed the whole family, have taken it into their heads to be very much attached to me, though I have known them only six days. The father (who is the manager and proprietor of the theatre) inclosed in a very polite note a free ticket for the season. The young lady is said to be the most literary of the beautiful, and the most beautiful of the literate. It may be so; my faculties and discernments are so completely jaundiced by vexation that the Virgin Mary and Mary Flanders, alias Moll, would appear in the same hues.

All last night, I was obliged to listen to the damned chatter of our mayor, a fellow that would certainly be a pantisocrat, were his head and heart as highly illuminated as his face. At present he is a High Churchman, and a Pittite, and is guilty (with a very large fortune) of so many rascalities in his public character, that he is obliged to drink three bottles of claret a day in order to acquire a stationary rubor, and prevent him from the trouble of running backwards and forwards for a blush once every five minutes. In the tropical latitudes of this fellow's nose was I obliged to fry. I wish you would write a lampoon upon him — in me it would be unchristian revenge.

Our tragedy is printed, all but the title-page. It will be complete by Saturday night.

God love you. I am in the queerest humour in the world, and am out of love with everybody.

S. T. COLERIDGE.

XXXVII. TO THE SAME.

To you alone, Southey, I write the first part of this letter. To yourself confine it.

" Is this handwriting altogether erased from your memory? To whom am I addressing myself? For whom am I now violating the rules of female delicacy?

Is it for the same Coleridge, whom I once regarded as a
sister her best-beloved Brother? Or for one who will
ridicule that advice from me, which he has *rejected* as
offered by his family? I will hazard the attempt. I
have no right, nor do I feel myself inclined to reproach
you for the Past. God forbid! You have already suffered too much from self-accusation. But I conjure you,
Coleridge, earnestly and solemnly conjure you to consider
long and deeply, before you enter into any rash schemes.
There is an Eagerness in your Nature, which is ever hurry-
ing you in the sad Extreme. I have heard that you mean
to leave England, and on a Plan so absurd and extravagant that were I for a moment to imagine it *true*, I should
be obliged to listen with a more patient Ear to suggestions, which I have rejected a thousand times with scorn
and anger. Yes! whatever Pain I might suffer, I should
be forced to exclaim, 'O what a noble mind is here *o'er-
thrown*, Blasted with ecstacy.' You have a country, does
it demand nothing of you? You have doting Friends!
Will you break their Hearts! There is a God — Coleridge! Though I have been told (*indeed* I do not believe
it) that you doubt of his existence and disbelieve a hereafter. No! you have too much sensibility to be an Infidel.
You know I never was rigid in my opinions concerning
Religion — and have always thought *Faith* to be only
Reason applied to a particular subject. In short, I am
the same Being as when you used to say, 'We thought
in all things alike.' I often reflect on the happy hours
we spent together and regret the Loss of your Society. I
cannot easily forget those whom I once loved — nor can
I easily form new Friendships. I find women in general
vain — all of the same Trifle, and therefore little and
envious, and (I am afraid) without sincerity ; and of the
other sex those who are offered and held up to my esteem
are very prudent, and very worldly. If you value my
peace of mind, you must *on no account* answer this let-

ter, or take the least notice of it. I *would* not for the
world *any part* of my Family should suspect that I have
written to you. My mind is sadly tempered by being
perpetually obliged to resist the solicitations of those
whom I love. I need not explain myself. Farewell,
Coleridge! I shall always feel that I have been your
Sister."

No name was signed, — it was from Mary Evans. I
received it about three weeks ago. I loved her, Southey,
almost to madness. Her image was never absent from
me for three years, for *more* than three years. My resolution has not faltered, but I want a comforter. I have
done nothing, I have gone into company, I was constantly
at the theatre here till they left us, I endeavoured to be
perpetually with Miss Brunton, I even hoped that her
exquisite beauty and uncommon accomplishments might
have cured one passion by another. The latter I could
easily have dissipated in her absence, and so have restored
my affections to her whom I do not love, but whom by
every tie of reason and honour I ought to love. I am
resolved, but wretched! But time shall do much. You
will easily believe that with such feelings I should have
found it no easy task to write to ——. I should have de-
tested myself, if after my first letter I had written coldly
— how could I write *as warmly?* I was vexed too and
alarmed by your letter concerning Mr. and Mrs. Roberts,
Shad, and little Sally. I was wrong, very wrong, in the
affair of Shad, and have given you reason to suppose that
I should assent to the innovation. I will most assuredly go
with you to America, on this plan, but remember, Southey,
this is *not our plan*, nor can I defend it. " Shad's children will be educated as ours, and the education we shall
give them will be such as to render them incapable of
blushing at the want of it in their parents " — *Perhaps!*
With this one word would every Lilliputian reasoner de-
molish the system. Wherever men *can* be vicious, some

will be. The leading idea of pantisocracy is to make men *necessarily* virtuous by removing all motives to evil — all possible temptation. "Let them dine with us and be treated with as much equality as they would wish, but perform that part of labour for which their education has fitted them." *Southey* should not have written this sentence. My friend, my noble and high-souled friend should have said to his dependents, "Be my slaves, and ye shall be my equals ; " to his wife and sister, "Resign the *name* of Ladyship and ye shall retain the *thing*." Again. Is every family to possess one of these unequal equals, these Helot Egalités? Or are the few you have mentioned, "with more toil than the peasantry of England undergo," to do for all of us "that part of labour which their education has fitted them for"? If your remarks on the other side are just, the inference is that the scheme of pantisocracy is impracticable, but I hope and believe that it is not a *necessary* inference. Your remark of the physical evil in the long infancy of men would indeed puzzle a Pangloss — puzzle him to account for the wish of a benevolent heart like yours to discover malignancy in its Creator. Surely every eye but an eye jaundiced by habit of peevish scepticism must have seen that the mothers' cares are repaid even to rapture by the mothers' endearments, and that the long helplessness of the babe is the *means* of our superiority in the filial and maternal affection and duties to the same feelings in the brute creation. It is likewise among other causes the *means* of society, that thing which makes them a little lower than the angels. If Mrs. S. and Mrs. F. go with us, they can at least prepare the food of simplicity for us. Let the married women do only what is absolutely convenient and customary for pregnant women or nurses. Let the husband do all the rest, and what will that all be? Washing with a machine and cleaning the house. One hour's addition to our daily labor, and *pantisocracy* in its most

perfect sense is practicable. That the greater part of our
female companions should have the task of maternal exertion at the same time is very *improbable ;* but, though
it were to happen, an infant is almost always sleeping,
and during its slumbers the mother may in the same room
perform the little offices of ironing clothes or making
shirts. But the hearts of the women are not *all* with us.
I do believe that Edith and Sarah are exceptions, but do
even they know the bill of fare for the day, every duty
that will be incumbent upon them?

All necessary knowledge in the branch of ethics is
comprised in the word justice : that the good of the whole
is the good of each individual, that, of course, it is each
individual's *duty* to be just, *because* it is his *interest.* To
perceive this and to assent to it as an abstract proposition
is easy, but it requires the most wakeful attentions of the
most reflective mind in all moments to bring it into practice. It is not enough that we have once swallowed it.
The *heart* should have *fed* upon the *truth*, as insects on a
leaf, till it be tinged with the colour, and show its food in
every the minutest fibre. In the book of pantisocracy I
hope to have comprised all that is good in Godwin, of
whom and of whose book I will write more fully in my
next letter (I think not so highly of him as you do, and I
have read him with the greatest attention). This will
be an advantage to the *minds* of our women.

What have been your feelings concerning the War with
America, which is now inevitable? To go from Hamburg will not only be a heavy additional expense, but
dangerous and uncertain, as nations at war are in the
habit of examining neutral vessels to prevent the impor-
tation of arms and seize subjects of the hostile governments. It is said that one cause of the ministers having
been so cool on the business is that it will prevent emigration, which it seems would be treasonable to a hostile
country. Tell me all you think on these subjects. What

think you of the difference in the prices of land as stated by Cowper from those given by the American agents? By all means read, ponder on Cowper, and when I hear your thoughts I will give you the result of my own.

> Thou bleedest, my poor Heart! and thy distress
> Doth Reason ponder with an anguished smile,
> Probing thy sore wound sternly, tho' the while
> Her eye be swollen and dim with heaviness.
> Why didst thou *listen* to Hope's whisper bland?
> Or, listening, why *forget* its healing tale,
> When Jealousy with feverish fancies pale
> Jarr'd thy fine fibres with a maniac's hand?
> Faint was that Hope, and rayless.   Yet 't was fair
> And sooth'd with many a dream the hour of rest:
> Thou should'st have loved it most, when most opprest,
> And nursed it with an agony of care,
> E'en as a mother her sweet infant heir
> That pale and sickly droops upon her breast![1]

When a man is unhappy he writes damned bad poetry, I find. My Imitations too depress my spirits — the task is arduous, and grows upon me. Instead of two octavo volumes, to do all I hoped to do two quartos would hardly be sufficient.

Of your poetry I will send you a minute critique, when I send you my proposed alterations. The sonnets are exquisite.[2] Banquo is not what it deserves to be. Towards the end it grows very flat, wants variety of imagery — you dwell too long on Mary, yet have made less of her than I expected. The other figures are not sufficiently distinct; indeed, the plan of the ode (after the first forty lines which are most truly sublime) is so evident an imitation of Gray's Descent of Odin, that I would rather

---

[1] This sonnet, afterwards headed, "On a Discovery made too late," was "first printed in *Poems*, 1796, as Effusion XIX., but in the Contents it was called, 'To my own Heart.'"

[2] "The Race of Banquo." Southey's *Poetical Works*, 1837, ii. 155.

Poetical Works, p. 34. See, too, Editor's Note, p. 571.

adopt Shakespeare's mode of introducing the figures themselves, and making the description now the Witches' and
now Fleance's.   I detest monodramas, but I never wished
to establish my judgment on the throne of critical despot-
ism.   Send me up the Elegy on the Exiled Patriots and
the Scripture Sonnets.   I have promised them to Flower.[1]
The first will do *good*, and more good in a paper than in
any other vehicle.

My thoughts are floating about in a most chaotic state.
I had almost determined to go down to Bath, and stay
two days, that I might say everything I wished.   You
mean to acquaint your aunt with the scheme?   As she
knows it, and knows that you know that she knows it,
justice cannot require it, but if your own comfort makes
it necessary, by all means do it, with all possible gentleness.   She has loved you tenderly; be firm, therefore, as
a rock, mild as the lamb.   I sent a hundred " Robes-
pierres " to Bath ten days ago and more.

Five hundred copies of " Robespierre " were printed.   A
hundred [went] to Bath ; a hundred to Kearsley, in London ; twenty-five to March, at Norwich ; thirty I have sold
privately (twenty-five of these thirty to Dyer, who found
it inconvenient to take fifty).   The rest are dispersed
among the Cambridge booksellers ; the delicacies of aca-
demic gentlemanship prevented me from disposing of more
than the five *propriâ personâ*.   Of course we only get
ninepence for each copy from the booksellers.   I expected
that Mr. Field would have sent for fifty, but have heard
nothing of it.   I sent a copy to him, with my respects,
and have made presents of six more.   How they sell in
London, I know not.   All that are in Cambridge will
sell — a great many are sold.   I have been blamed for
publishing it, considering the more important work I have
offered to the public.   *N'importe*.   'T is thought a very
aristocratic performance; you may suppose how hyper-

---

[1] The Editor of the *Cambridge Intelligencer*.

democratic my character must have been. The expenses
of paper, printing, and advertisements are nearly nine
pounds. We ought to have charged one shilling and sixpence a copy.

I presented a copy to Miss Brunton with these verses
in the blank leaf : [1] —

> Much on my early youth I love to dwell,
> Ere yet I bade that guardian dome farewell,
> Where first beneath the echoing cloisters pale,
> I heard of guilt and wondered at the tale !
> Yet though the hours flew by on careless wing
> Full heavily of Sorrow would I sing.
> Aye, as the star of evening flung its beam
> In broken radiance on the wavy stream,
> My pensive soul amid the *twilight* gloom
> Mourned with the breeze, O Lee Boo ! o'er thy tomb.
> Whene'er I wander'd, Pity still was near,
> Breath'd from the heart, and glitter'd in the tear :
> No knell, that toll'd, but fill'd my anguish'd eye,
> "And suffering Nature wept that *one* should die ! "
> Thus to sad sympathies I sooth'd my breast,
> Calm as the rainbow in the weeping West :
> When slumb'ring Freedom rous'd by high Disdain
> With giant fury burst her triple chain !
> Fierce on her front the blasting Dog star glow'd ;
> Her banners, like a midnight meteor, flow'd ;
> Amid the yelling of the storm-rent skies
> She came, and scatter'd battles from her eyes !
> Then Exultation woke the patriot fire
> And swept with wilder hand th' empassioned lyre ;
> Red from the Tyrants' wounds I shook the lance,
> And strode in joy the reeking plains of France !
> In ghastly horror lie th' oppressors low,
> And my Heart akes tho' Mercy struck the blow !
> With wearied thought I seek the amaranth Shade

[1] "To a Young Lady, with a Poem on the French Revolution." *Poetical Works*, p. 6.

Where peaceful Virtue weaves her *myrtle* braid.
And O! if Eyes, whose holy glances roll
The eloquent Messengers of the pure soul ;
If Smiles more cunning and a gentler Mien,
Than the love—wilder'd Maniac's brain hath seen
Shaping celestial forms in vacant air,
If *these* demand the wond'ring Poets' care —
If Mirth and soften'd Sense, and Wit refin'd,
The blameless features of a lovely mind ;
Then haply shall my trembling hand assign
No *fading* flowers to Beauty's saintly shrine.
Nor, Brunton! thou the blushing Wreath refuse,
Though harsh her notes, yet guileless is my Muse.
Unwont at Flattery's Voice to plume her wings.
A child of Nature, as she feels, she sings.

                                        S. T. C.

JES. COLL., CAMBRIDGE.

Till I dated this letter I never recollected that yesterday
was my birthday — twenty-two years old.

I have heard from my brothers — from him particularly
who has been friend, brother, father. 'T was all remonstrance and anguish, and suggestions that I am deranged!
Let me receive from you a letter of consolation ; for,
believe me, I am completely wretched.

                    Yours most affectionately,
                        S. T. COLERIDGE.

XXXVIII. TO ROBERT SOUTHEY.

                                    November, 1794.

My feeble and exhausted heart regards with a criminal
indifference the introduction of servitude into our society ;
but my judgment is not asleep, nor can I suffer your reason, Southey, to be entangled in the web which your feelings have woven. Oxen and horses possess not intellectual appetites, nor the powers of acquiring them. We are
therefore justified in employing their labour to our own
benefit : mind hath a divine right of sovereignty over body.

But who shall dare to transfer "from man to brute" to "from man to man"? To be employed in the toil of the field, while *we* are pursuing philosophical studies — can earldoms or emperorships boast so huge an inequality? Is there a human being of so torpid a nature as that placed in our society he would not feel it? A *willing* slave is the worst of slaves! His *soul* is a slave. Besides, I must own myself incapable of perceiving even the temporary *convenience* of the proposed innovation. The *men* do not want assistance, at least none that *Shad* can particularly give; and to the women, what assistance can little Sally, the *wife* of Shad, give more than any other of our married women? Is she to have no domestic cares of her own? No house? No husband to provide for? No children? *Because* Mr. and Mrs. Roberts are not likely to have children, I see less objection to their accompanying us. Indeed, indeed, Southey, I am fearful that Lushington's prophecy may not be altogether vain. "Your system, Coleridge, appears strong to the head and lovely to the heart; but depend upon it, you will never give your *women* sufficient strength of mind, liberality of heart, or vigilance of attention. *They* will spoil it."

I am extremely unwell; have run a nail into my heel, and before me stand "Embrocation for the throbbing of the head," "To be shaked up well that the ether may mix," "A wineglass full to be taken when faint." 'Sdeath! how I hate the labels of apothecary's bottles. Ill as I am, I must go out to supper. Farewell for a few hours.

'T is past one o'clock in the morning. I sat down at twelve o'clock to read the "Robbers" of Schiller.[1] I had read, chill and trembling, when I came to the part where the Moor fixes a pistol over the robbers who are asleep. I could read no more. My God, Southey, who is this Schiller, this convulser of the heart? Did he write his tragedy amid the yelling of fiends? I should not like to be

---

[1] Compare "Sonnet to the Author of The Robbers." *Poetical Works,* p. 34.

able to describe such characters. I tremble like an aspen
leaf. Upon my soul, I write to you because I am frightened. I had better go to bed. Why have we ever called
Milton sublime? that Count de Moor horrible wielder
of heart-withering virtues? Satan is scarcely qualified to
attend his execution as gallows chaplain.

Tuesday morning. — I have received your letter. Potter of Emanuel[1] drives me up to town in his phaeton on
Saturday morning. I hope to be with you by Wednesday
week. Potter is a "Son of Soul" — a poet of liberal sentiments in politics — yet (would you believe it?) possesses
six thousand a year independent.

I feel grateful to you for your sympathy. There is a
feverish distemperature of brain, during which some horrible phantom threatens our eyes in every corner, until,
emboldened by terror, we rush on it, and then — why then
we return, the heart indignant at its own palpitation!
Even so will the greater part of our mental miseries vanish before an effort. Whatever of mind we *will* to do, we
can do! What, then, palsies the will? The joy of grief.
A mysterious pleasure broods with dusky wings over the
tumultuous mind, "and the Spirit of God moveth on the
darkness of the waters." She *was very* lovely, Southey!
We formed each other's minds; our ideas were blended.
Heaven bless her! I cannot forget her. Every day her
memory sinks deeper into my heart.

[1] The date of this letter is fixed by that of Thursday, November 6, to George Coleridge. Both letters speak of a journey to town with Potter of Emanuel, but in writing to his brother he says nothing of a projected visit to Bath. There is no hint in either letter that he had made up his mind to leave the University for good and all. In a letter to Southey dated December 17, he says that "they are making a row about him at Jesus," and in a letter to Mary Evans, which must have been written a day or two later, he says, "I return to Cambridge to-morrow." From the date of the letter to George Coleridge of November 6 to December 11 there is a break in the correspondence with Southey, but from a statement in Letter XLIII. it appears plain that a visit was paid to the West in December, 1794. But whether he returned to Cambridge November 8, and for how long, is uncertain.

> Nutrito vulnere tabens
> Impatiensque mei feror undique, solus et excors,
> Et desideriis pascor!

I wish, Southey, in the stern severity of judgment, that the two mothers were *not* to go, and that the children stayed with them. Are you wounded by my want of feeling? No! how highly must I think of your rectitude of soul, that I should dare to say this to so affectionate a son! *That* Mrs. Fricker! We shall have her teaching the infants *Christianity*, — I mean, that mongrel whelp that goes under its name, — teaching them by stealth in some ague fit of superstition.

There is little danger of my being confined. *Advice* offered with *respect* from a brother; *affected coldness*, an assumed *alienation* mixed with involuntary bursts of *anguish* and disappointed *affection;* questions concerning the mode in which I would have it mentioned to my aged mother — these are the daggers which are plunged into *my* peace. Enough! I should rather be offering consolation to your sorrows than be wasting my feelings in egotistic complaints. " Verily my complaint is bitter, yet my stroke is heavier than my groaning."

God love you, my dear Southey!

S. T. COLERIDGE.

A friend of mine hath lately departed this life in a frenzy fever induced by anxiety. Poor fellow, a child of frailty like me! Yet he was amiable. I poured forth these incondite lines [1] in a moment of melancholy dissatisfaction : —

> ——! thy grave with aching eye I scan,
> And inly groan for Heaven's poor outcast — Man!
> 'T is tempest all, or gloom! In earliest youth

---

[1] " Lines on a Friend who died of a Frenzy Fever," etc. *Poetical Works*, p. 35. A copy of the same poem was sent on November 6 to George Coleridge.

If gifted with th' Ithuriel lance of Truth
He force to start amid the feign'd caress
Vice, siren-hag, in native ugliness;
A brother's fate shall haply rouse the tear,
And on he goes in heaviness and fear!
But if his fond heart call to Pleasure's bower
Some pigmy Folly in a careless hour,
The faithless Guest quick stamps th' enchanted ground,
And mingled forms of Misery threaten round:
Heart-fretting Fear, with pallid look aghast,
That courts the future woe to hide the past;
Remorse, the poison'd arrow in his side,
And loud lewd Mirth to Anguish close allied;
Till Frenzy, frantic child of moping Pain,
Darts her hot lightning-flash athwart the brain!
Rest, injur'd Shade! shall Slander, squatting near,
Spit her cold venom in a dead man's ear?
'T was thine to feel the sympathetic glow
In Merit's joy and Poverty's meek woe:
Thine all that cheer the moment as it flies,
The zoneless Cares and smiling Courtesies.
Nurs'd in thy heart the generous Virtues grew,
And in thy heart they wither'd! such chill dew
Wan Indolence on each young blossom shed;
And Vanity her filmy network spread,
With eye that prowl'd around in asking gaze,
And tongue that trafficked in the trade of praise!
Thy follies such the hard world mark'd them well.
Were they more wise, the proud who never fell?
Rest, injur'd Shade! the poor man's grateful prayer,
On heavenward wing, thy wounded soul shall bear!

As oft in Fancy's thought thy grave I pass,
And sit me down upon its recent grass,
With introverted eye I contemplate
Similitude of soul — perhaps of fate!
To me hath Heaven with liberal hand assign'd
Energic reason and a shaping mind,

The daring soul of Truth, the patriot's part,
And Pity's sigh, that breathes the gentle heart —
Sloth-jaundiced all ! and from my graspless hand
Drop Friendship's precious pearls, like hour-glass sand.
I weep, yet stoop not ! the faint anguish flows,
A dreamy pang in Morning's fev'rish doze !

Is that pil'd earth our Being's passless mound ?
Tell me, cold Grave ! is Death with poppies crown'd ?
Tir'd Sentinel ! with fitful starts I nod,
And fain would sleep, though pillow'd on a clod !

SONG.

When Youth his fairy reign began [1]
Ere Sorrow had proclaim'd me Man ;
While Peace the *present* hour beguil'd,
And all the lovely *Prospect* smil'd ;
Then, Mary, mid my lightsome glee
I heav'd the painless Sigh for thee !

And when, along the wilds of woe
My harass'd Heart was doom'd to know
The frantic burst of Outrage keen,
And the slow Pang that gnaws unseen ;
Then shipwreck'd on Life's stormy sea
I heav'd an anguish'd Sigh for thee !

But soon Reflection's hand imprest
A stiller sadness on my breast ;
And sickly Hope with waning eye
Was well content to droop and die :
I yielded to the stern decree,
Yet heav'd the languid Sigh for thee !

And though in distant climes to roam,
A wanderer from my native home,
I fain would woo a gentle Fair

[1] "The Sigh." *Poetical Works*, p. 20.

> To soothe the aching sense of care,
> Thy Image may not banish'd be —
> Still, Mary! still I sigh for thee!

S. T. C.

God love you.

XXXIX. TO THE SAME.

Autumn, 1794.

Last night, dear Southey, I received a special invitation from Dr. Edwards [1] (the great Grecian of Cambridge and heterodox divine) to drink tea and spend the evening. I there met a councillor whose name is Lushington, a democrat, and a man of the most powerful and Briarean intellect. I was challenged on the subject of pantisocracy, which is, indeed, the universal topic at the University. A discussion began and continued for six hours. In conclusion, Lushington and Edwards declared the system impregnable, supposing the assigned quantum of virtue and genius in the first individuals. I came home at one o'clock this morning in the honest consciousness of having exhibited closer argument in more elegant and appropriate language than I had ever conceived myself capable of. Then my heart smote me, for I saw your letter on the propriety of taking servants with us. I had answered that letter, and feel conviction that you will *perceive* the error into which the tenderness of your nature had led you. But other queries obtruded themselves on my understanding. The more perfect our system is, supposing the necessary premises, the more eager in anxiety am I that the necessary premises exist. O for that Lyncean eye that can discover in the acorn of Error the rooted and widely spreading oak of Misery! Quære: should not all who mean to

---

[1] Probably Thomas Edwards, LL. D., a Fellow of Jesus College, Cambridge, editor of Plutarch, *De Educatione Liberorum*, with notes, 1791, and author of " A Discourse on the Limits and Importance of Free Inquiry in Matters of Religion," 1792. *Natural Dictionary of Biography*, xvii. 130.

become members of our community be incessantly meliorating their temper and elevating their understandings? Qu.: whether a very respectable quantity of *acquired* knowledge (History, Politics, above all, *Metaphysics*, without which no man *can* reason but with women and children) be not a prerequisite to the improvement of the head and heart? Qu.: whether our Women have not been taught by us habitually to contemplate the littleness of individual comforts and a passion for the *novelty* of the scheme rather than a generous enthusiasm of Benevolence? Are they saturated with the Divinity of Truth sufficiently to be always wakeful? In the present state of their minds, whether it is not probable that the *Mothers* will tinge the minds of the infants with prejudication? The questions are meant merely as motives to you, Southey, to the strengthening the minds of the Women, and stimulating them to literary acquirements. But, Southey, there are *Children* going with us. Why did I never dare in my disputations with the unconvinced to hint at this circumstance? Was it not because I knew, even to certainty of conviction, that it is subversive of *rational* hopes of a permanent system? These children, — the little Frickers, for instance, and your brothers, — are they not already deeply tinged with the prejudices and errors of society? Have they not learned from their schoolfellows *Fear* and *Selfishness*, of which the necessary offsprings are Deceit and desultory Hatred? How are we to prevent them from infecting the minds of *our* children? By reforming their judgments? At so early an age, *can* they have *felt* the ill consequences of their errors in a manner sufficiently vivid to make this reformation practicable? How can we insure their silence concerning God, etc.? Is it possible *they* should enter into our *motives* for this silence? If not, we must produce their *Obedience* by *Terror.* *Obedience?* *Terror?* The repetition is sufficient. I need not inform you that they are as inadequate as inapplicable. I have told you, Southey, that I will accompany you on an *imperfect* system.   But must our system be thus necessarily imperfect ?   I ask the question that I may know whether or not I should write the Book of Pantisocracy.

I received your letter of Oyez; it brought a smile on a countenance that for these three weeks has been cloudy and stern in its solitary hours.   In company, wit and laughter are Duties.   Slovenly?   I could mention a lady of fashionable rank, and most fashionable ideas, who declared to Caldwell that I (S. T. Coleridge) was a man of the most *courtly* and polished manners, of the most *gentlemanly* address she had ever met with.   But I will not *crow!* Slovenly, indeed!

XL. TO THE REV. GEORGE COLERIDGE.

Thursday, November 6, 1794.

MY DEAR BROTHER, — Your letter of this morning gave me inexpressible consolation.   I thought that I perceived in your last the cold and freezing features of alienated affection.   Surely, said I, I have trifled with the spirit of love, and it has passed away from me! There is a vice of such powerful venom, that one grain of it will poison the overflowing goblet of a thousand virtues. This vice constitution seems to have implanted in me, and habit has made it almost Omnipotent.   It is *indolence !* [1] Hence, whatever web of friendship my presence may have woven, my absence has seldom failed to unravel.   Anxieties that stimulate others infuse an additional narcotic into my mind.   The appeal of duty to my judgment, and the pleadings of affection at my heart, have been heard indeed, and heard with deep regard.   Ah! that they had

---

[1] Compare " Lines on a Friend," etc., which accompanied this letter.

To me hath Heaven with liberal hand assigned
Energic reason and a shaping mind,

. . . .
Sloth-jaundiced all! and from my graspless hand
Drop Friendship's precious pearls, like hour-glass sand.

Poetical Works, p. 35.

been as constantly obeyed. But so it has been. Like
some poor labourer, whose night's sleep has but imperfectly
refreshed his overwearied frame, I have sate in drowsy
uneasiness, and doing nothing have thought what a deal
I had to do. But I trust that the kingdom of reason is
at hand, and even now cometh!

How often and how unkindly are the ebullitions of
youthful disputations mistaken for the result of fixed
principles. People have resolved that I am a dymocrat,
and accordingly look at everything I do through the
spectacles of prejudication. In the feverish distemperature of a *bigoted* aristocrat's brain, some phantom of
Dymocracy threatens him in every corner of my writings.

> And Hébert's atheist crew, whose maddening hand
> Hurl'd down the altars of the living God
> With all the infidel intolerance.[1]

"Are these lines in *character*," observed a sensible
friend of mine, "in a speech on the death of the man
whom it just became the fashion to style 'The ambitious
Theocrat'?" "I fear *not*," was my answer, "I gave way
to my feelings." The first speech of Adelaide,[2] whose
Automaton is this character? Who spoke through Le
Gendre's mouth,[3] when he says, "Oh, what a precious
name is Liberty To scare or cheat the simple into
slaves"? But in several parts I have, it seems, in the
strongest language boasted the impossibility of subdu-
ing France. Is not this sentiment highly characteristic?
Is it *forced* into the mouths of the speakers? Could I

---

[1] The lines occur in Barrère's
speech, which concludes the third
act of the "Fall of Robespierre."
Poetical Works, p. 225.

[2] "Fall of Robespierre," Act I.
l. 198.

O this new freedom! at how dear a price

We 've bought the seeming good! The
peaceful virtues
And every blandishment of private life,
The father's care, the mother's fond en-
dearment
All sacrificed to Liberty's wild riot.
            Poetical Works, p. 215.
[3] See "Fall of Robespierre," Act
I. l. 40. *Poetical Works*, p. 212.

have even omitted it without evident absurdity? But,
granted that it is my own opinion, is it an *anti-pacific* one?
I should have classed it among the anti-polemics.   Again,
are *all* who entertain and express this opinion dηmocrats?
God forbid!   They would be a formidable party indeed!
I know many violent anti-reformists, who are as violent
against the *war* on the ground that it may introduce that
reform, which they (perhaps not unwisely) imagine would
chant the dirge of our constitution.   Solemnly, my brother,
I tell you, I am *not* a dηmocrat.   I see, evidently, that the
present is *not* the highest state of society of which we are
capable.   And after a diligent, I may say an intense, study
of Locke, Hartley, and others who have written most wisely
on the nature of man, I appear to myself to see the point
of possible perfection, at which the world may perhaps be
destined to arrive.   But how to lead mankind from one
point to the other is a process of such infinite complexity, that in deep-felt humility I resign it to that Being
" Who shaketh the Earth out of her place, and the pillars
thereof tremble," " Who purifieth with Whirlwinds, and
maketh the Pestilence his Besom," Who hath said, " that
violence shall no more be heard of ; the people shall not
build and another inhabit ; they shall not plant and
another eat ; " " the wolf and the lamb shall feed together."
I have been asked what is the best conceivable mode of
meliorating society.   My answer has been this : " Slavery
is an abomination to my feeling of the head and the heart.
Did Jesus teach the *abolition* of it?   No!   He taught
those principles of which the necessary *effect* was to
abolish all slavery.   He prepared the *mind* for the reception before he poured the blessing."   You ask me what
the friend of universal equality should do.   I answer :
" Talk not politics.   *Preach the Gospel !* "

   Yea, my brother!   I have at all times in all places exerted my power in the defence of the Holy One of Nazareth
against the learning of the historian, the libertinism of

the wit, and (his worst enemy) the mystery of the bigot!
But I am an infidel, because I cannot thrust my head
into a *mud gutter*, and say, "How *deep* I am!" And
I am a dηmocrat, because I will not join in the male-
dictions of the despotist — because I will *bless all* men
and *curse* no one! I have been a fool even to madness;
and I am, therefore, an excellent hit for calumny to aim
her poisoned *probabilities* at! As the poor flutterer,
who by hard struggling has escaped from the bird-limed
thornbush, still bears the clammy incumbrance on his feet
and wings, so I am doomed to carry about with me the
sad mementos of past imprudence and anguish from
which I have been imperfectly released.

Mr. Potter of Emanuel drives me up to town in his
phaeton, on Saturday morning. Of course I shall see you
on Sunday. Poor Smerdon! the reports concerning his
literary plagiarism (as far as concerns *my* assistance) are
falsehoods. I have felt much for him, and on the morning I received your letter I poured forth these incondite
rhymes. Of course they are meant for a brother's eye.

Smerdon! thy grave with aching eye I scan, etc.[1]

God love you, dear brother, and your affectionate and
grateful

S. T. COLERIDGE.

XLI.   TO ROBERT SOUTHEY.

December 11, 1794.

MY DEAR SOUTHEY, — I sit down to write to you, not
that I have anything particular to say, but it is a relief,
and forms a very respectable part in my theory of "Es-
capes from the Folly of Melancholy." I am so habituated
to philosophizing that I cannot divest myself of it, even
when my own wretchedness is the subject. I appear to

[1] For full text of the "Lines on a Friend who died of a Frenzy Fe-ver," See Letter XXXVIII. See, too, *Poetical Works*, p. 35.

myself like a sick physician, feeling the pang acutely, yet
deriving a wonted pleasure from examining its progress
and developing its causes.

Your poems and Bowles' are my only morning companions. "The Retrospect!"[1] *Quod qui non prorsus
amat et deperit, illum omnes et virtutes et veneres odere!*
It is a most lovely poem, and in the next edition of your
works shall be a perfect one. The "Ode to Romance"[2]

---

[1] Southey's *Poetical Works*, 1837,
ii. 263.

[2] See *Poems by Robert Lovell, and
Robert Southey of Balliol College.*
Bath. Printed by A. Cruttwell, 1795,
p. 17. "Ode to Lycon," p. 77.
The last stanza runs thus:—

Wilt thou float careless down the stream
   of time,
  In sadness borne to dull oblivious shore,
Or shake off grief, and "build the lofty
   rhyme,"
  And live till time shall be no more?
If thy light bark have met the storms,
  If threatening cloud the sky deforms,
Let honest truth be vain; look back on
   me,
  Have I been "sailing on a Summer sea"?
Have only zephyrs fill'd my swelling sails,
  As smooth the gentle vessel glides
   along?
Lycon! I met unscar'd the wintry gales,
  And sooth'd the dangers with the song:
So shall the vessel sail sublime,
  And reach the port of fame adown the
   stream of time.
             BION [*i. e.* R. S.].
Compare the following unpub-
lished letter from Southey to Miss
Sarah Fricker:—

            October 18, 1794.
"Amid the pelting of the pitiless
storm" did I, Robert Southey, the
Apostle of Pantisocracy, depart
from the city of Bristol, my natal
place—at the hour of five in a wet
windy evening on the 17th of October,

1794, wrapped up in my father's old
great coat and my own cogitations.
Like old Lear I did not call the elements unkind,—and on I passed,
musing on the lamentable effects of
pride and prejudice—retracing all
the events of my past life—and
looking forward to the days to come
with pleasure.

Three miles from Bristol, an old
man of sixty, most royally drunk,
laid hold of my arm, and begged we
might join company, as he was
going to Bath. I consented, for he
wanted assistance, and dragged this
foul animal through the dirt, wind,
and rain! . . .

Think of me, with a mind so
fully occupied, leading this man
nine miles, and had I not led him
he would have lain down under a
hedge and probably perished.

I reached not Bath till nine
o'clock, when the rain pelted me
most unmercifully in the face. I rejoiced that my friends at Bath knew
not where I was, and was once
vexed at thinking that you would
hear it drive against the window
and be sorry for the way-worn traveller. Here I am, well, and satisfied
with my own conduct. . . .

My clothes are arrived. "I will
never see his face again [writes Miss

is the best of the odes. I dislike that to Lycon, excepting the last stanza, which is superlatively fine. The
phrase of " let honest truth be vain " is obscure. Of
your blank verse odes, " The Death of Mattathias " [1] is by
far the best. That you should ever write another, *Pul-
cher Apollo veta! Musæ prohibete venustæ!* They
are to poetry what dumb-bells are to music ; they can be
read only for *exercise*, or to make a man tired that he
may be sleepy. The sonnets are wonderfully inferior to
those which I possess of yours, of which that " To Valentine " [2] (" If long and lingering seem one little day The
motley crew of travellers among ") ; that on " The Fire " [3]
(not your last, a very so-so one) ; on " The Rainbow " [4]
(particularly the four last lines), and two or three others,
are all divine and fully equal to Bowles. Some parts of
" Miss Rosamund " [5] are beautiful — the *working* scene,
and that line with which the poem ought to have concluded, " And think who lies so cold and pale below."
Of the " Pauper's Funeral," [6] that part in which you have
done me the honour to imitate me is by far the worst ; the

Tyler], and, if he writes, will return
his letters unopened ; " to comment
on this would be useless. I feel
that strong conviction of rectitude
which would make me smile on the
rack. . . . The crisis is over — things
are as they should be ; my mother
vexes herself much, yet feels she is
right. Hostilities are commenced
with America ! so we must go to
some neutral fort — Hambro' or
Venice.

Your sister is well, and sends her
love to all ; on Wednesday I hope
to see you. Till then farewell,
            ROBERT SOUTHEY.
Bath, Sunday morning.

Compare, also, letter to Thomas
Southey, dated October 19, 1794.

Southey's Life and Correspondence,
i. 222.
    [1] *Poems,* 1795, p. 123.
    [2] See Southey's *Poetical Works,*
1837, ii. 91 : —

    " If heavily creep on one little day,
        The medley crew of travellers among."

    [3] *Poems,* 1795, p. 67.
    [4] *Poetical Works,* 1837, ii. 92.
    [5] " Rosamund to Henry ; written
after she had taken the veil."
Poems, 1795, p. 85.
    [6] *Poetical Works,* 1837, ii. 216.
Southey appears to have accepted
Coleridge's emendations. The varia-
tions between the text of the " Pauper's Funeral " and the *editio purgata* of the letter are slight and
unimportant.

thought has been so much better expressed by Gray. On the whole (like many of yours), it wants compactness and totality; the same thought is repeated too frequently in different words. That all these faults may be remedied by compression, my *editio purgata* of the poem shall show you.

> What! and not one to heave the pious sigh?
> Not one whose sorrow-swoln and aching eye,
> For social scenes, for life's endearments fled,
> Shall drop a tear and dwell upon the dead?
> Poor wretched Outcast! I will sigh for thee,
> And sorrow for forlorn humanity!
> Yes, I will sigh! but not that thou art come
> To the stern Sabbath of the silent tomb:
> For squalid Want and the black scorpion Care,
> (Heart-withering fiends) shall never enter there.
> I sorrow for the ills thy life has known,
> As through the world's long pilgrimage, alone,
> Haunted by Poverty and woe-begone,
> Unloved, unfriended, thou didst journey on;
> Thy youth in ignorance and labour past,
> And thy old age all barrenness and blast!
> Hard was thy fate, which, while it doom'd to woe,
> Denied thee wisdom to support the blow;
> And robb'd of all its energy thy mind,
> Ere yet it cast thee on thy fellow-kind,
> Abject of thought, the victim of distress,
> To wander in the world's wide wilderness.
> Poor Outcast! sleep in peace! The winter's storm
> Blows bleak no more on thy unsheltered form!
> Thy woes are past; thou restest in the tomb; —
> I pause . . . and ponder on the days to come.

Now! Is it not a beautiful poem? Of the sonnet, " No more the visionary soul shall dwell," [1] I wrote the

---

[1] In a letter from Southey to his brother Thomas, dated October 21, 1794, this sonnet " on the subject of our emigration " is attributed to Favell, a convert to pantisocracy who was still at Christ's Hospital. The

whole but the second and third lines. Of the "Old Man in the Snow,"[1] ten last lines *entirely*, and part of the four first. Those ten lines are, perhaps, the best I ever did write.

Lovell has no taste or simplicity of feeling. I remarked that when a man read Lovell's poems he *mus cus* (that is a rapid way of pronouncing "must curse"), but when he thought of Southey's, he'd "buy on!" For God's sake let us have no more Bions or Gracchus's. I abominate them! *Southey* is a name much more proper and handsome, and, I venture to prophesy, will be more *famous*. Your "Chapel Bell"[2] I love, and have made it, by a few alterations and the omission of one stanza (which, though beautiful *quoad se*, interrupted the *run* of the thought "I love to see the aged spirit soar"), a perfect poem. As it followed the "Exiled Patriots," I altered the second and fourth lines to, "So freedom taught, in high-voiced minstrel's weed;" "For cap and gown to leave the patriot's meed."

The last verse *now* runs thus:—

> " But thou, Memorial of monastic gall !
>   What fancy sad or lightsome hast *thou* given ?
> Thy vision-searing sounds alone recall
>   The prayer that *trembles* on a *yawn* to Heaven,
> And *this* Dean's gape, and *that* Dean's nasal tone."

Would not this be a fine subject for a wild ode?

> St. Withold footed thrice the Oulds,
> He met the nightmare and her nine foals;
> He bade her alight and her troth plight,
> And, "Aroynt thee, Witch!" he said.

first eight lines are included in the "Monody on Chatterton." See *Poetical Works*, p. 63, and Editor's Note, p. 563.

[1] Printed as Effusion XVI. in *Poems*, 1796. It was afterwards headed "Charity." In the preface he acknowledges that he was "indebted to Mr. Favell for the rough sketch." See *Poetical Works*, p. 45, and Editor's Note, p. 576.

[2] Southey's *Poetical Works*, ii. 143. In this instance Coleridge's corrections were not adopted.

I shall set about one when I am in a humour to abandon myself to all the diableries that ever met the eye of a Fuseli!

Le Grice has jumbled together all the quaint stupidity he ever wrote, amounting to about thirty pages, and published it in a book about the size and dimensions of children's twopenny books. The dedication is pretty. He calls the publication "Tineum;"[1] for what reason or with what meaning would give Madame Sphinx a complete victory over Œdipus.

A wag has handed about, I hear, an obtuse angle of wit, under the name of "An Epigram." 'T is almost as bad as the subject.

> "A tiny man of tiny wit
>   A tiny book has published.
> But not alas! one tiny bit
>   His tiny fame established."

TO BOWLES.[2]

My heart has thank'd thee, Bowles! for those soft strains,
That, on the still air floating, tremblingly
Woke in me Fancy, Love, and Sympathy!
For hence, not callous to a Brother's pains
Thro' Youth's gay prime and thornless paths I went;
And when the *darker* day of life began,
And I did roam, a thought-bewildered man!
Thy kindred Lays an healing solace lent,
Each lonely pang with dreamy joys combin'd,
And stole from vain REGRET her scorpion stings;
While shadowy PLEASURE, with mysterious wings,
Brooded the wavy and tumultuous mind,
Like that great Spirit, who with plastic sweep
Mov'd on the darkness of the formless Deep!

Of the following sonnet, the four *last* lines were written by Lamb, a man of uncommon genius. Have you

---

[1] Published in 1794.

[2] First version, printed in *Morn-* ing *Chronicle*, December 26, 1794. See *Poetical Works*, p. 40.

seen his divine sonnet of "O! I could *laugh* to hear the winter winds," etc. ?

SONNET.[1]

O gentle look, that didst my soul beguile,
Why hast thou left me ?   Still in some fond dream
Revisit my sad heart, auspicious smile !
As falls on closing flowers the lunar beam ;
What time in sickly mood, at parting day
I lay me down and think of happier years ;
Of joys, that glimmered in Hope's twilight ray,
Then left me darkling in a vale of tears.
O pleasant days of Hope — for ever flown !
Could I recall one ! — But that thought is vain.
Availeth not Persuasion's sweetest tone
To lure the fleet-winged travellers back again :
Anon, they haste to everlasting night,
Nor can a giant's arm arrest them in their flight.

The four last lines are beautiful, but they have no particular meaning which "that thought is *vain*" does not
convey.   And I cannot write without a *body* of *thought*.
Hence my poetry is crowded and sweats beneath a heavy
burden of ideas and imagery !   It has seldom ease.   The
little song ending with "I heav'd the painless sigh for
thee!" is an exception, and, accordingly, I like it the
best of all I ever wrote.   My sonnets to eminent contemporaries are among the better things I have written.
That to Erskine is a bad specimen.   I have written ten,
and mean to write six more.   In "Fayette" I unwittingly
(for I did not know it at the time) borrowed a thought
from you.

I will conclude with a little song of mine,[2] which has
no other merit than a pretty simplicity of silliness.

[1] First printed as Effusion XIV. in *Poems*, 1796. Of the four lines said to have been written by Lamb, Coleridge discarded lines 13 and 14, and substituted a favourite couplet, which occurs in more than one of his early poems. See *Poetical Works*, p. 23, and Editor's Note, p. 566.

[2] Imitated from the Welsh. See *Poetical Works*, p. 33.

If while my passion I impart,
  You deem my words untrue,
O place your hand upon my heart —
  Feel how it throbs for *you!*

Ah no! reject the thoughtless claim
  In pity to your Lover!
That thrilling touch would aid the flame
  It wishes to discover!

I am a complete necessitarian, and understand the subject as well almost as Hartley himself, but I go farther than Hartley, and believe the corporeality of *thought*, namely, that it is motion. Boyer thrashed Favell most cruelly the day before yesterday, and I sent him the following note of consolation: " I condole with you on the unpleasant motions, to which a certain uncouth automaton has been mechanized ; and am anxious to know the motives that impinged on its optic or auditory nerves so as to be communicated in such rude vibrations through the medullary substance of its brain, thence rolling their stormy surges into the capillaments of its tongue, and the muscles of its arm. The diseased violence of its thinking corporealities will, depend upon it, cure itself by exhaustion. In the mean time I trust that you have not been assimilated in degradation by losing the ataxy of your temper, and that necessity which dignified you by a sentience of the pain has not lowered you by the accession of anger or resentment."

God love you, Southey! My love to your mother!
                         S. T. COLERIDGE.

XLII. TO THE SAME.

Wednesday, December 17, 1794.

When I am unhappy a sigh or a groan does not feel
sufficient to relieve the oppression of my heart. I give
a long *whistle*. This by way of a detached truth.

" How infinitely more to be valued is integrity of heart
than effulgence of intellect ! " A noble sentiment, and
would have come home to me, if for " integrity " you had
substituted " energy." The skirmishes of sensibility are
indeed contemptible when compared with the well-dis-
ciplined phalanx of right-onward feelings. O ye invincible soldiers of virtue, who arrange yourselves under the
generalship of fixed principles, that you would throw up
your fortifications around my heart! I pronounce this a
very sensible, apostrophical, metaphorical rant.

I dined yesterday with Perry and Grey (the proprietor
and editor of the " Morning Chronicle ") at their house,
and met Holcroft. He either misunderstood Lovell, or
Lovell misunderstood him. I know not which, but it is
very clear to me that neither of them understands nor
enters into the views of our system. Holcroft opposes it
violently and thinks it not *virtuous*. His arguments were
such as Nugent and twenty others have used to us before
him ; they were *nothing*. There is a fierceness and dogmatism of conversation in Holcroft for which you receive
little compensation either from the veracity of his information, the closeness of his reasoning, or the splendour of his
language. He talks incessantly of metaphysics, of which
he appears to me to know nothing, to have read nothing.
He is ignorant as a scholar, and neglectful of the smaller
humanities as a man. Compare him with Porson! My
God! to hear Porson *crush* Godwin, Holcroft, etc. They
absolutely tremble before him ! I had the honour of working H. a little, and by my great *coolness* and command of
impressive language certainly *did him over*. " Sir! " said

he, " I never knew so much real wisdom and so much rank
error meet in one mind before!"　"Which," answered I,
" means, I suppose, that in some things, sir, I agree with
you, and in others I do not."　He absolutely infests you
with *atheism ;* and his arguments are such that the
nonentities of Nugent consolidate into oak or ironwood
by comparison!　As to his taste in poetry, he thinks
lightly, or rather contemptuously, of Bowles' sonnets ; the
language flat and prosaic and inharmonious, and the sentiments only fit for girls!　Come, come, Mr. Holcroft, as
much unintelligible metaphysics and as much bad criticism
as you please, but no *blasphemy* against the divinity of *a
Bowles !*　Porson idolizes the sonnets.　However it happened, I am higher in his good graces than he in mine.
If I am in town I dine with him and Godwin, etc., at
his house on Sunday.

I am astonished at your preference of the " Elegy."　I
think it the worst thing you ever wrote.

　　" Qui Gratio non odit, amet tua carmina, Avaro !" [1]

Why, 't is almost as bad as Lovell's " Farmhouse," and
that would be at least a thousand fathoms deep in the
dead sea of pessimism.

　　　　" The hard world scoff'd my woes, the chaste one's pride,
* Implied in　Mimic of virtue, mock'd my keen distress,
the second　* And Vice alone would shelter wretchedness.
line.　　　Even life is loathsome now," etc.

These two stanzas are exquisite, but the lovely thought of
the " hot sun," etc., as pitiless as proud prosperity loses
part of its beauty by the time being night.　It is among
the chief excellences of Bowles that his imagery appears
almost always prompted by surrounding scenery.

Before you write a poem you should say to yourself,
" What do I intend to be the character of this poem ;

[1] A parody of " Qui Bavinm non
odit, amet tua carmina, Mœvi."
Virgil, *Ecl.* iii. 90.　Gratio and
Avaro were signatures adopted by
Southey and Lovell in their joint
volume of poems published at Bristol in 1795.

which feature is to be predominant in it ? " So you make it unique. But in this poem now *Charlotte* speaks and now the Poet. Assuredly the stanzas of Memory, " three worst of fiends," etc., and "gay fancy fond and frolic " are altogether poetical. You have repeated the same rhymes ungracefully, and the thought on which you harp so long recalls too forcibly the Εὕδας βρέφος of Simonides. Unfortunately the " Adventurer " has made this sweet fragment an object of popular admiration. On the whole, I think it unworthy of your other " Botany Bay Eclogues," yet deem the two stanzas above selected superior almost to anything you ever wrote ; *quod est magna res dicere*, a great thing to say.

SONNET.[1]

Though king-bred rage with lawless Tumult rude
Have driv'n our *Priestley* o'er the ocean swell ;
Though Superstition and her wolfish brood
Bay his mild radiance, impotent and fell ;
Calm in his halls of brightness he shall dwell !
For lo ! Religion at his strong behest
Disdainful rouses from the Papal spell,
And flings to Earth her tinsel-glittering vest,
Her mitred state and cumbrous pomp unholy ;
And Justice wakes to bid th' oppression wail,
That ground th' ensnared soul of patient Folly ;
And from her dark retreat by Wisdom won,
Meek Nature slowly lifts her matron veil,
To smile with fondness on her gazing son !

[1] Of the six sonnets included in this letter, those to Burke, Priestley, and Kosciusko had already appeared in the *Morning Chronicle* on the 9th, 11th, and 16th of December, 1794. The sonnets to Godwin, Southey, and Sheridan were published on the 10th, 14th, and 29th of January, 1795. See *Poetical Works*, pp. 38, 39, 41, 42.

SONNET.

O what a loud and fearful shriek was there,
As though a thousand souls one death-groan poured !
Great *Kosciusko* 'neath an hireling's sword
The warriors view'd !   Hark ! through the list'ning air
(When pauses the tir'd Cossack's barbarous yell
Of triumph) on the chill and midnight gale
Rises with frantic burst or sadder swell
The " Dirge of Murder'd Hope ! " while Freedom pale
Bends in *such* anguish o'er her destined bier,
As if from eldest time some Spirit meek
Had gathered in a mystic urn each tear
That ever furrowed a sad Patriot's cheek,
And she had drench'd the sorrows of the bowl
Ev'n till she reel'd, intoxicate of soul!

Tell me which you like the best of the above two.   I
have written one to Godwin, but the mediocrity of the
eight first lines is *most miserably magazinish!* I have
plucked, therefore, these scentless road-flowers from the
chaplet, and entreat thee, thou river god of Pieria, to
weave into it the gorgeous water-lily from thy stream, or
the far-smelling violets on thy bank.   The last six lines
are these : —

Nor will I not thy holy guidance bless
And hymn thee, Godwin ! with an ardent lay ;
For that thy voice, in Passion's stormy day,
When wild I roam'd the bleak Heath of Distress,
Bade the bright form of Justice meet my way, —
And told me that her name was Happiness.

Give me your minutest opinion concerning the following sonnet, whether or no I shall admit it into the number. The move of bepraising a man by enumerating the
beauties of his polygraph is at least an original one ; so
much so that I fear it will be somewhat unintelligible to

those whose brains are not τοῦ ἀμείνονος πηλοῦ. (You have read S.'s poetry and know that the fancy displayed in it is sweet and delicate to the highest degree.)

TO R. B. SHERIDAN, ESQ.

Some winged Genius, Sheridan! imbreath'd
His various influence on thy natal hour:
My fancy bodies forth the Guardian Power,
His temples with Hymettian flowerets wreath'd;
And sweet his voice, as when o'er Laura's bier
Sad music trembled through Vauclusa's glade;
Sweet, as at dawn the lovelorn serenade
That bears soft dreams to Slumber's listening ear!
Now patriot Zeal and Indignation high
Swell the full tones! and now his eye-beams dance
Meanings of Scorn and Wit's quaint revelry!
Th' Apostate by the brainless rout adored,
Writhes inly from the bosom-probing glance,
As erst that nobler Fiend beneath great Michael's sword!

I will give the second number as deeming that it possesses *mind* : —

As late I roamed through Fancy's shadowy vale,
With wetted cheek and in a mourner's guise,
I saw the sainted form of Freedom rise:
He spake : — not sadder moans th' autumnal gale —
"Great Son of Genius! sweet to me thy name,
Ere in an evil hour with altered voice
Thou badst Oppression's hireling crew rejoice,
Blasting with wizard spell my laurell'd fame.
Yet never, Burke! thou drank'st Corruption's bowl!
Thee stormy Pity and the cherish'd lure
Of Pomp and proud *precipitance* of soul
Urged on with wild'ring fires. Ah, spirit pure!
That Error's mist had left thy purged eye;
So might I clasp thee with a Mother's joy."

ADDRESS TO A YOUNG JACKASS AND ITS TETHERED MOTHER.[1]

Poor little foal of an oppressed race!
I love the languid patience of thy face:
And oft with friendly hand I give thee bread,
And clap thy ragged coat and pat thy head.
But what thy dulled spirit hath dismay'd,
That never thou dost sport upon the glade?
And (most unlike the nature of things young)
That still to earth thy moping head is hung?
Do thy prophetic tears anticipate,
Meek Child of Misery, thy future fate?
The starving meal and all the thousand aches
That " patient Merit of the Unworthy takes " ?
Or is thy sad heart thrill'd with filial pain
To see thy wretched mother's lengthened chain?
And truly, very piteous is *her* lot,
Chained to a log upon a narrow spot,
Where the close-eaten grass is scarcely seen,
While sweet around her waves the tempting green!
Poor Ass! thy master should have learnt to show
Pity best taught by fellowship of Woe!
For much I fear me that *He* lives like thee
Half-famish'd in a land of Luxury!
How *askingly* its steps towards me bend!
It seems to say, " And have I then *one* friend? "
Innocent foal! thou poor, despis'd forlorn!
I hail thee Brother, spite of the fool's scorn!
And fain I 'd take thee with me in the Dell
Of high-souled Pantisocracy to dwell;
Where Toil shall call the charmer Health his bride,
And Laughter tickle Plenty's *ribless* side!
How thou wouldst toss thy heels in gamesome play,
And frisk about, as lamb or kitten gay.

[1] First published in the *Morning Chronicle*, December 30, 1794. An earlier draft, dated October 24, 1794, was headed " Monologue to a Young Jackass in Jesus Piece. Its Mother near it, chained to a Log." See *Poetical Works*, Appendix C, p. 477, and Editor's Note, p. 573.

> Yea, and more musically sweet to me
> Thy dissonant harsh bray of joy would be,
> Than *Banti's* warbled airs, that soothe to rest
> The tumult of a scoundrel Monarch's breast!

How do you like it?

I took the liberty — Gracious God! pardon me for the aristocratic frigidity of that expression — I indulged my feelings by sending this among my *Contemporary* Sonnets:

> Southey! Thy melodies steal o'er mine ear
> Like far-off joyance, or the murmuring
> Of wild bees in the sunny showers of Spring —
> Sounds of such mingled import as may cheer
> The lonely breast, yet rouse a mindful tear:
> Waked by the song doth Hope-born Fancy fling
> Rich showers of dewy fragrance from her wing,
> Till sickly Passion's drooping Myrtles sear
> Blossom anew!   But O! more thrill'd I prize
> Thy sadder strains, that bid in Memory's Dream
> The faded forms of past Delight arise:
> Then soft on Love's pale cheek the tearful gleam
> Of Pleasure smiles as faint yet beauteous lies
> The imaged Rainbow on a willowy stream.

God love you and your mother and Edith and Sara and Mary and little Eliza, etc., etc., etc., etc., etc., and

S. T. Coleridge.

[The following lines in Southey's handwriting are attached to this letter: —

> What though oppression's blood-cemented force
>   Stands proudly threatening arrogant in state,
>   Not thine his savage priests to immolate
> Or hurl the fabric on the encumber'd plain
> As with a whirlwind's fury.   It is thine
>   When dark Revenge masked in the form adored
>   Of Justice lifts on high the murderer's sword
> To save the erring victims from her shrine.

To Godwin.]

XLIII. TO THE SAME.

Monday morning, December, 1794.

MY DEAR SOUTHEY, — I will not say that you treat me coolly or mysteriously, yet assuredly you seem to look upon me as a man whom vanity, or some other inexplicable cause, has alienated from the system, or what could build so injurious a suspicion? Wherein, when roused to the recollection of my duty, have I shrunk from the performance of it? I hold my life and my feeble feelings as ready sacrifices to justice — κανκάω ὑπορᾶς γάρ. I dismiss a subject so painful to me as self-vindication ; painful to me only as addressing you on whose esteem and affection I have rested with the whole weight of my soul.

Southey! I must tell you that you appear to me to write as a man who is aweary of the world because it accords not with his ideas of perfection. Your sentiments look like the sickly offspring of disgusted pride. It flies not away from the couches of imperfection because the patients are fretful and loathsome.

Why, my dear, very dear Southey, do you wrap yourself in the mantle of self-centring resolve, and refuse to us your bounden quota of intellect? Why do you say, " *I, I, I* will do so and so," instead of saying, as you were wont to do, " It is all our duty to do so and so, for such and such reasons " ?

For God's sake, my dear fellow, tell me what we are to gain by taking a Welsh farm. Remember the principles and proposed consequences of pantisocracy, and reflect in what degree they are attainable by Coleridge, Southey, Lovell, Burnett, and Co., some five men *going partners* together? In the next place, supposing that we have proved the preponderating utility of our aspheterizing in Wales, let us by our speedy and united inquiries discover the sum of money necessary, whether such a farm with so very large a house is to be procured without launching our frail and unpiloted bark on a rough sea of anxieties. How much is necessary for the maintenance of so large a family — eighteen people for a year at least?

I have read my objections to Lovell. If he has not answered them altogether to my fullest conviction, he has however shown me the wretchedness that would fall on the majority of our party from any delay in so forcible a light, that if three hundred pounds be adequate to the commencement of the system (which I very much doubt), I am most willing to give up all my views and embark immediately with you.

If it be determined that we shall go to Wales (for which I now give my vote), in what time? Mrs. Lovell thinks it impossible that we should go in less than three months. If this be the case, I will accept of the reporter's place to the "Telegraph," live upon a guinea a week, and transmit the [? balance], finishing in the same time my "Imitations."

However, I will walk to Bath to-morrow morning and return in the evening.

Mr. and Mrs. Lovell, Sarah, Edith, all desire their best love to you, and are anxious concerning your health.

May God love you and your affectionate

S. T. COLERIDGE.

XLIV. TO MARY EVANS.

(?) December, 1794.

Too long has my heart been the torture house of suspense. After infinite struggles of irresolution, I will at last dare to request of you, Mary, that you will communicate to me whether or no you are engaged to Mr. ——. I conjure you not to consider this request as presumptuous indelicacy. Upon mine honour, I have made it with no other design or expectation than that of arming my fortitude by total hopelessness. Read this letter with benevolence — and consign it to oblivion.

For four years I have *endeavoured* to smother a very ardent attachment; in what degree I have succeeded you must know better than I can. With quick perceptions of moral beauty, it was impossible for me not to admire in you your sensibility regulated by judgment, your gaiety proceeding from a cheerful heart acting on the stores of a strong understanding. At first I voluntarily invited the recollection of these qualities into my mind. I made them the perpetual object of my reveries, yet I entertained no one sentiment beyond that of the immediate pleasure annexed to the thinking of you. At length it became a habit. I awoke from the delusion, and found that I had unwittingly harboured a passion which I felt neither the power nor the courage to subdue. My associations were irrevocably formed, and your image was blended with every idea. I thought of you incessantly; yet that spirit (if spirit there be that condescends to record the lonely beatings of my heart), that spirit knows that I thought of you with the purity of a brother. Happy were I, had it been with no more than a brother's ardour!

The man of dependent fortunes, while he fosters an attachment, commits an act of suicide on his happiness. I possessed no establishment. My views were very distant; I saw that you regarded me merely with the kindness of a sister. What expectations could I form? I formed no expectations. I was ever resolving to subdue the disquieting passion; still some inexplicable suggestion palsied my efforts, and I clung with desperate fondness to this phantom of love, its mysterious attractions and hopeless prospects. It was a faint and rayless hope![1] Yet it soothed my solitude with many a delightful day-dream. It was a faint and rayless hope! Yet I nursed it in my bosom with an agony of affection, even as a mother her

---

[1] Compare the last six lines of a sonnet, "On a Discovery made too late," sent in a letter to Southey, dated October 21, 1794. (Letter XXXVII.) See *Poetical Works*, p. 34, and Editor's Note, p. 571.

sickly infant. But these are the poisoned luxuries of a diseased fancy. Indulge, Mary, this my first, my last request, and restore me to *reality*, however gloomy. Sad and full of heaviness will the intelligence be; my heart will die within me. I shall, however, receive it with steadier resignation from yourself, than were it announced to me (haply on your marriage day!) by a stranger. Indulge my request; I will not disturb your peace by even a *look* of discontent, still less will I offend your ear by the whine of selfish sensibility. In a few months I shall enter at the Temple and there seek forgetful calmness, where only it can be found, in incessant and useful activity.

Were you not possessed of a mind and of a heart above the usual lot of women, I should not have written you sentiments that would be unintelligible to three fourths of your sex. But our feelings are congenial, though our attachment is doomed not to be reciprocal. You will not deem so meanly of me as to believe that I shall regard Mr. —— with the jaundiced eye of disappointed passion. God forbid! He whom you honour with your affections becomes sacred to me. I shall love him for *your* sake; the time may perhaps come when I shall be philosopher enough not to envy him for *his own*.

S. T. COLERIDGE.

I return to Cambridge to-morrow morning.

Miss EVANS, No. 17 Sackville Street, Piccadilly.

XLV. TO THE SAME.

December 24, 1794.

I have this moment received your letter, Mary Evans. Its firmness does honour to your understanding, its gentleness to your humanity. You condescend to accuse yourself — most unjustly! You have been altogether blameless. In my wildest day-dream of vanity, I never supposed that you entertained for me any other than a common friendship.

To love you, habit has made unalterable. This passion,
however, divested as it now is of all shadow of hope, will
lose its disquieting power. Far distant from you I shall
journey through the vale of men in calmness. He cannot
long be wretched, who dares be actively virtuous.

I have burnt your letters — forget mine; and that I
have pained you, forgive me!

May God infinitely love you!

S. T. COLERIDGE.

XLVI. TO ROBERT SOUTHEY.

December, 1794.

I am calm, dear Southey! as an autumnal day, when
the sky is covered with gray moveless clouds. To *love
her*, habit has made unalterable. I had placed her in the
sanctuary of my heart, nor can she be torn from thence
but with the strings that grapple it to life. This passion,
however, divested as it now is of all shadow of hope,
seems to lose its disquieting power. Far distant, and
never more to behold or hear of her, I shall sojourn in
the vale of men, sad and in loneliness, yet not unhappy.
He cannot be long wretched who dares be actively virtuous. I am well assured that she loves me as a favourite
brother. When she was present, she was to me only as a
very dear sister; it was in absence that I felt those gnaw-
ings of suspense, and that dreaminess of mind, which
evidence an affection more restless, yet scarcely less pure
than the fraternal. The struggle has been well nigh too
much for me; but, praised be the All-Merciful! the fee-
bleness of exhausted feelings has produced a calm, and
my heart stagnates into peace.

Southey! my ideal standard of female excellence rises
not above that woman. But all things work together
for good. Had I been united to her, the excess of my
affection would have effeminated my intellect. I should
have fed on her looks as she entered into the room, I

should have gazed on her footsteps when she went out
from me.

To lose her! I can rise above that selfish pang. But
to marry another. O Southey! bear with my weakness.
Love makes all things pure and heavenly like itself, —
but to marry a woman whom I do *not* love, to degrade
her whom I call my wife by making her the instrument
of low desire, and on the removal of a desultory appetite
to be perhaps not displeased with her absence! Enough!
These refinements are the wildering fires that lead me
into vice. Mark you, Southey! *I will do my duty.*

I have this moment received your letter. My friend,
you want but one quality of mind to be a perfect character. Your sensibilities are tempestuous; you feel *indignation* at weakness. Now Indignation is the handsome
brother of Anger and Hatred. His looks are " lovely in
terror," yet still remember *who* are his *relations.* I
would ardently that you were a necessitarian, and (believing in an all-loving Omnipotence) an optimist. That
puny imp of darkness yclept scepticism, how could it dare
to approach the hallowed fires that burn so brightly on
the altar of your heart?

Think you I wish to stay in town? I am all eagerness to leave it; and am resolved, whatever be the consequence, to be at Bath by Saturday. I thought of walking down.

I have written to Bristol and said I could not assign a
particular time for my leaving town. I spoke indefinitely
that I might not disappoint.

I am not, I presume, to attribute some verses addressed
to S. T. C., in the " Morning Chronicle," to you. To
whom? My dear Allen! wherein has he offended? He
did never promise to form one of our party. But of all
this when we meet. Would a pistol preserve integrity?
So concentrate guilt? no very philosophical mode of preventing it. I will write of indifferent subjects. Your

sonnet,[1] "Hold your mad hands!" is a noble burst of poetry; and — but my mind is weakened and I turn with selfishness of thought to those wilder songs that develop my lonely feelings. Sonnets are scarcely fit for the hard gaze of the public. I read, with heart and taste equally delighted, your prefatory sonnet.[2] I transcribe it, not so much to give you my corrections, as for the pleasure it gives me.

With wayworn feet, a pilgrim woe-begone,
  Life's upland steep I journeyed many a day,
  And hymning many a sad yet soothing lay,
Beguiled my wandering with the charms of song.
  Lonely my heart and rugged was my way,
Yet often plucked I, as I passed along,
The wild and simple flowers of poesy:
  And, as beseemed the wayward Fancy's child,
Entwined each random weed that pleased mine eye.
  Accept the wreath, Beloved! it is wild
  And rudely garlanded; yet scorn not thou
The humble offering, when the sad rue weaves
With gayer flowers its intermingled leaves,
  And I have twin'd the myrtle for thy brow!

It is a lovely sonnet. Lamb likes it with tears in his eyes. His sister has lately been very unwell, confined to her bed, dangerously. She is all his comfort, he hers. They dote on each other. Her mind is elegantly stored; her heart feeling. Her illness preyed a good deal on his spirits, though he bore it with an apparent equanimity as beseemed him who, like me, is a Unitarian Christian, and an advocate for the automatism of man.

---

[1] The first of six sonnets on the Slave Trade. Southey's *Poetical Works*, 1837, ii. 55.

[2] Prefixed as a dedication to Juvenile and Minor Poems. It is addressed to Edith Southey, and dated Bristol, 1796. Southey's *Poetical Works*, 1837, vol. ii. The text of 1837 differs considerably from the earlier version. Possibly in transcribing Coleridge altered the original to suit his own taste.

I was writing a poem, which when finished you shall
see, and wished him to describe the character and doctrines of Jesus Christ for me; but his low spirits prevented him.   The poem is in blank verse on the Nativity.
I sent him these careless lines, which flowed from my pen
extemporaneously : —

TO C. LAMB.[1]

Thus far my sterile brain hath framed the song
Elaborate and swelling : but the heart
Not owns it.   From thy spirit-breathing power
I ask not now, my friend ! the aiding verse,
Tedious to thee, and from thy anxious thought
Of dissonant mood.   In fancy (well I know)
Thou creepest round a dear-loved Sister's bed
With noiseless step, and watchest the faint look,
Soothing each pang with fond solicitude,
And tenderest tones, medicinal of love.
I too a Sister had, an only Sister —
She loved me dearly, and I doted on her !
On her soft bosom I reposed my cares
And gained for every wound a healing scar.
To her I pour'd forth all my puny sorrows,
(As a sick Patient in his Nurse's arms),
And of the heart those hidden maladies
That shrink ashamed from even Friendship's eye.
O ! I have woke at midnight and have wept
Because she was not !   Cheerily, dear Charles !
Thou thy best friend shalt cherish many a year :
Such high presages feel I of warm hope !
For not uninterested, the dear Maid
I 've view'd — her Soul affectionate yet wise,
Her polish'd wit as mild as lambent glories
That play around a holy infant's head.
He knows (the Spirit who in secret sees,
Of whose omniscient and all-spreading Love

[1] To a Friend [Charles Lamb], ["Religious Musings"].   *Poetical*
together with an Unfinished Poem   *Works*, p. 37.

Aught to *implore* were Impotence of mind)
That my mute thoughts are sad before his throne,
Prepar'd, when he his healing pay vouchsafes,
To pour forth thanksgiving with lifted heart,
And praise Him Gracious with a Brother's Joy !

Wynne is indeed a noble fellow. More when we meet.
          Your   S. T. COLERIDGE.

CHAPTER II

EARLY PUBLIC LIFE

1795–1796

CHAPTER II

XLVII. TO JOSEPH COTTLE.

Spring, 1795.

MY DEAR SIR, — Can you conveniently lend me five pounds, as we want a little more than four pounds to make up our lodging bill, which is indeed much higher than we expected; seven weeks and Burnett's lodging for twelve weeks, amounting to eleven pounds?

Yours affectionately,

S. T. COLERIDGE.

XLVIII. TO THE SAME.

July 31, 1795.

DEAR COTTLE, — By the thick smokes that precede the volcanic eruptions of Etna, Vesuvius, and Hecla, I feel an impulse to fumigate, at 25 College Street, one pair of stairs' room; yea, with our Oronoco, and, if thou wilt send me by the bearer four pipes, I will write a panegyrical epic poem upon thee, with as many books as there are letters in thy name. Moreover, if thou wilt send me "the copy-book," I hereby bind myself, by to-morrow morning, to write out enough copy for a sheet and a half.

God bless you.   S. T. C.

XLIX. TO THE SAME.

1795.

DEAR COTTLE, — Shall I trouble you (I being over the mouth and nose, in doing something of importance, at ——'s) to send your servant into the market and buy a pound of bacon, and two quarts of broad beans; and when he carries it down to College Street, to desire the maid to dress it for dinner, and tell her I shall be home by three o'clock? Will you come and drink tea with me? and I will endeavour to get the etc. ready for you.

Yours affectionately,
S. T. C.

L. TO ROBERT SOUTHEY.

October, 1795.

MY DEAR SOUTHEY, — It would argue imbecility and a latent wickedness in myself, if for a moment I doubted concerning your purposes and final determination. I write, because it is possible that I may suggest some idea to you which should find a place in your answer to your uncle, and I *write*, because in a letter I can express myself more connectedly than in conversation.

The former part of Mr. Hill's reasonings is reducible to this. It may not be vicious to entertain pure and virtuous sentiments; their criminality is confined to the promulgation (if we believe democracy to be pure and virtuous, to us it is so). Southey! Pantisocracy is not the question: its realization is distant — perhaps a miraculous millennium. What you have seen, or think that you have seen of the human heart, may render the formation even of a pantisocratic *seminary* improbable to you, but this is not the question. Were £300 a year offered to you as a man of the world, as one indifferent to absolute equality, but still on the supposition that you were commonly honest, I suppose it possible that doubts might arise; your mother, your brother, your Edith, would all crowd upon you, and certain misery might be weighed against distant, and perhaps unattainable happiness. But the point is, whether or no you can *perjure* yourself. There are men who hold the necessity and moral optimism of our religious establishment. Its peculiar dogmas they may disapprove, but of innovation they see dreadful and unhealable consequence; and they will not quit the Church for a few follies and absurdities, any more than for the same reason they would desert a valued friend. Such men I do not condemn. Whatever I may deem of their reasoning, their hearts and consciences I include not in the anathema. But you disapprove of an establishment altogether; you believe it iniquitous, a mother of crimes. It is impossible that *you* could uphold it by assuming the badge of affiliation.

My prospects are not bright, but to the eye of reason as bright as when we first formed our plan; nor is there any opposite inducement offered, of which you were not then apprized, or had cause to expect. Domestic happiness is the greatest of things sublunary, and of things celestial it is impossible, perhaps, for unassisted man to believe anything greater; but it is not strange that those things, which, in a pure form of society, will constitute our first blessings, should in its present morbid state be our most perilous temptations. "He that doth not love mother or wife less than me, is not worthy of me!"

This have I written, Southey, altogether disinterestedly. Your desertion or adhesion will in no wise affect my feelings, opinions, or conduct, and in a very inconsiderable degree my fortunes! That Being who is "in will, in deed, Impulse of all to all," whichever be your determination, will make it ultimately the best.

God love you, my dear Southey!

S. T. Coleridge.

LI. TO THOMAS POOLE.

My DEAR SIR, — God bless you ; or rather, God be praised for that he *has* blessed you !

On Sunday morning I was *married* at St. Mary's Redcliff, poor Chatterton's church! The thought gave a tinge of melancholy to the solemn joy which I felt, united to the woman whom I love best of all created beings. We are settled, nay, quite domesticated, at Clevedon, our comfortable cot !

Mrs. Coleridge ! I like to write the name. Well, as I was saying, Mrs. Coleridge desires her affectionate regards to you. I talked of you on my wedding night. God bless you ! I hope that some ten years hence you will believe and know of my affection towards you what I will not now profess.

The prospect around is perhaps more *various* than any in the kingdom. Mine eye gluttonizes the sea, the distant islands, the opposite coast! I shall assuredly write rhymes, let the nine Muses prevent it if they can. Cruikshank, I find, is married to Miss Buclé. I am happy to hear it. He will surely, I hope, make a good husband to a woman, to whom he would be a villain who should make a bad one.

I have given up all thoughts of the magazine, for various reasons. *Imprimis*, I must be connected with R. Southey in it, which I could not be with comfort to my feelings. *Secundo*, It is a thing of monthly *anxiety* and quotidian bustle. *Tertio*, It would cost Cottle an hundred pounds in buying paper, etc. — all on an uncertainty. *Quarto*, To publish a magazine for *one* year would be nonsense, and if I pursue what I mean to pursue, my school plan, I could not publish it for more than a year. *Quinto*, Cottle has entered into an engagement to give me a guinea and a half for every hundred lines of poetry

I write, which will be perfectly sufficient for my maintenance, I only amusing myself on mornings; and all my prose works he is eager to purchase. *Sexto,* In the course of half a year I mean to return to Cambridge (having previously taken my name off from the University control) and taking lodgings there for myself and wife, finish my great work of "Imitations," in two volumes. My former works may, I hope, prove somewhat of genius and of erudition. This will be better; it will show great industry and manly consistency; at the end of it I shall publish proposals for school, etc. Cottle has spent a day with me, and takes this letter to Bristol. My next will be long, and full of *something.* This is inanity and egotism. Pray let me hear from you, directing the letter to Mr. Cottle, who will forward it. My respectful and grateful remembrance to your mother, and believe me, dear Poole, your affectionate and mindful *friend,* shall I so soon dare to say? Believe me, my heart prompts it.

S. T. COLERIDGE.

LII. TO ROBERT SOUTHEY.[1]

Friday morning, November 13, 1795.

Southey, I *have* lost friends — friends who still cherish for me sentiments of high esteem and unextinguished tenderness. For the sum total of my misbehaviour, the Alpha and Omega of their accusations, is epistolary neglect. I never speak of them without affection, I never think of them without reverence. Not "to this catalogue," Southey, have I "added *your* name." You are *lost* to *me,* because you are lost to Virtue. As this will probably be the last time I shall have occasion to address you, I will begin at the beginning and regularly retrace your conduct

[1] This farewell letter of apology and remonstrance was not sent by post, but must have reached Southey's hand on the 13th of November, the eve of his wedding day. The original MS. is written on small foolscap. A first draft, or copy, of the letter was sent to Coleridge's friend, Josiah Wade.

and my own.   In the month of June, 1794, I first became
acquainted with your person and character.   Before I
quitted Oxford, we had struck out the leading features of
a pantisocracy.   While on my journey through Wales you
invited me to Bristol with the full hopes of realising it.
During my abode at Bristol the plan was matured, and I returned to Cambridge hot in the anticipation of that happy
season when we should remove the *selfish* principle from
ourselves, and prevent it in our children, by an abolition
of property ; or, in whatever respects this might be impracticable, by such similarity of property as would amount
to a *moral* sameness, and answer all the purposes of *abolition.*   Nor were you less zealous, and thought and expressed your opinion, that if any man embraced our system he must comparatively disregard "his father and
mother and wife and children and brethren and sisters,
yea, and his own life also, or he could not be our disciple."
In one of your letters, alluding to your mother's low spirits and situation, you tell me that "I cannot suppose any
individual feelings will have an undue weight with you,"
and in the same letter you observe (alas! your recent
conduct has made it a prophecy!), "God forbid that the
ebullience of *schematism* should be over.   It is the Pro-
methean fire that animates my soul, and when *that* is gone
all will be darkness.   I have *devoted* myself!"

Previously to my departure from Jesus College, and
during my melancholy detention in London, what convul-
sive struggles of feeling I underwent, and what sacrifices
I made, you know.   The liberal proposal from my family
affected me no further than as it pained me to wound a
revered brother by the positive and immediate refusal
which duty compelled me to return.   But there was a —
I need not be particular; you remember what a fetter I
burst, and that it snapt as if it had been a sinew of my
heart.   However, I returned to Bristol, and my addresses
to Sara, which I at first paid from principle, not feeling,

from feeling and from principle I renewed; and I met a reward more than proportionate to the greatness of the effort.   I love and I am beloved, and I am happy!

Your letter to Lovell (two or three days after my arrival at Bristol), in answer to some objections of mine to the Welsh scheme, was the first thing that alarmed me. Instead of "It is our duty," "Such and such are the reasons," it was "I and I" and "will and will," — sentences of gloomy and self-centering resolve.   I wrote you a friendly reproof, and in my own mind attributed this unwonted style to your earnest desires of realising our plan, and the angry pain which you felt when any appeared to oppose or defer its execution.   However, I came over to your opinions of the utility, and, in course, the duty of rehearsing our scheme in Wales, and, so, rejected the offer of being established in the Earl of Buchan's family.   To this period of our connection I call your more particular attention and remembrance, as I shall revert to it at the close of my letter.

We commenced lecturing.   Shortly after, you began to recede in your conversation from those broad principles in which pantisocracy originated.   I opposed you with vehemence, for I well knew that no notion of morality or its motives could be without consequences.   And once (it was just before we went to bed) you confessed to me that you had acted wrong.   But you relapsed; your manner became cold and gloomy, and pleaded with increased pertinacity for the wisdom of making Self an undiverging Center.   At Mr. Jardine's[1] your language was *strong indeed.* Recollect it.   You had left the table, and we were standing at the window.   Then darted into my mind the dread that you were meditating a separation.   At *Chepstow*[2]

[1] The Rev. David Jardine, Unitarian minister at Bath. Cottle lays the scene of the "inaugural sermons" on the corn laws and hair powder tax, which Coleridge deliv- ered in a blue coat and white waistcoat, in Mr. Jardine's chapel at Bath. *Early Recollections,* i. 179.

[2] If we may believe Cottle, the dispute began by Southey attacking

your conduct renewed my suspicion, and I was greatly
agitated, even to many tears.   But in Peircefield Walks[1]
you assured me that my suspicions were altogether un-
founded, that our differences were merely speculative, and
that you would certainly go into Wales.   I was glad and
satisfied.   For my heart was never bent from you but by
violent strength, and heaven knows how it leapt back to
esteem and love you.   But alas! a short time passed ere
your departure from our first principles became too fla-
grant.   Remember when we went to Ashton[2] on the straw-
berry party.   Your conversation with George Burnett on
the day following he detailed to me.   It scorched my
throat.   Your private resources were to remain your individual property, and everything to be separate except a
farm of five or six acres.   In short, we were to commence
partners in a petty farming trade.   This was the mouse
of which the mountain Pantisocracy was at last safely delivered.   I received the account with indignation and
loathings of unutterable contempt.   Such opinions were
indeed unassailable, — the javelin of argument and the
arrows of ridicule would have been equally misapplied; a
straw would have wounded them mortally.   I did not condescend to waste my intellect upon them; but in the most
express terms I declared to George Burnett my opinion
(and, Southey, next to my own existence, there is scarce
any fact of which at this moment I entertain less doubt),
to Burnett I declared it to be my opinion " *that you had
long laid a plot* of separation, and were now developing
it by proposing such a vile mutilation of our scheme as

Coleridge for his non-appearance at
a lecture which he had undertaken
to deliver in his stead.   The scene
of the quarrel is laid at Chepstow, on
the first day of the memorable excursion to Tintern Abbey, which
Cottle had planned to "gratify his
two young friends."   Southey had
been "dragged," much against the
grain, into this "detestable party of

pleasure," and was, no doubt, rendered doubly sore by his partner's
delinquency.   See *Early Recollections*, i. 40, 41.   See, also, letter from
Southey to Bedford, dated May 28,
1795.   *Life and Correspondence*, i.
239.

[1] At Chepstow.

[2] A village three miles W. S. W.
of Bristol.

you must have been conscious I should reject decisively
and with scorn." George Burnett was your most affectionate friend; I knew his unbounded veneration for you,
his personal attachment; I knew likewise his gentle dislike of *me*. Yet him I bade be the judge. I bade him
choose his associate. I would adopt the full system or depart. George, I presume, detailed of this my conversation what part he chose; from him, however, I received
your sentiments, viz.: that you would go into Wales, or
what place I liked. Thus your system of prudentials and
your apostasy were not sudden; these constant nibblings
had sloped your descent from virtue. "You received your
uncle's letter," I said — "what answer have you returned?" For to think with almost superstitious veneration of you had been such a deep-rooted habit of my soul
that even then I did not dream you could hesitate concerning so infamous a proposal. "None," you replied, "nor
do I know what answer I shall return." You went to
bed. George sat half-petrified, gaping at the pigmy virtue of his supposed giant. I performed the office of still-
struggling friendship by writing you my free sentiments
concerning the enormous guilt of that which your uncle's
doughty sophistry recommended.

On the next morning I walked with you towards Bath;
again I insisted on its criminality. You told me that you
had "little notion of guilt," and that "you had a pretty
sort of lullaby faith of your own." Finding you invulner-
able in conscience, for the sake of mankind I did not, however, quit the field, but pressed you on the difficulties of
your system. Your uncle's intimacy with the bishop, and
the hush in which you would lie for the two years previous
to your ordination, were the arguments (variously urged
in a long and desultory conversation) by which you solved
those difficulties. "But your 'Joan of Arc' — the sentiments in it are of the boldest order. What if the suspicions of the Bishop be raised, and he particularly questions

you concerning your opinions of the Trinity and the Redemption?" "Oh," you replied, "I am pretty well up to their jargon, and shall answer them accordingly." In fine, you left me fully persuaded that you would enter into Holy Orders. And, after a week's interval or more, you desired George Burnett to act independently of you, and *gave him an invitation to Oxford*. Of course, we both concluded that the matter was absolutely determined. Southey! I am not besotted that I should not know, nor hypocrite enough not to tell you, that you were diverted from being a Priest only by the weight of infamy which you perceived coming towards you like a rush of waters.

Then with good reason I considered you as one *fallen back into the ranks ;* as a man admirable for his abilities only, strict, indeed, in the lesser honesties, but, like the majority of men, unable to resist a strong temptation. *Friend* is a very sacred appellation. You were become an *acquaintance*, yet one for whom I felt no common tenderness. I could not forget what you had been. Your sun was set; your sky was clouded; but those clouds and that sky were yet tinged with the recent sun. As I considered you, so I treated you. I studiously avoided all particular subjects. I acquainted you with nothing relative to myself. Literary topics engrossed our conversation. You were too quick-sighted not to perceive it. I received a letter from you. "You have withdrawn your confidence from me, Coleridge. Preserving still the face of friendship when we meet, you yet avoid me and carry on your plans in secrecy." If by "the face of friendship" you meant that kindliness which I show to all because I feel it for all, your statement was perfectly accurate. If you meant more, you contradict yourself; for you evidently perceived from my manners that you were a "weight upon me" in company — an intruder, unwished and unwelcome. I pained you by "cold civility, the shadow which friendship leaves behind him." Since that letter I altered my conduct no otherwise than by avoiding you more. I still generalised, and spoke not of myself, except my proposed literary works. In short, I spoke to you as I should have done to any other man of genius who had happened to be my *acquaintance*. Without the farce and tumult of a rupture I wished you to sink into that class. "Face to face you never changed your manners to me." And yet I pained you by "cold civility." Egregious contradiction! Doubtless I always treated you with urbanity, and meant to do so; but I *locked up* my heart from you, and you perceived it, and I intended you to perceive it. "I planned works in conjunction with you." Most certainly; the *magazine* which, long before this, you had planned equally with me, and, if it had been carried into execution, would of course have returned you a third share of the profits. What had you done that should make you an unfit literary associate to me? Nothing. My opinion of you as a *man* was altered, not as a writer. Our Muses had not quarrelled. I should have read your poetry with equal delight, and corrected it with equal zeal if correction it needed. "I received you on my return from Shurton with my usual shake of the hand." You gave me your hand, and dreadful must have been my feelings if I had refused to take it. Indeed, so long had I known you, so highly venerated, so dearly loved you, that my hand would have taken yours *mechanically*. But is shaking the hand a mark of *friendship?* Heaven forbid! I should then be a hypocrite many days in the week. It is assuredly the pledge of acquaintance, and nothing more. But after this did I not with most scrupulous care avoid you? You know I did.

In your former letters you say that I made use of these words to you: "You will be retrograde that you may spring the farther forward." You have misquoted, Southey! You had talked of rejoining pantisocracy in about fourteen years. I exploded this probability, but as I saw you determined to leave it, hoped and wished it might be so — *hoped* that we might run backwards only to leap forward. Not to mention that during that conversation I had taken the weight and pressing urgency of your motives as truths granted; but when, on examination, I found them a show and mockery of unreal things, doubtless, my opinion of you *must* have become far less respectful. You quoted likewise the last sentence of my letter to you, as a proof that I approved of your design; you *knew* that sentence to imply no more than the pious confidence of optimism — however wickedly you might act, God would make it *ultimately* the best. You *knew* this was the meaning of it — I could find twenty parallel passages in the lectures. Indeed, such expressions applied to bad actions had become a habit of my conversation. You had named, not unwittingly, Dr. Pangloss. And Heaven forbid that I should not now have faith that however foul your stream may run here, yet that it will filtrate and become pure in its subterraneous passage to the Ocean of Universal Redemption.

Thus far had I written when the necessities of literary occupation crowded upon me, and I met you in Redcliff, and, unsaluted and unsaluting, passed by the man to whom for almost a year I had told my last thoughts when I closed my eyes, and the first when I awoke. But "ere this I have felt sorrow!"

I shall proceed to answer your letters, and first excriminate myself, and then examine your conduct. You charge me with having industriously trumpeted your uncle's letter. When I mentioned my intended journey to Clevedon with Burnett, and was asked by my immediate friends why *you* were not with us, should I have been silent and implied something mysterious, or have told an open untruth and made myself your accomplice? I could do neither; I answered that you were quite undetermined, but had some thoughts of returning to Oxford. To Danvers, indeed, and to Cottle I spoke more particularly, for

I knew their prudence and their love for you — and my
heart was very full. But to Mrs. Morgan I did not
mention it. She met me in the streets, and said : " So !
Southey is going into the Church ! 'T is all concluded, 't is
in vain to deny it ! " I answered : " You are mistaken ;
you must contradict ; Southey has received a splendid
offer, but he has not determined." This, I have some
faint recollection, was my answer, but of this particular
conversation my recollection is very faint. By what
means she received the intelligence I know not ; probably
from Mrs. Richardson, who might have been told it by
Mr. Wade. A considerable time after, the subject was
renewed at Mrs. Morgan's, Burnett and my Sara being
present. Mrs. M. told me that you had asserted to her,
that with regard to the Church you had barely hesitated,
that you might consider your uncle's arguments, that
you had given up no one principle — and that *I* was
more your friend than ever. I own I was roused to an
agony of passion ; nor was George Burnett undisturbed.
Whatever I said that afternoon (and since that time I
have but often repeated what I said, in gentler language)
George Burnett did give his *decided Amen* to. And I
said, Southey, that you had given up every principle —
that confessedly you were going into the law, more opposite to your avowed principles, if possible, than even the
Church — and that I had in my pocket a letter in which
you charged me with having withdrawn my friendship ;
and as to your barely hesitating about your uncle's proposal, I was obliged in my own defence to relate all that
passed between us, all on which I had founded a conviction so directly opposite.

I have, you say, distorted your conversation by " gross
misrepresentation and wicked and calumnious falsehoods.
It has been told me by Mrs. Morgan that I said : ' I have
seen my error ! I have been drunk with principle ! ' "
Just over the bridge, at the bottom of the High Street,

returning one night from Redcliff Hill, in answer to my
pressing contrast of your then opinions of the selfish
kind with what you had formerly professed, you said : " I
was intoxicated with the novelty of a system ! " That you
said, " I have seen my error," I never asserted.   It is
doubtless implied in the sentence which you did say, but
I never charged it to you as your expression.   As to your
reserving bank bills, etc., to yourself, the charge would
have been so palpable a lie that I must have been madman as well as villain to have been guilty of it.   If I
had, George Burnett and Sara would have contradicted
it.   I said that your conduct in little things had appeared
to me tinged with selfishness, and George Burnett attributed, and still does attribute, your defection to your
unwillingness to share your expected annuity with us.
As to the long catalogue of other lies, they not being
particularised, I, of course, can say nothing about them.
Tales may have been fetched and carried with embellish-
ments calculated to improve them in everything but the
truth.   I spoke " the plain and simple truth " alone.

And now for your conduct and motives.   My hand
trembles when I think what a series of falsehood and
duplicity I am about to bring before the conscience of
a man who has dared to write me that " his conduct has
been uniformly open."   I must revert to your first letter,
and here you say : —

" The plan you are going upon is not of sufficient importance to justify me to myself in abandoning a family,
who have none to support them but me."   The plan *you*
are going upon !   What plan was I meditating, save to
retire into the country with George Burnett and yourself,
and taking by degrees a small farm, there be *learning*
to get my own bread by my bodily labour — and then to
have all things in common — thus disciplining my body
and mind for the successful practice of the same thing
in America with more numerous associates ?   And even if

this should never be the case, ourselves and our children
would form a society sufficiently large.   And was not
this your own plan — the plan for the realising of which
you invited me to Bristol; the plan for which I abandoned
my friends, and every prospect, and every certainty, and
the woman whom I loved to an excess which you in your
warmest dream of fancy could never shadow out?   When
I returned from London, when you deemed pantisocracy
a *duty* — duty unaltered by numbers — when you said,
that, if others left it, you and George Burnett and your
brother would stand firm to the post of virtue — what then
were our circumstances?   Saving Lovell, our number
was the same, yourself and Burnett and I.   Our *prospects* were only an uncertain hope of getting thirty shillings a week between us by writing for some London
paper — for the remainder we were to rely on our agricultural exertions.   And as to your family you stood
precisely in the same situation as you now stand.   You
meant to take your mother with you, and your brother.
And where, indeed, would have been the difficulty?   She
would have earned her maintenance by her management
and savings — considering the matter even in this cold-
hearted way.   But when you broke from us our prospects
were brightening; by the magazine or by poetry we might
and should have got ten guineas a month.

But if you are acting right, I should be acting right in
imitating you.   What, then, would George Burnett do —
he " whom you seduced

> " With other promises and other vaunts
> Than to repent, boasting *you* could subdue
> Temptation ! "

He cannot go into the Church, for you did "give him
principles"! and I wish that you had indeed "learnt
from him how infinitely more to be valued is integrity of
heart than effulgence of intellect."   Nor can he go into
the law, for the same *principles* declare against it, and he

is not calculated for it. And his father will not support
any expense of consequence relative to his further education — for Law or Physic he could not take his degree in,
or be called to, without sinking of many hundred pounds.
What, Southey, was George Burnett to do?

Then, even if you had persisted in your design of taking
Orders, your motives would have been weak and shadowy
and vile ; but when you changed your ground for the Law
they were annihilated. No man dreams of getting bread
in the Law, till six or eight years after his first entrance
at the Temple. And how very few even then? Before
this time your brothers would have been put out, and the
money which you must of necessity have sunk in a wicked
profession would have given your brother an education,
and provided a premium fit for the first compting-house in
the world. But I hear that you have again changed your
ground. You do not now mean to study the Law, but to
maintain yourself by your writings and on your promised
annuity, which, you told Mrs. Morgan, would be more
than a hundred a year. Could you not have done the
same with *us* ? I neither have nor could deign to have a
hundred a year. Yet by my own exertions I will struggle
hard to maintain myself, and my wife, and my wife's
mother and my associate. Or what if you dedicated this
hundred a year to your family ? Would you not be precisely as I am ? Is not George Burnett accurate when he
undoubtedly ascribes your conduct to an unparticipating
propensity — to a total want of the boasted *flocci-nauci-
nihili-pilificating* sense? O selfish, money-loving man !
What principle have you not given up? Though death had
been the consequence, I would have spat in that man's
face and called him liar, who should have spoken that last
sentence concerning *you* nine months ago. For blindly
did I esteem you. O God! that *such a mind* should fall
in love with that low, dirty, gutter-grubbing trull, *Worldly
Prudence !*

Curse on all *pride!*   'T is a harlot that buckrams her-self up in virtue only that she may fetch a higher price. 'T is a rock where virtue may be planted, but cannot strike root.

Last of all, perceiving that your motives vanished at the first ray of examination, and that those accounts of your mother and family which had drawn easy tears down wrinkled cheeks had no effect on keener minds, your last resource has been to calumniate me.   If there be in nature a situation perilous to honesty, it is this, when a man has not heart to *be*, yet lusts to *seem* virtuous.   My *indolence* you assigned to Lovell as the reason for your quitting pantisocracy.   Supposing it true, it might in-deed be a reason for rejecting *me* from the system.   But how does this affect pantisocracy, that you should reject *it?*   And what has Burnett done, that he should not be a worthy associate?   He who leaned on you with all his head and with all his heart; he who gave his all for pantisocracy, and expected that pantisocracy would be at least bread and cheese to him.   But neither is the charge a true one.   My own lectures I wrote for myself, eleven in number, excepting a very few pages which most reluc-tantly you eked out for me.   And such pages!   I would not have suffered them to have stood in a lecture of yours. To *your* lectures I dedicated my whole mind and heart, and wrote one half in *quantity ;* but in quality you must be conscious that all the *tug* of brain was mine, and that your share was little more than transcription.   I wrote with vast exertion of all my intellect the parts in the " Joan of Arc," and I corrected that and other poems with greater interest than I should have felt for my own. Then my own poems, and the recomposing of my lectures, besides a sermon, and the correction of some poems for a friend.   I could have written them in half the time and with less expense of thought.   I write not these things boastfully, but to excriminate myself.   The truth is, you

sat down and wrote; I used to saunter about and think
what I should write. And we ought to appreciate our
comparative industry by the quantum of mental exertion,
not the particular mode of it — by the number of thoughts
collected, not by the number of lines through which these
thoughts are diffused. But I will suppose myself guilty
of the charge. How would an honest man have reasoned
in your letter and how acted? Thus: "Here is a man
who has abandoned all for what I believe to be virtue.
But he professed himself an imperfect being when he
offered himself an associate to me. He confessed that all
his valuable qualities were 'sloth-jaundiced,' and in his
letters is a bitter self-accuser. This man did not deceive
me. I accepted of him in the hopes of curing him, but I
half despair of it. How shall I act? I will tell him
fully and firmly, that much as I love him I love pantisocracy more, and if in a certain time I do not see this dis-
qualifying propensity subdued, I must and will reject
him." Such would have been an honest man's reasoning,
such his conduct. Did *you* act so? Did you even mention to me, "face to face," my indolence as a motive for
your recent conduct? Did you ever mention it in Peircefield Walks? and some time after, that night when you
scattered some heart-chilling sentiments, and in great
agitation I did ask you *solemnly* whether you disapproved
of anything in *my* conduct, and you answered, "Nothing.
I like you better now than at the commencement of our
friendship!" an answer which so startled Sara, that she
affronted you into angry silence by exclaiming, "What
a story!" George Burnett, I believe, was present. This
happened after all our lectures, after every one of those
proofs of indolence on which you must found your charge.
A charge which with what indignation did you receive
when brought against me by Lovell! Yet *then* there was
some shew for it. I *had* been criminally indolent. But
since then I have exerted myself more than I could have

supposed myself capable.   Enough! I heard for the
first time on Thursday that you were to set off for Lisbon
on Saturday morning.   It gives me great pain on many
accounts, but principally that those moments which should
be sacred to your affections may be disturbed by this
long letter.

Southey, as far as happiness will be conducive to your
virtue, which alone is final happiness, may you possess it!
You have left a large void in my heart.   I know no man
big enough to fill it.   Others I may love equally, and
esteem equally, and some perhaps I may admire as much.
But never do I expect to meet another man, who will
make me unite attachment for his person with reverence
for his heart and admiration of his genius.   I did not
only venerate you for your own virtues, I prized you as
the sheet-anchor of mine ; and even as a poet my vanity
knew no keener gratification than your praise.   But these
things are passed by like as when a hungry man dreams,
and lo! he feasteth, but he awakes and his soul is empty.

May God Almighty bless and preserve you ! and may
you live to know and feel and acknowledge that unless
we accustom ourselves to meditate adoringly on Him, the
source of all virtue, no virtue can be permanent.

Be assured that G. Burnett still loves you better than
he can love any other man, and Sara would have you
accept her love and blessing; accept it as the future husband of her best loved sister.   Farewell!

S. T. COLERIDGE.

LIII. TO JOSIAH WADE.[1]

NOTTINGHAM, Wednesday morning, January 27, 1796.

MY DEAR FRIEND, — You will perceive by this letter
that I have changed my route.   From Birmingham, which

---

[1] During the course of his tour
(January-February, 1796) to procure
subscribers for the *Watchman*, Coleridge wrote seven times to Josiah
Wade. Portions of these letters
have been published in Cottle's *Early*

I quitted on Friday last (four o'clock in the morning), I proceeded to Derby, stayed there till Monday morning, and am now at Nottingham. From Nottingham I go to Sheffield; from Sheffield to Manchester; from Manchester to Liverpool; from Liverpool to London; from London to Bristol. Ah, what a weary way! My poor crazy ark has been tossed to and fro on an ocean of business, and I long for the Mount Ararat on which it is to rest. At Birmingham I was extremely unwell. . . . Business succeeded very well there; about an hundred subscribers, I think. At Derby tolerably well. Mr. Strutt (the successor to Sir Richard Arkwright) tells me I may count on forty or fifty in Derby and round about.

Derby is full of curiosities, the cotton, the silk mills, Wright,[1] the painter, and Dr. Darwin, the everything, except the Christian![2] Dr. Darwin possesses, perhaps, a greater range of knowledge than any other man in Europe, and is the most inventive of philosophical men. He thinks in a *new* train on all subjects except religion. He bantered me on the subject of religion. I heard all his arguments, and told him that it was infinitely consoling to me, to find that the arguments which so great a man adduced against the existence of a God and the evidences of revealed religion were such as had startled me at fifteen, but had become the objects of my smile at twenty. Not one new objection — not even an ingenious one.

Recollections, i. 164–176, and in the " Biographical Supplement " to the *Biographia Literaria*, ii. 349–354. It is probable that Wade supplied funds for the journey, and that Coleridge felt himself bound to give an account of his progress and success.

[1] Joseph Wright, A R. A., known as Wright of Derby, 1736–1797. Two of his most celebrated pictures were *The Head of Ulleswater*, and *The Dead Soldier*. An excellent specimen of Wright's work, *An Experiment with the Air Pump*, was presented to the National Gallery in 1863.

[2] Compare *Biographia Literaria*, ch. i. " During my first Cambridge vacation I assisted a friend in a contribution for a literary society in Devonshire, and in that I remember to have compared Darwin's works to the Russian palace of ice, glittering, cold, and transitory." Coleridge's *Works*, Harper & Bros., 1853, iii. 155.

He boasted that he had never read one book in defence
of *such stuff*, but he had read all the works of infidels!
What should you think, Mr. Wade, of a man, who, having abused and ridiculed you, should openly declare that
he had heard all that your *enemies* had to say against
you, but had scorned to enquire the truth from any of
your own friends? Would you think him an honest
man? I am sure you would not. Yet of such are all
the infidels with whom I have met. They talk of a subject infinitely important, yet are proud to confess themselves profoundly ignorant of it. Dr. Darwin would have
been ashamed to have rejected Hutton's theory of the
earth[1] without having minutely examined it; yet what
is it to us *how* the earth was made, a thing impossible
to be known, and useless if known? This system the
doctor did not reject without having severely studied it;
but *all at once he makes up his mind* on such important subjects, as whether we be the outcasts of a blind
idiot called Nature, or the children of an all-wise and
infinitely good God; whether we spend a few miserable
years on this earth, and then sink into a clod of the valley, or only endure the anxieties of mortal life in order
to fit us for the enjoyment of immortal happiness. These
subjects are unworthy a philosopher's investigation. He
deems that there is a certain *self-evidence* in infidelity,
and becomes an atheist by intuition. Well did St. Paul
say: "Ye have an evil *heart* of unbelief." I had an
introductory letter from Mr. Strutt to a Mr. Fellowes of
Nottingham. On Monday evening when I arrived I found
there was a public dinner in honour of Mr. Fox's birthday,
and that Mr. Fellowes was present. It was a piece of
famous good luck, and I seized it, waited on Mr. Fellowes, and was introduced to the company. On the right
hand of the president whom should I see but an old Col-

[1] Dr. James Hutton, the author of *the Earth* was published at Edin-
the Plutonian theory. His *Theory of* burgh in 1795.

lege acquaintance? He hallooed out: " *Coleridge, by God!* " Mr. Wright, the president of the day, was his relation — a man of immense fortune. I dined at his house yesterday, and underwent the intolerable slavery of a dinner of three courses. We sat down at four o'clock, and it was six before the cloth was removed.

What lovely children Mr. Barr at Worcester has! After church, in the evening, they sat round and sang hymns so sweetly that they overwhelmed me. It was with great difficulty I abstained from weeping aloud — and the infant in Mrs. Barr's arms leaned forwards, and stretched his little arms, and stared and smiled. It seemed a picture of Heaven, where the different orders of the blessed join different voices in one melodious allelujah; and the baby looked like a young spirit just that moment arrived in Heaven, startling at the seraphic songs, and seized at once with wonder and rapture.

My kindest remembrances to Mrs. Wade, and believe me, with gratitude and unfeigned friendship, your

S. T. COLERIDGE.

LIV. TO JOSEPH COTTLE.

Redcliff Hill, February 22, 1796.

My dear Sir, — It is my duty and business to thank God for all his dispensations, and to believe them the best possible; but, indeed, I think I should have been more thankful, if he had made me a journeyman shoemaker, instead of an author by trade. I have left my friends; I have left plenty; I have left that ease which would have secured a literary immortality, and have enabled me to give the public works conceived in moments of inspiration, and polished with leisurely solicitude; and alas! for what have I left them? for —— who deserted me in the hour of distress, and for a scheme of virtue impracticable and romantic! So I am forced to write for bread; write the flights of poetic enthusiasm, when every minute I am hearing a groan from my wife. Groans, and complaints, and sickness! The present hour I am in a quick-set hedge of embarrassment, and whichever way I turn a thorn runs into me! The future is cloud and thick darkness! Poverty, perhaps, and the thin faces of them that want bread, looking up to me! Nor is this all. My happiest moments for composition are broken in upon by the reflection that I must make haste. I am too late! I am already months behind! I have received my pay beforehand! Oh, wayward and desultory spirit of genius! Ill canst thou brook a taskmaster! The tenderest touch from the hand of obligation wounds thee like a scourge of scorpions.

I have been composing in the fields this morning, and came home to write down the first rude sheet of my preface, when I heard that your man had brought a note from you. I have not seen it, but I guess its contents. I am writing as fast as I can. Depend on it you shall not be out of pocket for me! I feel what I owe you, and independently of this I love you as a friend; indeed, so much, that I regret, seriously regret, that you have been my copyholder.

If I have written petulantly, forgive me. God knows I am sore all over. God bless you, and believe me that, setting gratitude aside, I love and esteem you, and have your interest at heart full as much as my own.

S. T. COLERIDGE.

LV. TO THOMAS POOLE.

March 30, 1796.

MY DEAR POOLE, — For the neglect in the transmission of "The Watchman," you must blame George Burnett, who undertook the business. I however will myself see it sent this week with the preceding numbers. I am greatly obliged to you for your communication (on the Slave Trade in No. V.); it appears in this number, and

I am anxious to receive more from you, and likewise to know what you *dislike* in "The Watchman," and what you like; but particularly the former. You have not given me your opinion of "The Plot Discovered." [1]

Since last you saw me I have been well nigh distracted. The repeated and most injurious blunders of my printer out-of-doors, and Mrs. Coleridge's increasing danger at home, added to the gloomy prospect of so many mouths to open and shut like puppets, as I move the string in the eating and drinking way — but why complain to you? Misery is an article with which every market is so glutted, that it can answer no one's purpose to export it. *Alas! Alas! oh! ah! oh! oh!* etc.

I have received many abusive letters, post-paid, thanks to the friendly malignants! But I am perfectly callous to disapprobation, except when it tends to lessen profit. There, indeed, I am all one tremble of sensibility, marriage having taught me the wonderful uses of that vulgar commodity, yclept *bread*. "The Watchman" succeeds so as to yield a *bread-and-cheesish* profit. Mrs. Coleridge is recovering apace, and deeply regrets that she was deprived of seeing [you]. We are in our new house, where there is a bed at your service whenever you will please to delight us with a visit. Surely in spring you might force a few days into a sojourning with me.

Dear Poole, you have borne yourself towards me most kindly with respect to my epistolary ingratitude. But I know that you forbade yourself to feel resentment towards me because you had previously made my neglect ingratitude. A generous temper endures a great deal from one whom it has obliged deeply.

My poems are finished. I will send you two copies the

---

[1] The title of this pamphlet, which was published shortly after the *Conciones ad Populum*, was "The Plot Discovered; or, an Address to the People against Ministerial Treason. By S. T. Coleridge. Bristol, 1795." It had an outer wrapper with this half-title: "A Protest against Certain Wills. Bristol: Printed for the Author, November 28, 1795." It is reprinted in *Essays on His Own Times*, i. 56-98.

moment they are published. In the third number of
" The Watchman " there are a few lines entitled " The
Hour when we shall meet again," " *Dim hour that sleeps
on pillowy clouds afar*," which I think you will like. I
have received two or three letters from different *anonymi*,
requesting me to give more poetry. One of them writes : —

"Sir! I detest your principles ; your prose I think
very so-so ; but your poetry is so *exquisitely* beautiful, so
gorgeously sublime, that I take in your ' Watchman '
solely on account of it. In justice therefore to me and
some others of my stamp, I intreat you to give us more
verse and less democratic scurrility. Your admirer, —
not esteemer."

Have you read over Dr. Lardner on the Logos? It is,
I think, scarcely possible to read it and not be convinced.

I find that " The Watchman" comes more easy to me,
so that I shall begin about my Christian Lectures. I will
immediately order for you, unless you immediately coun-
termand it, Count Rumford's Essays ; in No. V. of " The
Watchman " you will see why. I have enclosed Dr. Beddoes's late pamphlets, neither of them as yet published.
The doctor sent them to me. I can get no one but the
doctor to agree with me in my opinion that Burke's " Letter to a Noble Lord " [1] is as contemptible in style as in
matter — it is sad stuff.

My dutiful love to your excellent mother, whom, believe
me, I think of frequently and with a pang of affection.
God bless you. I 'll try and venture to scribble a line
and a half every time the man goes with " The Watchman " to you.

N. B. The " Essay on Fasting " [2] I am ashamed of ;
but it is one of my misfortunes that I am obliged to publish *extempore* as well as compose. God bless you,

and S. T. COLERIDGE.

[1] The review of " Burke's Letter
to a Noble Lord," which appeared
in the first number of *The Watch-*
man, is reprinted in *Essays on His
Own Times*, i. 107-119.
[2] *Ibid*. 120-120.

LVI. TO THE SAME.

12th May, 1796.

Poole! The Spirit, who counts the throbbings of the solitary heart, knows that what my feelings ought to be, such they are. If it were in my power to give you anything which I have not already given, I should be oppressed by the letter now before me.[1] But no! I feel myself rich in being poor; and because I have nothing to bestow, I know how much I have bestowed. Perhaps I shall not make myself intelligible; but the strong and unmixed affection which I bear to you seems to exclude all emotions of gratitude, and renders even the principle of esteem latent and inert. Its presence is not perceptible, though its absence could not be endured.

Concerning the scheme itself, I am undetermined. Not that I am ashamed to receive — God forbid! I will make every possible exertion; my industry shall be at least commensurate with my learning and talents; — if these do not procure for me and mine the necessary comforts of life, I can receive as I would bestow, and, in either case — receiving or bestowing — be equally grateful to my Almighty Benefactor. I am undetermined, therefore — not because I receive with pain and reluctance, but — because I suspect that you attribute to others your own enthusiasm of benevolence; as if the sun should say, " With how rich a purple those opposite windows are burning!" But with God's permission I shall talk with you on this subject. By the last page of No. X. you will perceive that I have this day dropped " The Watchman." On Monday morning I

---

[1] The occasion of this " burst of affectionate feeling " was a communication from Poole that seven or eight friends had undertaken to subscribe a sum of £35 or £40 to be paid annually to the " author of the monody on the death of Chatter- ton," as " a trifling mark of their esteem, gratitude, and affection." The subscriptions were paid in 1796- 97, but afterwards discontinued on the receipt of the Wedgwood annuity. See *Thomas Poole and his Friends*, i. 142.

will go *per* caravan to Bridgewater, where, if you have a horse of tolerable meekness unemployed, you will let him meet me.

I should blame you for the exaggerated terms in which you have spoken of me in the Proposal, did I not perceive the motive. You wished to make it appear an offering — not a favour — and in excess of delicacy have, I fear, fallen into some grossness of flattery.

God bless you, my dear, very dear Friend. The widow [1] is calm, and amused with her beautiful infant. We are all become more religious than we were. God be ever praised for all things! Mrs. Coleridge begs her kind love to you. To your dear mother my filial respects.

S. T. COLERIDGE.

LVII. TO JOHN THELWALL.

May 13, 1796.

MY DEAR THELWALL, — You have given me the affection of a brother, and I repay you in kind. Your letters demand my friendship and deserve my esteem; the zeal with which you have attacked my supposed *delusions* proves that you are deeply interested for *me*, and interested even to agitation for what you believe to be *truth*. You deem that I have treated " systems and opinions with the furious prejudices of the conventicle, and the illiberal dogmatism of the cynic; " that I have " layed about me on this side and on that with the sledge hammer of abuse." I have, you think, imitated the " old sect in politics and morals " in their " outrageous violence," and have sunk into the " clownish fierceness of intolerant prejudice." I have " branded " the presumptuous children of scepticism " with vile epithets and hunted them down with abuse." " *These be hard words, Citizen! and I will be bold to say they are not to be justified* " by the unfortunate page

---

[1] Mrs. Robert Lovell, whose husband had been carried off by a fever about two years after his marriage with my aunt. — S. C.

which has occasioned them.   The only passage in it which
appears *offensive* (I am not now inquiring concerning the
truth or falsehood of this or the remaining passages) is
the following : " You have studied Mr. G.'s Essay on
Politi[cal] Jus[tice] — but to think filial affection folly,
gratitude a crime, marriage injustice, and the promiscuous
intercourse of the sexes right and wise, may class you
among the despisers of vulgar prejudices, but cannot increase the probability that you are a *patriot*.   But you
act up to your principles — so much the worse.   Your
principles are villainous ones.   I would not entrust my wife
or sister to you ; think you I would entrust my country ? "   My dear Thelwall ! how are these opinions connected with the conventicle more than with the Stoa, the
Lyceum, or the grove of Academus ?   I do not perceive
that to attack *adultery* is more characteristic of *Christian*
prejudices than of the prejudices of the disciples of Aristotle, Zeno, or Socrates.   In truth, the offensive sentence,
" Your principles are villainous," was suggested by the
Peripatetic Sage who divides bad men into two classes.
The first he calls " wet or intemperate sinners " — men
who are hurried into vice by their appetites, but *acknowledge* their actions to be vicious ; these are reclaimable.
The second class he names *dry* villains — men who are not
only vicious but who (the steams from the polluted heart
rising up and gathering round the head) have brought
themselves and others to believe that *vice* is *virtue*.   We
mean these men when we say men of bad *principles —
guilt* is out of the question.   I am a necessarian, and of
course deny the possibility of it.   However, a letter is not
the place for reasoning.   In some form or other, or by
some channel or other, I shall publish my critique on the
New Philosophy, and, I trust, shall demean myself not *un-
gently*, and disappoint your auguries. ... " But, you cannot be a patriot unless you are a Christian."   Yes, Thelwall, the disciples of Lord Shaftesbury and Rousseau as

well as of Jesus — but the man who suffers not his hopes
to wander beyond the objects of sense will in general be
sensual, and I again assert that a sensualist is not likely
to be a patriot. Have I tried these opinions by the double
test of argument and example? I *think* so. The first
would be too large a field, the second some following sentences of your letter forced me to. . . . *Gerrald*[1] you in-
sinuate is an *atheist*. Was he so, when he offered those
solemn prayers to God Almighty at the Scotch conventicle, and was this sincerity? But Dr. Darwin and (I suppose from his actions) Gerrald think sincerity a folly and
therefore vicious. Your atheistic brethren square their
moral systems exactly according to their inclinations.
Gerrald and Dr. Darwin are polite and good-natured men,
and willing to attain at good by attainable roads. They
deem insincerity a necessary virtue in the present imperfect state of our nature. Godwin, whose very heart is
cankered by the love of singularity, and who feels no dis-

---

[1] Compare *Conciones ad Populum*,
1795, p. 22. " Such is Joseph Gerrald! Withering in the sickly and
tainted gales of a prison, his healthful soul looks down from the citadel
of his integrity on his impotent per-
secutors. I saw him in the foul and
naked room of a jail; his cheek was
sallow with confinement, his body
was emaciated; yet his eye spake
the invincible purpose of his soul,
and he still sounded with rapture the
successes of Freedom, forgetful of
his own lingering martyrdom."

Together with four others, Gerrald
was tried for sedition at Edinburgh
in March, 1794. He delivered an
eloquent speech in his own defence,
but with the other prisoners was
convicted and sentenced to be transported for fifteen years. "In April
Gerrald was removed to London,
and committed to Newgate, where

Godwin and his other friends were
allowed to visit him. . . . In May,
1795, he was suddenly taken from
his prison and placed on board the
hulks, and soon afterwards sailed.
He survived his arrival in New
South Wales only five months. A
few hours before he died, he said to
the friends around him, 'I die in the
best of causes, and, as you witness,
without repining.'" Mrs. Shelley's
Notes, as quoted by Mr. C. Kegan
Paul in his *William Godwin*, i. 125.
See, too, "the very noble letter"
(January 23, 1794) addressed by
Godwin to Gerrald relative to his
defence. *Ibid*. i. 125. Lords Cock-
burn and Jeffrey considered the
conviction of these men a gross mis-
carriage of justice, and in 1844 a
monument was erected at the foot
of the Calton Hill, Edinburgh, to
their memory.

inclination to wound by abrupt harshness, pleads for absolute sincerity, because such a system gives him a frequent
opportunity of indulging his misanthropy. Poor Williams,[1] the Welsh bard (a very meek man), brought the
tear into my eye by a simple narration of the manner in
which Godwin insulted him under the pretence of reproof,
and Thomas Walker of Manchester told me that his indignation and contempt were never more powerfully excited than by an unfeeling and insolent speech of the said
Godwin to the poor Welsh bard. Scott told me some
shocking stories of Godwin. His base and anonymous attack on you is enough for me. At that time I had prepared a letter to him, which I was about to have sent to
the "Morning Chronicle," and I convinced Dr. Beddoes
by passages from the "Tribune" of the calumnious nature
of the attack. I was once and only once in company
with Godwin. He appeared to me to possess neither the
strength of intellect that discovers truth, nor the powers
of imagination that decorate falsehood ; he talked sophisms
in jejune language. I like Holcroft a thousand times better, and think him a man of much greater ability. Fierce,
hot, petulant, the very high priest of atheism, he hates
God "with all his heart, with all his mind, with all his
soul, and with all his strength." Every man not an atheist is only not a fool. " Dr. Priestley? there is a *petitesse*
in his mind. Hartley? pshaw ! *Godwin*, sir, is a thousand times a better metaphysician !" But this intolerance

[1] Edward Williams (Iolo Mor-
gangw), 1747–1826. His poems in
two volumes were published by subscription in 1794. Coleridge possessed a copy presented to him "by
the author," and on the last page of
the second volume he has scrawled
a single but characteristic marginal
note. It is affixed to a translation
of one of the "Poetic Triades."

"The three principal considerations
of poetical description : what is
obvious, what instantly engages the
affections, and what is strikingly
characteristic." The comment is as
follows : "I suppose, rather what we
recollect to have frequently seen in
nature, though not in the description
of it."

is founded on benevolence. (I had almost forgotten that horrible story about his son.)

. . . .

On the subject of using sugar, etc., I will write you a long and serious letter. This grieves me more than you [imagine]. I hope I shall be able by severe and un-adorned reasoning to convince you you are wrong.

Your remarks on my poems are, I think, just in general; there is a rage and affectation of double epithets. "Unshuddered, unaghasted" is, indeed, *truly* ridiculous. But why so violent against *metaphysics* in poetry? Is not Akenside's a metaphysical poem? Perhaps you do not like Akenside? Well, but *I do*, and so do a great many others. Why pass an act of *uniformity* against poets? I received a letter from a very sensible friend abusing love verses; another blaming the introduction of politics, "as wider from true poetry than the equator from the poles." "Some for each" is my motto. That poetry pleases which interests. My religious poetry interests the *religious*, who read it with rapture. Why? Because it awakes in them all the associations connected with a love of future existence, etc. A very dear friend of mine,[1] who is, in

[1] The allusion must be to Words-worth, but there is a difficulty as to dates. In a MS. note to the second edition of his poems (1797) Cole-ridge distinctly states that he had no personal acquaintance with Words-worth as early as March, 1796. Again, in a letter (Letter LXXXI.) to Estlin dated "May [? 1797]," but certainly written in May, 1798, Coleridge says that he has known Wordsworth for a year and some months. On the other hand, there is Mrs. Wordsworth's report of her hus-band's "impression" that he first met Coleridge, Southey, Sara, and Edith Fricker " in a lodging in Bris-tol in 1795," — an imperfect recol-lection very difficult to reconcile with other known facts. Secondly, there is Sara Coleridge's statement that "Mr. Coleridge and Mr. Wordsworth first met in the house of Mr. Pinney," in the spring or summer of 1795; and, thirdly, it would appear from a let-ter of Lamb to Coleridge, which be-longs to the summer of 1796, that "the personal acquaintance" with Wordsworth had already begun. The probable conclusion is that there was a first meeting in 1795, and occa-sional intercourse in 1796, but that intimacy and friendship date from the visit to Racedown in June, 1797.

my opinion, the best poet of the age (I will send you his poem when published), thinks that the lines from 364 to 375 and from 403 to 428 the best in the volume, — indeed, worth all the rest. And this man is a republican, and, at least, a *semi*-atheist. Why do you object to "shadowy of truth"? It is, I acknowledge, a Grecism, but, I think, an elegant one. Your remarks on the della-crusca place of emphasis are just in part. Where we wish to point out the *thing*, and the *quality* is mentioned merely as a decoration, this mode of emphasis is indeed absurd; therefore, I very patiently give up to critical vengeance "*high* tree," "*sore* wounds," and "*rough* rock;" but when you wish to dwell chiefly on the *quality* rather than the *thing*, then this mode is proper, and, indeed, is used in common conversation. Who says good *man*? Therefore, "*big* soul," "*cold* earth," "*dark* womb," and "*flamy* child" are all right, and introduce a variety into the versification, [which is] an advantage where you can attain it without any sacrifice of sense. As to harmony, it is all *association*. Milton is *harmonious* to me, and I absolutely nauseate Darwin's poems.

Yours affectionately,

S. T. COLERIDGE.

JOHN THELWALL,
  Beaufort Buildings, Strand, London.

LVIII. TO THOMAS POOLE.

May 29, 1796.

MY DEAR POOLE, — This said caravan does not leave Bridgewater till nine. In the market place stands the

---

Coleridge quotes Wordsworth in his "Lines from Shurton Bars," dated September, 1795, but the first trace of Wordsworth's influence on style and thought appears in "This Lime-Tree Bower my Prison," July, 1797. In May, 1796, Wordsworth could only have been "his very dear friend" *sensu poetico*. *Life of W. Wordsworth*, i. 111; Biographical Supplement to *Biographia Literaria*, chapter ii.; *Letters of Charles Lamb*, Macmillan, 1888, i. 6.

hustings. I mounted it, and, pacing the boards, mused on bribery, false swearing, and other foibles of election times. I have wandered, too, by the river Parret, which looks as filthy as if all the parrots of the House of Commons had been washing their consciences therein. Dear gutter of Stowey![1] Were I transported to Italian plains, and lay by the side of the streamlet that murmured through an orange grove, I would think of thee, dear gutter of Stowey, and wish that I were poring on thee!

So much by way of rant. I have eaten three eggs, swallowed sundries of tea and bread and butter, purely for the purpose of amusing myself! I have seen the horse fed. When at Cross, where I shall dine, I shall think of your happy dinner, celebrated under the auspices of humble independence, supported by brotherly love! I am writing, you understand, for no worldly purpose but that of avoiding anxious thoughts. Apropos of honey-pie, Caligula or Elagabalus (I forget which) had a dish of nightingales' tongues served up. What think you of the stings of bees? God bless you! My filial love to your mother, and fraternity to your sister. Tell Ellen Cruikshank that in my next parcel to you I will send my Haleswood poem to her. Heaven protect her and you and Sara and your mother and, like a bad shilling passed off between a handful of guineas,

Your affectionate friend and brother,

S. T. COLERIDGE.

P. S. — Don't forget to send by Milton [carrier] my old clothes, and linen *that once was clean, etcetera.* A pretty *periphrasis* that!

[1] On the side of the road, opposite to Poole's house in Castle Street, Nether Stowey, is a straight gutter through which a stream passes. See *Thomas Poole and his Friends,* i. 147.

LIX. TO JOHN THELWALL.

Wednesday, June 22, 1796.

DEAR THELWALL, — That I have not written you has been an act of self-denial, not indolence. I heard that you were electioneering, and would not be the occasion that any of your thoughts should diverge from that focus.

I wish very much to see you. Have you given up the idea of spending a few weeks or month at Bristol? You might be *making way* in your review of Burke's life and writings, and give us once or twice a week a lecture, which I doubt not would be crowded. We have a large and every way excellent library, to which I could make you a temporary subscriber, that is, I would get a subscription ticket transferred to you.

You are certainly well calculated for the review you meditate. Your answer to Burke is, I will not say, the best, for that would be no praise; it is certainly the only good one, and it is a very good one. In style and in *reflectiveness* it is, I think, your *chef d'œuvre.* Yet the " Peripatetic " [1] — for which accept my thanks — pleased me more because it let me into your heart; the poetry is frequently *sweet* and possesses the *fire* of feeling, but not enough (I think) of the *light* of fancy. I am sorry that you should entertain so degrading an opinion of me as to imagine that I *industriously* collected anecdotes unfavourable to the characters of great men. No, Thelwall, but I cannot shut my ears, and I have never given a moment's belief to any one of those stories unless when they were related to me at different times by professed democrats. My vice is of the opposite class, a precipitance in praise; witness my panegyric on Gerrald and that *black* gentleman Margarot in the " Conciones," and my foolish verses

---

[1] *The Peripatetic, or Sketches of the Heart, of Nature, and of Society,* a miscellany of prose and verse issued by John Thelwall, in 1793.

to Godwin in the " Morning Chronicle."[1]   At the same
time, Thelwall, do not suppose that I admit your pallia-
tions.   Doubtless I could fill a book with slanderous stories of *professed Christians*, but those very men would
allow they were acting contrary to Christianity; but, I
am afraid, an atheistic bad man manufactures his system
of principles with an eye to his peculiar propensities, and
makes his actions the criterion of what is virtuous, not
virtue the criterion of his actions.   Where the *disposition*
is not amiable, an acute understanding I deem no blessing.   To the last sentence in your letter I subscribe fully
and with all my inmost affections.   " He who thinks and
feels will be virtuous; and he who is absorbed in self
will be vicious, whatever may be his speculative opinions."
Believe me, Thelwall, it is not his atheism that has prejudiced me against Godwin, but Godwin who has, perhaps, *prejudiced* me against atheism.   Let me see you —
I already know a deist, and Calvinists, and Moravians
whom I love and reverence — and I shall leap forwards to
realise my *principles* by *feeling* love and honour for an
atheist.   By the bye, are you an atheist?   For I was told
that Hutton was an atheist, and procured his three massy
quartos on the principle of knowledge in the hopes of
finding some arguments in favor of atheism, but lo! I
discovered him to be a profoundly pious deist, — " independent of fortune, satisfied with himself, pleased with his
species, confident in his Creator."

God bless you, my dear Thelwall!   Believe me with
high esteem and *anticipated* tenderness,

Yours sincerely,   S. T. COLERIDGE.

P. S.   We have a hundred lovely scenes about Bristol,
which would make you exclaim, O admirable *Nature!*
and me, O Gracious *God!*

---

[1] January 10, 1795. See *Poetical*   one of those tried and transported
Works, p. 41, and Editor's Note, p.   with Gerrald.
575.   Margarot, a West Indian, was

Saturday, September 24, 1796.

MY DEAR, VERY DEAR POOLE, — The heart thoroughly
penetrated with the flame of virtuous friendship is in a
state of glory; but lest it should be exalted above measure there is given it a thorn in the flesh. I mean that
when the friendship of any person forms an essential
part of a man's happiness, he will at times be pestered
by the little jealousies and solicitudes of imbecile humanity. Since we last parted I have been gloomily
dreaming that you did not leave me so affectionately as
you were wont to do. Pardon this littleness of heart, and
do not think the worse of me for it. Indeed, my soul
seems so mantled and wrapped around by your love and
esteem, that even a dream of losing but the smallest
fragment of it makes me shiver, as though some tender
part of my nature were left uncovered in nakedness.

Last week I received a letter from Lloyd, informing
me that his parents had given their joyful concurrence to
his residence with me; but that, if it were possible that
I could be absent for three or four days, his father wished
particularly to see me. I consulted Mrs. Coleridge, who
advised me to go. . . . Accordingly on Saturday night I
went by the mail to Birmingham and was introduced to
the father, who is a mild man, very liberal in his ideas,
and in religion *an allegorizing Quaker*. I mean that all
the apparently irrational path of his sect he allegorizes
into significations, which for the most part you or I might
assent to. We became well acquainted, and he expressed himself "thankful to heaven that his son was
about to be with me." He said he would write to me
concerning money matters after his son had been some
time under my roof.

On Tuesday morning I was surprised by a letter from
Mr. Maurice, our medical attendant, informing me that

Mrs. Coleridge was delivered on Monday, September 19,
1796, half past two in the morning, of a SON, and that
both she and the child were uncommonly well.   I was
quite annihilated with the suddenness of the information, and retired to my own room to address myself to
my Maker, but I could only offer up to Him the silence
of stupefied feelings.   I hastened home, and Charles
Lloyd returned with me.   When I first saw the child,[1] I
did not feel that thrill and overflowing of affection which
I expected.   I looked on it with a melancholy gaze ; my
mind was intensely contemplative and my heart only sad.
But when two hours after I saw it at the bosom of its
mother, on her arm, and her eye tearful and watching
its little features, then I was thrilled and melted, and
gave it the KISS of a *father*. . . .   The baby seems
strong, and the old nurse has over-persuaded my wife to
discover a likeness of me in its face — no great compliment to me, for, in truth, I have seen handsomer babies
in my lifetime.   Its name is David Hartley Coleridge.
I hope that ere he be a man, if God destines him for continuance in this life, his head will be convinced of, and
his heart saturated with, the truths so ably supported by
that great master of *Christian* Philosophy.

Charles Lloyd wins upon me hourly ; his heart is uncommonly pure, his affection delicate, and his benevolence enlivened but not sicklied by sensibility.   He is
assuredly a man of great genius ; but it must be in *tête-
à-tête* with one whom he loves and esteems that his colloquial powers open ; and this arises not from reserve or
want of simplicity, but from having been placed in situations where for years together he met with no congenial
minds, and where the contrariety of his thoughts and
notions to the thoughts and notions of those around him
induced the necessity of habitually suppressing his feelings.   His joy and gratitude to Heaven for the circum-

---

[1] See *Poetical Works*, p. 66.

stance of his domestication with me I can scarcely describe to you; and I believe that his fixed plans are of being always with me. His father told me that if he saw that his son had formed habits of severe economy he should not insist upon his adopting any profession; as then his fair share of his (the father's) wealth would be sufficient for him.

My dearest Poole, can you conveniently receive us in the course of a week? We can both sleep in one bed, which we do now. And I have much, very much to say to you and consult with you about, for my heart is heavy respecting Derby,[1] and my feelings are so dim and huddled that though I can, I am sure, communicate them to you by my looks and broken sentences, I scarce know how to convey them in a letter. And Charles Lloyd wishes much to know you personally. I shall write on the other side of the paper two of Charles Lloyd's sonnets, which he wrote in one evening at Birmingham. The latter of them alludes to the conviction of the truth of Christianity, which he had received from me, for he had been, if not a deist, yet quite a sceptic.

Let me hear from you by post immediately; and give my kind love to that young man with the soul-beaming face,[2] which I recollect much better than I do his name.

God bless you, my dear friend.

Believe me, with deep affection, your

S. T. COLERIDGE.

---

[1] Early in the autumn of 1796, a proposal had been made to Coleridge that he should start a day school in Derby. Poole dissuaded him from accepting this offer, or rather, perhaps, Coleridge succeeded in procuring Poole's disapproval of a plan which he himself dreaded and disliked.

[2] Thomas Ward, at first the articled clerk, and afterwards partner in business and in good works, of Thomas Poole. He it was who transcribed in " Poole's Copying Book " Coleridge's letters from Germany, and much of his correspondence besides. See *Thomas Poole and his Friends*, i. 159, 160, 304, 305, etc.

LXI. TO CHARLES LAMB.[1]

[September 28, 1796.]

Your letter, my friend, struck me with a mighty horror. It rushed upon me and stupefied my feelings. You bid me write you a religious letter. I am not a man who would attempt to insult the greatness of your anguish by any other consolation. Heaven knows that in the easiest fortunes there is much dissatisfaction and weariness of spirit; much that calls for the exercise of patience and resignation; but in storms like these, that shake the dwelling and make the heart tremble, there is no middle way between despair and the yielding up of the whole spirit unto the guidance of faith. And surely it is a matter of joy that your faith in Jesus has been preserved; the Comforter that should relieve you is not far from you. But as you are a Christian, in the name of that Saviour, who was filled with bitterness and made drunken with wormwood, I conjure you to have recourse in frequent prayer to " his God and your God; " the God of mercies, and father of all comfort. Your poor father is, I hope, almost senseless of the calamity; the unconscious

---

[1] This letter, first printed in Gillman's *Life*, pp. 338–340, and since reprinted in the notes to Canon Ainger's edition of *Lamb's Letters* (i. 314, 315), was written in response to a request of Charles Lamb in his letter of September 27, 1796, announcing the "terrible calamities" which had befallen his family. "Write me," said Lamb, "as religious a letter as possible." In his next letter, October 3, he says, " Your letter is an inestimable treasure." But a few weeks later, October 24, he takes exception to the sentence, " You are a temporary sharer in human miseries that you may be an eternal partaker of the Divine nature." Lamb thought that the expression savoured too much of theological subtlety, and outstepped the modesty of weak and suffering humanity. Coleridge's " religious letter " came from his heart, but he was a born preacher, and naturally clothes his thoughts in rhetorical language. I have seen a note written by him within a few hours of his death, when he could scarcely direct his pen. It breathes the tenderest loving-kindness, but the expressions are elaborate and formal. It was only in poetry that he attained to simplicity.

instrument of Divine Providence knows it not, and your
mother is in heaven. It is sweet to be roused from a
frightful dream by the song of birds and the gladsome
rays of the morning. Ah, how infinitely more sweet to
be awakened from the blackness and amazement of a
sudden horror by the glories of God manifest and the
hallelujahs of angels.

As to what regards yourself, I approve altogether of
your abandoning what you justly call vanities. I look
upon you as a man called by sorrow and anguish and
a strange desolation of hopes into quietness, and a soul
set apart and made peculiar to God! We cannot arrive at
any portion of heavenly bliss without in some measure
imitating Christ; and they arrive at the largest inherit-
ance who imitate the most difficult parts of his character,
and, bowed down and crushed underfoot, cry in fulness
of faith, " Father, thy will be done."

I wish above measure to have you for a little while
here; no visitants shall blow on the nakedness of your
feelings; you shall be quiet, and your spirit may be
healed. I see no possible objection, unless your father's
helplessness prevent you, and unless you are necessary to
him. If this be not the case, I charge you write me that
you will come.

I charge you, my dearest friend, not to dare to encourage gloom or despair. You are a temporary sharer
in human miseries that you may be an eternal partaker
of the Divine nature. I charge you, if by any means
it be possible, come to me.

I remain your affectionate

S. T. COLERIDGE

LXII. TO THOMAS POOLE.

Saturday night, November 5, 1796.

Thanks, my heart's warm thanks to you, my beloved
friend, for your tender letter! Indeed, I did not deserve

so kind a one; but by this time you have received my last.

To live in a beautiful country, and to enure myself as much as possible to the labour of the field, have been for this year past my dream of the day, my sigh at midnight. But to enjoy these blessings *near* you, to see you daily, to tell you all my thoughts in their first birth, and to hear yours, to be mingling identities with you as it were, — the vision-wearing fancy has indeed often pictured such things, but *hope* never dared whisper a promise. Disappointment! Disappointment! dash not from my trembling hand the bowl which almost touches my lips. Envy me not this immortal draught, and I will forgive thee all thy persecutions. Forgive thee! Impious! *I will bless thee*, black-vested minister of optimism, stern pioneer of happiness! Thou hast been " *the cloud* " before me from the day that I left the flesh-pots of Egypt, and was led through the way of a wilderness — the cloud that hast been guiding me to a land flowing with milk and honey — the milk of innocence, the honey of friendship!

I wanted such a letter as yours, for I am very unwell. On Wednesday night I was seized with an intolerable pain from my right temple to the tip of my right shoulder, including my right eye, cheek, jaw, and that side of the throat. I was nearly frantic, and ran about the house naked, endeavouring by every means to excite sensations in different parts of my body, and so to weaken the enemy by creating division. It continued from one in the morning till half past five, and left me pale and fainting. It came on fitfully, but not so violently, several times on Thursday, and began severer threats towards night; but I took between sixty and seventy drops of laudanum,[1]

---

[1] Coleridge must have resorted occasionally to opiates long before this. In an unpublished letter to his brother George, dated November 21, 1791, he says, "Opium never used to have any disagreeable effects on me." Most likely it was given to him at Christ's Hospital, when he

and *sopped* the Cerberus, just as his mouth began to open. On Friday it only *niggled*, as if the chief had departed from a conquered place, and merely left a small garrison behind, or as if he had evacuated the Corsica,[1] and a

was suffering from rheumatic fever. In the sonnet on " Pain," which belongs to the summer of 1790, he speaks of "frequent pangs," of " seas of pain," and in the natural course of things opiates would have been prescribed by the doctors. Testimony of this nature appears at first sight to be inconsistent with statements made by Coleridge in later life to the effect that he began to take opium in the second year of his residence at Keswick, in consequence of rheumatic pains brought on by the damp climate. It was, however, the first commencement of the secret and habitual resort to narcotics which weighed on memory and conscience, and there is abundant evidence that it was not till the late spring of 1801 that he could be said to be under the dominion of opium. To these earlier indulgences in the "accursed drug," which probably left no "disagreeable effects," and of which, it is to be remarked, he speaks openly, he seems to have attached but little significance.

Since the above note was written, Mr. W. Aldis Wright has printed in the *Academy*, February 24, 1894, an extract from an unpublished letter from Coleridge to the Rev. Mr. Edwards of Birmingham, recently found in the Library of Trinity College, Cambridge. It is dated Bristol, "12 March, 1795" (read "1796"), and runs as follows : —

"Since I last wrote you, I have been tottering on the verge of madness — my mind overbalanced on the *e contra* side of happiness — the blunders of my associate [in the editing of the *Watchman*, G. Burnett], etc., etc., abroad, and, at home, Mrs. Coleridge dangerously ill. . . . Such has been my situation for the last fortnight — I have been obliged to take laudanum almost every night."

[1] The news of the evacuation of Corsica by the British troops, which took place on October 21, 1796, must have reached Coleridge a few days before the date of this letter. Corsica was ceded to the British, June 18, 1794. A declaration of war on the part of Spain (August 19, 1796) and a threatened invasion of Ireland compelled the home government to withdraw their troops from Corsica. In a footnote to chapter xxv. of his *Life of Napoleon Bonaparte*, Sir Walter Scott quotes from Napoleon's memoirs compiled at St. Helena the "odd observation" that "the crown of Corsica must, on the temporary annexation of the island to Great Britain, have been surprised at finding itself appertaining to the successor of Fingal." Sir Walter's patriotism constrained him to add the following comment : " Not more, we should think, than the diadem of France and the iron crown of Lombardy marvelled at meeting on the brow of a Corsican soldier of fortune."

In the *Biographia Literaria*, 1847, ii. 380, the word is misprinted Corrica, but there is no doubt as to the reading of the MS. letter, or to the allusion to contemporary history.

few straggling pains only remained. But *this morning*
he returned in full force, and his name is Legion. Giant-
fiend of a hundred hands, with a shower of arrowy death-
pangs he transpierced me, and then he became a wolf,
and lay a-gnawing at my bones! I am not mad, most
noble Festus, but in sober sadness I have suffered this
day more bodily pain than I had before a conception of.
My right cheek has certainly been placed with admirable
exactness under the focus of some invisible burning-glass,
which concentrated all the rays of a Tartarean sun. My
medical attendant decides it to be altogether nervous, and
that it originates either in severe application, or excessive
anxiety. My beloved Poole! in excessive anxiety, I believe it might originate. I have a blister under my right
ear, and I take twenty-five drops of laudanum every five
hours, the ease and *spirits* gained by which have enabled
me to write you this flighty but not exaggerated account.
With a gloomy wantonness of imagination I had been
coquetting with the hideous *possibles* of disappointment.
I drank fears like wormwood, yea, made myself drunken
with bitterness; for my ever - shaping and distrustful
mind still mingled gall-drops, till out of the cup of hope
I almost *poisoned* myself with despair.

Your letter is dated November 2d; I wrote to you
November 1st. Your sister was married on that day;
and on that day several times I felt my heart overflowed
with such tenderness for her as made me repeatedly ejac-
ulate prayers in her behalf. Such things are strange.
It may be superstitious to think about such correspond-
ences; but it is a superstition which softens the heart and
leads to no evil. We will call on your dear sister as soon
as I am quite well, and in the mean time I will write a few
lines to her.

I am anxious beyond measure to be in the country as
soon as possible. I would it were possible to get a temporary residence till Adscombe is ready for us. I would

that it could be that we could have three rooms in Bill Poole's large house for the winter. Will you try to look out for a fit servant for us — simple of heart, physiognomically handsome, and scientific in vaccimulgence? That last word is a new one, but soft in sound and full of expression. Vaccimulgence! I am pleased with the word. Write to me all things about yourself. Where I cannot advise I can condole and communicate, which doubles joy, halves sorrow.

Tell me whether you think it at all possible to make any terms with William Poole. You know I would not wish to touch with the edge of the nail of my great toe the line which should be but half a barley-corn out of the niche of the most trembling delicacy. I will write Cruikshank to-morrow, if God permit me.

God bless and protect you, friend, brother, beloved!

S. T. COLERIDGE.

Sara's best love, and Lloyd's. David Hartley is well, saving that he is sometimes inspired by the god Æolus, and like Isaiah, "his bowels sound like an harp." My filial love to your dear mother. Love to Ward. Little Tommy, I often think of thee.

LXIII. TO THE SAME.

Monday night, November 7, 1796.

MY DEAREST POOLE, — I wrote you on Saturday night under the immediate inspiration of laudanum, and wrote you a flighty letter, but yet one most accurately descriptive both of facts and feelings. Since then my pains have been lessening, and the greater part of this day I have enjoyed perfect ease, only I am totally inappetent of food, and languid, even to an inward perishing.

I wrote John Cruikshank this morning, and this moment I have received a letter from him. My letter written before the receipt of his contains everything I would write in answer to it, and I do not like to write to him superfluously, lest I should break in on his domestic terrors and solitary broodings with regard to Anna Cruikshank.[1] May the Father and lover of the meek preserve that meek woman, and give her a safe and joyful deliverance !

I wrote this morning a short note of congratulatory kindliness to your sister, and shall be eager to call on her, when *Legion* has been thoroughly exorcised from my temple and cheeks. Tell Cruikshank that I have received his letter, and thank him for it.

A few lines in your last letter betokened, I thought, a wounded spirit. Let me know the particulars, my beloved friend. I shall forget and lose my own anxieties while I am healing yours with cheerings of sympathy.

I met with the following sonnet in some very dull poems, among which it shone like a solitary star when the night is dark, and *one* little space of blue uninvaded by the floating blackness, or, if a *terrestrial* simile be required, like a red carbuncle on a negro's nose. From the languor and exhaustion to which pain and my frequent doses of laudanum have reduced me, it suited the feeble temper of [my] mind, and I have transcribed it on the other page. I amused myself the other day (having some *paper* at the printer's which I could employ no other way) in selecting twenty-eight sonnets,[2] to bind up with Bowles's. I charge sixpence for them, and have sent you five to dispose of. I have only printed two hundred, as my paper held out to no more ; and dispose of them privately, just. enough to pay the printing. The essay which I have written at the beginning I like. . . . I have likewise sent you Burke's pamphlet which was given to me ; it has all his excellences without any of his faults.

[1] It was to this lady that the lines "On the Christening of a Friend's Child" were addressed. *Poetical Works*, p. 83.

[2] See Letter LXVIII., p. 206, note.

This parcel I send to-morrow morning, enclosed in a parcel to Bill Poole of Thurston.

God love you, my affectionate brother, and your affectionate

S. T. COLERIDGE.

SONNET.

With passive joy the moment I survey
When welcome Death shall set my spirit free.
My soul! the prospect brings no fear to thee,
But soothing Fancy rises to pourtray
The dear and parting words my Friends will say :
With secret Pride their heaving Breast I see,
And count the sorrows that will flow for me.
And now I hear my lingering knell decay
And mark the Hearse!   Methinks, with moisten'd eye,
CLARA beholds the sad Procession move
That bears me to the Resting-place of Care,
And sighs, " Poor youth ! thy Bosom well could love,
And well thy Numbers picture Love's despair."
Vain Dreams! yet such as make it sweet to die.

LXIV. TO JOHN THELWALL.

Saturday, November 19, [1796].
Oxford Street, Bristol.

MY DEAR THELWALL, — Ah me ! literary adventure is but bread and cheese by chance.   I keenly sympathise with you.   Sympathy, the only poor consolation I can offer you.   Can no plan be suggested? . . . Of course you have read the " Joan of Arc." [1]   Homer is the poet for the warrior, Milton for the religionist, Tasso for women, Robert Southey for the patriot.   The first and fourth

---

[1] The preface to the quarto edition of Southey's *Joan of Arc* is dated Bristol, November, 1795, but the volume did not appear till the following spring. Coleridge's contribution to Book II. was omitted from the second (1797) and subsequent editions. It was afterwards republished, with additions, in *Sibylline Leaves* (1817) as " The Destiny of Nations."

books of the "Joan of Arc" are to me more interesting
than the same number of lines in any poem whatever. But
you and I, my dear Thelwall, hold different creeds in
poetry as well as religion. *N'importe!* By the bye, of
your works I have now all, except your "Essay on Animal Vitality" which I never had, and your *Poems*, which
I bought on their first publication, and lost them. From
these poems I should have supposed our poetical tastes
more nearly alike than, I find, they are. The poem on the
Sols [?] flashes genius through Strophe I, Antistrophe I,
and Epode I. The rest I do not perhaps understand,
only I love these two lines : —

> " Yet sure the verse that shews the friendly mind
> To Friendship's ear not harshly flows."

Your larger *narrative* affected me greatly. It is admirably written, and displays strong sense animated by feeling, and illumined by imagination, and neither in the
thoughts nor rhythm does it encroach on poetry.

There have been two poems of mine in the new
"Monthly Magazine," [1] with my name ; indeed, I make it
a scruple of conscience never to publish anything, however trifling, without it. Did you like them? The first
was written at the desire of a beautiful little aristocrat ;
consider it therefore as a lady's poem. Bowles (the bard
of my idolatry) has written a poem lately without plan
or meaning, but the component parts are divine. It is
entitled "Hope, an Allegorical Sketch." I will copy
two of the stanzas, which must be peculiarly interesting
to you, virtuous high-treasonist, and your friends the
democrats.

---

[1] The lines "On a late Connu-
bial Rupture" were printed in the
Monthly Magazine for September,
1796. The well-known poem beginning "Low was our pretty Cot"
appeared in the following number.
It was headed, "Reflections on entering into active Life. A Poem
which affects not to be Poetry."

" But see, as one awaked from deadly trance,
   With hollow and dim eyes, and stony stare,
Captivity with faltering step advance!
   Dripping and knotted was her coal-black hair:
For she had long been hid, as in the grave;
   No sounds the silence of her prison broke,
Nor one companion had she in her cave
   Save Terror's dismal shape, that no word spoke,
But to a stony coffin on the floor
With lean and hideous finger pointed evermore.

" The lark's shrill song, the early village chime,
   The upland echo of the winding horn,
The far-heard clock that spoke the passing time,
   Had never pierced her solitude forlorn:
At length released from the deep dungeon's gloom
   She feels the fragrance of the vernal gale,
She sees more sweet the living landscape bloom,
   And while she listens to Hope's tender tale,
She thinks her long-lost friends shall bless her sight,
And almost faints for joy amidst the broad daylight."

The last line is exquisite.

Your portrait of yourself interested me. As to me, my
face, unless when animated by immediate eloquence, expresses great sloth, and great, indeed, almost idiotic good-
nature. 'T is a mere carcass of a face;[1] fat, flabby, and
expressive chiefly of inexpression. Yet I am told that
my eyes, eyebrows, and forehead are physiognomically
good; but of this the deponent knoweth not. As to my
shape, 't is a good shape enough if measured, but my gait
is awkward, and the walk of the whole man indicates *indolence capable of energies*. I am, and ever have been, a
great reader, and have read almost everything — a library

---

[1] Compare the following lines
from an early transcript of " Happiness " now in my possession: —

" Ah! doubly blest if Love supply
   Lustre to the now heavy eye,
And with unwonted spirit grace
   That fat vacuity of face."

The transcriber adds in a footnote,
" The author was at this time, at
seventeen, remarkable for a plump
face."

   The " Reminiscences of an Octo-
genarian " (The Rev. Leapidge
Smith), contributed to the *Leisure
Hour*, convey a different impression:
" In person he was a tall, dark, handsome young man, with long, black,
flowing hair; eyes not merely dark,

cormorant. I am *deep* in all out of the way books, whether of the monkish times, or of the puritanical era. I have read and digested most of the historical writers; but I do not *like* history. Metaphysics and poetry and " facts of mind," that is, accounts of all the strange phantasms that ever possessed " your philosophy ; " dreamers, from Thoth the Egyptian to Taylor the English pagan, are my darling studies. In short, I seldom read except to amuse myself, and I am almost always reading. Of useful knowledge, I am a so-so chemist, and I love chemistry. All else is *blank ;* but I *will* be (please God) an horticulturalist and a farmer. I compose very little, and I absolutely hate composition, and such is my dislike that even a sense of duty is sometimes too weak to overpower it.

I cannot breathe through my nose, so my mouth, with sensual thick lips, is almost always open. In conversation I am impassioned, and oppose what I deem error with an eagerness which is often mistaken for personal asperity; but I am ever so swallowed up in the *thing* that I perfectly forget my *opponent.* Such am I. I am just going to read Dupuis' twelve octavos,[1] which I have got from London. I shall read only one octavo a week, for I cannot *speak* French at all and I read it slowly.

My wife is well and desires to be remembered to you and your *Stella* and little ones. N. B. Stella (among the Romans) was a man's name. All the *classics* are against you ; but our Swift, I suppose, is authority for this unsexing.

Write on the receipt of this, and believe me as ever, with affectionate esteem,   Your sincere friend,

S. T. Coleridge.

---

but black, and keenly penetrating ; a fine forehead, a deep-toned, harmonious voice ; a manner never to be forgotten, full of life, vivacity, and kindness; dignified in person and, added to all these, exhibiting the elements of his future greatness." — *Leisure Hour,* 1870, p. 651.

[1] *Origine de tous les Cultes, ou Religion universelle.*

P. S. I have enclosed a five-guinea note. The five shillings over please to lay out for me thus. In White's (of Fleet Street or the Strand, I forget which — O ! the Strand I believe, but I don't know which), well, in White's catalogue are the following books : —

4674. Iamblichus,[1] Proclus, Porphyrius, etc., one shilling and sixpence, one little volume.

4686. Juliani Opera, three shillings : which two books you will be so kind as to purchase for me, and send down with the twenty-five pamphlets. But if they should unfortunately be sold, in the same catalogue are : —

2109. Juliani Opera, 12s. 6d.

676. Iamblichus de Mysteriis, 10s. 6d.

2681. Sidonius Apollinaris, 6s.

And in the catalogue of Robson, the bookseller in New Bond Street, Plotini Opera, a Ficino, £1.1.0, making altogether £2.10.0.

If you can get the two former little books, costing only four and sixpence, I will rest content with them ; if they are gone, be so kind as to purchase for me the others I mentioned to you, amounting to two pounds, ten shillings ; and, as in the course of next week I shall send a small parcel of books and manuscripts to my very dear Charles Lamb of the India House, I shall be enabled to convey the money to you in a letter, which he will leave at your house. I make no apology for this commission, because I feel (to use a vulgar phrase) that I would do as much for you. P. P. S. Can you buy them time enough to send down with your pamphlets ? If not, make a parcel *per se.* I hope your hurts from the fall are not serious ; you have given a *proof* now that you are no *Ippokrite,* but I forgot that you are not a Greekist, and perchance you hate puns ; but, in Greek, *Krites* signifies a judge and *hippos* a

---

[1] Thelwall executed his commission. The Iamblichus and the Julian were afterwards presented by Coleridge to his son Derwent. They are still in the possession of the family.

horse. Hippocrite, therefore, may mean a *judge of horses.*
My dear fellow, I laugh more and talk more nonsense in
a week than [most] other people do in a year.   Farewell.
JOHN THELWALL,
Beaufort Buildings, Strand, London.

LXV. TO THOMAS POOLE.[1]

Sunday morning, December 11, 1796.

MY BELOVED POOLE, — The sight of your villainous
hand-scrawl was a great comfort to me.   How have you
been diverted in London ?   What of the theatres ?   And
how found you your old friends ?   I dined with Mr. King
yesterday week.   He is *quantum suff :* a pleasant man,
and (my wife says) very handsome.   Hymen lies in the
arms of Hygeia, if one may judge by your sister ; she
looks remarkably well !   But has she not caught some
complaint in *the head ?*   Some *scurfy* disorder ?   For her
hair was filled with an odious white Dandruff.   ("N. B.
Nothing but powder," Mrs. King.)   About myself, I
have so much to say that I really can say nothing.   I
mean to work *very hard* — as Cook, Butler, Scullion,
Shoe-cleaner, occasional Nurse, Gardener, Hind, Pig-pro-
tector, Chaplain, Secretary, Poet, Reviewer, and *omnium-
botherum* shilling-Scavenger.   In other words, I shall
keep no servant, and will cultivate my land-acre and my
wise-acres, as well as I can.   The motives which led to
this determination are numerous and weighty ; I have

[1] The three letters to Poole, dated
December 11, 12, and 13, relative
to Coleridge's residence at Stowey,
were published for the first time in
Thomas Poole and his Friends. The
long letter of expostulation, dated
December 13, which is in fact a
continuation of that dated December 12, is endorsed by Poole : " An
angry letter, but the breach was
soon healed." Either on Coleridge's
account or his own it was among
the few papers retained by Poole
when, to quote Mrs. Sandford, " in
1836 he placed the greater number of the letters which he had received from S. T. Coleridge at the
disposal of his literary executors
for biographical purposes." *Thomas
Poole and his Friends,* i. 182-193.
Mrs. Sandford has kindly permitted
me to reprint it *in extenso.*

thought much and calmly, and calculated time and money
with unexceptionable accuracy; and at length determined
not to take the charge of Charles Lloyd's mind on me.
Poor fellow! he still hopes to live with me — is now at
Birmingham.   I wish that little cottage by the roadside
were gettable?   That with about two or three rooms — it
would quite do for us, as we shall occupy only *two rooms*.
I will write more fully on the receipt of yours.   God love
you and

S. T. COLERIDGE.

LXVI. TO THE SAME.

December 12, 1796.

You tell me, my dear Poole, that my residence near
you would give you great pleasure, and I am sure that if
you had any objections on your own account to my settling near Stowey you would have mentioned them to me.
Relying on this, I assure you that a disappointment would
try my philosophy.   Your letter did indeed give me unexpected and most acute pain.   I will make the cottage
do.   We want but three rooms.   If Cruikshank have
promised more than his circumstances enable him to perform, I am sure that I can get the other purchased by my
friends in Bristol.   I mean, the place at Adscombe.   I
wrote him pressingly on this head some ten days ago;
but he has returned me no answer.   Lloyd has obtained
his father's permission and will return to me.   He is willing to be his own servant.   As to Acton, 't is out of the
question.   In Bristol I have Cottle and Estlin (for Mr.
Wade is going away) willing and eager to serve me; but
how they can serve me more effectually at Acton than at
Stowey, I cannot divine.   If I live at Stowey, you indeed
can serve me effectually, by assisting me in the acquirement of agricultural practice.   If you can instruct me to
manage an acre and a half of land, and to raise in it, with
my own hands, all kinds of vegetables and grain, enough

for myself and my wife and sufficient to feed a pig or two with the refuse, I hope that you will have served me *most* effectually by placing me out of the necessity of being served. I receive about forty guineas yearly from the " Critical Review " and the new " Monthly Magazine." It is hard if by my greater works I do not get twenty more. I know how little the human mind requires when it is tranquil, and in proportion as I should find it difficult to simplify my wants it becomes my duty to simplify them. For there must be a vice in my nature, which woe be to me if I do not cure. The less meat I eat the more healthy I am ; and strong liquors of any kind always and perceptibly injure me. Sixteen shillings would cover all the weekly expenses of my wife, infant, and myself. This I say from my wife's own calculation.

But whence this sudden revolution in your opinions, my dear Poole ? You saw the cottage that was to be our temporary residence, and thought we might be *happy* in it, and now you hurry to tell me that we shall not even be *comfortable* in it. You tell me I shall be " too far from my *friends*," that is, Cottle and Estlin, for I have no other in Bristol. In the name of Heaven, *what can* Cottle or Estlin [do] for me ? They do nothing who do not teach me how to be independent of any except the Almighty Dispenser of sickness and health. And " too far from the press." With the printing of the review and the magazine I have no concern ; and, if I publish any work on my own account, I will send a fair and faultless copy, and Cottle promises to correct the press for me. Mr. King's family may be very worthy sort of people, for aught I know ; but assuredly I can employ my time wiselier than to gabble with my tongue to beings with whom neither my head nor heart can commune. My habits and feelings have suffered a total alteration. I *hate* company except of my dearest friends, and systematically avoid it ; and when in it keep silence as far as social humanity will permit me.

Lloyd's father, in a letter to me yesterday, enquired how
I should live without any companions. I answered him
not an hour before I received your letter : —

"I shall have six companions: My Sara, my babe, my
own shaping and disquisitive mind, my books, my beloved
friend Thomas Poole, and lastly, Nature looking at me
with a thousand looks of beauty, and speaking to me in
a thousand melodies of love. If I were capable of being
tired with all these, I should then detect a vice in my
nature, and would fly to habitual solitude to eradicate it."

Yes, my friend, while I opened your letter my heart
was glowing with enthusiasm towards you. How little
did I expect that I should find you earnestly and vehemently persuading me to prefer Acton to Stowey, and in
return for the loss of your society recommending *Mr.
King's* family as "very pleasant neighbours." Neighbours! Can mere juxtaposition form a neighbourhood?
As well should the louse in my head call himself my
friend, and the flea in my bosom style herself my love!

On Wednesday week we must leave our house, so that
if you continue to dissuade me from settling near Stowey
I scarcely know what I shall do. Surely, my beloved
friend, there must be some reason which you have not yet
told me, which urged you to send this hasty and heart-
chilling letter. I suspect that something has passed
between your sister and dear mother (in whose illness I
sincerely sympathise with you).

I have never considered my settlement at Stowey in
any other relation than its advantages to myself, and they
would be great indeed. My objects (assuredly wise ones)
were to learn agriculture (and where should I get instructed except at Stowey?) and to be where I can communicate in a literary way. I must conclude. I pray you
let me hear from you immediately. God bless you and
                                     S. T. COLERIDGE.

LXVII. TO THE SAME.

I wrote the former letter immediately on receipt of
yours, in the first flutter of agitation. The tumult of my
spirits has now subsided, but the Damp struck into my
very heart ; and there I feel it. O my God ! my God !
where am I to find rest ? Disappointment follows disappointment, and Hope seems given me merely to prevent
my becoming callous to Misery. Now I know not where
to turn myself. I was on my way to the City Library,
and wrote an answer to it there. Since I have returned
I have been poring into a book, as a shew for not looking at my wife and the baby. By God, I dare not look
at them. Acton ! The very name makes me grind my
teeth ! What am I to do there ?

"You will have a good garden ; you may, I doubt not,
have ground." But am I not ignorant as a child of everything that concerns the garden and the ground ? and shall
I have one human being there who will instruct me ?
The House too — what should I do with it ? We want
but two rooms, or three at the furthest. And the country
around is intolerably flat. I would as soon live on the
banks of a Dutch canal ! And no one human being near
me for whom I should, or could, care a rush ! No one
walk where the beauties of nature might endear solitude to
me ! There is one Ghost that I *am* afraid of ; with that I
should be perpetually haunted in this same cursed Acton —
the hideous Ghost of departed Hope. O Poole ! how could
you make such a proposal to me ? I have compelled
myself to reperuse your letter, if by any means I may be
able to penetrate into your motives. I find three reasons
assigned for my not settling at Stowey. The first, the
distance from my friends and the Press. This I answered
in the former letter. As to my friends, what can they do
for me ? And as to the Press, even if Cottle had not

promised to correct it for me, yet I might as well be fifty
miles from it as twelve, for any purpose of correcting.
Secondly, the expense of moving. Well, but I must
move to Acton, and what will the difference be? Perhaps three guineas. . . . I would give three guineas that
you had not assigned this reason. Thirdly, the wretchedness of that cottage, which alone we can get. But
surely, in the house which I saw, *two* rooms may be
found, which, by a little green list and a carpet, and a
slight alteration in the fireplace, may be made to exclude
the cold : and this is all we want. Besides, it will be but
for a while. If Cruikshank cannot buy and repair
Adscombe, I have no doubt that my friends here and at
Birmingham would, some of them, purchase it. So much
for the reasons : but these cannot be the real reasons.
I was with you for a week, and then we talked over the
whole scheme, and you approved of it, and I gave up
Derby. More than nine weeks have elapsed since then,
and you saw and examined the cottage, and you knew
every other of these reasons, if reasons they can be called.
Surely, surely, my friend, something has occurred which
you have not mentioned to me. Your mother has manifested a strong dislike to our living near you — or something or other ; for the reasons you have assigned tell
me nothing except that there are reasons which you have
not assigned.

Pardon, if I write vehemently. I meant to have written calmly ; but bitterness of soul came upon me. Mrs.
Coleridge has observed the workings of my face while I
have been writing, and is entreating to know what is the
matter. I dread to show her your letter. I dread it.
My God! my God! What if she should dare to think
that my most beloved friend has grown cold towards me !

Tuesday morning, 11 o'clock. — After an unquiet and
almost sleepless night, I resume my pen. As the sentiments over leaf came into my heart, I will not suppress

them. I would keep a letter by me which I wrote to a
mere acquaintance, lest anything unwise should be found
in it; but my friend ought to know not only what my
sentiments are, but what my feelings were.

I am, indeed, perplexed and cast down. My first plan,
you know, was this — My family was to have consisted of
Charles Lloyd, my wife and wife's mother, my infant, the
servant, and myself.

My means of maintaining them — Eighty pounds a year
from Charles Lloyd, and forty from the Review and Magazine. My time was to have been divided into four parts:
1. Three hours after breakfast to studies with C. L. 2.
The remaining hours till dinner to our garden. 3. From
after dinner till tea, to letter-writing and domestic quietness. 4. From tea till prayer-time to the reviews, magazines, and other literary labours.

In this plan I calculated nothing on my garden but
amusement. In the mean time I heard from Birmingham
that Lloyd's father had declared that he should insist on
his son's returning to him at the close of a twelvemonth.
What am I to do then? I shall be again afloat on the
wide sea, unpiloted and unprovisioned. I determined to
devote *my whole day* to the acquirement of practical
horticulture, to part with Lloyd immediately, and live
without a servant. Lloyd intreated me to give up the
Review and Magazine, and devote the evenings to him,
but this would be to give up a permanent for a temporary
situation, and after subtracting £40 from C. Ll.'s £80 in
return for the Review business, and then calculating the
expense of a servant, a less severe mode of general living,
and Lloyd's own board and lodging, the remaining £40
would make but a poor figure. And what was I to do
at the end of a twelvemonth? In the mean time Mrs.
Fricker's son could not be got out as an apprentice — he
was too young, and premiumless, and no one would take
him; and the old lady herself manifested a great aversion

to leaving Bristol. I recurred therefore to my first promise of allowing her £20 a year; but all her furniture
must of course be returned, and enough only remains to
furnish one bedroom and a kitchen-parlour.

If Charles Lloyd and the servant went with me I must
have bought new furniture to the amount of £40 or £50,
which, if not Impossibility in person, was Impossibility's
first cousin. We determined to live by ourselves. We
arranged our time, money, and employments. We found
it not only practicable *but easy;* and Mrs. Coleridge
entered with enthusiasm into the scheme.

To Mrs. Coleridge the nursing and sewing only would
have belonged; the rest I took upon myself, and since
our resolution have been learning the practice. With
only two rooms and two people — their wants severely
simple — no great labour can there be in their waiting upon
themselves. Our washing we should put out. I should
have devoted my whole head, heart, and body to my acre
and a half of garden land, and my evenings to literature.
Mr. and Mrs. Estlin approved, admired, and applauded
the scheme, and thought it not only highly virtuous, but
highly prudent. In the course of a year and a half, I
doubt not that I should feel myself independent, for my
bodily strength would have increased, and I should have
been weaned from animal food, so as never to touch it
but once a week; and there can be no shadow of a doubt
that an acre and a half of land, divided properly, and
managed properly, would maintain a small family in
everything but clothes and rent. What had I to ask of
my friends? Not money; for a temporary relief of my
want is nothing, removes no gnawing of anxiety, and de-
bases the dignity of man. Not their interest. What
could their interest (supposing they had any) do for me?
I can accept no place in state, church, or dissenting meeting. Nothing remains possible but a school, or writer to a
newspaper, or my present plan. I could not love the man

who advised me to keep a school, or write for a newspaper.
He must have a hard heart. What then could I ask of
my friends? What of Mr. Wade? Nothing. What of
Mr. Cottle? Nothing. . . . What of Thomas Poole? O!
a great deal. Instruction, daily advice, society — everything necessary to my feelings and the realization of my
innocent independence. You know it would be impossible for me to learn *everything* myself. To pass across
my garden once or twice a day, for five minutes, to set
me right, and cheer me with the sight of a friend's face,
would be more to me than hundreds. Your letter was
not a kind one. One week only and I must leave my
house, and yet in one week you advise me to alter the
plan which I had been three months framing, and in
which you must have known by the letters I wrote you,
during my illness, that I was interested even to an excess
and violence of Hope. And to abandon this plan for darkness and a renewal of anxieties which might be fatal to
me! Not one word have you mentioned how I am to
live, or even exist, supposing I were to go to Acton.
Surely, surely, you do not advise me to lean with the
whole weight of my necessities on the Press? Ghosts
indeed! I should be haunted with ghosts enough — the
ghosts of Otway and Chatterton, and the phantasms of a
wife broken-hearted, and a hunger-bitten baby! O Thomas
Poole! Thomas Poole! if you did but know what a
Father and a Husband must feel who toils with his brain
for uncertain bread! I dare not think of it. The evil
face of Frenzy looks at me. The husbandman puts his
seed in the ground, and the goodness, power, and wisdom
of God have pledged themselves that he shall have bread,
and health, and quietness in return for industry, and
simplicity of wants and innocence. The AUTHOR scatters
his seed — with aching head, and wasted health, and all
the heart-leapings of anxiety; and the follies, the vices,
and the fickleness of man promise him printers' bills and

the Debtors' Side of Newgate as full and sufficient payment.

Charles Lloyd is at Birmingham. I hear from him daily. In his yesterday's letter he says: " My dearest friend, everything seems clearing around me. My friends enter fully into my views. They seem altogether to have abandoned any ambitious views on my account. My health has been very good since I left you; and I own I look forward with more pleasure than ever to a permanent connection with you. Hitherto I could only look forward to the pleasures of a year. All beyond was dark and uncertain. My father now completely acquiesces in my abandoning the prospect of any profession or trade. If God grant me health, there now remains no obstacle to a completion of my most sanguine wishes." Charles Lloyd will furnish his own room, and feels it his duty to be in all things his own servant. He will put up a press-bed, so that one room will be his bedchamber and parlour; and I shall settle with him the hours and seasons of our being together, and the hours and seasons of our being apart. But I shall rely on him for nothing except his own maintenance.

As to the poems, they are Cottle's property, not mine. There is no obstacle from me — no new poems intended to be put in the volume, except the " Visions of the Maid of Orleans." . . . But literature, though I shall never abandon it, will always be a secondary object with me. My poetic vanity and my political *furor* have been exhaled; and I would rather be an expert, self-maintaining gardener than a Milton, if I could not unite both.

My *friend*, wherein I have written impetuously, pardon me! and consider what I have suffered, and still am suffering, in consequence of your letter. . . .

Finally, my Friend! if your opinion of me and your attachment to me remain unaltered, and if you have assigned the true reasons which urged you to dissuade me from a settlement at Stowey, and if indeed (provided such settlement were consistent with my good and happiness), it would give you unmixed pleasure, I adhere to Stowey, and consider the time from last evening as a distempered dream. But if any circumstances have occurred that have lessened your love or esteem or confidence ; or if there be objections to my settling in Stowey on your own account, or any other objections than what you have urged, I doubt not you will declare them openly and unreservedly to me, in your answer to this, which I shall expect with a total incapability of doing or thinking of anything, till I have received it. Indeed, indeed, I am very miserable.   God bless you and your affectionate

S. T. COLERIDGE.

Tuesday, December 13, 1796.

LXVIII. TO JOHN THELWALL.

December 17, 1796.

MY DEAR THELWALL, — I should have written you long ere this, had not the settlement of my affairs previous to my leaving Bristol and the organization of my *new plan* occupied me with bulky anxieties that almost excluded everything but self from my thoughts. And, besides, my health has been very bad, and remains so. A nervous affection from my right temple to the extremity of my right shoulder almost distracted me, and made the frequent use of laudanum absolutely necessary. And, since I have subdued this, a rheumatic complaint in the back of my head and shoulders, accompanied with sore throat and depression of the animal spirits, has convinced me that a man may change bad lodgers without bettering himself. I write these things, not so much to apologise for my silence, or for the pleasure of complaining, as that you may know the reason why I have not given you a " strict account " how I have disposed of your books. This I will shortly do, with all the veracity which that solemn incantation, "*upon your honour*," must necessarily have conjured up.

Your second and third part promise great things.   I

have counted the subjects, and by a nice calculation find
that eighteen Scotch doctors would write fifty-four quarto
volumes, each choosing his thesis out of your syllabus.
May you do good by them, and moreover enable yourself to
do more good, I *should* say, to continue to do good. *My
farm* will be a garden of one acre and a half, in which
I mean to raise vegetables and corn enough for myself
and wife, and feed a couple of snouted and grunting
cousins from the refuse. My evenings I shall devote to
literature; and, by reviews, the magazine, and the other
shilling - scavenger employments, shall probably gain
forty pounds a year; which economy and self - denial,
gold-beaters, shall hammer till it cover my annual expenses. Now, in favour of this scheme, I shall say nothing,
for the more vehement my ratiocinations were, previous
to the experiment, the more ridiculous my failure would
appear; and if the scheme deserve the said ratiocinations
I shall live down all your objections. I doubt not that
the time will come when all our utilities will be directed
in one simple path. That time, however, is not come; and
imperious circumstances point out to each one his particular road. Much good may be done in all. I am not *fit*
for *public* life; yet the light shall stream to a far distance from my cottage window. Meantime, *do you* uplift
the *torch* dreadlessly, and show to mankind the face of
that idol which they have worshipped in darkness! And
now, my dear fellow, for a little sparring about poetry.
My first *sonnet*[1] *is obscure;* but you ought to distinguish
between obscurity residing in the uncommonness of the
thought, and that which proceeds from thoughts unconnected and language not adapted to the expression of

---

[1] "Sonnet composed on a journey homeward, the author having re-ceived intelligence of the birth of a son. September 20, 1796."

The opening lines, as quoted in the letter, differ from those pub-lished in 1797, and again from a copy of the same sonnet sent in a letter to Poole, dated November 1, 1796. See *Poetical Works*, p. 66, and Editor's Note, p. 582.

them. Where you do find out the meaning of my poetry, can you (in general, I mean) alter the language so as to make it more perspicuous — the thought remaining the same? By "dreamy semblance" I *did* mean semblance of some unknown past, like to a dream, and not "a semblance *presented* in a dream." I meant to express that ofttimes, for a second or two, it flashed upon my mind that the then company, conversation, and everything, had occurred before with all the precise circumstances; so as to make reality appear a semblance, and the present like a dream in sleep. Now this thought is obscure; because few persons have experienced the same feeling. Yet several have; and they were proportionably delighted with the lines, as expressing some strange sensations, which they themselves had never ventured to communicate, much less had ever seen developed in poetry. The lines I have altered to, —

> Oft o'er my brain does that strange rapture roll
> Which makes the present (while its brief fit last)
> Seem a mere semblance of some unknown past,
> Mixed with such feelings as distress the soul
> When dreaming that she dreams.[1]

Next as to "mystical." Now that the thinking part of man, that is, the soul, existed previously to its appearance in its present body may be very wild philosophy, but it is very intelligible poetry; inasmuch as "soul" is an orthodox word in all our poets, they meaning by "soul" a being inhabiting our body, and playing upon it, like a musician enclosed in an organ whose keys were placed inwards. Now this opinion I do not hold; not that I am a materialist, but because I am a Berkleyan. Yet as you, who are not a Christian, wished you were, that we might meet in heaven, so I, who did not believe in this descending and incarcerated soul, yet said if my baby had died before I

---

[1] Coleridge's *Poetical Works*, p. 66.

had seen him I should have *struggled* to believe it. Bless
me ! a commentary of thirty-five lines in defence of a sonnet ! and I do not like the sonnet much myself.   In some
(indeed, in many of my poems) there is a garishness and
swell of diction which I hope that my poems in future, if
I write any, will be clean of, but seldom, I think, any *con-
ceits*.   In the second edition, now printing, I have swept
the book with the expurgation-besom to a fine tune, having
omitted nearly one third.   As to Bowles, I affirm that the
manner of his accentuation in the words " broad daylight " (three long syllables) is a beauty, as it admirably
expresses the captive's dwelling on the sight of noon with
rapture and a kind of wonder.

> The common sun, the air, the skies
> To him are opening paradise.
>
> GRAY.

But supposing my defence not tenable ; yet how a blunder
in metre stamps a man Italian or Della Cruscan I cannot perceive.   As to my own poetry, I do confess that it
frequently, both in thought and language, deviates from
" nature and simplicity."   But that Bowles, the most
tender, and, with the exception of Burns, the only *always
natural* in our language, that *he* should not escape the
charge of Della Cruscanism, — this cuts the skin and surface of my heart.   " Poetry to have its highest relish must
be impassioned."   True.   But, firstly, poetry ought not
always to have its *highest* relish ; and, secondly, judging of
the cause from its effect, poetry, though treating on lofty
and abstract truths, ought to be deemed *impassioned* by
him who reads it with impassioned feelings.   Now Collins's " Ode on the Poetical Character," — that part of it,
I should say, beginning with " The band (as faery legends
say) Was wove on that creating day," — has inspired and
whirled *me* along with greater agitations of enthusiasm
than any the most *impassioned* scene in Schiller or Shake-

speare, using "impassioned" in its confined sense, for writing in which the human passions of pity, fear, anger, revenge, jealousy, or love are brought into view with their workings. Yet I consider the latter poetry as more valuable, because it gives *more general* pleasure, and I judge of all things by their utility. I feel strongly and I think strongly, but I seldom feel without thinking or think without feeling Hence, though my poetry has in general a hue of tenderness or passion over it, yet it seldom exhibits unmixed and simple tenderness or passion. My philosophical opinions are blended with or deduced from my feelings, and this, I think, peculiarises my style of writing, and, like everything else, it is sometimes a beauty and sometimes a fault. But do not let us introduce an Act of Uniformity against Poets. I have room enough in *my* brain to admire, aye, and almost equally, the *head* and fancy of Akenside, and the heart and fancy of Bowles, the solemn lordliness of Milton, and the divine chit-chat of Cowper.[1] And whatever a man's excellence is, that will be likewise his fault.

There were some verses of yours in the last "Monthly Magazine" with which I was much pleased — calm good sense combined with *feeling*, and conveyed in harmonious verse and a chaste and pleasing imagery. I wish much, very much, to see your other poem. As to your Poems which you informed me in the accompanying letter that you had sent in the same parcel with the pamphlets, whether or no your verses had more than their *proper number of feet* I cannot say; but certain it is, that somehow or other they *marched off*. No "Poems by John Thelwall" could I find. When I charged you with anti-

---

[1] Compare Lamb's letter to Coleridge, December 5, 1796. "I am glad you love Cowper. I could forgive a man for not enjoying Milton, but I would not call that man my friend who should be offended with the 'divine chit-chat of Cowper.'" Compare, too, letter of December 10, 1796, in which the origin of the phrase is attributed to Coleridge. *Letters of Charles Lamb*, i. 52, 54. See, too, Canon Ainger's note, i. 316.

religious bigotry, I did not allude to your pamphlet, but
to passages in your letters to me, and to a circumstance
which Southey, I *think*, once mentioned, that you had asserted that the name of *God* ought never to be produced
in poetry.[1] Which, to be sure, was carrying hatred *to
your Creator very far indeed.*

My dear Thelwall! " It is the principal felicity of life
and the chief glory of manhood to speak out fully on all
subjects." I will avail myself of it. I will express *all*
my feelings, but will previously take care to make my feelings benevolent. Contempt is hatred without fear; anger, hatred accompanied with apprehension. But because
hatred is always evil, contempt must be always evil, and a
good man ought to speak *contemptuously* of nothing. I
am sure a wise man will not of opinions which have been
held by men, in *other* respects at least, confessed of more
powerful intellect than himself. 'T is an assumption of
infallibility ; for if a man were wakefully mindful that
what he now thinks foolish he may himself hereafter think
wise, it is not in nature that he should *despise* those who
now believe what it is possible he may himself hereafter
believe ; and if he deny the possibility he must *on that
point* deem himself infallible and immutable. Now, in
your letter of yesterday, you speak with *contempt* of two
things: old age and the Christian religion ; though religion was believed by Newton, Locke, and Hartley, after
intense investigation, which in each had been preceded by
unbelief. This does not prove its truth, but it should save
its followers from *contempt,* even though through the infirmities of mortality they should have *lost their teeth.* I
call that man a bigot, Thelwall, whose intemperate zeal,
for or against any opinions, leads him to contradict himself
in the space of half a dozen lines. Now this you appear

[1] "Southey misrepresented me.
My maxim was and is that the name
of God should not be introduced into
Love Sonnets." MS. Note by John
Thelwall.

to me to have done. I will write fully to you now, because I shall never renew the subject. I shall not be idle
in defence of the religion I profess, and my books will be
the place, not my letters. You say the Christian is a *mean*
religion. Now the religion which Christ taught is simply,
first, that there is an omnipresent Father of infinite
power, wisdom, and goodness, in whom we all of us move
and have our being; and, secondly, that when we appear
to men to die we do not utterly perish, but after this life
shall continue to enjoy or suffer the consequences and natural effects of the habits we have formed here, whether
good or evil. This is the Christian *religion*, and all of
the Christian *religion*. That there is no *fancy* in it I
readily grant, but that it is mean and deficient in *mind*
and *energy* it were impossible for me to admit, unless I
admitted that there *could be* no dignity, intellect, or force
in anything but *atheism*. But though it appeal not itself
to the fancy, the truths which it teaches admit the highest
exercise of it. Are the " innumerable multitude of angels
and archangels " less splendid beings than the countless
gods and goddesses of Rome and Greece? And can you
seriously think that Mercury from Jove equals in poetic
sublimity " the mighty angel that came down from heaven,
whose face was as it were the sun and his feet as pillars
of fire : who set his right foot on the sea, and his left foot
on the earth. And he sent forth a loud voice ; and when
he had sent it forth, seven thunders uttered their voices :
and when the seven thunders had uttered their voices, the
mighty Angel[1] lifted up his hand to heaven, and sware by
Him that liveth for ever and ever that *Time* was no more " ?
Is not Milton a sublimer poet than Homer or Virgil ? Are
not his personages more sublimely clothed, and do you not
know that there is not perhaps *one page* in *Milton's* Par-

[1] Revelation x. 1–6. Some words and sentences of the original are omitted, either for the sake of brev-ity, or to heighten the dramatic ef-fect.

adise Lost in which he has not borrowed his imagery from
the *Scriptures?* I allow and rejoice that *Christ* appealed
only to the understanding and the affections; but I affirm
that after reading Isaiah, or St. Paul's "Epistle to the
Hebrews," Homer and Virgil are disgustingly *tame* to me,
and Milton himself barely tolerable. You and I are very
differently organized if you think that the following (putting serious belief out of the question) is a mean flight of
impassioned eloquence in which the Apostle marks the difference between the Mosaic and Christian Dispensation:
" For ye are not come unto the mount that might be
touched" (that is, a material and earthly place) "and
that burned with fire, nor unto blackness, and tempest,
and the sound of a trumpet, and the voice of words; which
voice they that heard entreated that the word should not
be spoken to them any more. But ye are come unto
Mount Sion, and unto the city of the living God, to an
innumerable company of angels, to God the Judge of all,
and to the spirits of just men made perfect." [1] *You* may
prefer to all this the quarrels of Jupiter and Juno, the
whimpering of wounded Venus, and the jokes of the celes-
tials on the lameness of Vulcan. Be it so (the difference
in our tastes it would not be difficult to account for from
the different feelings which we have associated with these
ideas); I shall continue with Milton to say that

> " Zion Hill
> Delights me more, and Siloa's brook that flow'd
> Fast by the oracle of God ! "

" Visions fit for slobberers!" If infidelity do not lead
to sensuality, which in every case except yours I have observed it to do, it always takes away all respect for those
who become unpleasant from the infirmities of disease or
decaying nature. *Exempli gratiâ,* "the aged are *slobberers.*" [2] The only vision which Christianity holds forth

---

[1] Hebrews xii. 18, 19, 22, 23.

[2] " In reading over this after an in-   terval of twenty-three years I was
wondering what I could have said

is indeed peculiarly adapted to these *slobberers*. Yes, to
these lowly and despised and perishing slobberers it pro-
claims that their "corruptible shall put on *incorruption*,
and their mortal put on *immortality*."

"Morals to the Magdalen and Botany Bay." Now,
Thelwall, I presume that to preach morals to the virtuous is not quite so requisite as to preach them to the
vicious. "The sick need a physician." Are morals
which would make a prostitute a wife and a sister,
which would restore her to inward peace and purity; are
morals which would make drunkards sober, the ferocious
benevolent, and thieves honest, *mean morals?* Is it a
despicable trait in our religion, that its professed object
is to heal the broken-hearted and give wisdom to the
poor man? It preaches *repentance*. What repentance?
Tears and sorrow and a repetition of the same crimes?
No, a " repentance unto good works;" a repentance that
completely does away all superstitious terrors by teaching
that the past is nothing in itself, that, if the mind *is* good,
that it *was* bad imports nothing. " It is a religion for
democrats." It certainly teaches in the most explicit terms
the rights of man, his right to wisdom, his right to an equal
share in all the blessings of nature; it commands its disciples to go everywhere, and everywhere to preach these
rights; it commands them never to use the arm of flesh, to
be perfectly non-resistant; yet to hold the promulgation
of *truth* to be a law above law, and in the performance of
this office to defy " wickedness in high places," and cheerfully to endure ignominy, and wretchedness, and torments,
and death, rather than *intermit* the performance of it; yet,
while enduring ignominy, and wretchedness, and torments,
and death, to feel nothing but sorrow, and pity, and love

that looked like contempt of age.
May not slobberers have referred not
to age but to the drivelling of de-
cayed intellect, which is surely an
ill guide in matters of understanding
and consequently of faith?" MS.
Note by John Thelwall, 1819.

for those who inflicted them; wishing their oppressors to be altogether such as they, " excepting these bonds." Here is *truth* in theory and in practice, a union of energetic *action* and more energetic *suffering.* For activity amuses; but he who can *endure* calmly must possess the seeds of true greatness. For all his animal spirits will of necessity fail him; and he has only his mind to trust to. These doubtless are morals for all the lovers of mankind, who wish to *act* as well as *speculate;* and that you should allow this, and yet, not three lines before call the same *morals mean,* appears to me a gross self-contradiction symptomatic of bigotry. I write freely, Thelwall; for, though *personally* unknown, I really love you, and can count but few human beings whose hand I would welcome with a more hearty grasp of friendship. I suspect, Thelwall, that you never read your Testament, since your understanding was matured, without carelessness, and previous contempt, and a somewhat like hatred. Christianity regards morality as a process. It finds a man vicious and unsusceptible of noble motives and gradually leads him, at least desires to lead him, to the height of disinterested virtue; till, in relation and proportion to his faculties and power, he is perfect " even as our Father in heaven is perfect." There is no resting-place for morality. Now I will make one other appeal, and have done forever with the subject. There is a passage in Scripture which comprises the whole process, and each component part, of Christian morals. Previously let me explain the word faith. By faith I understand, first, a deduction from experiments in favour of the existence of something not experienced, and, secondly, the motives which attend such a deduction. Now motives, being selfish, are only the beginning and the *foundation*, necessary and of first-rate importance, yet made of vile materials, and hidden beneath the splendid superstructure.

" Now giving all diligence, add to your faith *fortitude,*

and to *fortitude knowledge,* and to knowledge purity, and to purity patience,[1] and to patience godliness,[2] and to

[1] Patience — permit me as a definition of the word to quote one sentence from my first Address, p. 20. "Accustomed to regard all the affairs of man as a process, they never hurry and they never pause." In his not possessing *this* virtue, all the horrible excesses of Robespierre did, I believe, originate. — MS. note to text of letter by S. T. Coleridge.

[2] Godliness — the belief, the habitual and efficient belief, that we are always in the presence of our universal Parent. I will translate literally a passage [the passage is from Voss's *Luise.* I am enabled by the courtesy of Dr. Garnett, of the British Museum, to give an exact reference : *Luise, ein ländliches Gedicht in drei Idyllen,* von Johann Heinrich Voss, Königsberg, MDCCXCV. Erste Idylle, pp. 41–45, lines 303–339. — E. H. C.] from a German hexameter poem. It is the speech of a country clergyman on the birthday of his daughter. The *latter part* fully expresses the spirit of godliness, and its connection with brotherly-kindness. (Pardon the harshness of the language, for it is translated *totidem verbis.*)

"Yes! my beloved daughter, I am cheerful, cheerful as the birds singing in the wood here, or the squirrel that hops among the airy branches around its young in their nest. To-day it is eighteen years since God gave me my beloved, now my only child, so intelligent, so pious, and so dutiful. How the time flies away! Eighteen years to come — how far the space extends itself before us! and how does it vanish when we look back upon it! It was but yesterday, it seems to me, that as I was plucking flowers here, and offering praise, on a sudden the joyful message came, 'A daughter is born to us.' Much since that time has the Almighty imparted to us of good and evil. But the evil itself was good ; for his loving-kindness is infinite. Do you recollect [to his wife] as it once had rained after a long drought, and I (Louisa in my arms) was walking with thee in the freshness of the garden, how the child snatched at the rainbow, and kissed me, and said : 'Papa! there it rains flowers from heaven! Does the blessed God strew these that we children may gather them up?' 'Yes!' I answered, 'full-blowing and heavenly blessings does the Father strew who stretched out the bow of his favour; flowers and fruits that we may gather them with thankfulness and joy. *Whenever I think of that great Father then my heart lifts itself up and swells with active impulse towards all his children, our brothers who inhabit the earth around us; differing indeed from one another in powers and understanding, yet all dear children of the same parent, nourished by the same Spirit of animation, and ere long to fall asleep, and again to wake in the common morning of the Resurrection ; all who have loved their fellow-creatures, all shall rejoice with Peter, and Moses, and Confucius, and Homer, and Zoroaster, with Socrates who died for truth, and also with the noble Mendelssohn who teaches that the divine one was never crucified.'*"

Mendelssohn is a German Jew by parentage, and *deist* by election.

godliness brotherly-kindness, and to brotherly-kindness universal love." [1]

I hope, whatever you may think of godliness, you will like the *note* on it.   I need not tell you, that godliness is God-*like*ness, and is paraphrased by Peter " that ye may be partakers of the divine nature," that is, act from a love of order and happiness, not from any self-respecting motive ; from the excellency into which you have exalted your *nature*, not from the *keenness* of mere *prudence*. " Add to your faith fortitude, and to fortitude knowledge, and to knowledge purity, and to purity patience, and to patience godliness, and to godliness brotherly-kindness, and to brotherly-kindness universal love." Now, Thelwall, putting *faith* out of the question (which, by the bye, is not mentioned as a virtue, but as the leader to them), can you mention a virtue which is not here enjoined ? and supposing the precepts embodied in the practice of any one human being, would not perfection be personified ? I write these things not with any expectation of making you a Christian.   I should smile at my own folly, if I conceived it even in a friendly day-dream.

.   .   .   .

"The ardour of undisciplined benevolence seduces us into malignity," and, while you accustom yourself to speak so *contemptuously* of doctrines you do not accede to, and persons with whom you do not accord, I must doubt whether even your *brotherly-kindness* might not be made more perfect.   That is surely *fit* for a man which his mind after sincere examination approves, which animates his conduct, soothes his sorrows, and heightens his pleasures.   Every good and earnest Christian declares that all this is true of the *visions* (as you please to style

He has written some of the most acute books possible in favour of natural immortality, and Germany deems him her profoundest metaphysician, with the exception of the most unintelligible Immanuel Kant. — MS. note to text of letter by S. T. Coleridge.

[1] 2 Peter i. 5–7.

them, God knows why) of Christianity. Every earnest
Christian, therefore, is on a level with slobberers. Do not
charge me with dwelling on one expression. These expressions are always indicative of the habit of feeling.
You possess fortitude and purity, and a large portion of
brotherly-kindness and universal love; drink with un-
quenchable thirst of the two latter virtues, and acquire
patience; and then, Thelwall, should *your* system be
true, all that can be said is that (if both our systems
should be found to increase our own and our fellow-creatures' happiness), " Here lie and did lie the *all* of John
Thelwall and S. T. Coleridge. They were both humane,
and happy, but the former was the more knowing; " and
if my system should prove true, we, I doubt not, shall
both meet in the kingdom of heaven, and I, with transport in my eye, shall say, " I *told* you so, my *dear* fellow."
But seriously, the faulty habit of feeling, which I have
endeavoured to point out in you, I have detected in at
least as great degree in my own practice, and am struggling to subdue it. I rejoice that the bankrupt honesty
of the public has paid even the small dividend you mentioned. As to your second part, I will write you about
it in a day or two, when I give you an account how I
have disposed of your first. My dear little baby! and
my wife thinks that he already begins to flutter the
callow wings of his intellect. Oh, the wise heart and
foolish head of a mother! Kiss your little girl for me,
and tell her if I knew her I would love her; and then I
hope in your next letter you will convey *her love* to me
and my Sara. Your dear boy, I trust, will return with
rosy cheeks. Don't you suspect, Thelwall, that the little
atheist Madam Stella has an abominable *Christian* kind
of *heart?* My Sara is much interested about her; and I
should not wonder if they were to be sworn sister-seraphs
in the heavenly Jerusalem. Give my love to her.

I have sent you some loose sheets which Charles Lloyd

and I printed together, intending to make a volume, but
I gave it up and cancelled them.[1]   Item, Joan of Arc,
with only the passage of my writing cut out for the printers, as I am printing it in my second edition, with very
great alterations and an addition of four hundred lines, so
as to make it a complete and independent poem, entitled,
" The Progress of Liberty," or " The Visions of the Maid
of Orleans."   Item, a sheet of sonnets[2] collected by me for
the use of a few friends, who paid the printing.   There
you will see my opinion of sonnets.   Item, Poem by C.
Lloyd[3] on the death of one of your " slobberers," a very
venerable old lady, and a Quaker.   The book is dressed
like a rich Quaker, in costly raiment but unornamented.
The loss of her almost killed my poor young friend ; for
he doted on her from his infancy.   Item, a poem of
mine on Burns[4] which was printed to be dispersed among

---

[1] They were criticised by Lamb in his letter to Coleridge Dec. 10, 1796 (xxxi. of Canon Ainger's edition), but in a passage first printed in the *Atlantic Monthly* for February, 1891. The explanatory notes there printed were founded on a misconception, but the matter is cleared up in the *Athenæum* for June 13, 1891, in the article, " A Letter of Charles Lamb."

[2] The reference is to a pamphlet of sixteen pages containing twenty-eight sonnets by Coleridge, Southey, Lloyd, Lamb, and others, which was printed for private circulation towards the close of 1796, and distributed among a few friends. Of this selection of sonnets, which was made " for the purpose of binding them up with the sonnets of the Rev. W. L. Bowles," the sole surviving copy is now in the Dyce Collection of the South Kensington Museum. On the fly-leaf, in Coleridge's handwriting,

is a " presentation note " to Mrs. Thelwall. For a full account of this curious and interesting volume, see Coleridge's *Poetical and Dramatic Works*, 4 vols., 1877–1880, ii. 377–379 ; also, *Poetical Works* (1893), 542–544.

[3] A folio edition of " *Poems on the Death of Priscilla Farmer*, by her grandson Charles Lloyd," was printed at Bristol in 1796. The volume was prefaced by Coleridge's sonnet, " The piteous sobs which choke the virgin's breast," and contained Lamb's " Grandame." As Mr. Dykes Campbell has pointed out, it is to this " magnificent folio " that Charles Lamb alludes in his letter of December 10, 1796 (incorrectly dated 1797), when he speaks of " my granny so gaily decked," and records " the odd coincidence of two young men in one age carolling their grandmothers." *Poetical Works*, note 99, p. 583.

[4] " To a friend (C. Lamb) who had

friends. It was addressed to Charles Lamb. Item,
(Shall I give it thee, blasphemer? No! I won't, but) to
thy Stella I do present the poems of my youth for a keep-
sake. Of this parcel I do entreat thy acceptance. I have
another Joan of Arc, so you have a *right* to the one enclosed. Postscript. Item, a humorous "Droll" on S. Ireland, of which I have likewise another. Item, a strange
poem written by an astrologer here, who *was* a man of
fine genius, which, at intervals, he still discovers. But,
ah me! Madness smote with her hand and stamped with
her feet and swore that he should be hers, and hers he is.
He is a man of fluent eloquence and general knowledge,
gentle in his manners, warm in his affections; but unfortunately he has received a few rays of supernatural light
through a crack in his upper story. I *express* myself un-
feelingly; but indeed my heart always aches when I think
of him. Item, some verses of Robert Southey to a college cat.[1] And, finally, the following lines by thy affectionate friend,

S. T. COLERIDGE.

TO A YOUNG MAN

WHO ABANDONED HIMSELF TO A CAUSELESS AND INDOLENT MEL-
ANCHOLY.[2]

Hence that fantastic wantonness of woe,
  O youth to partial Fortune vainly dear!
To plunder'd Want's half-sheltered hovel go,
  Go, and some hunger-bitten infant hear
  Moan haply in a dying mother's ear.

[1] Printed in the *Annual Anthology* for 1799.

[2] These lines, which were published with the enlarged title "To
a Young Man of Fortune who had
abandoned himself to an indolent and
causeless melancholy," may have
been addressed to Charles Lloyd.

The last line, "A prey to the
throned murderess of mankind," was
afterwards changed to "A prey to
tyrants, murderers of mankind."
The reference is, doubtless, to Cath-
erine of Russia. Her death had
taken place a month before the date

declared his intention of writing no
more poetry." *Poetical Works*, p.
69. See, too, Editor's Note, p. 583.

Or seek some *widow's* grave ; whose dearer part
   Was slaughtered, where o'er his uncoffin'd limbs
The flocking flesh-birds scream'd ! Then, while thy heart
   Groans, and thine eyes a fiercer sorrow dims,
Know (and the truth shall kindle thy young mind),
   What Nature makes thee mourn she bids thee heal.
O abject ! if, to sickly dreams resign'd,
   All effortless thou leave Earth's common weal
A prey to the thron'd Murderess of Mankind !

After the first five lines these two followed : —

   Or when the cold and dismal fog-damps brood
   O'er the rank church-yard with sere elm-leaves strew'd,
   Pace round some *widow's* grave, etc.

These they rightly omitted. I love sonnets ; but *upon my honour* I do not love *my* sonnets.

N. B. — Direct your letters, S. T. Coleridge, Mr. Cottle's, High Street, Bristol.

LXIX. TO THOMAS POOLE.

Sunday morning [? December 18, 1796.]

MY DEAR POOLE, — I wrote to you with improper impetuosity ; but I had been dwelling so long on the circumstance of living near you, that my mind was thrown by your letter into the feelings of those distressful dreams [1] where we imagine ourselves falling from precipices. I

of this letter, but possibly when Coleridge wrote the lines the news had not reached England. It is not a little strange that Coleridge should write and print so stern and uncompromising a rebuke to his intimate and disciple before there had been time for coolness and alienation on either side. Very possibly the reproof was aimed in the first instance against himself, and afterwards he permitted it to apply to Lloyd.

[1] Compare the line, " From precipices of distressful sleep," which occurs in the sonnet, "No more my visionary soul shall dwell," which is attributed to Favell in a letter of Southey's to his brother Thomas, dated October 24, 1795. Southey's *Life and Correspondence*, i. 224. See, also, Editor's Note to "Monody on the Death of Chatterton," *Poetical Works*, p. 563.

seemed falling from the summit of my fondest desires, whirled from the height just as I had reached it.

We shall want none of the Woman's furniture; we have enough for ourselves. What with boxes of books, and chests of drawers, and kitchen furniture, and chairs, and our bed and bed-linen, etc., we shall have enough to fill a small waggon, and to-day I shall make enquiry among my trading acquaintance, whether it would be cheaper to hire a waggon to take them straight to Stowey, than to put them in the Bridgwater waggon. Taking in the double trouble and expense of putting them in the drays to carry them to the public waggon, and then seeing them packed again, and again to be unpacked and packed at Bridgwater, I much question whether our goods would be good for anything. I am very poorly, not to say ill. My face monstrously swollen — my recondite eye sits distent quaintly, behind the flesh-hill, and looks as little as a tomtit's. And I have a sore throat that prevents my eating aught but spoon-meat without great pain. And I have a rheumatic complaint in the back part of my head and shoulders. Now all this demands a small portion of Christian patience, taking in our present circumstances. My apothecary says it will be madness for me to walk to Stowey on Tuesday, as, in the furious zeal of a new convert to economy, I had resolved to do. My wife will stay a week or fortnight after me; I think it not improbable that the weather may break up by that time. However, if I do not get worse, I will be with you by Wednesday or Thursday at the furthest, so as to be there before the waggon. Is there any grate in the house? I should think we might Rumfordize one of the chimneys. I shall bring down with me a dozen yards of green list. I can endure cold, but not a cold room. If we can but contrive to make two rooms *warm* and *wholesome*, we will laugh in the faces of gloom and ill-lookingness.

I shall lose the post if I say a word more. You thor-

oughly and in every nook and corner of your heart forgive
me for my letters ? Indeed, indeed, Poole, I know no
one whom I esteem more — no one friend whom I love so
much. But bear with my infirmities! God bless you,
and your grateful and affectionate

S. T. COLERIDGE.

LXX. TO JOHN THELWALL.

December 31, 1796.

Enough, my dear Thelwall, of theology. In my book on
Godwin, I compare the two systems, his and Jesus', and
that book I am sure you will read with attention. I entirely
accord with your opinion of Southey's " Joan." The ninth
book is execrable, and the poem, though it frequently reach
the *sentimental*, does not display the *poetical-sublime*.
In language at once natural, perspicuous, and dignified
in manly pathos, in soothing and sonnet-like description,
and, above all, in character and *dramatic* dialogue,
Southey is unrivalled ; but as certainly he does not possess opulence of imaginative lofty-paced harmony, or that
toil of thinking which is necessary in order to plan a
whole. Dismissing mock humility, and hanging your
mind as a looking-glass over my idea-pot, so as to image
on the said mind all the bubbles that boil in the said idea-
pot (there 's a damned long-winded metaphor for you), I
think that an admirable poet might be made by *amalga-
mating him* and *me*. I *think* too much for a *poet*, he too
little for a *great* poet. But he abjures *feeling*. Now (as
you say) they must go together. Between ourselves the
enthusiasm of friendship is not with S. and me. We
quarrelled and the quarrel lasted for a twelvemonth. We
are now reconciled ; but the cause of the difference was
solemn, and " the blasted oak puts not forth its buds
anew." We are *acquaintances*, and feel *kindliness* towards each other, but I do not *esteem* or *love* Southey,
as I must esteem and love the man whom I dared call by

the holy name of *friend :* and vice versâ Southey of me.
I say no more. It is a painful subject, and do you say
nothing. I mention this for obvious reasons, but let it
go no farther. It is a painful subject. Southey's direction at present is R. Southey, No. 8 West-gate Buildings,
Bath, but he leaves Bath for London in the course of a
week. You imagine that I know Bowles personally. I
never saw him but once, and when I was a boy and in
Salisbury market-place.

The passage in your letter respecting your mother
affected me greatly. Well, true or false, heaven is a less
gloomy idea than annihilation. Dr. Beddoes and Dr.
Darwin think that *Life* is utterly inexplicable, writing as
materialists. You, I understand, have adopted the idea
that it is the result of organised matter acted on by external stimuli. As likely as any other system, but you
assume the thing to be proved. The "capability of being
stimulated into sensation" . . . is my definition of
animal life. Monro believes in a plastic, immaterial
nature, all-pervading.

> And what if all of animated nature
> Be but organic harps diversely framed,
> That tremble into thought, as o'er them sweeps
> Plastic and vast, etc.

(By the bye, that is the favourite of *my* poems ; do you
like it ?) Hunter says that the *blood* is the life, which is
saying nothing at all ; for, if the blood were *life,* it could
never be otherwise than life, and to say it is *alive* is
saying nothing ; and Ferriar believes in a *soul,* like an
orthodox churchman. So much for physicians and sur-
geons ! Now as to the metaphysicians. Plato says it is
harmony. He might as well have said a fiddlestick's end ;
but I love Plato, his dear, *gorgeous* nonsense ; and I,
though last not least, I do not know what to think about
it. On the whole, I have rather made up my mind that I

am a mere *apparition*, a naked spirit, and that life is,
I myself I; which is a mighty clear account of it. Now I
have written all this, not to express my ignorance (that is
an accidental effect, not the final cause), but to shew you
that I want to see your essay on "Animal Vitality," of
which Bowles the surgeon spoke in high terms. Yet *he*
believes in a *body* and a *soul*. Any book may be left at
Robinson's for *me*, "to be put into the next parcel, to be
sent to 'Joseph Cottle, bookseller, Bristol.'" Have you
received an "Ode"[1] of mine from Parsons? In your
next letter tell me what you think of the *scattered* poems
I sent you. Send me any poems, and I will be minute in
criticism. For, O Thelwall, even a long-winded abuse is
more consolatory to an *author's* feelings than a short-
breathed, asthma-lunged panegyric. Joking apart, I
would to God we could sit by a fireside and joke *vivâ
voce*, face to face — Stella and Sara, Jack Thelwall and
I. As I once wrote to my dear friend, T. Poole, "repeating —

'Such verse as Bowles, heart-honour'd poet, sang,
That wakes the Tear, yet steals away the Pang,
Then, or with Berkeley or with Hobbes romance it,
Dissecting Truth with metaphysic lancet.
Or, drawn from up those dark unfathom'd wells,
In wiser folly clink the Cap and Bells.
How many tales we told! what jokes we made!
Conundrum, Crambo, Rebus, or Charade;
Ænigmas that had driven the Theban[2] mad,
And Puns, then best when exquisitely bad;
And I, if aught of archer vein I hit
With my own laughter stifled my own wit.'"[3]

[1] The *Ode on the Departing Year*.   [3] *Poetical Works*, p. 459.
[2] Œdipus.

CHAPTER III

THE STOWEY PERIOD

1797–1798

CHAPTER III

LXXI. TO REV. J. P. ESTLIN.

[STOWEY, 1797.]

MY DEAR FRIEND, — I was indeed greatly rejoiced at the first sight of a letter from you; but its contents were painful. Dear, dear Mrs. Estlin! Sara burst into an agony of tears that she *had* been so ill. Indeed, indeed, we hover about her, and think and talk of her, with many an interjection of prayer. I do not wonder that you have acquired a distaste to London — your associations must be painful indeed. But God be praised! you shall look back on those sufferings as the vexations of a dream! Our friend, T. Poole, particularly requests me to mention how deeply he condoles with you in Mrs. Estlin's illness, how fervently he thanks God for her recovery. I assure you he was extremely affected. We are all remarkably well, and the child grows fat and strong. Our house is better than we expected — there is a comfortable bedroom and sitting-room for C. Lloyd, and another for us, a room for Nanny, a kitchen, and outhouse. Before our door a clear brook runs of very soft water; and in the back yard is a nice *well* of fine spring water. We have a very pretty garden, and large enough to find us vegetables and employment, and I am already an expert gardener, and both my hands can exhibit a callum as testimonials of their industry. We have likewise a sweet orchard, and at the end of it T. Poole has made a gate, which leads into his garden, and from thence either through the tan yard into his house, or else through his orchard over a fine meadow into the garden of a Mrs. Cruikshank, an old acquaintance, who married on the same day as I, and has got a little girl a little younger than David Hartley. Mrs. Cruikshank is a sweet little woman, of the same size as my Sara, and they are extremely cordial. T. Poole's mother behaves to *us* as a kind and tender mother. She is very fond indeed of my wife, so that, you see, I ought to be happy, and, thank God, I am so. . . .

LXXII. TO JOHN THELWALL.

STOWEY NEAR BRIDGEWATER, SOMERSET.
February 6, 1797.

I thank you, my dear Thelwall, for the parcel, and your letters. Of the contents I shall speak in the order of their importance. First, then, of your scheme of a school, I approve it; and fervently wish, that you may find it more easy of accomplishment than my fears suggest. But try, by all means, try. Have hopes without expectations to hazard disappointment. Most of our patriots are tavern and parlour patriots, that will not avow their principles by any decisive action ; and of the few who would wish to do so, the larger part are unable, from their children's expectancies on rich relations, etc., etc. May these remain enough for your Stella to employ herself on ! Try, by all means, try. For your comfort, for your progressiveness in literary excellence, in the name of everything that is happy, and in the name of everything that is miserable, I would have you do anything honest rather than lean with the whole weight of your necessities on the Press. Get bread and cheese, clothing and housing independently of it ; and you may then safely trust to it for beef and strong beer. You will find a country life a happy one ; and you might live

comfortably with an hundred a year. Fifty pounds you might, I doubt not, gain by *reviewing* and furnishing miscellanies for the different magazines ; you might safely speculate on twenty pounds a year or more from your compositions published separately — $50+20 = £70$; and by severe economy, a little garden labour, and a pigstye, this would do. And, if the education scheme did not succeed, and I could get *engaged* by any one of the Reviews and the new "Monthly Magazine," I would *try* it, and begin to farm by little and slow degrees. You perceive that by the Press I mean merely *writing without a certainty*. The other is as secure as anything else could be to *you*. With health and spirits it would stand ; and without health and spirits every other mode of maintenance, as well as reviewing, would be impracticable. You are going to Derby ! I shall be with you in spirit. Derby is no common place ; but where you will find *citizens* enough to fill your lecture-room puzzles me. Dr. Darwin will no doubt excite your respectful curiosity. On the whole, I think, he is the first *literary* character in Europe, and the most original-minded man. Mrs. Crompton is an angel ; and Dr. Crompton a truly honest and benevolent man, possessing good sense and a large portion of humour. I never think of him without respect and tenderness ; never (for, thank Heaven ! I abominate Godwinism) without gratitude. William Strutt [1] is a man of stern aspect, but

[1] William and Joseph Strutt were the sons of Jedediah Strutt, of Derby. The eldest, William, was the father of Edward Strutt, created Lord Belper in 1856. Their sister, Elizabeth, who had married William Evans of Darley Hall, was at this time a widow. She had been struck by Coleridge's writings, or perhaps had heard him preach when he visited Derby on his *Watchman* tour, and was anxious to engage him as tutor to her children. The offer was actually made, but the relations on both sides intervened, and she was reluctantly compelled to withdraw her proposal. By way of consolation, she entertained Coleridge and his wife at Darley Hall, and before he left presented him with a handsome sum of money and a store of baby-linen, worth, if one may accept Coleridge's valuation, a matter of forty pounds. *Thomas Poole and his Friends,* i. 152-154 ; *Estlin Letters,* p. 13.

strong, very strong abilities. Joseph Strutt every way amiable. He deserves his wife — which is saying a great deal — for she is a sweet-minded woman, and one that you would be apt to recollect whenever you met or used the words lovely, handsome, beautiful, etc. " While smiling Loves the shaft display, And lift the playful torch elate." Perhaps you may be so fortunate as to meet with a Mrs. Evans whose seat is at Darley, about a mile from Derby. Blessings descend on her! emotions crowd on me at the sight of her name. We spent five weeks at her house, a sunny spot in our life. My Sara sits and thinks and thinks of her and bursts into tears, and when I turn to her says, " I was thinking, my dear, of Mrs. Evans and Bessy " (that is, her daughter). I mention this to you, because things are characterized by their effects. She is no common being who could create so warm and lasting an interest in *our* hearts; for *we* are no common people. Indeed, indeed, Thelwall, she is without exception the greatest *woman* I have been fortunate enough to meet with in my brief pilgrimage through life.

At Nottingham you will surely be more likely to obtain audiences; and, I doubt not, you will find a hospitable reception there. I was treated by many families with kindliness, by some with a zeal of affection. Write me if you go and when you go. Now for your pamphlet. It is well written, and the doctrine sound, although sometimes, I think, deduced falsely. For instance (p. iii.): It is *true* that all a man's children, " however begotten, whether in marriage or out," are his heirs in nature, and ought to be so in true policy; but, instead of tacitly allowing that I meant by it to encourage what Mr. B.[1] and the

[1] Probably Jacob Bryant, 1715–1804, author of *An Address to Dr. Priestley upon his Doctrine of Philosophical Necessity*, 1780; *Treatise on the Authenticity of the Scriptures*, 1792; *The Sentiments of Philo-Judæus concerning the Logos or Word of God*, 1797, etc. Allibone's *Dictionary*, i. 270.

priests would call licentiousness (and which surely, Thelwall, in the *present state of society* you must allow to be injustice, inasmuch as it deprives the woman of her respectability in the opinions of her neighbours), I would have shown that such a law would of all others operate most powerfully in *favour* of *marriage ;* by which word I mean not the effect of spells uttered by conjurers, but permanent cohabitation useful to society as the best conceivable means (in the present state of society, at least) of ensuring nurture and systematic education to infants and children. We are but frail beings at present, and want such motives to the practice of our duties. Unchastity may be no vice, — I think it is, — but it may be no vice, abstractly speaking ; yet from a variety of causes unchaste women are almost without exception careless mothers. *Wife* is a solemn name to me because of its influence on the more solemn duties of *mother.* Such passages (p. 30 is another of them) are offensive. They are mere *assertions*, and of course can convince no person who thinks differently ; and they give pain and irritate. I write so frequently to you on this subject, because I have reason to *know* that passages of this order did give very general offence in your first part, and have operated to retard the sale of the second. If they had been arguments or necessarily connected with your main argument, I am not the man, Thelwall, who would oppose the filth of prudentials merely to have it swept away by the indignant torrent of your honesty. But as I said before, they are mere *assertions ;* and certainly their truth is not self-evident. With the exception of these passages, the pamphlet is the best I have read since the commencement of the war ; warm, not fiery, well-seasoned without being dry, the periods harmonious yet avoiding metrical harmony, and the ornaments so dispersed as to set off the features of truth without turning the attention on themselves. I account for its slow sale partly from

your having compared yourself to Christ in the first
(which gave great offence, to my knowledge, although
very foolishly, I confess), and partly from the sore and
fatigued state of men's minds, which disqualifies them for
works of principle that exert the intellect without agita-
ting the passions.   But it has not been reviewed yet, has
it?   I read your narrative and was almost sorry I had
read it, for I had become much interested, and the abrupt
" no more " jarred me.   I never heard before of your
variance with Horne Tooke.   Of the poems, the two
Odes are the best.   Of the two Odes, the last, I think;
it is in the best style of Akenside's best Odes.   Several
of the sonnets are pleasing, and whenever I was pleased
I paused, and imaged you in my mind in your captivity.
. . . _My Ode_ [1] by this time you are conscious that you
have praised too highly.   With the exception of " I un-
partaking of the evil thing," which line I do not think
injudiciously weak, I accede to all your remarks, and
shall alter accordingly.   Your remark that the line on
the Empress had more of Juvenal than Pindar _flashed
itself_ on my mind.   I had admired the line before, but
I became immediately of your opinion, and that criticism
has convinced me that your nerves are exquisite _electro-
meters_ [2] of taste.   You forgot to point out to me that the

---

[1] "Ode to the Departing Year,"
published in the _Cambridge Intelli-
gencer_, December 24, 1796.   The
lines on the " Empress," to which
Thelwall objected, are in the first
epode : —

> No more on Murder's lurid face
> The Insatiate Hag shall gloat with drunken
>   eye.
>   _Poetical Works_, p. 79.

[2] Compare the well-known description of Dorothy Wordsworth,
in a letter to Cottle of July, 1797 :
" W. and his exquisite sister are
with me.   She is a woman, indeed,
— in mind I mean, and heart.   Her
information various.   Her eye watch-
ful in minutest observation of nature;
and her taste a perfect electrometer.
It bends, protrudes, and draws in, at
subtlest beauties and most recondite
faults."

Bennett's, or the gold leaf electroscope, is an instrument for " detect-
ing the presence, and determining
the kind of electricity in any body."
Two narrow strips of gold leaf are
attached to a metal rod, terminating
in a small brass plate above, contained in a glass shade, and these

whole childbirth of Nature is at once ludicrous and disgusting, an epigram smart yet bombastic. The review
of Bryant's pamphlet is good — the sauce is better than
the fish. Speaking of Lewis's death, surely you forget
that the legislature of France were to act by *laws* and
not by general morals ; and that they violated the law
which they themselves had made. I will take in the " Corresponding Society Magazine." That good man, James
Losh, has just published an admirable treatise translated from the French of Benjamin Constant,[1] entitled,
" Consideration on the Strength of the Present Government of France." " Woe to that country when crimes
are punished by crimes, and where men murder in the
name of justice." I apply this to the death of the mistaken but well-meaning Lewis.[2] I never go to Bristol.
From seven till half past eight I work in my garden ;
from breakfast till twelve I read and compose, then read
again, feed the pigs, poultry, etc., till two o'clock ; after
dinner work again till tea ; from tea till supper, *review*.
So jogs the day, and I am happy. I have society — *my
friend* T. Poole, and as many acquaintances as I can dis-
pense with. There are a number of very pretty young

under certain conditions of the application of positive and negative
electricity diverge or collapse.

The gold leaf electroscope was
invented by Abraham Bennett in
1786. Cottle's *Early Recollections*,
i. 252; Ganot's *Physics*, 1870, p.
631.

[1] His tract *On the Strength of
the Existing Government (the Directory) of France, and the Necessity
of supporting it*, was published in
1796.

The translator, James Losh, described by Southey as " a provincial
counsel," was at one time resident in
Cumberland, and visited Coleridge
at Greta Hall. At a later period he

settled at Jesmond, Newcastle. His
name occurs among the subscribers
to *The Friend. Letters from the Lake
Poets*, p. 453.

[2] Compare stanzas eight and nine
of " The Mad Ox : " —

Old Lewis ('t was his evil day)
  Stood trembling in his shoes ;
The ox was his — what could he say ?
  His legs were stiffened with dismay,
The ox ran o'er him mid the fray,
  And gave him his death's bruise.

The baited ox drove on (but here,
  The Gospel scarce more true is,
My muse stops short in mid career —
  Nay, gentle reader, do not sneer !
I could chuse but drop a tear,
  A tear for good old Lewis !)
        Poetical Works, p. 134.

women in Stowey, all musical, and I am an immense
favourite : for I pun, conundrumize, *listen*, and dance.
The last is a recent acquirement. We are very happy,
and my little David Hartley grows a sweet boy and has
high health ; he laughs at us till he makes us weep for
very fondness. You would smile to see my eye rolling
up to the ceiling in a lyric fury, and on my knee a diaper
pinned to warm. I send and receive to and from Bristol
every week, and will transcribe that part of your last
letter and send it to Reed.

I raise potatoes and all manner of vegetables, have an
orchard, and shall raise corn with the spade, enough for
my family. We have two pigs, and ducks and geese. A
cow would not answer the keep : for we have whatever
milk we want from T. Poole. God bless you and your
affectionate

S. T. COLERIDGE.

LXXIII. TO JOSEPH COTTLE.[1]

June, 1797.

MY DEAR COTTLE, — I am sojourning for a few days
at Racedown, the mansion of our friend Wordsworth,
who has received Fox's " Achmed." He returns you his
acknowledgments, and presents his kindliest respects to

[1] The probable date of this letter is Thursday, June 8, 1797. On
Monday, June 5, Coleridge breakfasted with Dr. Toulmin, the Unitarian minister at Taunton, and on the
evening of that or the next day he
arrived on foot at Racedown, some
forty miles distant. Mrs. Wordsworth, in a letter to Sara Coleridge,
dated November 7, 1845, conveys
her husband's recollections of this
first visit in the following words :
" Your father," she says, " came
afterwards to visit us at Racedown,
where I was living with my sister.
We have both a distinct remembrance of his arrival. He did not
keep to the high road, but leaped
over a high gate and bounded down
the pathless field, by which he cut
off an angle. We both retain the
liveliest possible image of his appearance at that moment. My poor
sister has just been speaking of it to
me with much feeling and tenderness." A portion of this letter, of
which I possess the original MS., was
printed by Professor Knight in his
Life of Wordsworth, i. 111.

you. I shall be home by Friday — not to-morrow — but the next Friday. If the "Ode on the Departing Year" be not reprinted, please to *omit* the lines from "When shall scepter'd slaughter cease," to "For still does Madness roam on Guilt's bleak dizzy height," inclusive.[1] The first epode is to end at the words "murderer's fate." Wordsworth admires my tragedy, which gives me great hopes. Wordsworth has written a tragedy himself. I speak with heartfelt sincerity, and (I think) unblinded judgment, when I tell you that I feel myself *a little man by his side*, and yet do not think myself the less man than I formerly thought myself. His drama is absolutely wonderful. You know I do not commonly speak in such abrupt and unmingled phrases, and therefore will the more readily believe me. There are in the piece those *profound* touches of the human heart which I find three or four times in "The Robbers" of Schiller, and often in Shakespeare, but in Wordsworth there are no *inequalities*. T. Poole's opinion of Wordsworth is that he is the greatest man he ever knew; I coincide.

It is not impossible, that in the course of two or three months I may see you. God bless you, and

S. T. COLERIDGE.

Thursday. — Of course, with the lines you omit the notes that relate to them.

Mr. COTTLE, Bookseller, High Street, Bristol.

LXXIV. TO ROBERT SOUTHEY.

July, 1797.

DEAR SOUTHEY, — You are acting kindly in your exertions for Chatterton's sister; but I doubt the success. Chatterton's or Rowley's poems were never popular. The very circumstance which made them so much talked of,

---

[1] This passage, which for some reason Cottle chose to omit, seems to imply that the second edition of the poems had not appeared by the beginning of June.

their *ancientness*, prevented them from being generally
read, in the degree, I mean, that Goldsmith's poems or
even Rogers' thing upon memory has been. The sale was
never very great. Secondly, the London Edition and the
Cambridge Edition, which are now both of them the
property of London booksellers, are still in hand, and
these booksellers will " hardly exert their interest for a
rival." *Thirdly, these are bad times.* Fourthly, all who
are sincerely zealous for Chatterton, or who from knowledge of her are interested in poor Mrs. Newton, will come
forwards first, and if others should drop in but slowly,
Mrs. Newton will either receive no benefit at all from
those her friends, or one so long procrastinated, from the
necessity of waiting for the complement of subscribers,
that it may at last come too late. For these reasons I am
almost inclined to think a *subscription* simply would be
better. It is unpleasant to cast a damp on anything;
but that benevolence alone is likely to be beneficent which
calculates. If, however, you continue to entertain higher
hopes than I, believe me, I will shake off my sloth, and
use my best muscles in gaining subscribers. I will certainly write a preliminary essay, and I will *attempt* to
write a poem on the life and death of Chatterton, but the
Monody *must not be reprinted*. Neither this nor the
Pixies' Parlour would have been in the second edition, but
for dear Cottle's solicitous importunity. Excepting the
last eighteen lines of the Monody, which, though deficient
in chasteness and severity of diction, breathe a pleasing
spirit of romantic feeling, there are not five lines in either
poem which might not have been written by a man who
had lived and died in the self-same St. Giles' cellar, in
which he had been first suckled by a drab with milk
and gin. The Pixies is the least disgusting, because the
subject leads you to expect nothing, but on a life and
death so full of heart-going *realities* as poor Chatterton's,
to find such shadowy nobodies as cherub-winged *Death*,

Trees of *Hope*, bare-bosomed *Affection* and simpering *Peace*, makes one's blood circulate like ipecacuanha. But so it is. A young man by strong feelings is impelled to write on a particular subject, and this is all his feelings do for him. They set him upon the business and then they leave him. He has such a high idea of what poetry ought to be, that he cannot conceive that such things as his natural emotions may be allowed to find a place in it; his learning therefore, his fancy, or rather conceit, and all his powers of buckram are put on the stretch. It appears to me that strong feeling is not so requisite to an author's being profoundly pathetic as taste and good sense.

Poor old Whag! his mother died of a dish of clotted cream, which my mother sent her as a present.

I rejoice that your poems are all sold. In the ballad of "Mary the Maid of the Inn," you have properly enough made the diction colloquial, but "*engages* the eye," applied to a gibbet, strikes me as *slipshoppish* from the unfortunate meaning of the word "engaging." Your praise of my Dedication [1] gave me great pleasure. From the ninth to the fourteenth the five lines are flat and prosish, and the versification ever and anon has too much of the rhyme couplet cadence, and the metaphor [2] on

---

[1] . . . Such, O my earliest friend!
Thy lot, and such thy brothers too enjoy.
At distance did ye climb life's upland road,
Yet cheered and cheering: now fraternal
    love
Hath drawn you to one centre.

Poetical Works, p. 81, l. 9–14.

[2] . . . and some most false,
False, and fair-foliaged as the Manchineel,
Have tempted me to slumber in their shade
E'en mid the storm; then breathing sub-
    tlest damp
Mixed their own venom with the rain from
    Heaven,
That I woke poisoned,

Poetical Works, p. 82, l. 25–30.

Compare Lamb's humorous reproach in a letter to Coleridge, September, 1797: "For myself I must spoil a little passage of Beaumont and Fletcher's to adapt it to my feelings: —

. . . I am prouder
That I was once your friend, tho' now forgot,
Than to have had another true to me.

"If you don't write to me now, as I told Lloyd, I shall get angry, and call you hard names — Manchineel, and I don't know what else." *Letters of Charles Lamb*, i. 83.

the diverse sorts of friendship is *hunted down*, but the poem is dear to me, and in point of taste I place it next to " Low was our pretty Cot," which I think the best of my poems.

I am as much a Pangloss as ever, only less contemptuous than I used to be, when I argue how unwise it is to feel contempt for anything.

I had been on a visit to Wordsworth's at Racedown, near Crewkerne, and I brought him and his sister back with me, and here I have *settled them*. By a combination of curious circumstances a gentleman's seat, with a park and woods, elegantly and completely furnished, with nine lodging rooms, three parlours, and a hall, in the most beautiful and romantic situation by the seaside, four miles from Stowey, — this we have got for Wordsworth at the *rent of twenty-three pounds a year, taxes included!* The park and woods are *his* for all purposes *he* wants them, and the large gardens are altogether and entirely his. Wordsworth is a very great man, the only man to whom *at all times* and *in all modes of excellence* I feel myself inferior, the only one, I mean, whom *I have yet met with*, for the London *literati* appear to me to be very much like little potatoes, that is, *no great things*, a compost of nullity and dullity.

Charles Lamb has been with me for a week.[1] He left me Friday morning. The second day after Wordsworth came to me, dear Sara accidentally emptied a skillet of boiling milk on my foot, which confined me during the whole time of C. Lamb's stay and still prevents me from all *walks* longer than a furlong. While Wordsworth, his sister, and Charles Lamb were out one evening, sitting in the arbour of T. Poole's garden[2] which communicates with

[1] Charles Lamb's visit to the cottage of Nether Stowey lasted from Friday, July 7, to Friday, July 14, 1797.

[2] According to local tradition, the lime-tree bower was at the back of the cottage, but according to this letter it was in Poole's garden.

mine I wrote these lines, with which I am pleased. (I
heard from C. Lamb of Favell and Le Grice.[1] Poor
Allen! I knew nothing of it.[2] As to Rough,[3] he is a
wonderful fellow ; and when I returned from the army,
cut me for a month, till he saw that other people *were as
much* attached as before.)

> Well, they are gone, and here must I remain,
> Lam'd by the scathe of fire, lonely and faint,
> This lime-tree bower my prison ! They, meantime
> My Friends,[4] whom I may never meet again,

From either spot the green ram-
parts of Stowey Castle and the
" airy ridge " of Dowseborough are
full in view.

[1] " He [Le Grice] and Favell . . .
wrote to the Duke of York, when
they were at college, for commis-
sions in the army. The Duke good-
naturedly sent them." *Autobiography of Leigh Hunt*, p. 72.

[2] Possibly he alludes to his ap-
pointment as deputy-surgeon to the
Second Royals, then stationed in
Portugal.

His farewell letter to Coleridge
(undated) has been preserved and
will be read with interest.

PORTSMOUTH.

MY BELOVED FRIEND, — Farewell ! I shall never think of you
but with tears of the tenderest affection. Our routes in life have
been so opposite, that for a long
time past there has not been that
intercourse between us which our
mutual affection would have otherwise occasioned. But at this serious moment, all your kindness and
love for me press upon my memory
with a weight of sensation I can
scarcely endure.

. . . .

You have heard of my destination,
I suppose. I am going to Portugal
to join the Second Royals, to which
I have been appointed Deputy-Surgeon. What fate is in reserve for
me I know not. I should be more
indifferent to my future lot, if it
were not for the hope of passing
many pleasant hours, in times to
come, in your society.

Adieu ! my dearest fellow. My
love to Mrs. C. Health and fraternity to young David.

Yours most affectionate,
R. ALLEN.

[3] A friend and fellow-collegian
of Christopher Wordsworth at Trinity College, Cambridge. He was a
member of the " Literary Society "
to which Coleridge, C. Wordsworth,
Le Grice, and others belonged. He
afterwards became a sergeant-at-
law. He was an intimate friend of
H. Crabb Robinson. See H. C.
Robinson's *Diary*, *passim*. See, too,
*Social Life at the English Universi-
ties*, by Christopher Wordsworth,
M. A., Fellow of Peterhouse, Cambridge, 1874, Appendix.

[4] Not, as has been supposed,

On springy [1] heath, along the hill-top edge
Wander delighted, and look down, perchance,
On that same rifted Dell, where many an ash
Twists its wild limbs beside the ferny [2] rock
Whose plumy ferns forever nod and drip,
Spray'd by the waterfall.   But chiefly thou
My gentle-hearted *Charles!* thou who had pin'd
And hunger'd after Nature many a year,
In the great City pent, winning thy way
With sad yet bowed soul, through evil and pain
And strange calamity!   Ah! slowly sink
Behind the western ridge, thou glorious Sun!
Shine in the slant heaven of the sinking orb,
Ye purple heath-flowers! richlier burn, ye clouds
Live in the yellow Light, ye distant groves!
Struck with joy's deepest calm, and gazing round
On [3] the wide view, may gaze till all doth seem
Less gross than bodily ; a living thing
That acts upon the mind, and with such hues
As clothe the Almighty Spirit, when He makes
Spirits perceive His presence !

                          A delight
Comes sudden on my heart, and I am glad
As I myself were there ! nor in the bower

Charles and Mary Lamb, but Wordsworth and his sister Dorothy. Mary Lamb was not and could not have been at that time one of the party. The version sent to Southey differs both from that printed in the *Annual Anthology* of 1800, and from a copy in a contemporary letter sent to C. Lloyd. It is interesting to note that the words, "My sister, and my friends," ll. 47 and 53, which gave place in the *Anthology* to the thrice-repeated, "My gentle-hearted Charles," appear, in a copy sent to Lloyd, as "My Sara and my friend." It was early days for him to address Dorothy Wordsworth as "My sister," but in forming friendships Coleridge did not "keep to the high road, but leaped over a gate and bounded" from acquaintance to intimacy. *Poetical Works*, p. 92. For version of "This Lime-Tree Bower my Prison," sent to C. Lloyd, see *Ibid.*, Editor's Note, p. 591.

[1] "Elastic, I mean." — S. T. C.

[2] "The ferns that grow in moist places grow five or six together, and form a complete 'Prince of Wales's Feathers,' — that is, plumy." — S. T. C.

[3] "You remember I am a *Berkleian*." — S. T. C.

Want I sweet sounds or pleasing shapes. I watch'd
The sunshine of each broad transparent leaf
Broke by the shadows of the leaf or stem
Which hung above it : and that walnut-tree
Was richly ting'd, and a deep radiance lay
Full on the ancient ivy, which usurps
Those fronting elms, and now with blackest mass
Makes their dark foliage gleam a lighter hue
Through the late twilight : and though the rapid bat
Wheels silent by, and not a swallow titters,
Yet still the solitary humble bee
Sings in the bean-flower ! Henceforth I shall know
That Nature ne'er deserts the wise and pure ;
No scene so narrow, but may well employ
Each faculty of sense, and keep the heart
Awake to Love and Beauty ! and sometimes
'T is well to be bereav'd of promised good,
That we may lift the soul and contemplate
With lively joy the joys we cannot share.
My Sister and my Friends ! when the last rook
Beat its straight path along the dusky air
Homewards, I bless'd it ! deeming its black wing
Cross'd like a speck the blaze of setting day
While ye stood gazing ; or when all was still,
Flew creaking o'er your heads, and had a charm
For you, my Sister and my Friends, to whom
No sound is dissonant which tells of Life.

I would make a shift by some means or other to visit
you, if I thought that you and Edith Southey would return with me. I think — indeed, I am almost certain —
that I could get a one-horse chaise free of all expense. I
have driven back Miss Wordsworth over forty miles of
execrable roads, and have been always very cautious, and
am now no inexpert whip. And Wordsworth, at whose
house I now am for change of air, has commissioned me
to offer you a suite of rooms at this place, which is called
" All-foxen ; " and so divine and wild is the country that

I am sure it would increase your stock of images, and three weeks' absence from Christchurch will endear it to you; and Edith Southey and Sara may not have another opportunity of seeing one another, and Wordsworth is very solicitous to know you, and Miss Wordsworth is a most exquisite young woman in her mind and heart. I pray you write me immediately, directing Stowey, near Bridgewater, as before.

God bless you and your affectionate

S. T. COLERIDGE.

LXXV. TO JOHN THELWALL.

Saturday morning [October 16], 1797.

My dear Thelwall, — I have just received your letter, having been absent a day or two, and have already, before I write to you, written to Dr. Beddoes. I would to Heaven it were in my power to serve you; but alas! I have neither money or influence, and I suppose that at last I must become a Unitarian minister, as a less evil than starvation. For I get nothing by literature. . . . You have my wishes and, what is very liberal in me for such an atheist reprobate, my prayers. I can *at times* feel strongly the beauties you describe, in themselves and for themselves; but more frequently *all things* appear *little*, all the knowledge that can be acquired child's play; the universe itself! what but an immense heap of *little* things? I can contemplate nothing but *parts*, and parts are all *little!* My mind feels as if it ached to behold and know something *great*, something *one* and *indivisible*. And it is only in the faith of that that rocks or waterfalls, mountains or caverns, give me the sense of sublimity or majesty! But in this faith *all things* counterfeit infinity.

> " Struck with the deepest calm of joy," [1] I stand
> Silent, with swimming sense; and gazing round

---

[1] " This Lime-Tree Bower," l. 38. *Poetical Works*, p. 93.

> On the wide landscape, gaze till all doth seem
> Less gross than bodily, a living Thing
> Which acts upon the mind and with such hues
> As clothe th' Almighty Spirit, where He makes
> Spirits perceive His presence ! . . .

It is but seldom that I raise and spiritualize my intellect to this height; and at other times I adopt the Brahmin creed, and say, " It is better to sit than to stand, it is better to lie than to sit, it is better to sleep than to wake, but Death is the best of all ! "   I should much wish, like the Indian Vishnu, to float about along an infinite ocean cradled in the flower of the Lotus, and wake once in a million years for a few minutes just to know that I was going to sleep a million years more.   I have put this feeling in the mouth of Alhadra, my Moorish Woman.   She is going by moonlight to the house of Velez, where the band turn off to wreak their vengeance on Francesco, but

> She moved steadily on,
> Unswerving from the path of her resolve.

A Moorish priest, who has been with her and then left her to seek the men, had just mentioned the owl, " Its note comes dreariest in the fall of the year."   This dwells on her mind, and she bursts into this soliloquy : —

> The [1] hanging woods, that touch'd by autumn seem'd
> As they were blossoming hues of fire and gold, —
> The hanging woods, most lovely in decay,
> The many clouds, the sea. the rock, the sands,
> Lay in the silent moonshine ; and the owl,
> (Strange ! very strange !) the scritch owl only waked,
> Sole voice, sole eye of all that world of beauty !
> Why such a thing am I ?   Where are these men ?
> I need the sympathy of human faces
> To beat away this deep contempt for all things,
> Which quenches my revenge.   Oh ! would to Alla

[1] "Osorio," Act V., Sc. 1, l. 39. *Poetical Works*, p. 507.

The raven and the sea-mew were appointed
To bring me food, or rather that my soul
Could drink in life from universal air!
It were a lot divine in some small skiff,
Along some ocean's boundless solitude,
To float for ever with a careless course,
And think myself the only being alive!

I do not wonder that your poem procured you kisses
and hospitality. It is indeed a very sweet one, and I have
not only admired your genius more, but I have loved *you*
better since I have read it. Your sonnet (as you call it,
and, being a freeborn Briton, who shall prevent you from
calling twenty-five blank verse lines a sonnet, if you have
taken a bloody resolution so to do) — your sonnet I am
much pleased with; but the epithet " downy " is probably
more applicable to Susan's upper lip than to her bosom,
and a mother is so holy and divine a being that I cannot
endure any *corporealizing* epithets to be applied to her
or any body of her — besides, damn epithets! The last
line and a half I suppose to be miswritten. What can
be the meaning of " Or scarce one leaf to cheer," etc.?
" Cornelian virtues " — pedantry! The " melancholy
fiend," villainous in itself, and inaccurate; it ought to
be the "fiend that makes melancholy." I should have
written it thus (or perhaps something better), " but with
matron cares *drives away heaviness;* " and in your similes,
etc., etc., a little *compression* would make it a beautiful
poem. *Study compression!*

I presume you mean decorum by *Harum* Dick. An
affected fellow at Bridgwater called truces " trusses." I
told him I admired his pronunciation, for that lately they
had been found " to suspend ruptures without curing
them."

There appeared in the " Courier " the day before yesterday a very sensible vindication of the conduct of the
Directory. Did you see it?

Your news respecting Mrs. E. did not surprise me. I saw it even from the first week I was at Darley. As to the other event, our non-settlement at Darley, I suspect, had little or nothing to do with it — but the *cause* of our non-settlement there might perhaps — O God! O God! I wish (but what is the use of *wishing?*) — I wish that Walter Evans may have talent enough to appreciate Mrs. Evans, but I suspect his intellect is not tall enough even to measure hers.

Hartley is well, and *will not* walk or run, having discovered the art of crawling with wonderful ease and rapidity. Wordsworth and his sister are well. I want to see your wife. God bless her! . . .

Oh, my Tragedy! it is finished, transcribed, and to be sent off to-day; but I have no hope of its success, or even of its being acted.

God bless, etc., .

S. T. COLERIDGE.

MR. JOHN THELWALL, Derby.

LXXVI. TO THE SAME.

Saturday morning. Bridgwater.
[Autumn, 1797.]

MY DEAR THELWALL, — Yesterday morning I miss'd the coach, and was ill and could not walk. This morning the coach was completely full, but I was not ill, and so did walk; and here I am, footsore very, and weary somewhat. With regard to the business, I mentioned it at Howell's; but I perceive he is absolutely powerless. Chubb I would have called on, but there are the Assizes, and I find he is surrounded in his own house by a mob of visitors whom it is scarcely possible for him to leave, long enough at least for the conversation I want with him. I will write him to-morrow morning, and shall have an answer the same day, which I will transmit to you on Monday, but you *cannot* receive it till Tuesday night. If, therefore, you leave Swansea before that time, or, in case of accident, before Wednesday night, leave directions with the postmaster to have your letter forwarded.

I go for Stowey immediately, which will make my walk forty-one miles. The Howells desire to be remembered to you kindly.

I am sad at heart about you on many accounts, but chiefly anxious for this present business. The aristocrats seem to persecute *even Wordsworth*.[1] But we will at least not yield without a struggle; and if I cannot get you near me, it shall not be for want of a trial on my part. But perhaps I am passing the worn-out spirits of a *fag*-walk for the real aspect of the business.

God love you, and believe me affectionately your friend,

S. T. COLERIDGE.

MR. THELWALL,
To be left at the Post Office, Swansea,
    Glamorganshire.

LXXVII. TO THE SAME.

[Autumn, 1797.]

DEAR THELWALL, — This is the first hour that I could write to you anything decisive. I have received an answer from Chubb, intimating that he will undertake the office of procuring you a cottage, provided it was thought *right* that you should settle *here;* but this (that is the whole difficulty) he left for T. Poole and me to settle, and he acquainted Poole with this determination. Consequently,

---

[1] Thelwall's visit brought Coleridge and Wordsworth into trouble. At the instance of a "titled Dogberry," Sir Philip Hale of Cannington, a government spy was sent to watch the movements of the supposed conspirators, and, a more serious matter, Mrs. St. Albyn, the owner of Alfoxden, severely censured her tenant for having sublet the house to Wordsworth. See letter of explanation and remonstrance from Poole to Mrs. St. Albyn, September 16, 1797. *Thomas Poole and his Friends*, i. 240. See, too, Cottle's *Early Recollections*, i. 319, and for apocryphal anecdotes about the spy, etc., *Biographia Literaria*, cap. x.

the whole returns to its former situation; and the hope
which I had entertained, that you could have settled without any the remotest interference of Poole, *has vanished.*
To such interference on his part there are insuperable
difficulties: the whole malignity of the aristocrats will
converge to him as to the one point; his tranquillity will
be perpetually interrupted, his business and his credit
hampered and distressed by vexatious calumnies, the ties
of relationship weakened, perhaps broken; and, lastly, his
poor old mother made miserable — the pain of the stone
aggravated by domestic calamity and quarrels betwixt her
son and those neighbours with whom and herself there
have been peace and love for these fifty years. Very
great odium T. Poole incurred by bringing *me* here. My
peaceable manners and known attachment to Christianity had almost worn it away when Wordsworth came,
and he, likewise by T. Poole's agency, settled here. You
cannot conceive the tumult, calumnies, and apparatus of
threatened persecutions which this event has occasioned
round about us. If *you*, too, should come, I am afraid
that even riots, and dangerous riots, might be the consequence. Either of us separately would perhaps be toler-
ated, but *all three* together, what can it be less than plot
and damned conspiracy — a school for the propagation of
Demagogy and Atheism? And it deserves examination,
whether or no as moralists we should be justified in haz-
arding the certain evil of calling forth malignant passions
for the contingent good, that might result from our living
in the same neighbourhood? Add to which, that in point
of the *public interest*, we must take into the balance the
Stowey Benefit Club. Of the present utility of this T.
Poole thinks highly; of its possible utility, very, very highly
indeed; but the interests, nay, perhaps the existence of
this club, is interwoven with his character as a peaceable
and *undesigning* man; certainly, any future and greater
excellence which he hopes to realize in and through the

society will vanish like a dream of the morning. If, therefore, you can get the land and cottage near Bath of which you spoke to me, I would advise it on many accounts ; but if you still see the arguments on the other side in a stronger light than those which I have stated, come, but not yet. Come in two or three months — take lodgings at Bridgwater — familiarise the people to your name and appearance, and, when the *monstrosity* of the thing is gone off, and the people shall have begun to consider you as a man whose mouth won't eat them, and whose pocket is better adapted for a bundle of sonnets than the transportation or ambush place of a French army, then you may take a house ; but indeed (I say it with a very sad but a very clear conviction), at *present* I see that much evil and little good would result from your settling here.

I am unwell. This business has, indeed, preyed much on my spirits, and I have suffered for you more than I hope and trust you will suffer yourself.

God love you and yours.

S. T. COLERIDGE.

Mr. Thelwall,
To be left at the Post Office, Swansea, Glamorganshire.

LXXVIII. TO WILLIAM WORDSWORTH.

Tuesday morning, January, 1798.

My dear Wordsworth, — You know, of course, that I have accepted the magnificent liberality of Josiah and Thomas Wedgwood.[1] I accepted it on the presumption

---

[1] Their proposal was to settle on Coleridge "an annuity for life of £150, to be regularly paid by us, no condition whatever being annexed to it." See letter of Josiah Wedgwood to Coleridge, dated January 10, 1798. *Thomas Poole and his Friends*, i. 258. An unpublished letter from Thelwall to Dr. Crompton dated Llyswen, March 3, 1798, contains one of several announcements of "his good fortune," made by Coleridge at the time to his numerous friends.

To Dr. Crompton, Eton House, Nr. Liverpool.
Llyswen, 3d March, 1798.
I am surprised you have not heard the particulars of Coleridge's good

that I had talents, honesty, and propensities to perse-
verant effort. If I have hoped wisely concerning myself,
I have acted justly. But dismissing severer thoughts,
believe me, my dear fellow! that of the pleasant ideas
which accompanied this unexpected event, it was not the
least pleasant, nor did it pass through my mind the last
in the procession, that I should at least be able to trace
the spring and early summer at Alfoxden with you, and
that wherever your after residence may be, it is probable
that you will be within the reach of my tether, lengthened as it now is. The country round Shrewsbury is
rather tame. My imagination has clothed it with all its
summer attributes; but I still can see in it no possibility
beyond that of *beauty*. The Society here were sufficiently
eager to have me as their minister, and, I think, would

fortune. It is not a legacy, but a
gift. The circumstances are thus
expressed by himself in a letter of
the 30th January: "I received an invitation from Shrewsbury to be the
Unitarian minister, and at the same
time an order for £100 from Thomas
and Josiah Wedgwood. I accepted
the former and returned the latter
in a long letter explanatory of my
motive, and went off to Shrewsbury,
where they were on the point of
electing me unanimously and with
unusual marks of affection, where I
received an offer from T. and J.
Wedgwood of an annuity of £150
to be legally settled on me. Astonished, agitated, and feeling as I
could not help feeling, I accepted
the offer in the same worthy spirit,
I hope, in which it was made, and
this morning I have returned from
Shrewsbury." This letter was written in a great hurry in Cottle's shop
in Bristol, in answer to one which a
friend of mine had left for him there,
on his way from Llyswen to Gosport,
and you will perceive that it has a
dash of the obscure not uncommon
to the rapid genius of C. Whether
he did or did not accept the cure of
Unitarian Souls, it is difficult from
the account to make out. I suppose
he did not, for I know his aversion
to preaching God's holy word for
hire, which is seconded not a little, I
expect, by his repugnance to all regular routine and application. I also
hope he did not, for I know he cannot preach very often without travelling from the pulpit to the Tower.
Mount him but upon his darling
hobby-horse, " the republic of God's
own making," and away he goes like
hey-go-mad, spattering and splash-
ing through thick and thin and scat-
tering more *levelling* sedition and
constructive treason than poor Gilly
or myself ever dreamt of. He
promised to write to me again in a
few days; but, though I answered his
letter directly, I have not heard from
him since.

have behaved kindly and respectfully, but I perceive
clearly that without great courage and perseverance in the
use of the monosyllable *No!* I should have been plunged in
a very Maelstrom of visiting — whirled round, and round,
and round, never changing yet always moving.   Visiting
with all its pomp and vanities is the mania of the place ;
and many of the congregation are both rich and expensive.
I met a young man, a Cambridge undergraduate.   Talking of plays, etc., he told me that an acquaintance of his
was printing a translation of one of Kotzebue's tragedies,
entitled, " Benyowski." [1]   The name startled me, and upon
examination I found that the story of my " Siberian
Exiles " has been already dramatized.   If Kotzebue has
exhibited no greater genius in it than in his negro slaves,
I shall consider this as an unlucky circumstance; but the
young man speaks enthusiastically of its merits.   I have
just read the " Castle Spectre," and shall bring it home
with me.   I will begin with its defects, in order that my
" But " may have a charitable transition.   1. Language ;
2. Character ; 3. Passion ; 4. Sentiment ; 5. Conduct.
(1.) Of styles, some are pleasing durably and on reflection, some only in transition, and some are not pleasing at
all ; and to this latter class belongs the " Castle Spectre." [2]
There are no felicities in the humorous passages ; and in
the serious ones it is Schiller Lewis-ized, that is, a flat,
flabby, unimaginative bombast oddly sprinkled with colloquialisms.   (2.) No character at all.   The author in a
postscript lays claim to *novelty* in *one* of his characters,
that of Hassan.   Now Hassan is a negro, who *had* a
warm and benevolent heart; but having been kidnapped
from his country and barbarously used by the Christians,
becomes a misanthrope.   This is all !!   (3.) Passion —

[1] *Count Benyowsky, or the Conspiracy of Kamtschatka, a Tragi-
comedy.* Translated from the German by the Rev. W. Render, teacher
of the German Language in the University of Cambridge. Cambridge,
1798.

[2] Coleridge's copy of Monk Lewis'
play is dated January 20, 1798.

horror! agonizing pangs of conscience! Dreams full of
hell, serpents, and skeletons; starts and attempted mur-
ders, etc., but positively, not *one* line that marks even a
superficial knowledge of human feelings could I discover.
(4.) Sentiments are moral and humorous. There is a
book called the "Frisky Songster," at the end of which
are two chapters: the first containing *frisky* toasts and
sentiments, the second, "*Moral* Toasts," and from these
chapters I suspect Mr. Lewis has stolen all his sentimen-
tality, moral and humorous. A very fat friar, renowned
for gluttony and lubricity, furnishes abundance of jokes
(all of them abdominal *vel si quid infra*), jokes that would
have stunk, had they been fresh, and alas! they have the
very *sæva mephitis* of *antiquity* on them. *But* (5.) the
Conduct of the Piece is, I think, *good;* except that the
first act is *wholly* taken up with explanation and narration. This play proves how accurately you conjectured
concerning *theatric* merit. The merit of the "Castle
Spectre" consists wholly in its *situations*. These are all
borrowed and all absolutely *pantomimical;* but they are
admirably managed for stage effect. There is not much
bustle, but *situations* for ever. The whole plot, machinery,
and incident are borrowed. The play is a mere patch-
work of plagiarisms; but they are very well worked up,
and for stage effect make an excellent *whole*. There is a
pretty little ballad-song introduced, and Lewis, I think has
great and peculiar excellence in these compositions. The
simplicity and naturalness is his own, and not imitated;
for it is made to subsist in congruity with a language
perfectly modern, the language of his own times, in the
same way that the language of the writer of "Sir
Cauline" was the language of *his* times. This, I think,
a rare merit: at least, I find, *I* cannot attain this innocent nakedness, except by *assumption*. I resemble the
Duchess of Kingston, who masqueraded in the character
of "Eve before the Fall," in flesh-coloured Silk. This

play struck me with utter hopelessness. It would [be easy] to produce these situations, but not in a play so [constructed] as to admit the permanent and closest beauties of style, passion, and character. To admit panto-mimic tricks, the plot itself must be pantomimic. Harle-quin cannot be had unaccompanied by the Fool.

I hope to be with you by the middle of next week. I must stay over next Sunday, as Mr. Row is obliged to go to Bristol to seek a house. He and his family are honest, sensible, pleasant people. My kind love to Dorothy, and believe me, with affectionate esteem, yours sincerely,

S. T. COLERIDGE.[1]

LXXIX.   TO JOSEPH COTTLE.

Stowey, March 8, 1798.

My DEAR COTTLE, — I have been confined to my bed for some days through a fever occasioned by the stump of a tooth. . . . I thank you, my dear friend, for your late kindness, and in a few weeks will either repay you in money or by verses, as you like. With regard to Lloyd's verses, it is curious that *I* should be applied to to be " per-suaded to resign, and in hope that I might " *consent* to *give up* a number of poems which were published at the earnest request of the author, who assured me that the circum-stance was " of no trivial import to his happiness." Times change and people change; but let us keep our souls in quietness! I have no objection to any disposal of C. Lloyd's poems, except that of their being republished with mine. The motto which I had prefixed, " Duplex," etc.,[2] from Groscollius, has placed me in a ridiculous situation; but it was a foolish and presumptuous start of affection-

---

[1] The following memoranda, pre-sumably in Wordsworth's handwrit-ing, have been scribbled on the outside sheet of the letter: "Tea — Thread fine — needles Silks — Strainer for starch — Mustard — Ba-sil's shoes — Shoe horn.

" The sun's course is short, but clear and blue the sky."

[2] " Duplex nobis vinculum, et ami-citiæ et similium junctarumque Ca-mœnarum; quod utinam neque mors solvat, neque temporis longinquitas."

ateness, and I am not unwilling to incur punishments due
to my folly. By past experiences we build up our moral
being. How comes it that I have never heard from dear
Mr. Estlin, my fatherly and brotherly friend? This idea
haunted me through my sleepless nights, till my sides were
sore in turning from one to the other, as if I were hoping
to turn from the idea. The Giant Wordsworth — God
love him! Even when I speak in the terms of admiration due to his intellect, I fear lest those terms should
keep out of sight the amiableness of his manners. . . .
He has written more than 1,200 lines of a blank verse,
superior, I hesitate not to aver, to anything in our language which any way resembles it. Poole (whom I feel
so consolidated with myself that I seem to have no occasion to speak of him out of myself) thinks of it as likely
to benefit mankind much more than anything Wordsworth
has yet written. With regard to my poems, I shall prefix the "Maid of Orleans," 1,000 lines, and three blank
verse poems, making all three about 200, and I shall utterly leave out perhaps a larger quantity of lines; and I
should think it would answer to you in a pecuniary way to
print the third edition humbly and cheaply. My alterations in the "Religious Musings" will be considerable, and
will lengthen the poem. Oh, Poole desires you *not* to
mention his house to any one unless you hear from him
again, as since I have been writing a thought has struck
us of letting it to an inhabitant of the village, which we
should prefer, as we should be certain that his manners
would be severe, inasmuch as he would be a Stow-ic.

God bless you and

S. T. C.

LXXX. TO THE REV. GEORGE COLERIDGE.

April, 1798.

MY DEAR BROTHER, — An illness, which confined me
to my bed, prevented me from returning an immediate

answer to your kind and interesting letter. My indisposition originated in the stump of a tooth over which some matter had formed; this affected my eye, my eye my stomach, my stomach my head, and the consequence was a general fever, and the sum of pain was considerably increased by the vain attempts of our surgeon to extract the offending member. Laudanum gave me repose, not sleep; but you, I believe, know how divine that repose is, what a spot of enchantment, a green spot of fountain and flowers and trees in the very heart of a waste of sands! God be praised, the matter has been absorbed; and I am now recovering apace, and enjoy that newness of sensation from the fields, the air, and the sun which makes convalescence almost repay one for disease. I collect from your letter that our opinions and feelings on political subjects are more nearly alike than you imagine them to be. Equally with you (and perhaps with a deeper conviction, for my belief is founded on actual experience), equally with you I deprecate the moral and intellectual habits of those men, both in England and France, who have modestly assumed to themselves the exclusive title of Philosophers and Friends of Freedom. I think them at least *as* distant from greatness as from goodness. If I know my own opinions, they are utterly untainted with French metaphysics, French politics, French ethics, and French theology. As to *the Rulers* of France, I see in their views, speeches, and actions nothing that distinguishes them to their advantage from other animals of the same species. History has taught me that rulers are much the same in all ages, and under all forms of government; they are as bad as they dare to be. The vanity of ruin and the curse of blindness have clung to them like an hereditary leprosy. Of the French Revolution I can give my thoughts most adequately in the words of Scripture: "A great and strong wind rent the mountains, and brake in pieces the rocks before the Lord; but the Lord was not in the wind; and

after the wind an earthquake; and after the earthquake a
fire; and the Lord was not in the fire;" and now (believing that no calamities are permitted but as the means of
good) I wrap my face in my mantle and wait, with a subdued and patient thought, expecting to hear "the still
small voice" which is of God.   In America (I have received my information from unquestionable authority) the
morals and domestic habits of the people are daily deteri-
orating; and one good consequence which I expect from
revolution is that individuals will see the necessity of individual effort; that they will act as good Christians, rather
than as citizens and electors; and so by degrees will purge
off that error, which to me appears as wild and more pernicious than the πάγχρυσον and panacea of the alchemists,
the error of attributing to governments a talismanic influence over our virtues and our happiness, as if governments
were not rather effects than causes.   It is true that all effects react and become causes, and so it must be in some
degree with governments; but there are other agents which
act more powerfully because by a nigher and more continuous agency, and it remains true that governments are
more the *effect* than the cause of that which we are.   Do
not therefore, my brother, consider me as an enemy to
government and its rulers, or as one who says they are
evil.   I do not say so.   In my opinion it were a species of
blasphemy!   Shall a nation of drunkards presume to bab-
ble against sickness and the headache?   I regard governments as I regard the abscesses produced by certain fevers
— they are necessary consequences of the disease, and by
their pain they increase the disease; but yet they are in
the wisdom and goodness of Nature, and not only are they
physically necessary as effects, but also as causes they are
morally necessary in order to prevent the utter dissolution
of the patient.   But what should we think of a man who
expected an absolute cure from an ulcer that only prevented his dying.   Of guilt I say nothing, but I believe

most steadfastly in original sin; that from our mothers'
wombs our understandings are darkened; and even where
our understandings are in the light, that our organization
is depraved and our volitions imperfect; and we sometimes see the good without wishing to attain it, and of-
tener *wish* it without the energy that wills and performs.
And for this inherent depravity I believe that the *spirit*
of the Gospel is the sole cure; but permit me to add, that
I look for the spirit of the Gospel "neither in the mountain, nor at Jerusalem."

You think, my brother, that there can be but two *parties* at present, for the Government and against the Government. It may be so. I am of no party. It is true I
think the present Ministry weak and unprincipled men;
but I would not with a safe conscience vote for their
removal; I could point out no substitutes. I think very
seldom on the subject; but as far as I have thought, I am
inclined to consider the aristocrats as the most respectable of our three factions, because they are more decorous.
The Opposition and the Democrats are not only vicious,
they wear the *filthy garments* of vice.

> He that takes
> Deep in his soft credulity the stamp
> Design'd by loud declaimers on the part
> Of liberty, themselves the slaves of lust,
> Incurs derision for his easy faith
> And lack of knowledge, and with cause enough:
> For when was public virtue to be found
> Where private was not? Can he love the whole
> Who loves no part? He be a *nation's* friend,
> Who is, in truth, the friend of *no* man there?
> Can he be strenuous in his country's cause
> Who slights the charities, for whose dear sake
> That country, if at all, must be belov'd?
> COWPER.[1]

I am prepared to suffer without discontent the consequences of my follies and mistakes; and unable to con-

[1] *The Task*, Book V., "A Winter's Morning Walk."

ceive how that which I am of Good could have been without that which I have been of evil, it is withheld from me to regret anything. I therefore consent to be deemed a Democrat and a Seditionist. A man's character follows him long after he has ceased to deserve it; but I have snapped my squeaking baby-trumpet of sedition, and the fragments lie scattered in the lumber-room of penitence. I wish to be a good man and a Christian, but I am no Whig, no Reformist, no Republican, and because of the multitude of fiery and undisciplined spirits that lie in wait against the public quiet under these titles, because of them I chiefly accuse the present ministers, to whose folly I attribute, in a great measure, their increased and increasing numbers. You think differently, and if I were called upon by you to prove my assertions, although I imagine I could make them appear plausible, yet I should feel the insufficiency of my data. The Ministers may have had in their possession facts which alter the whole state of the argument, and make my syllogisms fall as flat as a baby's card-house. And feeling this, my brother! I have for some time past withdrawn myself totally from the consideration of *immediate causes*, which are infinitely complex and uncertain, to muse on fundamental and general causes the " causæ causarum." I devote myself to such works as encroach not on the anti-social passions — in poetry, to elevate the imagination and set the affections in right tune by the beauty of the inanimate impregnated as with a living soul by the presence of life — in prose to the seeking with patience and a slow, very slow mind, "Quid sumus, et quidnam victuri gignimus," — what our faculties are and what they are capable of becoming. I love fields and woods and mountains with almost a visionary fondness. And because I have found benevolence and quietness growing within me as that fondness has increased, therefore I should wish to be the means of implanting it in others, and to destroy the

bad passions not by combating them but by keeping them
in inaction.

> Not useless do I deem
> These shadowy sympathies with things that hold
> An inarticulate Language; for the Man —
> Once taught to love such objects as excite
> No morbid passions, no disquietude,
> No vengeance, and no hatred — needs must feel
> The joy of that pure principle of love
> So deeply, that, unsatisfied with aught
> Less pure and exquisite, he cannot choose
> But seek for objects of a kindred love
> In fellow-nature and a kindred joy.
> Accordingly he by degrees perceives
> His feelings of aversion softened down;
> A holy tenderness pervade his frame!
> His sanity of reason not impair'd,
> Say, rather, that his thoughts now flowing clear
> From a clear fountain flowing, he looks round,
> He seeks for good; and finds the good he seeks.
>   WORDSWORTH.[1]

I have laid down for myself two maxims, and, what is
more I am in the habit of regulating myself by them.
With regard to others, I never controvert opinions except
after some intimacy, and when alone with the person, and
at the happy time when we both seem awake to our own
fallibility, and then I rather state my reasons than argue
against his.   In general conversation to find out the
opinions common to us, or at least the subjects on which
difference of opinion creates no uneasiness, such as
novels, poetry, natural scenery, local anecdotes, and (in a
serious mood and with serious men) the general evidences
of our religion.   With regard to myself, it is my habit,
on whatever subject I think, to endeavour to discover all
the good that has resulted from it, that does result, or
that can result.   To this I bind down my mind, and after
long meditation in this tract slowly and gradually make

---

[1] A later version of these lines is   fourth book of "The Excursion."
to be found at the close of the   Works of Wordsworth, 1889, p. 467.

up my opinions on the quantity and nature of the evil. I consider this as the most important rule for the regulation of the intellect and the affections, as the only means of preventing the passions from turning reason into a hired advocate. I thank you for your kindness, and propose in a short time to walk down to you : but my wife must forego the thought, as she is within five or six weeks of lying-in. She and my child, whose name is David Hartley, are remarkably well. You will give my duty to my mother, and love to my brothers, to Mrs. S. and G. Coleridge.

Excuse my desultory style and illegible scrawl, for I have written you a long letter, you see, and am in truth too weary to write a fair copy of it, or rearrange my ideas, and I am anxious you should know me as I am.

God bless you, from your affectionate brother,

S. T. COLERIDGE.

LXXXI. TO REV. J. P. ESTLIN.[1]

May [? 1798].

MY DEAR FRIEND, — I write from Cross, to which place I accompanied Mr. Wordsworth, who will give you this

[1] In the series of letters to Dr. Estlin, contributed to the privately printed volumes of the Philobiblon Society, the editor, Mr. Henry A. Bright, dates this letter *May* (? 1797). A comparison with a second letter to Estlin. dated May 14, 1798 (Letter LXXXII.), with a letter to Poole, dated May 28, 1798 (Letter LXXXIV.), with a letter to Charles Lamb belonging to the spring of 1798 (Letter LXXXV.), and with an entry in Dorothy Wordsworth's journal for May 16, 1798, affords convincing proof that the date of the letter should be May. 1798.

The MS. note of November 10, 1810, to which a previous reference has been made, connects a serious quarrel with Lloyd, and consequent distress of mind, with the retirement to "the lonely farm-house," and a first recourse to opium. If, as the letters intimate, these events must be assigned to May, 1798, it follows that "Kubla Khan" was written at the same time, and not, as Coleridge maintained in the Preface of 1816, "in the summer of 1797."

It would, indeed, have been altogether miraculous if, before he had written a line of "Christabel," or "The Ancient Mariner," either in an actual dream, or a dreamlike reverie, it had been "given to him" to divine the enchanting images of "Kubla Khan," or attune his mysterious vision to consummate melody.

letter. We visited Cheddar, but his main business was to
bring back poor Lloyd, whose infirmities have been made
the instruments of another man's darker passions. But
Lloyd (as we found by a letter that met us in the road)
is off for Birmingham. Wordsworth proceeds, lest possibly Lloyd may not be gone, and likewise to see his own
Bristol friends, as he is so near them. I have now known
him a year and some months, and my admiration, I might
say my awe, of his intellectual powers has increased even
to this hour, and (what is of more importance) he is a
tried good man. On one subject we are habitually silent ;
we found our data dissimilar, and never renewed the subject. It is his practice and almost his nature to convey
all the truth he knows without any attack on what he sup-
poses falsehood, if that falsehood be interwoven with virtues or happiness. He loves and venerates Christ and
Christianity. I wish he did more, but it were wrong indeed if an incoincidence with one of our wishes altered
our respect and affection to a man of whom we are, as it
were, instructed by one great Master to say that not being
against us he is for us. His genius is most *apparent* in
poetry, and rarely, except to me in *tête-à-tête*, breaks forth
in conversational eloquence. My best and most affectionate wishes attend Mrs. Estlin and your little ones, and believe me, with filial and fraternal friendship, your grateful

S. T. COLERIDGE.

REV. J. P. ESTLIN,
    St. Michael's Hill, Bristol.

LXXXII. TO THE SAME.

Monday, May 14, 1798.

MY DEAR FRIEND, — I ought to have written to you
before ; and have done very wrong in not writing. But I
have had many sorrows and some that bite deep ; calumny
and ingratitude from men who have been fostered in the
bosom of my confidence ! I pray God that I may sanctify

these events by forgiveness and a peaceful spirit full of love. This morning, half-past one, my wife was safely delivered of a fine boy;[1] she had a remarkably good time, better if possible than her last, and both she and the child are as well as can be. By the by, it is only three in the morning now. I walked in to Taunton and back again, and performed the divine services for Dr. Toulmin. I suppose you must have heard that his daughter, in a melancholy derangement, suffered herself to be swallowed up by the tide on the sea-coast between Sidmouth and Bere. These events cut cruelly into the hearts of old men; but the good Dr. Toulmin bears it like the true practical Christian, — there is indeed a tear in his eye, but *that* eye is lifted up to the Heavenly Father. I have been too neglectful of practical religion — I mean, actual and stated prayer, and a regular perusal of scripture as a morning and evening duty. May God grant me grace to amend this error, for it is a grievous one! Conscious of frailty I almost wish (I say it confidentially to you) that I had become a stated minister, for indeed I find true joy after a sincere prayer; but for want of habit my mind wanders, and I cannot *pray* as often as I ought. Thanksgiving is pleasant in the performance; but prayer and distinct confession I find most serviceable to my spiritual health when I can do it. But though all my doubts are done away, though Christianity is my *passion*, it is too much my *intellectual* passion, and therefore will do me but little good in the hour of temptation and calamity.

My love to Mrs. E. and the dear little ones, and ever, O ever, believe me, with true affection and gratitude,

        Your filial friend,   S. T. COLERIDGE.

[1] Berkeley Coleridge, born May 14, 1798, died February 10, 1799.

LXXXIII. TO THOMAS POOLE.

Monday, May 14, 1798.
Morning, 10 o'clock.

My DEAREST FRIEND, — I have been sitting many minutes with my pen in my hand, full of prayers and wishes for you, and the house of affliction in which you have so trying a part to sustain — but I know not what to *write*. May God support you! May he restore your brother — but above all, I pray that he will make us able to cry out with a fervent sincerity : Thy will be done! I have had lately some sorrows that have cut more deeply into my heart than they ought to have done, and I have found religion, and *commonplace religion* too, my restorer and my comfort, giving me gentleness and calmness and dignity! Again and again, may God be with you, my best, dear friend! and believe me, my Poole! dearer, to my understanding and affections unitedly, than all else in the world!

It is almost painful and a thing of fear to tell you that I have another boy; it will bring upon your mind the too affecting circumstance of poor Mrs. Richard Poole! The prayers which I have offered for her have been a relief to my own mind; I would that they could have been a consolation to her. Scripture seems to teach us that our fervent prayers are not without efficacy, even for others ; and though my reason is perplexed, yet my internal feelings impel me to a humble faith, that it is possible and consistent with the divine attributes.

Poor Dr. Toulmin! he bears his calamity like one in whom a faith through Jesus is the *Habit* of the whole man, of his affections still more than of his convictions. The loss of a dear child in so frightful a way cuts cruelly with an old man, but though there is a tear and an anguish in his eye, that eye is raised to heaven.

Sara was safely delivered at half past one this morning

— the boy is already almost as large as Hartley. She had an astonishingly good time, better if possible than her last ; and excepting her weakness, is as well as ever. The child is strong and shapely, and has the paternal beauty in his upper lip. God be praised for all things.

Your affectionate and entire friend,

S. T. COLERIDGE.

LXXXIV. TO THE SAME.

Sunday evening [May 20, 1798].

MY DEAREST POOLE, — I was all day yesterday in a distressing perplexity whether or no it would be wise or consolatory for me to call at your house, or whether I should write to your mother, as a Christian friend, or whether it would not be better to wait for the exhaustion of that grief which must have its way.

So many unpleasant and shocking circumstances have happened to me in my immediate knowledge within the last fortnight, that I am in a nervous state, and the most trifling thing makes me weep. Poor Richard ! May Providence heal the wounds which it hath seen good to inflict !

Do you wish me to see you to-day ? Shall I call on you ? Shall I stay with you? or had I better leave you uninterrupted ? In all your sorrows as in your joys, I am, indeed, my dearest Poole, a true and faithful sharer !

May God bless and comfort you all !

S. T. COLERIDGE.

LXXXV. TO CHARLES LAMB.[1]

[Spring of 1798.]

DEAR LAMB, — Lloyd has informed me through Miss Wordsworth that you intend no longer to correspond with

[1] The original MS. of this letter, which was preserved by Coleridge, is, doubtless, a copy of that sent by post. Besides this, only three of Coleridge's letters to Lamb have been preserved, — the " religious letter "

me. This has given me little pain; not that I do not love
and esteem you, but on the contrary because I am confident that your intentions are pure. You are performing
what you deem a duty, and humanly speaking have that
merit which can be derived from the performance of a
painful duty. Painful, for you would not without struggles abandon me in behalf of a man [1] who, wholly ignorant
of all but your name, became attached to you in consequence of my attachment, caught *his* from *my* enthusiasm,
and learned to love you at my fireside, when often while I
have been sitting and talking of your sorrows and afflictions I have stopped my conversations and lifted up wet
eyes and prayed for you. No! I am confident that
although you do not think as a wise man, you feel as a
good man.

From you I have received little pain, because for you
I suffer little alarm. I cannot say this for your friend;
it appears to me evident that his feelings are vitiated,
and that his ideas are in their combination merely the
creatures of those feelings. I have received letters from
him, and the best and kindest wish which, as a Christian,
I can offer in return is that he may feel remorse.

Some brief resentments rose in my mind, but they did
not remain there; for I began to think almost immediately, and my resentments vanished. There has resulted
only a sort of fantastic scepticism concerning my own
consciousness of my own rectitude. As dreams have impressed on him the sense of reality, my sense of reality
may be but a dream. From his letters it is plain that
he has mistaken the heat and bustle and swell of self-
justification for the approbation of his conscience. I am
certain that *this* is not the case with me, but the human
heart is so wily and inventive that possibly it may be

of 1796, a letter concerning the quarrel with Wordsworth, of May, 1812
[Letter CLXXXIV.], and one written in later life (undated, on the par-

ticulars of Hood's *Odes to Great
People*).

[1] Charles Lloyd.

cheating me, who am an older warrior, with some newer stratagem. When I wrote to you that my Sonnet to Simplicity [1] was not composed with reference to Southey, you answered me (I believe these were the words): " It was a lie too gross for the grossest ignorance to believe ; " and I was not angry with you, because the asser-

[1] The three sonnets of " Nehemiah Higginbottom " were published in the *Monthly Magazine* for November, 1797. Compare his letter to Cottle (*E. R.* i. 289) which Mr. Dykes Campbell takes to have been written at the same time.

" I sent to the *Monthly Magazine*, three mock sonnets in ridicule of my own Poems, and Charles Lloyd's and Charles Lamb's, etc., etc., exposing that affectation of unaffectedness, of jumping and misplaced accent, in commonplace epithets, flat lines forced into poetry by italics (signifying how well and mouthishly the author would read them), puny pathos, etc., etc. The instances were all taken from myself and Lloyd and Lamb. I signed them 'Nehemiah Higginbottom.' I hope they may do good to our young bards."

The publication of these sonnets in November, 1797, cannot, as Mr. Dykes Campbell points out (*Poetical Works*, p. 599), have been the immediate cause of the breach between Coleridge and Lamb which took place in the spring or early summer of 1798, but it seems that during the rise and progress of this quarrel the Sonnet on Simplicity was the occasion of bitter and angry words. As Lamb and Lloyd and Southey drew together, they drew away from Coleridge, and Southey, who had only been formally reconciled with his brother-in-law, seems to have re-

garded this sonnet as an ill-natured parody of his earlier poems. In a letter to Wynn, dated November 20, 1797, he says, " I am aware of the danger of studying simplicity of language," and he proceeds to quote some lines of blank verse to prove that he could employ the " grand style " when he chose.

A note from Coleridge to Southey, posted December 8, 1797, deals with the question, and would, if it had not been for Lloyd's " tittle-tattle," have convinced both Southey and Lamb that in the matter they were entirely mistaken.

I am sorry, Southey! very sorry that I wrote or published those sonnets — but 'sorry' would be a tame word to express my feelings, if I had written them with the motives which you have attributed to me. I have not been in the habit of treating our separation with levity — nor ever since the first moment thought of it without deep emotion — and how could you apply to yourself a sonnet written to ridicule infantine simplicity, vulgar colloquialisms, and lady-like friendships ? I have no conception, neither I believe could a passage in your writings have suggested to me or any man the notion of *your* 'plainting plaintively.' I am sorry that I wrote thus, because I am sorry to perceive a disposition in you to believe evil of me,

tion which the grossest ignorance would believe a lie the Omniscient knew to be truth. This, however, makes me cautious not too hastily to affirm the falsehood of an assertion of Lloyd's that in Edmund Oliver's [1] love-fit, leaving college, and going into the army he had no sort of allusion to or recollection of my love-fit, leaving college, and going into the army, and that he never thought of my person in the description of Oliver's person in the first letter of the second volume. This cannot appear stranger to me than my assertion did to you, and therefore I will suspend my absolute faith.

of which your remark to Charles Lloyd was a painful instance. I say this to you, because I shall say it to no other being. I feel myself wounded and hurt and write as such. I believe in my letter to Lloyd I forgot to mention that the Editor of the *Morning Post* is called Stuart, and that he is the brother-in-law of Mackintosh. Yours sincerely,

S. T. COLERIDGE.

Thursday morning.

Post-mark, Dec. 8, 1797.

MR. SOUTHEY, No. 23 East Street, Red Lion Square, London.

[1] Charles Lloyd's novel, *Edmund Oliver*, was published at Bristol in 1798. It is dedicated to "His friend Charles Lamb of the India House." He says in the Preface: "The incidents relative to the army were given me by an intimate friend who was himself eye-witness of one of them." The general resemblance between the events of Coleridge's earlier history and the story of Edmund Oliver is not very striking, but apart from the description of "his person" in the first letter of the second volume, which is close enough, a single sentence from Edmund Oliver's journal, i. 245, betrays the malignant nature of the attack. "I have at all times a strange dreaminess about me which makes me indifferent to the future, if I can by any means fill the present with sensations, — with that dreaminess I have gone on here from day to day; if at any time thought-troubled, I have swallowed some spirits, or had recourse to my laudanum." In the same letter, the account which Edmund Oliver gives of his sensations as a recruit in a regiment of light horse, and the vivid but repulsive picture which he draws of his squalid surroundings in "a pot-house in the Borough," leaves a like impression that Coleridge confided too much, and that Lloyd remembered "not wisely but too well." How Coleridge regarded Lloyd's malfeasance may be guessed from one of his so-called epigrams.

TO ONE WHO PUBLISHED IN PRINT WHAT HAD BEEN INTRUSTED TO HIM BY MY FIRESIDE.

Two things hast thou made known to half the nation,
My secrets and my want of penetration:
For oh! far more than all which thou hast penned,
It shames me to have called a wretch, like thee, my friend!

Poetical Works, p. 448.

I wrote to you not that I wish to hear from you, but that I wish you to write to Lloyd and press upon him the propriety, nay the necessity, of his giving me a meeting either *tête-à-tête* or in the presence of all whose esteem I value. This I owe to my own character; I owe it to him if by any means he may even yet be extricated. He assigned as reasons for his rupture my vices; and he is either right or wrong. If right, it is fit that others should know it and follow his example; if wrong, he has acted very wrong. At present, I may expect everything from his heated mind rather than continence of language, and his assertions will be the more readily believed on account of his former enthusiastic attachment, though with wise men this would cast a hue of suspicion over the whole affair; but the number of wise men in the kingdom would not puzzle a savage's arithmetic — you may tell them in every [community] on your fingers. I have been unfortunate in my connections. Both you and Lloyd became acquainted with me when your minds were far from being in a composed or natural state, and you clothed my image with a suit of notions and feelings which could belong to nothing human. You are restored to comparative saneness, and are merely wondering what is become of the Coleridge with whom you were so passionately in love; *Charles Lloyd's* mind has only changed his disease, and he is now arraying his ci-devant Angel in a flaming San Benito — the whole ground of the garment a dark brimstone and plenty of little devils flourished out in black. Oh, me! Lamb, " even in laughter the heart is sad!" My kindness, my affectionateness, he deems wheedling; but, if after reading all my letters to yourself and to him, you can suppose him wise in his treatment and correct in his accusations of me, you think worse of human nature than poor human nature, bad as it is, deserves to be thought of.

God bless you and   S. T. COLERIDGE.

CHAPTER IV

A VISIT TO GERMANY

1798–1799

CHAPTER IV

A VISIT TO GERMANY

1798-1799

THE letters which Coleridge wrote from Germany were, with few exceptions, addressed either to his wife or to Poole. They have never been published in full, but during his life and since his death various extracts have appeared in print. The earlier letters descriptive of his voyage, his two visits to Hamburg, his interviews with Klopstock, and his settlement at Ratzeburg were published as "Satyrane's Letters," first in November-December, 1809, in Nos. 14, 16, and 18 of "The Friend," and again, in 1817, in the "Biographia Literaria" (ii. 183–253). Two extracts from letters to his wife, dated respectively January 14 and April 8, 1799, appeared in No. 19 of "The Friend," December 28, 1809, as "Christmas Indoors in North Germany," and "Christmas Out of Doors." In 1828, Coleridge placed a selection of unpublished letters from Germany in the hands of the late S. C. Hall, who printed portions of two (dated "Clausthal, May 17, 1799") in the "Amulet" of 1829, under the title of "Fragments of a Journal of a Tour over the Brocken, by S. T. Coleridge." The same extract is included in Gillman's "Life of Coleridge," pp. 125, 138.

After Coleridge's death, Mr. Hall published in the "New Monthly Magazine" (1835, No. 45, pp. 211–226) the three last letters from Germany, dated May 17, 18, and 19, which include the "Tour over the Brocken." Selections from Coleridge's letters to Poole of April 8 and May 6, 1799, were published by Mrs. Sandford in "Thomas Poole and his Friends" (i. 295–299), and four letters from Poole to Coleridge are included in the same volume (pp. 277–294). A hitherto unpublished letter from Coleridge to his wife, dated January 14, 1799, appeared in "The Illustrated London News," April 29, 1893. For further particulars relative to Coleridge's life in Germany, see Carlyon's "Early Years," etc., 1856, i. 26–198, *passim*, and Brandl's "Life of Coleridge," 1887, pp. 230–252.

LXXXVI. TO THOMAS POOLE.

September 15, 1798.

MY VERY DEAR POOLE, — We have arrived at Yarmouth just in time to be hurried into the packet — and four or five letters of recommendation have been taken away from me, owing to their being wafered. Wedgwood's luckily were not.

I am at the point of leaving my native country for the first time — a country which God Almighty knows is dear to me above all things for the love I bear to you. Of many friends whom I love and esteem, my head and heart have ever chosen you as the friend — as the one being in whom is involved the full and whole meaning of that sacred title. God love you, my dear Poole! and your faithful and most affectionate

S. T. COLERIDGE.

P. S. We may be only two days, we may be a fortnight going. The same of the packet that returns. So do not let my poor Sara be alarmed if she do not hear from me. I will write alternately to you and her, twice every week during my absence. May God preserve us, and make us continue to be joy, and comfort, and wisdom, and virtue to each other, my dear, dear Poole!

LXXXVII. TO HIS WIFE.

HAMBURG, September 19, 1798.

Over what place does the moon hang to your eye, my
dearest Sara ? To me it hangs over the left bank of the
Elbe, and a long trembling road of moonlight reaches from
thence up to the stern of our vessel, and there it ends. We
have dropped anchor in the middle of the stream, thirty
miles from Cuxhaven, where we arrived this morning at
eleven o'clock, after an unusually fine passage of only
forty-eight hours. The Captain agreed to take all the
passengers up to Hamburg for ten guineas; my share
amounted only to half a guinea. We shall be there, if no
fogs intervene, to-morrow morning. Chester was ill the
whole voyage ; Wordsworth shockingly ill ; his sister worst
of all, and I neither sick nor giddy, but gay as a lark.
The sea rolled rather high, but the motion was pleasant to
me. The stink of a sea cabin in a packet (what with the
bilge-water, and what from the crowd of sick passengers)
is horrible. I remained chiefly on deck. We left Yarmouth Sunday morning, September 16, at eleven o'clock.
Chester and Wordsworth ill immediately. Our passengers were : ‡ Wordsworth, * Chester, S. T. Coleridge, a
Dane, second Dane, third Dane, a Prussian, a Hanoverian and * his servant, a German tailor and his * wife, a
French ‡ emigrant and * French servant, * two English
gentlemen, and ‡ a Jew. All these with the prefix * were
sick, those marked ‡ horribly sick. The view of Yarmouth from the sea is interesting ; besides, it was English ground that was flying away from me. When we
lost sight of land, the moment that we quite lost sight of
it and the heavens all round me rested upon the waters,
my dear babes came upon me like a flash of lightning ; I
saw their faces [1] so distinctly ! This day enriched me with

[1] In a letter dated November 1,
1798, Mrs. Coleridge acquaints her
husband with the danger and the
disfigurement from small-pox which

characters, and I passed it merrily. Each of those characters I will delineate to you in my journal, which you and
Poole alternately will receive regularly as soon as I arrive
at any settled place, which will be in a week. Till then I
can do little more than give you notice of my safety and
my faithful affection to you (but the journal will commence from the day of my arrival at London, and give
every day's occurrence, etc.). I have it written, but I
have neither paper or time to transcribe it. I trust nothing to memory. The Ocean is a noble thing by night;
a beautiful white cloud of foam at momentary intervals
roars and rushes by the side of the vessel, and stars of
flame dance and sparkle and go out in it, and every now
and then light detachments of foam dart away from the
vessel's side with their galaxies of stars and scour out of
sight like a Tartar troop over a wilderness. What these
stars are I cannot say; the sailors say they are fish spawn,
which is phosphorescent. The noisy passengers swear in
all their languages, with drunken hiccups, that I shall
write no more, and I must join them. Indeed, they present a rich feast for a dramatist. My kind love to Mrs.
Poole (with what wings of swiftness would I fly home if
I could find something in Germany to do her good!). Remember me affectionately to Ward, and my love to the
Chesters (Bessy, Susan, and Julia) and to Cruickshank,
etc., etc., Ellen and Mary when you see them, and to
Lavinia Poole and Harriet and Sophy, and be sure to give
my kind love to Nanny. I associate so much of Hartley's
infancy with her, so many of his figures, looks, words, and
antics with her form, that I shall never cease to think of
her, poor girl! without interest. Tell my best good friend,
my dear Poole! that all his manuscripts, with Wordsworth's Tragedy, are safe in Josiah Wedgwood's hands;

had befallen her little Berkeley. "The dear child," she writes, "is getting strength every hour; but 'when you lost sight of land, and the faces of your children crossed you like a flash of lightning,' you saw *that* face for the last time."

and they will be returned to him together. Good-night,
my dear, dear Sara! — "every night when I go to bed,
and every morning when I rise," I will think with yearning love of you and of my blessed babies! Once more,
my dear Sara! good-night.

Wednesday afternoon, four o'clock. — We are safe in
Hamburg — an ugly city that stinks in every corner,
house, and room worse than cabins, sea-sickness, or bilge-
water! The hotels are all crowded. With great difficulty we have procured a very filthy room at a large expense; but we shall move to-morrow. We get very excellent claret for a trifle — a guinea sells at present for more
than twenty-three shillings here. But for all particulars
I must refer your patience to my journal, and I must get
some proper paper — I shall have to pay a shilling or
eighteenpence with every letter. N. B. Johnson the
bookseller, without any poems sold to him, but purely out
of affection conceived for me, and as part of anything I
might do for him, gave me an order on Remnant at Hamburg for thirty pounds. The "Epea Pteroenta," an Essay
on Population, and a "History of Paraguay," will come
down for me directed to Poole, and for Poole's reading.
Likewise I have desired Johnson to print in quarto [1] a little
poem of mine, one of which quartos must be sent to my
brother, Rev. G. C., Ottery St. Mary, carriage paid. Did
you receive my letter directed in a different hand, with
the 30*l.* banknote? The "Morning Post" and Magazine
will come to you as before. If not regularly, Stuart desires that you will write to him. I pray you, my dear
love! read Edgeworth's "Essay on Education" — read it
heart and soul, and if you approve of the mode, teach
Hartley his letters. I am very desirous that you should
teach him to read; and they point out some easy modes.

---

[1] "Fears in Solitude, written in
1798, during the alarm of an invasion.
To which are added, France, an Ode;
and Frost at Midnight. By S. T.
Coleridge. London : Printed for J.
Johnson, in St. Paul's Churchyard.
1798."

J. Wedgwood informed me that the Edgeworths were most miserable when children; and yet the father in his book is ever vapouring about their happiness. However, there are very good things in the work — and some nonsense.

Kiss my Hartley and Bercoo baby brodder (kiss them for their dear father, whose heart will never be absent from them many hours together). My dear Sara! I think of you with affection and a desire to be home, and in the full and noblest sense of the word, and after the antique principles of *Religion*, unsophisticated by Philosophy, will be, I trust, your husband faithful unto death,

S. T. COLERIDGE.

Wednesday night, eleven o'clock. — The sky and colours of the clouds are quite English, just as if I were coming out of T. Poole's homeward with you in my arm.

LXXXVIII. TO THE SAME.

[RATZEBURG], October 20, 1798.

. . . But I must check these feelings and write more collectedly. I am well, my dear Love! very well, and my situation is in all respects comfortable. My room is large and healthy; the house commands an enchanting prospect. The pastor is worthy and a learned man — a widower with eight children, five of whom are at home. The German language is spoken here in the utmost purity. The children often stand round my sofa and chatter away; and the little one of all corrects my pronunciation with a pretty pert lisp and self-sufficient tone, while the others laugh with no little joyance. The Gentry and Nobility here pay me almost an adulatory attention. There is a very beautiful little woman — less, I think, than you — a Countess Kilmansig;[1] her father is our Lord Howe's cousin. She

---

[1] According to Burke's *Peerage*, Howe, and father of the Admiral, Emanuel Scoope, second Viscount "Our Lord Howe," married, in 1719,

is the wife of a very handsome man, and has two fine little children. I have quite won her heart by a German poem which I wrote. It is that sonnet, "Charles! my slow heart was only sad when first," and considerably dilated with new images, and much superior in the German to its former dress. It has excited no small wonder here for its purity and harmony. I mention this as a proof of my progress in the language — indeed, it has surprised myself; but I want to be home, and I work hard, very hard, to shorten the time of absence. The little Countess said to me, "Oh! Englishmen be always sehr gut fathers and husbands. I hope dat you will come and lofe my little babies, and I will sing to you and play on the guitar and the pianoforte; and my dear huspan he sprachs sehr gut English, and he lofes England better than all the world." (Sehr gut is very good; sprach, speaks or talks.) She is a sweet little woman, and, what is very rare in Germany, she has perfectly white, regular, French teeth. I could give you many instances of the ridiculous partiality, or rather madness, for the English. One of the first things which strikes an Englishman is the German cards. They are very different from ours; the court cards have two heads, a very convenient thing, as it prevents the necessity of turning the cards and betraying your hand, and are smaller and cost only a penny; yet the envelope in which they are sold has "Wahrlich Englische Karten," that is, genuine *English* cards. I bought some sticking-plaister yesterday; it cost twopence a very large piece, but it was three-halfpence farthing too dear — for indeed it looked like a nasty rag of black silk which cat or mouse

Mary Sophia, daughter of Baron Kielmansegge, Master of the Horse to George I. Coleridge's countess must have been a great-granddaughter of the baron. In her reply to this letter, dated December 13, 1798, Mrs. Coleridge writes: "I am very proud to hear that you are so forward in the language, and that you are so gay with the ladies. You may give my respects to them, and say that I am not at all jealous, for I know my dear Samuel in her affliction will not forget entirely his most affectionate wife, Sara Coleridge."

dung had stained and spotted — but this was " Königl. Pat.
Engl. Im. Pflaster," that is, Royal Patent *English Orna-
ment* Plaister. They affect to write English over their
doors. One house has " English Lodgement and Caffee
Hous!" But the most amusing of all is an advertisement
of a quack medicine of the same class with Dr. Solomon's
and Brody's, for the spirits and all weakness of mind and
body. What, think you? "A wonderful and secret
Essence extracted with patience and God's blessing from
the English Oaks, and from that part thereof which the
heroic sailors of that Great Nation call the Heart of Oak.
This invaluable and infallible Medicine has been godlily
extracted therefrom by the slow processes of the Sun and
magnetical Influences of the Planets and fixed Stars."
This is a literal translation. At the concert, when I entered, the band played " Britannia rule the waves," and at
the dinner which was given in honour of Nelson's victory,
twenty-one guns were fired by order of the military Governor, and between each firing the military band played
an English tune. I never saw such enthusiasm, or heard
such tumultuous shouting, as when the Governor gave as
a toast, "The Great Nation." By this name they always
designate England, in opposition to the same title self-
assumed by France. The military Governor is a pleasant man, and both he and the Amtmann (*i. e.* the civil
regent) are particularly attentive to me. I am quite domesticated in the house of the latter; his first wife was an
English woman, and his partiality for England is without
bounds. God bless you, my Love! Write me a very,
very long letter; write me all that can cheer me; all that
will make my eyes swim and my heart melt with tenderness! Your faithful and affectionate husband,

S. T. COLERIDGE.

P. S.   A dinner lasts not uncommonly three hours!

LXXXIX. TO THE SAME.

RATZEBURG, November 26, 1798.

Another and another and yet another post day ; and
still Chester greets me with, " No letters from England ! "
A knell, that strikes out regularly four times a week.
How is this, my Love ? Why do you not write to me ? Do
you think to shorten my absence by making it insupporta-
ble to me ? Or perhaps you anticipate that if I received
a letter I should idly turn away from my German to *dream*
of you — of you and my beloved babies ! Oh, yes ! I
should indeed dream of you for hours and hours ; of you,
and of beloved Poole, and of the infant that sucks at your
breast, and of my dear, dear Hartley. You would be
present, you would be with me in the air that I breathe ;
and I should cease to see you only when the tears rolled
out of my eyes, and this naked, undomestic room became
again visible. But oh, with what leaping and exhilarated
faculties should I return to the objects and realities of my
mission. But now — nay, I cannot describe to you the
gloominess of thought, the burthen and sickness of heart,
which I experience every post day. Through the whole
remaining day I am incapable of everything but anxious
imaginations, of sore and fretful feelings. The Hamburg
newspapers arrive here four times a week ; and almost
every newspaper commences with, " *Schreiben aus London* — They write from London." This day's, with
schreiben aus London, vom November 13. But I am certain that you have written more than once ; and I stum-
ble about in dark and idle conjectures, how and by what
means it can have happened that I have not received your
letters. I recommence my journal, but with feelings that
approach to disgust — for in very truth I have nothing
interesting to relate.

XC. TO THE SAME.

December 2, 1798.

Sunday Evening. — God, the Infinite, be praised that my babes are alive. His mercy will forgive me that late and all too slowly I raised up my heart in thanksgiving. At first and for a time I wept as passionately as if they had been dead; and for the whole day the weight was heavy upon me, relieved only by fits of weeping. I had long expected, I had passionately expected, a letter; I received it, and my frame trembled. I saw your hand, and all feelings of mind and body crowded together. Had the news been cheerful and only " We are as you left us," I must have wept to have delivered myself of the stress and tumult of my animal sensibility. But when I read the danger and the agony — My dear Sara! my love! my wife! — God bless you and preserve us. I am well; but a stye, or something of that kind, has come upon and enormously swelled my eyelids, so that it is painful and improper for me to read or write. In a few days it will now disappear, and I will write at length (now it forces me to cease). To-morrow I will write a line or two on the other side of the page to Mr. Roskilly.

I received your letter Friday, November 31. I cannot well account for the slowness. Oh, my babies! Absence makes it painful to be a father.

My life, believe and know that I pant to be home and with you.

S. T. COLERIDGE.

December 3. — My eyes are painful, but there is no doubt but they will be well in two or three days. I have taken physic, eat very little flesh, and drink only water, but it grieves me that I cannot read. I need not have troubled my poor eyes with a superfluous love to my dear Poole.

XCI. TO THE REV. MR. ROSKILLY.[1]

RATZEBURG, Germany, December 3, 1798.

MY DEAR SIR, — There is an honest heart out of Great Britain that enters into your good fortune with a sincere and lively joy. May you enjoy life and health — all else you have, — a good wife, a good conscience, a good temper, sweet children, and competence ! The first glass of wine I drink shall be a bumper — not to you, no ! but to the Bishop of Gloucester ! God bless him !

Sincerely your friend,

S. T. COLERIDGE.

XCII. TO THOMAS POOLE.

January 4, 1799 — Morning, 11 o'clock.

My friend, my dear friend ! Two hours have past since I received your letter. It was so frightfully long since I received one ! ! My body is weak and faint with the beating of my heart. But everything affects me more than it ought to do in a foreign country. I cried myself blind about Berkeley, when I ought to have been on my knees in the joy of thanksgiving. The waywardness of the pacquets is wonderful. On December the seventh Chester received a letter from his sister dated November 27. Yours is dated November 22, and I received it only this morning. I am quite well, calm and industrious. I now read German as English, — that is, without any *mental* translation as I read. I likewise understand all that is said to me, and a good deal of what they say to each other.

[1] The " Rev. Mr. Roskilly " had been curate-in-charge of the parish of Nether Stowey, and the occasion of the letter was his promotion to the Rectory of Kempsford in Gloucestershire. Mrs. S. T. Coleridge, in a late letter (probably 1843) to her sister, Mrs. Lovell, writes : " In March [1800] I and the child [Hart-ley] left him [S. T. C.] in London, and proceeded to Kempsford in Gloucestershire, the Rectory of Mr. Roskilly ; remained there a month. Papa was to have joined us there, but did not." See *Thomas Poole and his Friends*, i. 25-27, and *Letters from the Lake Poets*, p. 6.

On very trivial and on metaphysical subjects I can talk *tolerably* — so, so ! — but in that conversation, which is between both, I bungle most ridiculously.   I owe it to my industry that I can read old German, and even the old low German, better than most of even the educated natives.   It has greatly enlarged my knowledge of the English language.   It is a great bar to the amelioration of Germany, that through at least half of it, and that half composed almost wholly of Protestant States, from whence alone amelioration can proceed, the agriculturists and a great part of the artizans talk a language as different from the language of the higher classes (in which all books are written) as the Latin is from the Greek.   The differences are greater than the affinities, and the affinities are darkened by the differences of pronunciation and spelling.   I have written twice to Mr. Josiah Wedgwood,[1] and in a few days will follow a most voluminous letter, or rather series of letters, which will comprise a history of the bauers or peasants collected, not so much from books as from oral communications from the Amtmann here — (an Amtmann is a sort of perpetual Lord Mayor, uniting in himself Judge and Justice of Peace over the bauers of a certain district).   I have enjoyed great advantages in this place, but I have paid dear for them.   Including *all* expenses, I have not lived at less than two pounds a week. Wordsworth (from whom I receive long and affectionate letters) has enjoyed scarcely one advantage, but his expenses have been considerably less than they were in England.   Here I shall stay till the last week in January, when I shall proceed to Göttingen, where, all expenses included, I can live for 15 shillings a week.   For these last two months I have drunk nothing but water, and I

---

[1] In his letter of January 20, 1799, Josiah Wedgwood acknowledges the receipt of a letter dated November 29, 1798, but adds that an earlier letter from Hamburg had not come to hand. A third letter, dated Göttingen, May 21, 1799, was printed by Cottle in his *Reminiscences*, 1848, p. 425.

eat but little animal food. At Göttingen I shall hire lodging for two months, buy my own cold beef at an eating-house, and dine in my chamber, which I can have at a dollar a week. And here at Göttingen I must endeavour to unite the advantages of advancing in German and doing something to repay myself. My dear Poole! I am afraid that, supposing I return in the first week of May, my whole expenses [1] from Stowey to Stowey, including books and clothes, will not have been less than 90 *pounds!* and if I buy ten pounds' worth more of books it will have been a hundred. I despair not but with intense application and regular use of time, to which I have now almost accustomed myself, that by three months' residence at Göttingen

[1] Miss Meteyard, in her *Group of Englishmen*, 1871, p. 99, gives extracts from the account-current of Messrs. P. and O. Von Axen, the Hamburg agents of the Wedgwoods. According to her figures, Coleridge drew £125 from October 20 to March 29, 1799, and, "conjointly with Wordsworth," £106 10s. on July 8, 1799. Mr. Dykes Campbell, in a footnote to his *Memoir*, p. xliv., combats Miss Meteyard's assertion that these sums were advanced by the Wedgwoods to Coleridge and Wordsworth, and argues that Wordsworth merely drew on the Von Axens for sums already paid in from his own resources. Coleridge, he thinks, had only his annuity to look to, but probably anticipated his income. In a MS. note-book of 1798-99, Coleridge inserted some concise but not very business-like entries as to expenditures and present resources, but says nothing as to receipts.

"March 25th, being Easter Monday, Chester and S. T. C., in a damn'd dirty hole in the Burg Strasse at Göttingen, possessed at that moment eleven Louis d'ors and two dollars. When the money is spent in common expenses S. T. Coleridge will owe Chester 5 pounds 12 shillings.

"NOTE. — From September 8 to April 8 I shall have spent £90, of which £15 was in Books; and Cloathes, mending and making, £10.

"May 10. We have 17 Louis d'or, of which, as far as I can at present calculate, 10 belong to Chester."

The most probable conclusion is that both Coleridge and Chester were fairly well supplied with money when they left England, and that the £178 10s. which Coleridge received from the Von Axens covered some portion of Chester's expenses in addition to his own. I may add that a recent collation of the autograph letter of Coleridge to Josiah Wedgwood dated May 21, 1799, Göttingen, with the published version in Cottle's *Reminiscences*, pp. 425-429, fully bears out Mr. Campbell's contention, that though Coleridge anticipated his annuity, be was not the recipient of large sums over and above what was guaranteed to him.

I shall have *on paper* at least *all* the materials if not the
whole structure of a work that will repay me.   The work
I have planned, and I have imperiously excluded all
waverings about other works.   That is the disease of my
mind — it is comprehensive in its conceptions, and wastes
itself in the contemplations of the many things which it
might do.   I am aware of the disease, and for the next
three months (if I cannot cure it) I will at least suspend
its operation.   This book is a life of Lessing, and inter-
weaved with it a true state of German literature in its rise
and present state.   I have already written a little life from
three different biographies, divided it into years, and at
Göttingen I will read his works regularly according to the
years in which they were written, and the controversies,
religious and literary, which they occasioned.   But of this
say nothing to any one.   The journey to Germany has certainly *done me good*.   My habits are less irregular and
my *mind* more in my own power.   But I have much still
to do!   I did, indeed, receive great joy from Roskilly's
good fortune, and in a little note to my dear Sara I joined
a note of congratulation to Roskilly.   O Poole! you are a
noble heart as ever God made!   Poor ——! he is passing through a fiery discipline, and I would fain believe
that it will end in his peace and utility.   Wordsworth is
divided in his mind, — unquietly divided between the
neighbourhood of Stowey and the North of England.   He
cannot think of settling at a distance from me, and I have
told him that I cannot leave the vicinity of Stowey.   His
chief objection to Stowey is the want of books.   The Bristol Library is a hum, and will do us little service; and he
thinks that he can procure a house near Sir Gilford Lawson's by the Lakes, and have free access to his immense
library.   I think it better once in a year to walk to Cambridge, in the summer vacation — perhaps I may be able
to get rooms for nothing, and there for a couple of months
read like a Turk on a given plan, and return home with a

mass of materials which, with dear, *independent* Poetry, will fully employ the remaining year. But this is idle prating about a future. But indeed, it is time to be looking out for a house for me — it is not possible I can be either comfortable or useful in so small a house as that in Lime Street. If Woodlands can be gotten at a reasonable price, I would have it. I will now finish my long-neglected journal.

Sara, I suppose, is at Bristol — on Monday I shall write to her. The frost here has been uncommonly severe. For two days it was 20 degrees under the freezing point. Wordsworth has left Goslar, and is on his road into higher Saxony to cruise for a pleasanter place ; he has made but little progress in the language. I am interrupted, and if I do not conclude shall lose the post. Give my kind love to your dear mother. Oh, that I could but find her comfortable on my return. To Ward remember me affectionately — likewise remember to James Cole ; and my grateful remembrances to Mrs. Cole for her kindness during my wife's domestic troubles. To Harriet, Sophia, and Lavinia Poole — to the Chesters — to Mary and Ellen Cruickshank — in short, to all to whom it will give pleasure remember me affectionately.

My dear, dear Poole, God bless us !

S. T. COLERIDGE.

P. S. The Amtmann, who is almost an Englishman and an idolizer of our nation, desires to be kindly remembered to you. He told me yesterday that he had dreamt of you the night before.

XCIII. TO HIS WIFE.

RATZEBURG, Monday, January 14, 1799.

MY DEAREST LOVE, — Since the wind changed, and it became possible for me to have letters, I lost all my tranquillity. Last evening I was absent in company, and when

I returned to solitude, restless in every fibre, a novel which I attempted to read seemed to interest me so extravagantly that I threw it down, and when it was out of my hands I knew nothing of what I had been reading. This morning I awoke long before light, feverish and unquiet. I was certain in my mind that I should have a letter from you, but before it arrived my restlessness and the irregular pulsation of my heart had quite wearied me down, and I held the letter in my hand like as if I was stupid, without attempting to open it. "Why don't you read the letter?" said Chester, and I read it. Ah, little Berkeley — I have misgivings, but my duty is rather to comfort you, my dear, dear Sara! I am so exhausted that I could sleep. I am well, but my spirits have left me. I am completely homesick. I must walk half an hour, for my mind is too scattered to continue writing. I entreat and entreat you, Sara! take care of yourself. If you are well, I think I could frame my thoughts so that I should not sink under other losses. You do right in writing me the truth. Poole is kind, but you do right, my dear! In a sense of *reality* there is always comfort. The workings of one's imagination ever go beyond the worst that nature afflicts us with; they have the terror of a superstitious circumstance. I express myself unintelligibly. Enough that you write me always the whole truth. Direct your next letter thus: An den Herrn Coleridge, à la Poste Restante, Göttingen, Germany. If God permit I shall be there before this day three weeks, and I hope on May-day to be once more at Stowey. My motives for going to Göttingen I have written to Poole. I hear as often from Wordsworth as letters can go backward and forward in a country where fifty miles in a day and night is expeditious travelling! He seems to have employed more time in writing English than in studying German. No wonder! for he might as well have been in England as at Goslar, in the situation which he chose and with his unseeking manners. He has now left

it, and is on his journey to Nordhausen. His taking his
sister with him was a wrong step; it is next but impossible for any but married women, or in the suit of married
women, to be introduced to any company in Germany. Sister here is considered as only a name for mistress. Still,
however, male acquaintance he might have had, and had I
been at Goslar I would have had them; but W., God love
him! seems to have lost his spirits and almost his inclination for it. In the mean time his expenses have been almost less than they [would have been] in England; mine
have been very great, but I do not despair of returning to
England with somewhat to pay the whole. O God! I do
languish to be at home.

I will endeavour to give you some idea of Ratzeburg,
but I am a wretched describer. First you must imagine
a lake, running from south to north about nine miles in
length, and of very various breadths — the broadest part
may be, perhaps, two or three miles, the narrowest scarce
more than half a mile. About a mile from the southern-
most point of the lake, that is, from the beginning of the
lake, is the island-town of Ratzeburg.

• is Ratzeburg; ◸ is our house on the hill; from the
bottom of the hill there lies on the lake a slip of land,
scarcely two stone-throws wide, at the end of which is a
little bridge with a superb military
gate, and this bridge joins Ratzeburg to the slip of land — you pass
through Ratzeburg up a little hill,
and down the hill, and this brings you to another bridge,
narrow, but of an immense length, which communicates
with the other shore.

The water to the south of Ratzeburg is called the little
lake and the other the large lake, though they are but one
piece of water. This little lake is very beautiful, the
shores just often enough green and bare to give the proper
effect to the magnificent *groves* which mostly fringe them.
The views vary almost every ten steps, such and so beautiful are the turnings and windings of the shore — they
unite beauty and magnitude, and can be but expressed by
feminine grandeur! At the north of the great lake, and
peering over, you see the seven church-towers of Lubec,
which is twelve or fourteen miles from Ratzeburg. Yet
you see them as distinctly as if they were not three miles
from you. The worse thing is that Ratzeburg is built entirely of bricks and tiles, and is therefore all red — a clump
of brick-dust red — it gives you a strong idea of perfect
neatness, but it is not beautiful.[1] In the beginning or
middle of October, I forget which, we went to Lubec in
a boat. For about two miles the shores of the lake are
exquisitely beautiful, the woods now running into the
water, now retiring in all angles. After this the left
shore retreats, — the lake acquires its utmost breadth,
and ceases to be beautiful. At the end of the lake is
the river, about as large as the river at Bristol, but
winding in infinite serpentines through a dead flat, with
willows and reeds, till you reach Lubec, an old fantastic
town. We visited the churches at Lubec — they were
crowded with gaudy gilded figures, and a profusion of
pictures, among which were always the portraits of the
popular pastors who had served the church. The pastors here wear white ruffs exactly like the pictures of
Queen Elizabeth. There were in the Lubec churches
a very large attendance, but almost *all women.* The
genteeler people dressed precisely as the English; but

[1] A portion of this description of Ratzeburg is included in No. III. of *Satyrane's Letters*, originally pub- lished in No. 10 of *The Friend*, December 21, 1809.

behind every lady sat her maid, — the caps with gold
and silver combs. Altogether, a Lubec church is an
amusing sight. In the evening I wished myself a painter,
just to draw a German Party at cards. One man's long
pipe rested on the table, by the fish-dish; another who
was shuffling, and of course had both hands employed,
held his pipe in his teeth, and it hung down between
his thighs even to his ankles, and the distortion which
the attitude and effort occasioned made him a most
ludicrous phiz. . . . [If it] had been possible I would
have loitered a week in those churches, and found incessant amusement. Every picture, every legend cut out in
gilded wood-work, was a history of the manners and feelings of the ages in which such works were admired and
executed.

As the sun both rises and sets over the little lake by
us, both rising and setting present most lovely spectacles.[1] In October Ratzeburg used at sunset to appear
completely beautiful. A deep red light spread over all,
in complete harmony with the red town, the brown-red
woods, and the yellow-red reeds on the skirts of the lake
and on the slip of land. A few boats, paddled by single
persons, used generally to be floating up and down in the
rich light. But when first the ice fell on the lake, and the
whole lake was frozen one large piece of thick transparent
glass — O my God! what sublime scenery I have beheld.
Of a morning I have seen the little lake covered with mist;
when the sun peeped over the hills the mist broke in the
middle, and at last stood as the waters of the Red Sea are
said to have done when the Israelites passed; and between
these two walls of mist the sunlight burst upon the ice in
a straight road of golden fire, all across the lake, intolerably bright, and the walls of mist partaking of the light in

[1] The following description of the   *The Friend*, December 28, 1809, as
frozen lake was thrown into a literary   "Christmas Indoors in North Ger-
shape and published in No. 19 of   many."

a *multitude* of colours. About a month ago the vehemence of the wind had shattered the ice; part of it, quite shattered, was driven to shore and had frozen anew; this was of a deep blue, and represented an agitated sea — the water that ran up between the great islands of ice shone of a yellow-green (it was at sunset), and all the scattered islands of *smooth* ice were *blood*, intensely bright *blood;* on some of the largest islands the fishermen were pulling out their immense nets through the holes made in the ice for this purpose, and the fishermen, the net-poles, and the huge nets made a part of the glory! O my God! how I wished you to be with me! In skating there are three pleasing circumstances — firstly, the infinitely subtle particles of ice which the skate cuts up, and which creep and run before the skater like a low mist, and in sunrise or sunset become coloured; second, the shadow of the skater in the water seen through the transparent ice; and thirdly, the melancholy undulating sound from the skate, not without variety; and, when very many are skating together, the sounds give an impulse to the icy trees, and the woods all round the lake *tinkle.* It is a pleasant amusement to sit in an ice stool (as they are called) and be driven along by two skaters, faster than most horses can gallop. As to the customs here, they are nearly the same as in England, except that [the men] never sit after dinner [and only] drink at dinner, which often lasts three or four hours, and in noble families is divided into three gangs, that is, walks. When you have sat about an hour, you rise up, each lady takes a gentleman's arm, and you walk about for a quarter of an hour — in the mean time another course is put upon the table; and, this in great dinners, is repeated three times. A man here seldom sees his wife till dinner, — they take their coffee in separate rooms, and never eat at breakfast; only as soon as they are up they take their coffee, and about eleven o'clock eat a bit of bread and butter with the coffee. The men at least take a pipe.

Indeed, a pipe at breakfast is a great addition to the comfort of life. I shall [smoke at] no other time in England. Here I smoke four times a day — 1 at breakfast, 1 half an hour before dinner, 1 in the afternoon at tea, and 1 just before bed-time — but I shall give it all up, unless, as before observed, you should happen to like the smoke of a pipe at breakfast. Once when I first came here I smoked a pipe immediately after dinner; the pastor expressed his surprise: I expressed mine that he could smoke before breakfast. "O Herr Gott!" (that is, Lord God) quoth he, "it is delightful; it invigorates the frame and *it clears out the mouth so*." A common amusement at the German Universities is for a number of young men to smoke out a candle! that is, to fill a room with tobacco smoke till the candle goes out. Pipes are quite the rage — a pipe of a particular kind, that has been smoked for a year or so, will sell here for twenty guineas — the same pipe when new costs four or five. They are called Meerschaum.

God bless you, my dear Love! I will soon write again.

S. T. COLERIDGE.

Postscript. Perhaps you are in Bristol. However, I had better direct it to Stowey. My love to Martha and your mother and your other sisters. Once more, my dearest Love, God love and preserve us through this long absence! O my dear Babies! my Babies!

XCIV. TO THE SAME.

Bei dem Radermacher Gohring, in der Bergstrasse, Göttingen,
March 12, 1799. Sunday Night.

MY DEAREST LOVE, — It has been a frightfully long time since we have heard from each other. I have not written, simply because my letters could have gone no further than Cuxhaven, and would have stayed there to the [no] small hazard of their being lost. Even now the mouth of the Elbe is so much choked with ice that the

English Pacquets cannot set off. Why need I say how anxious this long interval of silence has made me ! I have thought and thought of you, and pictured you and the little ones so often and so often that my imagination is tired down, flat and powerless, and I languish after home for hours together in vacancy, my feelings almost wholly unqualified by *thoughts*. I have at times experienced such an extinction of *light* in my mind — I have been so forsaken by all the *forms* and *colourings* of existence, as if the *organs* of life had been dried up; as if only simply Being remained, blind and stagnant. After I have recovered from this strange state and reflected upon it, I have thought of a man who should lose his companion in a desart of sand, where his weary Halloos drop down in the air without an echo. I am deeply convinced that if I were to remain a few years among objects for whom I had no affection I should wholly lose the powers of intellect. Love is the vital air of my genius, and I have not seen one human being in Germany whom I can conceive it *possible* for me to *love*, no, not *one ;* in my mind they are an unlovely race, these Germans.

We left Ratzeburg, Feb. 6, in the Stage Coach. This was not the coldest night of the century, because the night following was two degrees colder — the oldest man living remembers not such a night as Thursday, Feb. 7. This whole winter I have heard incessant complaints of the unusual cold, but I have felt very little of it. But *that night!* My God! Now I know what the pain of cold is, and what the danger. The pious care of the German Governments that none of their loving subjects should be suffocated is admirable ! On Friday morning when the light dawned, the Coach looked like a shapeless idol of suspicion with an hundred eyes, for there were at least so many holes in it. And as to rapidity! We left Ratzeburg at 7 o'clock Wednesday evening, and arrived at Lüneburg — i. e., 35 English miles — at 3 o'clock on

Thursday afternoon. This is a fair specimen! In England I used to laugh at the "flying waggons;" but, compared with a German Post Coach, the metaphor is perfectly justifiable, and for the future I shall never meet a flying waggon without thinking respectfully of its speed. The whole country from Ratzeburg almost to Einbeck — *i. e.*, 155 English miles — is a flat, objectless, hungry heath, bearing no marks of cultivation, except close by the towns, and the only remarks which suggested themselves to me were that it was cold — very cold — shocking cold — never felt it so cold in my life! Hanover is 115 miles from Ratzeburg. We arrived there Saturday evening.

The Herr von Döring, a nobleman who resides at Ratzeburg, gave me letters to his brother-in-law at Hanover, and by the manner in which he received me I found that they were not *ordinary* letters of recommendation. He pressed me exceedingly to stay a week in Hanover, but I refused, and left it on Monday noon. In the mean time, however, he had introduced me to all the great people and presented me "as an English gentleman of first-rate character and talents" to Baron Steinburg, the Minister of State, and to Von Brandes, the Secretary of State and Governor of Göttingen University. The first was amazingly *perpendicular*, but civil and polite, and gave me letters to Heyne, the head Librarian, and, in truth, the real *Governor* of Göttingen. Brandes likewise gave me letters to Heyne and Blumenbach, who are his brothers-in-law. Baron Steinburg offered to present me to the Prince (Adolphus), who is now in Hanover; but I deferred the honour till my return. I shall make Poole laugh when I return with the visiting-card which the Baron left at my inn.

The two things worth seeing in Hanover are (1) the conduit representing Mount Parnassus, with statues of Apollo, the Muses, and a great many others; flying horses, rhinoceroses, and elephants, etc.; and (2) a bust of Leibnitz — the first for its excessive absurdity, ugliness, and indecency — (absolutely I could write the most humorous octavo volume containing the description of it with a commentary) — the second — *i. e.* the bust of Leibnitz — impressed on my soul a sensation which has ennobled it.   It is the face of a god! and Leibnitz was almost more than a man in the wonderful capaciousness of his judgment and imagination!   Well, we left Hanover on Monday noon, after having paid a most extravagant bill.   We lived with Spartan frugality, and paid with Persian pomp!   But I was an Englishman, and visited by half a dozen noblemen and the Minister of State.   The landlord could not dream of affronting me by anything like a reasonable charge!   On the road we stopped with the postillion always, and our expenses were nothing. Chester and I made a very hearty dinner of cold beef, etc., and both together paid only fourpence, and for coffee and biscuits only threepence each.   In short, a man may travel cheap in Germany, but he must avoid great towns and not be visited by Ministers of State.

In a village some four miles from Einbeck we stopped about 4 o'clock in the morning.   It was pitch dark, and the postillion led us into a room where there was not a ray of light — we could not see our hand — but it felt extremely warm.   At length and suddenly the lamp came, and we saw ourselves in a room thirteen strides in length, strew'd with straw, and lying by the side of each other on the straw twelve Jews.   I assure you it was curious. Their dogs lay at their feet.   There was one very beautiful boy among them, fast asleep, with the softest conceivable opening of the mouth, with the white beard of his grandfather upon his cheek — a fair, rosy cheek.

This day I called with my letters on the Professor Heyne, a little, hopping, over-civil sort of a thing, who talks very fast and with fragments of coughing between every ten words.   However, he behaved very courteously

to me. The next day I took out my matricula, and commenced student of the University of Göttingen. Heyne
has honoured me so far that he has given me the right,
which properly only professors have, of sending to the
Library for an indefinite number of books in my own
name.

On Saturday evening I went to the concert. Here the
other Englishmen introduced themselves. After the concert Hamilton, a Cambridge man, took me as his guest to
the Saturday Club, *where what is called* the first class of
students meet and sup once a week. Here were all the
nobility and three Englishmen. Such an evening I never
passed before — roaring, kissing, embracing, fighting,
smashing bottles and glasses against the wall, singing —
in short, such a scene of uproar I never witnessed before,
no, not even at Cambridge. I drank nothing, but all except two of the Englishmen were drunk, and the party
broke up a little after one o'clock in the morning. I
thought of what I had been at Cambridge and of what I
was, of the wild bacchanalian sympathy with which I had
formerly joined similar parties, and of my total inability
now to do aught but meditate, and the feeling of the deep
alteration in my moral being gave the scene a melancholy
interest to me.

We are quite well. Chester will write soon to his
family; in the mean time he sends duty, love, and remembrance to all to whom they are due. I have drunk no
wine or fermented liquor for more than three months, in
consequence of which I am apt to be wakeful; but then I
never feel any oppression after dinner, and my spirits are
much more equable, blessings which I esteem inestimable!
My dear Hartley — my Berkeley — how intensely do I
long for you! My Sara, O my dear Sara! To Poole,
God bless him! to dear Mrs. Poole and Ward, kindest
love, and to all love and remembrance.

                                    S. T. COLERIDGE.

XCV. TO THOMAS POOLE.

April 6, 1799.

MY DEAREST POOLE, — Your two letters, dated January 24 and March 15,[1] followed close on each other. I was still enjoying "the livelier impulse and the dance of thought" which the first had given me when I received the second. At the time, in which I read Sara's lively account of the miseries which herself and the infant had undergone, all was over and well — there was nothing to *think* of — only a mass of pain was brought suddenly and closely within the sphere of my perception, and I was made to suffer it over again. For this bodily frame is an imitative thing, and touched by the imagination gives the hour which is past as faithfully as a repeating watch. But Death — the death of an infant — of one's own infant! I read your letter in calmness, and walked out into the open fields, oppressed, not by my feelings, but by the riddles which the thought so easily proposes, and solves — never!

---

[1] A letter from Mrs. Coleridge to her husband, dated March 25, 1799, followed Poole's letter of March 15. (*Thomas Poole and his Friends*, i. 280.) She writes : —

"MY DEAREST LOVE, — I hope you will not attribute my long silence to want of affection. If you have received Mr. Poole's letter you will know the reason and acquit me. My darling infant left his wretched mother on the 10th of February, and though the leisure that followed was intolerable to me, yet I could not employ myself in reading or writing, or in any way that prevented my thoughts from resting on him. This parting was the severest trial that I have ever yet undergone, and I pray to God that I may never live to behold the death of another child. For, O my dear Samuel, it is a suffering beyond your conception! You will feel and lament the death of your child, but you will only recollect him a baby of fourteen weeks, but I am his mother and have carried him in my arms and have fed him at my bosom, and have watched over him by day and by night for nine months. I have seen him twice at the brink of the grave, but he has returned and recovered and smiled upon me like an angel,— and now I am lamenting that he is gone ! "

In her old age, when her daughter was collecting materials for a life of her father, Mrs. Coleridge wrote on the back of the letter : —

"No secrets herein. I will not burn it for the sake of my sweet Berkeley."

A parent — in the strict and exclusive sense a parent! —
to me it is a *fable* wholly without meaning except in the
moral which it suggests — a fable of which the moral is
God. Be it so — my dear, dear friend! Oh let it be so!
La Nature (says Pascal) "La Nature confond les Pyr-
rhoniens, et la Raison confond les Dogmatistes. Nous
avons une impuissance à prouver invincible à tout le Dog-
matisme. Nous avons une idée de la verité invincible
à tout le Pyrrhonisme." I find it wise and human to
believe, even on slight evidence, opinions, the contrary of
which cannot be proved, and which promote our happiness
without hampering our intellect. My baby has not lived
in vain — this life has been to him what it is to all of us
— education and development! Fling yourself forward
into your immortality only a few thousand years, and how
small will not the difference between one year old and
sixty years appear! Consciousness! — it is no otherwise
necessary to our conceptions of future continuance than as
connecting the present link of our being with the one immediately preceding it; and *that* degree of consciousness,
that small portion of *memory*, it would not only be arro-
gant, but in the highest degree absurd, to deny even to a
much younger infant. 'T is a strange assertion that the
essence of identity lies in *recollective* consciousness.
'T were scarcely less ridiculous to affirm that the eight
miles from Stowey to Bridgwater consist in the eight mile-
stones. Death in a doting old age falls upon my feelings
ever as a more hopeless phenomenon than death in infancy;
but *nothing* is hopeless. What if the vital force which I
sent from my arm into the stone as I flung it in the air
and skimmed it upon the water — what if even that did
not perish! It was *life!* — it was a particle of *being!* —
it was power! and how could it perish? *Life, Power,
Being!* Organization may and probably is their *effect* —
their *cause* it *cannot* be! I have indulged very curious
fancies concerning that force, that swarm of motive powers

which I sent out of my body into that stone, and which,
one by one, left the untractable or already possessed mass,
and — but the German Ocean lies between us. It is all
too far to send you such fancies as these! Grief, indeed, —

> Doth love to dally with fantastic thoughts,
> And smiling like a sickly Moralist,
> Finds some resemblance to her own concern
> In the straws of chance, and things inanimate.[1]

But I cannot truly say that I grieve — I am perplexed
— I am sad — and a little thing — a very trifle — would
make me weep — but for the death of the baby I have
not wept! Oh this strange, strange, strange scene-shifter
Death! — that giddies one with insecurity and so unsub-
stantiates the living things that one has grasped and han-
dled! Some months ago Wordsworth transmitted me a
most sublime epitaph. Whether it had any reality I cannot say. Most probably, in some gloomier moment he had
fancied the moment in which his sister might die.

EPITAPH.

> A slumber did my spirit seal,
> I had no human fears;
> She seemed a thing that could not feel
> The touch of earthly years.
> No motion has she now, no force,
> She neither hears nor sees:
> Mov'd round in Earth's diurnal course
> With rocks, and stones, and trees!

XCVI. TO HIS WIFE.

GÖTTINGEN, in der Wendestrasse, April 8, 1799.

It is one of the discomforts of my absence, my dearest
Love! that we feel the same calamities at different times —
I would fain write words of consolation to you; yet I
know that I shall only fan into new activity the pang
which was growing dead and dull in your heart. Dear

[1] From "Osorio," Act V. Sc. 1. *Poetical Works*, p. 506.

little Being! he had existed to me for so many months
only in dreams and reveries, but in them existed and still
exists so livelily, so like a real thing, that although I know
of his death, yet when I am alone and have been long
silent, it seems to me as if I did not understand it. Methinks there is something awful in the thought, what an
unknown being one's own infant is to one — a fit of
sound — a flash of light — a summer gust that is as it were
created in the bosom of the calm air, that rises up we
know not how, and goes we know not whither! But we
say well; it goes! it is gone! and only in states of society
in which the revealing voice of our most inward and
abiding nature is no longer listened to (when we sport
and juggle with abstract phrases, instead of representing
our feelings and ideas), only then we say it *ceases!* I
will not believe that it ceases — in this moving, stirring,
and harmonious universe — I *cannot* believe it! Can
cold and darkness come from the sun? where the sun is
not, there is cold and darkness! But the living God is
everywhere, and works everywhere — and where is there
room for death? To look back on the life of my baby,
how short it seems! but consider it referently to non-
existence, and what a manifold and majestic *Thing* does
it not become? What a multitude of admirable actions,
what a multitude of *habits* of actions it learnt even before
it saw the light! and who shall count or conceive the
infinity of its thoughts and feelings, its hopes, and fears,
and joys, and pains, and desires, and presentiments, from
the moment of its birth to the moment when the glass,
through which we saw him darkly, was broken — and he
became suddenly invisible to us? Out of the Mount that
might not be touched, and that burnt with fire, out of
darkness, and blackness, and tempest, and with his own
Voice, which they who heard entreated that they might
not hear it again, the most high God forbade us to use his
name vainly. And shall we who are Christians, shall we

believe that he himself uses his own power vainly? That
like a child he builds palaces of mud and clay in the
common road, and then he destroys them, as weary of his
pastime, or leaves them to be trod under by the hoof of
Accident? That God works by *general* laws are to me
words without meaning or worse than meaningless —
ignorance, and imbecility, and limitation must wish in
generals. What and who are these horrible shadows
necessity and general law, to which God himself must
offer *sacrifices* — hecatombs of sacrifices? I feel a deep
conviction that these shadows exist not — they are only the
dreams of reasoning pride, that would fain find solutions
for all difficulties without faith — that would make the
discoveries which lie thick sown in the path of the eternal
Future unnecessary; and so conceiting that there is suffi-
ciency and completeness in the narrow present, weakens
the presentiment of our wide and ever widening immortality. God works in each for all — most true — but
more comprehensively true is it, that he works in all for
each. I confess that the more I think, the more I am dis-
contented with the doctrines of Priestley. He builds the
whole and sole hope of future existence on the words and
miracles of Jesus — yet doubts or denies the future existence of infants — only because according to his own system of materialism he has not discovered how they can be
made *conscious*. But Jesus has declared that *all* who
are in the grave shall arise — and that those who should
arise to perceptible progression must be ever as the infant
which He held in his arms and blessed. And although
the *Man* Jesus had never appeared in the world, yet I am
Quaker enough to believe, that in the heart of every man
the Christ would have revealed himself, the Power of the
Word, that was even in the wilderness. To me who am
absent this faith is a real consolation, — and the few, the
slow, the quiet tears which I shed, are the accompani-
ments of high and solemn thought, not the workings of

pain or sorrow. When I return indeed, and see the
vacancy that has been made — when nowhere anything
corresponds to the form which will perhaps for ever dwell
on my mind, then it is possible that a keener pang will
come upon me. Yet I trust, my love! I trust, my dear
Sara! that this event which has forced us to think of the
death of what is most dear to us, as at all times probable,
will in many and various ways be good for us. To have
shared — nay, I should say — to have divided with any
human being any one deep sensation of joy or of sorrow,
sinks deep the foundations of a lasting love. When in
moments of fretfulness and imbecility I am disposed to
anger or reproach, it will, I trust, be always a restoring
thought — " We have wept over the same little one," —
and with whom I am angry? With her who so patiently
and unweariedly sustained my poor and sickly infant
through his long pains — with her, who, if I too should
be called away, would stay in the deep anguish over my
death-pillow! who would never forget me!" Ah, my
poor Berkeley! A few weeks ago an Englishman desired
me to write an epitaph on an infant who had died before
its christening. While I wrote it, my heart with a deep
misgiving turned my thoughts homewards.

ON AN INFANT, WHO DIED BEFORE ITS CHRISTENING.

> Be rather than be *call'd* a Child of God !
> Death whisper'd. With assenting Nod
> Its head upon the Mother's breast
> The baby bow'd, and went without demur,
> Of the kingdom of the blest
> Possessor, not Inheritor.

It refers to the second question in the Church Catechism.
We are well, my dear Sara. I hope to be home at the
end of ten or eleven weeks. If you should be in Bristol,
you will probably be shewn by Mr. Estlin three letters
which I have written to him altogether — and one to

Mr. Wade. Mr. Estlin will permit you to take the letters to Stowey that Poole may see them, and Poole will
return them. I have no doubt but I shall repay myself
by the work which I am writing, to such an amount, that
I shall have spent out of my income only fifty pounds at
the end of August. My love to your sisters — and love
and duty to your mother. God bless you, my love! and
shield us from deeper afflictions, or make us resigned unto
them (and perhaps the latter blessedness is greater than
the former).

Your affectionate and faithful husband,

S. T. COLERIDGE.

XCVII. TO THE SAME.

April 23, 1799.

MY DEAR SARA, — Surely it is unnecessary for me to
say how infinitely I languish to be in my native country,
and with how many struggles I have remained even so
long in Germany! I received your affecting letter, dated
Easter Sunday; and, had I followed my impulses, I should
have packed up and gone with Wordsworth and his sister,
who passed through (and only passed through) this place
two or three days ago. If they burn with such impatience
to return to their native country, *they* who are all to each
other, what must I feel with everything pleasant and
everything valuable and everything dear to me at a distance — here, where I may truly say my only amusement
is — to labour! But it is, in the strictest sense of the
word, impossible to collect what I have to collect in less
than six weeks from this day; yet I read and transcribe
from eight to ten hours every day. Nothing could support me but the knowledge that if I return now we shall
be embarrassed and in debt; and the moral certainty that
having done what I am doing we shall be more than
cleared — not to add that so large a work with so great a
quantity and variety of information from sources so scat-

tered and so little known, even in Germany, will of course
establish my character for industry and erudition certainly; and, I would fain hope, for reflection and genius.
This day in June I hope and trust that I shall be in England. Oh that the vessel could but land at Shurton Bars!
Not that I should wish to see you and Poole immediately
on my landing.   No! — the sight, the touch of my native
country, were sufficient for one *whole* feeling, the most
deep unmingled emotion — but then and after a lonely walk
of three miles — then, first of *all*, whom I knew, to see
you and my *Friend!* It lessens the delight of the thought
of my return that I must get at you through a tribe of
acquaintances, damping the freshness of one's joy! My
poor little baby! At this time I see the corner of the
room where his cradle stood — and his cradle too — and
I cannot help seeing him in the cradle.   Little lamb!
and the snow would not melt on his limbs! I have some
faint recollections that he had that difficulty of breathing
once before I left England — or was it Hartley? "A
child, a child is born, and the fond heart dances; and yet
the childless are the most happy." At Christmas [1] I saw a
custom which pleased and interested me here.   The children make little presents to their parents, and to one another, and the parents to the children.   For three or four
months before Christmas the girls are all busy, and the
boys save up their pocket-money, to make or purchase
these presents.   What the present is to be is cautiously
kept secret, and the girls have a world of contrivances to
conceal it, such as working when they are at a visit, and
the others are not with them, and getting up in the morning long before light, etc.   Then on the evening before
Christmas Day, one of the parlours is lighted up by the
children, into which the parents must not go.   A great yew

---

[1] The following description of the
Christmas-tree, and of Knecht Rupert, was originally published, almost
verbatim, in No. 19 of the original
issue of *The Friend*, December 28,
1809.

bough is fastened on the table at a little distance from the
wall, a multitude of little tapers are fastened in the bough,
but not so as to burn it, till they are nearly burnt out, and
coloured paper, etc., hangs and flutters from the twigs.
Under this bough the children lay out in great neatness
the presents they mean for their parents, still concealing
in their pockets what they intend for each other.   Then
the parents are introduced, and each presents his little
gift — and then they bring out the others, and present
them to each other with kisses and embraces.   Where I saw
the scene there were eight or nine children of different
ages; and the eldest daughter and the mother wept aloud
for joy and tenderness, and the tears ran down the cheek
of the father, and he clasped all his children so tight to
his heart, as if he did it to stifle the sob that was rising
within him.   I was very much affected, and the shadow of
the bough on the wall, and arching over on the ceiling,
made a pretty picture — and then the raptures of the
very little ones, when at last the twigs and thread-leaves
began to catch fire and snap!   Oh that was a delight for
them!   On the next day in the great parlour the parents
lay out on the tables the presents for the children; a scene
of more sober joy succeeds, as, on this day, after an old
custom, the mother says privately to each of her daughters,
and the father to each of his sons, that which he has observed most praiseworthy, and that which he has observed
most faulty in their conduct.   Formerly, and still in all
the little towns and villages through the whole of North
Germany, these presents were sent by all the parents of the
village to some one fellow, who, in high buskins, a white
robe, a mask, and an enormous flax wig, personates Knecht
Rupert, that is, the servant Rupert.   On Christmas night
he goes round to every house and says that Jesus Christ
his Master sent him there; the parents and older children
receive him with great pomp of reverence, while the little
ones are most terribly frightened.   He then enquires for

the children, and according to the character which he hears
from the parent he gives them the intended presents, as if
they came out of Heaven from Jesus Christ; or, if they
should have been bad children, he gives the parents a rod,
and, in the name of his Master Jesus, recommends them
to use it frequently. About eight or nine years old, the
children are let into the secret; and it is curious, how
faithfully they all keep it. There are a multitude of
strange superstitions among the bauers; — these still survive in spite of the efforts of the Clergy, who in the north
of Germany, that is, in the Hanoverian, Saxon, and Prussian dominions, are almost all Deists. But they make little or no impressions on the bauers, who are wonderfully
religious and fantastically superstitious, but not in the
least priest-rid. But in the Catholic countries of Germany the difference is vast indeed! I met lately an intelligent and calm-minded man who had spent a considerable
time at Marburg in the Bishopric of Paderborn in West-
phalia. He told me that bead-prayers to the Holy Virgin
are universal, and universally, too, are magical powers
attributed to one particular formula of words which are
absolutely jargons; at least, the words are to be found in
no known language. The peasants believe it, however, to
be a prayer to the Virgin, and happy is the man among
them who is made confident by a priest that he can repeat
it perfectly; for heaven knows what terrible calamity
might not happen if any one should venture to repeat it
and blunder. Vows and pilgrimages to particular images
are still common among the bauers. If any one dies before the performance of his vow, they believe that he hov-
ers between heaven and *earth*, and at times hobgoblins his
relations till they perform it for him. Particular saints
are believed to be eminently favourable to particular
prayers, and he assured me solemnly that a little before
he left Marburg a lady of Marburg had prayed and given
money to have the public prayers at St. Erasmus's Chapel

to St. Erasmus — for what, think you? — that the baby,
with which she was then pregnant, might be a boy with
light hair and rosy cheeks. When their cows, pigs, or
horses are sick they take them to the Dominican monks,
who transcribe *texts out of the holy books*, and perform
exorcisms. When men or women are sick they give largely
to the Convent, who on good conditions dress them in
Church robes, and lay a particular and highly venerated
Crucifix on their breast, and perform a multitude of antic
ceremonies. In general, my informer confessed that they
cured the persons, which he seemed to think extraordinary,
but which I think very natural. Yearly on St. Blasius's
Day unusual multitudes go to receive the Lord's Supper;
and while they are receiving it the monks hold a Blasius's
Taper (as it is called) before the forehead of the kneeling
person, and then pray to St. Blasius to drive away all
headaches for the ensuing year. Their wishes are often
expressed in this form : " Mary, Mother of God, make her
Son do so and so." Yet with all this, from every information which I can collect (and I have had many opportunities of collecting various accounts), the peasants in
the Catholic countries of Germany, but especially in Aus-
tria, are far better off, and a far happier and livelier race,
than those in the Protestant lands. . . . I fill up the sheet
with scattered customs put down in the order in which I
happened to see them. The peasant children, wherever I
have been, are dressed warm and tight, but very ugly ;
the dress looks a frock coat, some of coarse blue cloth,
some of plaid, buttoned behind — the row of buttons running down the back, and the seamless, buttonless fore-part
has an odd look. When the peasants marry, if the girl is of
a good character, the clergyman gives her a Virgin Crown
(a tawdry, ugly thing made of gold and silver tinsel, like
the royal crowns in shape). This they wear with cropped,
powdered, and pomatumed hair — in short, the bride looks
ugliness personified. While I was at Ratzeburg a girl

came to beg the pastor to let her be married in this crown,
and she had had two bastards! The pastor refused, of
course. I wondered that a reputable farmer should marry
her; but the pastor told me that where a female bauer is
the heiress, her having had a bastard does not much stand
in her way; and yet, though little or no infamy attaches to
it, the number of bastards is but small — two in seventy
has been the average of Ratzeburg among the peasants.
By the bye, the bells in Germany are not rung as ours,
with ropes, but two men stand, one on each side of the bell,
and each pushes the bell away from him with his foot. In
the churches, what is a baptismal font in our churches is a
great Angel with a bason in his hand; he draws up and
down with a chain like a lamp. In a particular part of
the ceremony down comes the great stone Angel with the
bason, presenting it to the pastor, who, having taken *quant.
suff.*, up flies my Angel to his old place in the ceiling
— you cannot conceive how droll it looked. The graves
in the little village churchyards are in square or paral-
lelogrammic wooden cases — they look like boxes without
lids — and thorns and briars are woven over them, as is
done in some parts of England. Perhaps you recollect
that beautiful passage in Jeremy Taylor's Holy Dying,
"and the Summer brings briers to bud on our graves."
The shepherds with iron soled boots walk before the sheep,
as in the East — you know our Saviour says — "My
Sheep follow me." So it is here. The dog and the shepherd walk first, the shepherd with his romantic fur, and
generally knitting a pair of white worsted gloves — he
walks on and his dog by him, and then follow the sheep
winding along the roads in a beautiful *stream!* In the
fields I observed a multitude of poles with bands and
trusses of straw tied round the higher part and the top —
on enquiry we found that they were put there for the owls
to perch upon. And the owls? They catch the field
mice, who do amazing damage in the light soil all through-

out the north of Germany.   The gallows near Göttingen, like that near Ratzeburg, is three great stone pillars, square, like huge tall chimneys, and connected with each other at the top by three iron bars with hooks to them — and near them is a wooden pillar with a wheel on the top of it on which the head is exposed, if the person instead of being hung is beheaded.   I was frightened at first to see such a multitude of bones and skeletons of sheep, oxen, and horses, and bones as I imagined of men for many, many yards all round the gallows. I found that in Germany the hangman is by the laws of the Empire infamous — these hangmen form a caste, and their families marry with each other, etc. — and that all dead cattle, who have died, belong to them, and are carried by the owners to the gallows and left there.   When their cattle are bewitched, or otherwise desperately sick, the peasants take them and tie them to the gallows — drowned dogs and kittens, etc., are thrown there — in short, the grass grows rank, and yet the bones overtop it (the fancy of *human* bones must, I suppose, have arisen in my ignorance of comparative anatomy). God bless you, my Love !   I will write again speedily. When I was at Ratzeburg I wrote one wintry night in bed, but never sent you, three stanzas which, I dare say, you will think very silly, and so they are : and yet they were not written without a yearning, yearning, yearning *Inside* — for my yearning affects more than my *heart.* I feel it all within me.

I.

If I had but two little wings,
And were a little feath'ry bird,
To you I 'd fly, my dear !
But thoughts like these are idle things —
And I stay here.

II.

But in my sleep to you I fly :
I 'm always with you in my sleep —

The World is all one's own.
But then one wakes — And where am I ? —
All, all alone !

III.

Sleep stays not, though a monarch bids :
So I love to wake ere break of day :
For though my sleep be gone,
Yet while 't is dark, one shuts one's lids,
And still dreams on !¹

If Mrs. Southey be with you, remember me with all kindness and thankfulness for their attention to you and Hartley. To dear Mrs. Poole give my filial love. My love to Ward. Why should I write the name of Tom Poole, except for the pleasure of writing it ? It grieves me to the heart that Nanny is not with you — I cannot bear changes — Death makes enough !

God bless you, my dear, dear wife, and believe me with eagerness to clasp you to my heart, your ever faithful husband,

S. T. COLERIDGE.

XCVIII. TO THOMAS POOLE.

May 6, 1799, Monday morn.

My dear Poole, my dear Poole ! — I am homesick. Society is a burden to me ; and I find relief only in labour. So I read and transcribe from morning till night, and never in my life have I worked so hard as this last month, for indeed I must sail over an ocean of matter with almost spiritual speed, to do what I have to do in the time in which I *will* do it or leave it undone ! O my God, how I long to be at home ! My *whole Being* so yearns after you, that when I think of the moment of our meeting, I catch the fashion of German joy, rush into

---

¹ First published in *Annual An-thology* of 1800, under the signature *Cordomi*. See *Poetical Works*, p. 146, and Editor's Note, p. 621.

your arms, and embrace you. Methinks my hand would
swell if the whole force of my feeling were crowded there.
Now the Spring comes, the vital sap of my affections
rises as in a tree! And what a gloomy Spring! But a
few days ago all the new buds were covered with snow ;
and everything yet looks so brown and wintry, that yesterday the roses (which the ladies carried on the ram-
parts, their promenade), beautiful as they were, so little
harmonized with the general face of nature, that they
looked to me like silk and made roses. But these leaf-
less Spring Woods! Oh, how I long to hear you whistle
to the Rippers![1] There are a multitude of nightingales
here (poor things! they sang in the snow). I thought
of my own[2] verses on the nightingale, only because I
thought of Hartley, my *only* Child. Dear lamb! I
hope he won't be dead before I get home. There are
moments in which I have such a power of life within me,
such a *conceit* of it, I mean, that I lay the blame of my
child's death to my absence. *Not intellectually ;* but I
have a strange sort of sensation, as if, while I was present,
none could die whom I entirely loved, and doubtless it
was no absurd idea of yours that there may be unions and
connections out of the visible world.

Wordsworth and his sister passed through here, as I
have informed you. I walked on with them five English
miles, and spent a day with them. They were melancholy
and hypped. W. was affected to tears at the thought
of not being near me — wished me of course to live in
the North of England near Sir Frederick Vane's great
library.[3] I told him that, independent of the expense of
removing, and the impropriety of taking Mrs. Coleridge

---

[1] The men who rip the oak bark
from the logs for tanning.

[2] My dear babe,
Who capable of no articulate sound,
Mars all things with his imitative lisp,
How he would place his hand beside his
    ear,

His little hand, the small forefinger up,
And bid us listen.

— " The Nightingale, a Conversation Poem," written in April, 1798.
Poetical Works, p. 133.

[3] Hutton Hall, near Penrith.

to a place where she would have no acquaintance, two
insurmountable objections, the library was no inducement
to me — for I wanted old books chiefly, such as could be
procured anywhere better than in a gentleman's new
fashionable collection.   Finally I told him plainly that
you had been the man in whom *first* and in whom alone
I had felt an *anchor !*   With all my other connections I
felt a dim sense of insecurity and uncertainty, terribly
incompatible.   W. was affected *to tears*, very much affected ; but he deemed the vicinity of a library absolutely
necessary to his health, nay to his existence.   It is painful to me, too, to think of not living near him ; for he is
a *good* and *kind* man, and the only one whom in *all*
things I feel my superior — and you will believe me when
I say that I have few feelings more pleasurable than to
find myself, in intellectual faculties, an inferior.

But my resolve is fixed, *not to leave you till you leave
me !*   I still think that Wordsworth will be disappointed
in his expectation of relief from reading without society ;
and I think it highly probable that where I live, there he
will live ; unless he should find in the North any person
or persons, who can feel and understand him, and recip-
rocate and react on him.   My many weaknesses are of
some advantage to me ; they unite me more with the
great mass of my fellow-beings — but dear Wordsworth
appears to me to have hurtfully segregated and isolated
his being.   Doubtless his delights are more deep and
sublime ; but he has likewise more hours that prey upon
the flesh and blood.   With regard to *Hancock's* house, if
I can get no place within a mile or two of Stowey I must
try to get that ; but I confess I like it not — not to say
that it is not altogether pleasant to live directly opposite
to a person who had behaved so rudely to Mrs. Coleridge.
But these are in the eye of reason trifles, and if no other
house can be got — in my eye, too, they shall be trifles.

.   .   .   .

O Poole! I am homesick. Yesterday, or rather yesternight, I dittied the following horrible ditty; but my poor Muse is quite gone — perhaps she may return and meet me at Stowey.

> 'T is sweet to him who all the week
> Through city-crowds must push his way,
> To stroll alone through fields and woods,
> And hallow thus the Sabbath-day.
>
> And sweet it is, in summer bower,
> Sincere, affectionate, and gay,
> One's own dear children feasting round,
> To celebrate one's marriage day.
>
> But what is all to his delight,
> Who having long been doomed to roam,
> Throws off the bundle from his back,
> Before the door of his own home?
>
> Home-sickness is no baby pang —
> This feel I hourly more and more:
> There 's only musick in thy wings,
> Thou breeze that play'st on Albion's Shore.[1]

The Professors here are exceedingly kind to all the Englishmen, but to me they pay the most flattering attentions, especially Blumenbach and Eichhorn. Nothing can be conceived more delightful than Blumenbach's lectures, and, in conversation, he is, indeed, a most interesting man. The learned Orientalist Tychsen[2] has given me instruction in the Gothic and Theotuscan languages, which I can now read pretty well; and hope in the course

---

[1] First published in the *Annual Anthology* of 1800. See *Poetical Works*, p. 146, and Editor's Note, p. 621. According to Carlyon the lines were dictated by Coleridge and inscribed by one of the party in the "Stammbuch" of the Wernigerode Inn. *Early Years*, i. 66.

[2] Olaus Tychsen, 1734–1815, was "Professor of Oriental Tongues" at Rostock, in Mecklenburg-Schwerin.

of a year to be thoroughly acquainted with all the languages of the North, both German and Celtic. I find
being learned is a mighty easy thing, compared with any
study else. My God! a miserable poet must he be, and
a despicable metaphysician, whose acquirements have not
cost him more trouble and reflection than all the learning
of Tooke, Porson, and Parr united. With the advantage
of a great library, learning is nothing — methinks, merely
a sad excuse for being idle. Yet a man gets reputation
by it, and reputation gets money; and for reputation I
don't care a damn, but money — yes — money I must get
by all honest ways. Therefore at the end of two or three
years, if God grant me life, expect to see me come out
with some horribly learned book, full of manuscript quota-
tions from Laplandish and Patagonian authors, possibly,
on the striking resemblance of the Sweogothian and San-
scrit languages, and so on! N. B. Whether a sort of
parchment might not be made of old shoes; and whether
apples should not be grafted on oak saplings, as the fruit
would be the same as now, but the wood far more valuable? *Two ideas of mine.* — To extract *aqua fortis* from
cucumbers is a discovery not yet made, but sugar from
bete, oh! all Germany is mad about it. I have seen the
sugar sent to Blumenbach from Achard [1] the great chemist, and it is good enough. They say that an hundred
pounds weight of *bete* will make twelve pounds of sugar,
and that there is no expense in the preparation. It is the
Beta altissima, belongs to the *Beta vulgaris,* and in Germany is called *Runkelrübe.* Its leaves resemble those of
the common red *bete.* It is in shape like a clumsy nine
pin and about the size of a middling turnip. The flesh
is white but has rings of a reddish cast. I will bring over
a quantity of the seed.

.   .   .   .

[1] F. C. Achard, born in 1754, was sugar, molasses, and vinous spirit
author of an "Instruction for making from Beet-root."

A stupid letter! — I believe my late proficiency in learning has somewhat stupified me, but live in hopes of one better worth postage. In the last week of June, I trust, you will see me. Chester is well and desires love and duty to his family. To your dear Mother and to Ward give my kind love, and to all who ask after me.

My dear Poole! don't let little Hartley die before I come home. That's silly — true — and I burst into tears as I wrote it. Yours

S. T. COLERIDGE.

CHAPTER V

FROM SOUTH TO NORTH

1799–1800

XCIX. TO ROBERT SOUTHEY.

NETHER STOWEY, July 29, 1799.

I AM doubtful, Southey, whether the circumstances which impel me to write to you ought not to keep me silent, and, if it were only a feeling of delicacy, I should remain silent, for it is good to do all things in faith. But I have been absent, Southey! ten months, and if *you* knew that domestic affection was hard upon me, and that my own health was declining, would you not have shootings within you of an affection which ("though fallen, though changed") has played too important a part in the event of our lives and the formation of our character, ever to be *forgotten?* I am perplexed what to write, or how to state the object of my writing. Any participation in each other's moral being I do not wish, simply because I know enough of the mind of man to know that [it] is impossible. But, Southey, we have similar talents, sentiments nearly similar, and kindred pursuits; we have likewise, in more than one instance, common objects of our esteem and love. I pray and intreat you, if we should meet at any time, let us not withhold from each other the outward expressions of daily kindliness; and if it be no longer in your power to soften your opinions, make your feelings at least more tolerant towards me — (a debt of humility which assuredly we all of us owe to our most feeble, imperfect, and self-deceiving nature). We are

few of us good enough to know our own hearts, and as to
the hearts of others, let us struggle to hope that they are
better than we think them, and resign the rest to our
common Maker. God bless you and yours.

S. T. Coleridge.

[Southey's answer to this appeal has not been preserved,
but its tenor was that Coleridge had slandered him to
others. In his reply Coleridge " avers on his honour as a
man and a gentleman " that he never charged Southey
with " aught but deep and implacable enmity towards himself," and that his authorities for this accusation were
those on whom Southey relied, that is, doubtless, Lloyd
and Lamb. He appeals to Poole, the " repository " of
his every thought, and to Wordsworth, " with whom he
had been for more than one whole year almost daily and
frequently for weeks together," to bear him out in this
statement. A letter from Poole to Southey dated August
8, and forwarded to Minehead by " special messenger,"
bears ample testimony to Coleridge's disavowal. " Without entering into particulars," he writes, " I will say generally, that in the many conversations I have had with
Coleridge concerning yourself, he has never discovered
the least personal enmity against, but, on the contrary,
the strongest affection for you stifled only by the untoward events of your separation." Poole's intervention
was successful, and once again the cottage opened its
doors to a distinguished guest. The Southeys remained
as visitors at Stowey until, in company with their host,
they set out for Devonshire.]

C. TO THOMAS POOLE.

EXETER, Southey's Lodgings, Mr. Tucker's, Fore Street Hill,
September 16, 1799.[1]

MY DEAR POOLE, — Here I am just returned from a
little tour[2] of five days, having seen rocks and waterfalls,
and a pretty river or two; some wide landscapes, and a
multitude of ash-tree dells, and the blue waters of the
"roaring sea," as little Hartley says, who on Friday fell
down stairs and injured his arm. 'T is swelled and
sprained, but, God be praised, not broken. The views of
Totness and Dartmouth are among the most impressive
things I have ever seen; but in general what of Devonshire I have lately seen is tame to Quantock, Porlock,
Culbone, and Linton. So much for the country! Now
as to the inhabitants thereof, they are bigots, unalphabeted
in the first feelings of liberality; of course in all they speak
and all they do not speak, they give good reasons for the
opinions which they hold, viz. they hold the propriety of
slavery, an opinion which, being generally assented to by
Englishmen, makes Pitt and Paul the first among the
moral fitnesses of things. I have three brothers, that is
to say, relations by gore. Two are parsons and one is a

[1] The Coleridges were absent from
Stowey for about a month. For
the first fortnight they were guests
of George Coleridge at Ottery. The
latter part of the time was spent with
the Southeys in their lodgings at
Exeter. It was during this second
visit that Coleridge accompanied
Southey on a walking tour through
part of Dartmoor and as far as Dartmouth.

[2] Coleridge took but few notes
during this tour. In 1803 he retran-
scribed his fragmentary jottings and
regrets that he possessed no more,
"though we were at the interesting Bovey waterfall [Becky Fall],
through that wild dell of ashes
which leads to Ashburton, most like
the approach to upper Matterdale."
"I have," he adds, "at this moment
very distinct visual impressions of
the tour, namely of Torbay, the
village of Paignton with the Castle." Southey was disappointed in
South Devon, which he contrasts
unfavourably with the North of
Somersetshire, but for "the dell of
ashes" he has a word of praise.
*Selections from Letters of Robert Sou-
they*, i. 84.

colonel. George and the colonel, good men as times go —
very good men — but alas! we have neither tastes nor
feelings in common. This I wisely learnt from their conversation, and did not suffer them to learn it from mine.
What occasion for it? Hunger and thirst — roast fowls,
mealy potatoes, pies, and clouted cream! bless the inven-
tors of them! An honest philosopher may find therewith
preoccupation for his mouth, keeping his heart and brain,
the latter in his scull, the former in the pericardium
some five or six inches from the roots of his tongue!
Church and King! Why I drink Church and King, mere
cutaneous scabs of loyalty which only ape the king's evil,
but affect not the interior of one's health. Mendicant
sores! it requires some little caution to keep them open,
but they heal of their own accord. Who (such a friend
as I am to the system of fraternity) could refuse such a
toast at the table of a clergyman and a colonel, his brother? So, my dear Poole! I live in peace. Of the other
party, I have dined with a Mr. Northmore, a pupil of
Wakefield, who possesses a fine house half a mile from
Exeter. In his boyhood he was at my father's school.
. . . But Southey and self called upon him as authors —
he having edited a Tryphiodorus and part of Plutarch,
and being a notorious anti-ministerialist and free-thinker.
He welcomed us as he ought, and we met at dinner Hucks
(at whose house I dine Wednesday), the man who toured
with me in Wales and afterwards published his " Tour,"
Kendall, a poet, who really looks like a man of genius,
pale and gnostic, has the merit of being a Jacobin or so,
but is a shallowist — and finally a Mr. Banfill, a man of
sense, information, and various literature, and most perfectly a gentleman — in short a pleasant man. At his
house we dine to-morrow. Northmore himself is an honest, vehement sort of a fellow who splutters out all his
opinions like a fiz-gig, made of gunpowder not thoroughly
dry, sudden and explosive, yet ever with a certain adhe-

sive blubberliness of elocution.   Shallow! shallow!   A
man who can read Greek well, but shallow!   Yet honest,
too, and who ardently wishes the well-being of his fellow-
men, and believes that without more liberty and more
equality this well-being is not possible.   He possesses a
most noble library.   The victory at Novi![1]   If I were a
good caricaturist I would sketch off Suwarrow in a car of
conquest drawn by huge crabs!!   With what retrograde
majesty the vehicle advances!   He may truly say he
came off with *éclat*, that is, a claw!   I shall be back at
Stowey in less than three weeks. . . .

We hope your dear mother remains well.   Give my
filial love to her.   God bless her!   I beg my kind love to
Ward.   God bless you and

S. T. Coleridge.

Monday night.

CI. TO ROBERT SOUTHEY.

Stowey, Tuesday evening, October 15, 1799.

It is fashionable among our philosophizers to assert the
existence of a surplus of misery in the world, which, in
my opinion, is no proof that either systematic thinking
or unaffected self-observation is fashionable among them.
But Hume wrote, and the French imitated him, and we
the French, and the French us; and so philosophisms fly
to and fro, in series of imitated imitations — shadows of
shadows of shadows of a farthing-candle placed between
two looking-glasses.   For in truth, my dear Southey! I
am harassed with the rheumatism in my head and shoulders, not without arm-and-thigh-twitches — but when the
pain intermits it leaves my sensitive frame *so* sensitive!
My enjoyments are so deep, of the fire, of the candle, of
the thought I am thinking, of the old folio I am reading,

---

[1] Suwarrow, at the head of the Austro-Russian troops, defeated the French under Joubert at Novi near Alessandria, in North Italy, August 15, 1799.

and the silence of the silent house is so *most and very
delightful*, that upon my soul ! the rheumatism is no such
bad thing as *people make for*.   And yet I have, and do
suffer from it, in much pain and sleeplessness and often
sick at stomach through indigestion of the food, which I
eat from compulsion.   Since I received your former letter, I have spent a few days at Upcott;[1] but was too
unwell to be comfortable, so I returned yesterday.   Poor
Tom ![2] he has an adventurous calling.   I have so wholly
forgotten my geography that I don't know where Ferrol
is, whether in France or Spain.   Your dear mother must
be very anxious indeed.   If he return safe, it will have
been good.   God grant he may!

Massena ![3] and what say you of the resurrection and
glorification of the Saviour of the East after his trials in
the wilderness ?   (I am afraid that this is a piece of blasphemy ; but it was in simple verity such an infusion of
animal spirits into me.)   Buonaparte ! Buonaparte ! dear,
dear, *dear* Buonaparte !   It would be no bad fun to hear
the clerk of the Privy Council read this paragraph before
Pitt, etc.   " You ill-looking frog-voiced reptile ! mind you
lay the proper emphasis on the third *dear*, or I 'll split
your clerkship's skull for you !"   Poole ordered a paper.
He has *found out*, he says, why the *newspapers* had become so indifferent to him.   *Inventive* Genius !   He begs
his kind remembrances to you.   In consequence of the
news he burns like Greek Fire, under all the wets and
waters of this health-and-harvest destroying weather.   He
flames while his barley smokes.   " See ! " he says, " how it

[1] A temporary residence of Josiah
Wedgwood, who had taken it on lease
in order to be near his newly purchased property at Combe Florey,
in Somersetshire. Meteyard's *Group
of Englishmen*, 1871, p. 107.

[2] Southey's brother, a midshipman on board the Sylph gun-brig.

A report had reached England that
the Sylph had been captured and
brought to Ferrol.   *Southey's Life
and Correspondence*, ii. 30.

[3] Marshal Massena defeated the
Russians under Prince Korsikov at
Zurich, September 25, 1799.

grows out again, ruining the prospects of those who had cut it down!" You are harvest-man enough, I suppose, to understand the metaphor. Jackson [1] is, I believe, out of all doubt a bad man. Why is it, if it be, and I fear it is, why is it that the studies of music and painting are so unfavourable to the human heart? Painters have been commonly very clever men, which is not so generally the case with musicians, but both alike are almost uniformly debauchees. It is superfluous to say how much your account of Bampfylde [2] interested me. Predisposition to madness gave him a cast of originality, and he had a species of *taste* which only genius could give; but his genius does not appear a *powerful* or *ebullient* faculty (nearer to Lamb's than to the Gebir-man [Landor], so I judge from the few specimens *I* have seen). If you think otherwise, you are right I doubt not. I shall be glad to give Mr. and Mrs. Keenan [3] the right hand of welcome with looks and tones in *fit* accompaniment. For the wife of a man

[1] William Jackson, organist of Exeter Cathedral, 1730–1803, a musical composer and artist. He published, among other works, *The Four Ages with Essays*, 1798. See letter of Southey to S. T. Coleridge, October 3, 1799, *Southey's Life and Correspondence*, ii. 26.

[2] John Codrington Warwick Bampfylde, second son of Richard Bampfylde, of Poltimore, was the author of *Sixteen Sonnets*, published in 1779. In the letter of October 3 (see above) Southey gives an interesting account of his eccentric habits and melancholy history. In a prefatory note to four of Bampfylde's sonnets, included by Southey in his *Specimens of the Later English Poets*, he explains how he came to possess the copies of some hitherto unpublished poems.

"Jackson of Exeter, a man whose various talents made all who knew him remember him with regret, designed to republish the little collection of Bampfylde's Sonnets, with what few of his pieces were still unedited.

"Those poems which are here first printed were transcribed from the originals in his possession."

"Bampfylde published his Sonnets at a very early age; they are some of the most original in our language. He died in a private mad-house, after twenty years' confinement." *Specimens of the Later English Poets*, 1808, iii. 434.

[3] "A sister of General McKinnon, who was killed at Ciudad Rodrigo." In the same letter to Coleridge (see above) Southey says that he looked up to her with more respect because the light of Buonaparte's countenance had shone upon her.

of genius who sympathises effectively with her husband in his habits and feelings is a *rara avis* with me; though a vast majority of her own sex and too many of ours will scout her for a *rara piscis*. If I am well enough, Sara and I go to Bristol in a few days. I hope they will not come in the mean time. It is singularly unpleasant to me that I cannot renew our late acquaintances in Exeter without creating very serious uneasinesses at Ottery, Northmore is so preëminently an offensive character to the aristocrats. He sent Paine's books as a present to a clergyman of my brother's acquaintance, a Mr. Markes. This was silly enough. . . .

I will set about "Christabel" with all speed; but I do not think it a fit opening poem. What I think would be a fit opener, and what I would humbly lay before you as the best plan of the next Anthologia, I will communicate shortly in another letter entirely on this subject. Mohammed I will not forsake; but my money-book I must write first. In the last, or at least in a late "Monthly Magazine" was an Essay on a Jesuitic conspiracy and about the Russians. There was so much genius in it that I suspected William Taylor for the author; but the style was so nauseously affected, so absurdly pedantic, that I was half-angry with myself for the suspicion. Have you seen Bishop Prettyman's book? I hear it is a curiosity. You remember Scott the attorney, who held such a disquisition on my simile of property resembling matter rather than blood? and eke of St. John? and you remember, too, that I shewed him in my face that there was no room for him in my heart? Well, sir! this man has taken a most deadly hatred to me, and how do you think he revenges himself? He imagines that I write for the "Morning Post," and he goes regularly to the coffee-houses, calls for the paper, and reading it he observes aloud, "What damn'd stuff of poetry is always crammed in this paper! such damn'd silly nonsense! I wonder what coxcomb it is that writes it! I wish the paper was kicked out of the coffee-house." Now, but for Cruik-shank, I could play Scott a precious trick by sending to Stuart, " The Angry Attorney, a True Tale," and I know more than enough of Scott's most singular parti-coloured rascalities to make a most humorous and biting satire of it.

I have heard of a young Quaker who went to the Lobby, with a monstrous military cock-hat on his head, with a scarlet coat and up to his mouth in flower'd muslin, swear-ing too most bloodily — all " that he might not be unlike other people!" A Quaker's son getting himself christen'd to avoid being remarkable is as *improbable* a lie as ever self-delusion permitted the heart to impose on the under-standing, or the understanding to invent without the con-sent of the heart. But so it is. Soon after Lloyd's arri-val at Cambridge I understand Christopher Wordsworth wrote his uncle, Mr. Cookson,[1] that Lloyd was going to read Greek with him. Cookson wrote back recommending caution, and whether or no an intimacy with so marked a character might not be prejudicial to his academical inter-ests. (This is his usual mild manner.) Christopher Wordsworth returned for answer that Lloyd was by no means a democrat, and as a proof of it, transcribed the most favourable passages from the " Edmund Oliver," and here the *affair* ended. You remember Lloyd's own account of this story, of course, more accurately than I, and can therefore best judge how far my suspicions of falsehood and exaggeration were well-founded. My dear Southey! the having a bad heart and not having a good one are different things. That Charles Lloyd has a bad heart, I do not even think; but I venture to say, and that openly, that he has not a good one. He is unfit to be any man's friend, and to all but a very guarded man he is a

[1] Dr. Cookson, Canon of Windsor and Rector of Forncett, Norfolk. Dorothy Wordsworth passed much of her time under his roof before she finally threw in her lot with her brother William in 1795.

perilous *acquaintance*. *Your* conduct towards him, while
it is wise, will, I doubt not, be gentle. Of confidence he
is not worthy; but social kindness and communicativeness
purely intellectual can do you no harm, and may be the
means of benefiting his character essentially. *Aut ama
me quia sum Dei, aut ut sim Dei*, said St. Augustin, and
in the laxer sense of the word "Ama" there is wisdom in
the expression notwithstanding its wit. Besides, it is the
way of *peace*. From Bristol perhaps I go to London, but
I will write you where I am.   Yours affectionately,

S. T. COLERIDGE.

I have great affection for Lamb, but I have likewise
a perfect Lloyd-and-Lambophobia! Independent of the
irritation attending an epistolary controversy with them,
their *prose* comes so damn'd dear! Lloyd especially
writes with a woman's fluency in a large rambling hand,
most dull though profuse of feeling. I received from
them in last quarter letters so many, that with the postage I might have bought Birch's Milton. — Sara will write
soon.   Our love to Edith and your mother.

CII. TO THE SAME.

KESWICK,[1] Sunday, November 10, 1799.

MY DEAR SOUTHEY, — I am anxious lest so long
silence should seem unaffectionate, or I would not, hav-

---

[1] The journal, or notes for a journal, of this first tour in the Lake
Country, leaves a doubt whether
Coleridge and Wordsworth slept at
Keswick on Sunday, November 10,
1799, or whether they returned to
Cockermouth. It is certain that
they passed through Keswick again
on Friday, November 15, as the following entry testifies: —

"1 mile and ½ from Keswick, a
Druidical circle. On the right the
road and Saddleback; on the left a
fine but unwatered vale, walled by
grassy hills and a fine black crag
standing single at the terminus as
sentry. Before me, that is, towards
Keswick, the mountains stand, one
behind the other, in orderly array,
as if evoked by and attentive to the
white-vested wizards." It was from
almost the same point of view that,
thirty years afterwards, his wife, on
her journey south after her daugh-

ing so little to say, write to you from such a distant corner of the kingdom. I was called up to the North by alarming accounts of Wordsworth's health, which, thank God! are but little more than alarms. *Since* I have visited the Lakes and in a pecuniary way have made the trip answer to me. From hence I go to London, having had (by accident here) a sort of offer made to me of a pleasant kind, which, if it turn out well, will enable me and Sara to reside in London for the next four or five months — a thing I wish extremely on many and important accounts. So much for myself. In my last letter I said I would give you my reasons for thinking "Christabel," *were* it finished, and finished as spiritedly as it commences, yet still an improper opening poem. My reason is it cannot be expected to please all. *Those* who dislike it will deem it extravagant ravings, and go on through the rest of the collection with the feeling of disgust, and it is not impossible that were it liked by any it would still not harmonise with the *real-life* poems that follow. It ought, I think, to be the last. The first ought *me judice* to be a poem in couplets, didactic or satirical, such a one as the lovers of genuine poetry would call sensible and entertaining, such as the ignoramuses and Pope-admirers would deem genuine poetry. I had planned such a one, and, but for the absolute necessity of scribbling prose, I should have written it. The great and master fault of the last "Anthology" was the want of arrangement. It is called a collection, and meant to be continued annually; yet was distinguished in nothing from any other single volume of poems equally good. Yours ought to have been a cabinet with proper compartments, and papers in them, whereas it was only the papers. Some such arrangement as this should have been adopted: First. Satirical and Didactic. 2. Lyrical. 3. Narrative. 4. Levities.

ter's marriage, took a solemn farewell of the Vale of Keswick once so strange, but then so dear and so familiar.

> "Sic positi quoniam suaves miscetis odores,
>   Neve inter vites corylum sere" —

is, I am convinced, excellent advice of Master Virgil's.
N. B. A good motto! 'T is from Virgil's seventh Eclogue.

> " Populus Alcidæ gratissima, vitis Iaccho,
>   Formosæ myrtus Veneri, sua laurea Phœbo;
>   Phyllis amat corylos."

But still, my dear Southey! it goes grievously against
the grain with me, that *you* should be editing antholo-
gies. I would to Heaven that you could afford to write
nothing, or at least to publish nothing, till the completion
and publication of the " Madoc." I feel as certain, as my
mind dare feel on any subject, that it would lift you with
a spring into a reputation that would give immediate sale
to your after compositions and a license of writing more
at ease. Whereas " Thalaba " would gain you (for a time
at least) more ridiculers than admirers, and the " Madoc "
might in consequence be welcomed with an *ecce iterum*.
Do, do, my dear Southey! publish the " Madoc " *quam
citissime*, not hastily, but yet speedily. I will instantly
publish an Essay on Epic Poetry in reference to it. I
have been reading the Æneid, and there you will be all
victorious, excepting the importance of Æneas and his
connection with events existing in Virgil's time. This
cannot be said of " Madoc." There are other faults in
the construction of your poem, but nothing compared to
those in the Æneid. Homer I shall read too.

(No signature.)

CIII. TO THE SAME.

December 9, [1799].

MY DEAR SOUTHEY, — I pray you in your next give
me the particulars of your health. I hear accounts so
contradictory that I know only enough to be a good deal
frightened. You will surely think it your duty to sus-

pend all intellectual exertion; as to money, you will get
it easily enough. You may easily make twice the money
you receive from Stuart by the use of the scissors; for
your name is prodigiously high among the London publishers. I would to God your health permitted you to
come to London. You might have lodgings in the same
house with us. And this I am certain of, that not even
Kingsdown is a more healthy or airy place. I have
enough for us to do that would be mere child's work to
us, and in which the women might assist us essentially,
by the doing of which we might easily get a hundred and
fifty pounds each before the first of April. This I speak,
not from guess but from absolute conditions with booksellers. The principal work to which I allude would be
likewise a great source of amusement and profit to us in
the execution, and assuredly we should be a mutual comfort to each other. This I should *press* on you were not
Davy at Bristol, but he is indeed an admirable young
man; not only must he be of comfort to you, but in
whom can you place such reliance as a medical man?
But for Davy, I should advise your coming to London;
the difference of expense for three months could not be
above fifty pounds. I do not see how it could be half as
much. But I pray you write me all particulars, how
you have been, how you are, and what you think the particular nature of your disease.

Now for poor George.[1] Assuredly I am ready and
willing to become his bondsman for five hundred pounds
if, on the whole, you think the scheme a good one. I see
enough of the boy to be fully convinced of his goodness
and well-intentionedness; of his present or probable
talents I know little. To remain all his life an under
clerk, as many have done, and earn fifty pounds a year in
his old age with a trembling hand—alas! that were a
dreary prospect. No creature under the sun is so helpless,

---

[1] George Fricker, Mrs. Coleridge's younger brother.

so unfitted, I should think, for any other mode of life as a clerk, a mere clerk. Yet still many have begun so and risen into wealth and importance, and it is not impossible that before his term closed we might be able, if nought better offered, perhaps to procure him a place in a public office. We might between us keep him neat in clothes from our own wardrobes, I should think, and I am ready to allow five guineas this year, in addition to Mr. Savary's twelve pounds. More I am not justified to *promise*. Yet still I think it matter of much reflection with you. The commercial prospects of this country are, in my opinion, gloomy; our present commerce is enormous: that it must diminish after a peace is certain, and should any accident injure the West India trade, and give to France a para-mountship in the American affections, that diminution would be vast indeed, and, of course, great would be the number of clerks, etc., wholly out of employment. This is no visionary speculation; for we are consulting concerning a *life*, for probably fifty years. I should have given a more intense conviction to the goodness of the former scheme of apprenticing him to a printer, and would make every exertion to raise my share of the money wanting. How-ever, all this is talk at random. I leave it to you to decide. What does Charles Danvers think? He has been very kind to George. But to whom is he not kind, that body — blood — bone — muscle — nerve —heart and head — good man! I lay final stress on his opinion in almost everything except verses; those I know more about than he does — "God bless him, to use a vulgar phrase." This is a quotation from Godwin, who used these words in conversation with me and Davy. The pedantry of atheism tickled me hugely. Godwin is no great things in intellect; but in heart and manner he is all the better for having been the husband of Mary Woll-stonecraft. Why did not George Dyer (who, by the bye,

has written a silly milk-and-water life of you,[1] in which
your talents for *pastoral* and *rural* imagery are extolled,
and in which you are asserted to be a republican), why
did not George Dyer send to the "Anthology" that poem
in the last "Monthly Magazine?" It is so very far
superior to anything I have ever seen of his, and might
have made some atonement for his former transgressions.
God love him, he is a very good man; but he ought not
to degrade himself by writing lives of living characters
for Phillips; and all his friends make wry faces, peeping
out of the pillory of his advertisemental notes. I hold to
my former opinion concerning the *arrangement* of the
"Anthology," and the booksellers with whom *I* have
talked coincide with me. On this I am decided, that all
the *light* pieces should be put together under one title with
a motto[2] thus: "*Nos hæc novimus esse nihil — Phillis
amat Corylos.*" I am afraid that I have scarce poetic
enthusiasm enough to finish "Christabel;" but the poem,
with which Davy is so much delighted, I probably may
finish time enough. I shall probably *not* publish my
letters, and if I do so, I shall most certainly *not* publish
any verses in them. Of course, I expect to see them in
the "Anthology." As to title, I should wish a fictitious

[1] A gossiping account of the early
history and writings of "Mr. Robert
Southey" appeared in *Public Characters for* 1799–1800, a humble fore-
runner of *Men of the Time*, published by Richard Phillips, the
founder of the *Monthly Magazine*,
and afterwards knighted as a sheriff
of the city of London. Possibly
Coleridge was displeased at the
mention of his name in connection
with Pantisocracy, and still more by
the following sentence: "The three
young poetical friends, Lovel, Southey, and Coleridge, married three
sisters. Southey is attached to domestic life, and, fortunately, was
very happy in his matrimonial connection." It was Sir Richard Phillips, the "knight" of Coleridge's
anecdote, who told Mrs. Barbauld
that he would have given "nine
guineas a sheet for the last hour
and a half of his conversation."
Letters, Conversations, etc., 1836, ii.
131, 132.

[2] "These various pieces were rear-
ranged in three volumes under the
title of *Minor Poems*, in 1815, with
this motto, *Nos hæc novimus esse
nihil.*" *Poetical Works of Robert
Southey*, 1837, ii., xii.

one or none ; were I sure that I could finish the poem I
spoke of. I do not know how to get the conclusion of
Mrs. Robinson's poem for you. Perhaps it were better
omitted, and I mean to put the thoughts of that concert
poem into smoother metre. Our " Devil's Thoughts "
have been admired far and wide, most *enthusiastically*
admired. I wish to have my name in the collection at all
events ; but I should better like it to better poems than
these I have been hitherto able to give you. But I will
write again on Saturday. Supposing that Johnson should
mean to do nothing more with the " Fears in Solitude "
and the two accompanying poems, would they be excluded
from the plan of your " Anthology ? " There were not
above two hundred sold, and what is that to a newspaper
circulation ? Collins's Odes were thus reprinted in Dodsley's Collection. As to my future residence, I can say
nothing — only this, that to be near you would be a
strong motive with me for my wife's sake as well as myself. I think it not impossible that a number might be
found to go with you and settle in a warmer climate.
My kind love to your wife. Sara and Hartley arrived
safe, and here they are, No. 21 Buckingham Street,
Strand. God bless you, and your affectionate

S. T. COLERIDGE.

Thursday evening.

P. S. Mary Hayes [1] is writing the " Lives of Famous
Women," and is now about your friend *Joan.* She begs
you to tell her what books to consult, or to communicate
something to her. This from Tobin, who sends his love.

---

[1] Mary Hayes, a friend of Mary
Wollstonecraft, whose opinions she
advocated with great zeal, and
whose death she witnessed. Among
other works, she wrote a novel, *Me-*
moirs of Emma Courtney, and *Fe-*
male Biography, or Memoirs of Illus-
trious and Celebrated Women. Six
volumes. London : R. Phillips.
1803.

CIV. TO THE SAME.

Tuesday night, 12 o'clock [December 24], **1799**.

MY DEAR SOUTHEY, — My Spinosism (if Spinosism it be, and i' faith 't is very like it) disposed me to consider this big city as that part of the supreme One which the prophet Moses was allowed to see — I should be more disposed to pull off my shoes, beholding Him in a *Bush*, than while I am forcing my reason to believe that even in theatres *He* is, yea! even in the Opera House. Your " Thalaba " will beyond all doubt bring you two hundred pounds, if you will sell it at once; but *do* not print at a venture, under the notion of selling the edition. I assure you that Longman regretted the bargain he made with Cottle concerning the second edition of the " Joan of Arc," and is indisposed to similar negotiations ; but most and very eager to have the property of your works at almost any price. If you have not heard it from Cottle, why, you may hear it from me, that is, the arrangement of Cottle's affairs in London. The whole and total copyright of your " Joan," and the first volume of your poems (exclusive of what Longman had before given), was taken by him at three hundred and seventy pounds. You are a strong swimmer, and have borne up poor Joey with all his leaden weights about him, his own and other people's! Nothing has answered to him but your works. By me he has lost somewhat — by Fox, Amos, and himself *very much*. I can sell your "Thalaba" quite as well in your absence as in your presence. I am employed from I-rise to I-set [1] (that is, from nine in the morning to twelve at night), a pure scribbler. My mornings to booksellers' compilations, after dinner to Stuart, who pays *all* my expenses here, let them be what they will; the earnings of the morning go to make up an hundred and fifty pounds for my year's expenditure ; for, supposing *all clear* my year's (1800) allowance

---

[1] He used the same words in a letter to Poole dated December 31,   1799. T'   as *Poole and his Friends,*   :

is anticipated. But this I can do by the first of April (at which time I leave London). For Stuart I write often his leading paragraphs on Secession, Peace, Essay on the new French Constitution,[1] Advice to Friends of Freedom, Critiques on Sir W. Anderson's Nose, Odes to Georgiana D. of D. (horribly misprinted), Christmas Carols, etc., etc., — anything not bad in the paper, that is not yours, is mine. So if any verses there strike you as worthy the " Anthology," "do me the honour, sir!" However, in the course of a week I *do mean* to conduct a series of essays in that paper which may be of public utility. So much for myself, except that I long to be out of London; and that my Xstmas Carol is a quaint performance, and, in as strict a sense as is *possible*, an Impromptu, and, had I done all I had planned, that " Ode to the Duchess "[2] would have been a better thing than it is — it being somewhat dull-ish, etc. I have bought the " Beauties of the Anti-jaco-bin," and attorneys and counsellors advise me to prosecute, and offer to undertake it, so as that I shall have neither trouble or expense. They say it is a clear case, etc.[3] I

[1] " Essay on the New French Con-stitution," *Essays on His Own Times*, i. 183-189.

[2] The Ode appeared in the *Morn-ing Post*, December 24, 1799. The stanzas in which the Duchess com-memorated her passage over Mount St. Gothard appeared in the *Morn-ing Post*, December 21. They were inscribed to her children, and it was the last stanza, in which she antici-pates her return, which suggested to Coleridge the far-fetched conceit that maternal affection enabled the Duchess to overcome her aristocratic prejudices, and "hail Tell's chapel and the platform wild." It runs thus : —

Hope of my life ! dear *children* of my heart!

That anxious heart to each fond feeling true,
To you still pants each pleasure to impart,
And soon — oh transport — reach its home and you.

From a transcript in my possession of which the opening lines are in the handwriting of Mrs. H. N. Cole-ridge.

[3] The libel of which Coleridge justly complained was contained in these words : "Since this time (that is, since leaving Cambridge) he has left his native country, commenced citizen of the world, left his poor children fatherless and his wife des-titute. *Ex his disce* his friends Lamb and Southey." *Biographia Literaria*, 1817, vol. i. chapter i. p. 70, n.

will speak to Johnson about the " Fears in Solitude." If
he gives them up they are yours. That dull ode has been
printed often enough, and may now be allowed to " sink
with dead swoop, and to the bottom *go*," to quote an admired author; but the two others will do with a little
trimming.

My dear Southey! I have said nothing concerning that
which most oppresses me. Immediately on my leaving
London I fall to the " Life of Lessing; " till that is done,
till I have given the Wedgwoods some proof that I am
endeavouring to do well for my fellow-creatures, I cannot
stir. That being done, I would accompany you, and see
no impossibility of forming a pleasant little colony for a
few years in Italy or the South of France. Peace will
soon come. God love you, my dear Southey! I would
write to Stuart, and give up his paper immediately. You
should do nothing that did not absolutely *please* you. Be
idle, be very idle! The habits of your mind are such that
you will necessarily do much; but be as idle as you can.

Our love to dear Edith. If you see Mary, tell her that
we have received our trunk. Hartley is quite well, and
my talkativeness is his, without diminution on my side.
'T is strange, but certainly many things go in the blood,
beside gout and scrophula. Yesterday I dined at Longman's and met Pratt, and that honest piece of prolix dullity and nullity, young Towers, who desired to be remembered to you. To-morrow Sara and I dine at Mister
Gobwin's, as Hartley calls him, who gave the philosopher
such a rap on the shins with a ninepin that Gobwin in
huge pain *lectured* Sara on his boisterousness. I was not
at home. *Est modus in rebus.* Moshes is somewhat too
rough and noisy, but the cadaverous silence of Godwin's
children is to me quite catacombish, and, thinking of Mary
Wollstonecraft, I was oppressed by it the day Davy and I
dined there.

God love you and   S. T. COLERIDGE.

CV. TO THE SAME.

MY DEAR SOUTHEY, — No day passes in which I do not as it were yearn after you, but in truth my occupations have lately swoln above smothering point. I am over mouth and nostrils. I have inclosed a poem which Mrs. Robinson gave me for your "Anthology." She is a woman of undoubted genius. There was a poem of hers in this morning's paper which both in metre and matter pleased me much. She overloads everything; but I never knew a human being with so *full* a mind — bad, good, and indifferent, I grant you, but full and overflowing. This poem I *asked* for you, because I thought the metre stimulating and some of the stanzas really *good*. The first line of the twelfth would of itself redeem a worse poem.[1] I think you will agree with me, but should you not, yet still put it *in*, my dear fellow! for my sake, and out of respect to a woman-poet's feelings. Miss Hayes I have seen. Charles Lloyd's conduct has been atrocious beyond what you stated. Lamb himself confessed to me that during the time in which he kept up his ranting, sentimental correspondence with Miss Hayes, he frequently read her letters in company, as a subject for *laughter*, and then sate down and answered them quite *à la Rousseau!* Poor Lloyd! Every hour new-creates him; he is his own posterity in a perpetually flowing series, and his body unfortunately retaining an external identity, *their* mutual contradictions and disagreeings are united under one name, and of course are called lies, treachery, and rascality! I would not give him up, but that the same circumstances which have wrenched his morals prevent in him any salu-

[1] Mrs. Robinson (" Perdita ") contributed two poems to the *Annual Anthology* of 1800, " Jasper " and " The Haunted Beach." The line which caught Coleridge's fancy, the first of the twelfth stanza, runs thus: —

" Pale Moon! thou Spectre of the Sky."
Annual Anthology, 1800, p. 168.

tary exercise of genius.   And therefore he is not worth to the world that I should embroil and embrangle myself in his interests.

Of Miss Hayes' intellect I do not think so highly as you, or rather, to speak sincerely, I think not *contemptuously* but certainly *despectively* thereof.   Yet I think you likely in this case to have judged better than I; for to hear a thing, ugly and petticoated, ex-syllogize a God with cold-blooded precision, and attempt to run religion through the body with an icicle, an icicle from a Scotch Hog-trough ! *I* do not endure it; my eye beholds phantoms, and " nothing is, but what is not."

By your last I could not find whether or no you still are willing to execute the " History of the Levelling Principle."   Let me hear.   Tom Wedgwood is going to the Isle of St. Nevis.   As to myself, Lessing out of the question; I must stay in England. . . . Dear Hartley is well, and in high force; he sported of his own accord a theologico-astronomical hypothesis.   Having so perpetually heard of good boys being put up into the sky when they are dead, and being now beyond measure enamoured of the lamps in the streets, he said one night coming through the streets, " Stars are dead lamps, they be'nt naughty, they are put up in the sky."   Two or three weeks ago he was talking to himself while I was writing, and I took down his soliloquy.   It would make a most original poem.

You say, I illuminize.   I think that property will some time or other be modified by the predominance of intellect, even as rank and superstition are now modified by and subordinated to property, that much is to be hoped of the future ; but first those particular modes of property which more particularly stop the diffusion must be done away, as injurious to property itself ; these are priesthood and the too great patronage of Government.   Therefore, if to act on the belief that all things are the process, and that inapplicable truths are moral falsehoods, be to illuminize, why

then I illuminize! I know that I have been obliged to
illuminize so late at night, or rather mornings, that eyes
have smarted as if I had *allum in eyes!* I believe I have
misspelt the word, and ought to have written Alum; that
aside, 't is a *humorous pun!*

Tell Davy that I will soon write. God love him! You
and I, Southey! know a good and great man or two in this
world of ours.

God love you, my dear Southey, and your affectionate
S. T. COLERIDGE.

My kind love to Edith. Let me hear from you, and do
not be angry with me that I don't answer your letters
regularly.

CVI. TO THE SAME.

(Early in 1800.)

MY DEAR SOUTHEY, — I shall give up this Newspaper
business; it is too, too fatiguing. I have attended the
Debates twice, and the first time I was twenty-five hours
in activity, and that of a very unpleasant kind; and the
second time, from ten in the morning till four o'clock the
next morning. I am sure that you will excuse my silence,
though indeed after two such letters from you I cannot
scarcely excuse it myself. First of the book business. I
find a resistance which I did not expect to the *anonymous-
ness* of the publication. Longman seems confident that
a work on such a subject without a name would not do.
Translations and perhaps Satires are, he says, the only
works that booksellers now venture on *without a name.*
He is very solicitous to have your "Thalaba," and wonders
(most wonderful!) that you do not write a novel. That
would be the thing! and truly, if by no more pains than a
"St. Leon"[1] requires you could get four hundred pounds!!

---

[1] *St. Leon* was published in 1799. *William Godwin, his Friends and
Contemporaries,* i. 330.

or half the money, I say so too! If we were together we
might easily *toss up* a novel, to be published in the name
of one of us, or *two*, if that were all, and then christen 'em
by lots.   As sure as ink flows in my pen, by help of an
amanuensis I could write a volume a week — and Godwin
got four hundred pounds! for it — think of that, Master
Brooks.   I hope that some time or other you will write a
novel on that subject of yours!   I mean the " Rise and
Progress of a *Laugher*" — Le Grice in your eye — the
effect of Laughing on taste, manners, morals, and happiness! But as to the Jacobin Book, I must wait till I hear
from you.   Phillips would be very glad to engage you to
write a school book for him, the History of Poetry in all
nations, about 400 pages; but this, too, *must* have your
name.   He would give sixty pounds.   If poor dear Burnett were with you, he might do it under your eye and
with your instructions as well as you or I could do it, but
it is *the name.* Longman remarked acutely enough, " The
booksellers scarcely pretend to judge the merits of the
book, but we know the *saleableness* of the name! and as
they continue to buy most books on the calculation of a
first edition of a thousand copies, they are seldom much
mistaken; for the name gives them the excuse for sending
it to all the Gemmen in Great Britain and the Colonies,
from whom they have standing orders for new books of
reputation."   This is the secret why books published by
country booksellers, or by authors on their own account, so
seldom succeed.

As to my schemes of residence, I am as unfixed as yourself, only that we are under the absolute necessity of fixing
somewhere, and that somewhere will, I suppose, be Stowey.
There are all my books and all our furniture.   In May I
am under a kind of engagement to go with Sara to Ottery.
My family wish me to fix there, but *that* I must decline in
the names of public liberty and individual free-agency.
Elder brothers, not senior in intellect, and not sympathis-

ing in main opinions, are subjects of occasional visits, not temptations to a co-township. But if you go to Burton, Sara and I will waive the Ottery plan, if possible, and spend May and June with you, and perhaps July; but she must be settled in a house by the latter end of July, or the first week in August. Till we are with you, Sara means to spend five weeks with the Roskillies, and a week or two at Bristol, where I shall join her. She will leave London in three weeks at least, perhaps a fortnight; and I shall give up lodgings and billet myself free of expense at my friend Purkis's, at Brentford. This is my present plan. O my dear Southey! I would to God that your health did not enforce you to migrate — we might most assuredly continue to fix a residence somewhere, which might possess a sort of centrality. Alfoxden would make two houses sufficiently divided for unimpinging independence.

Tell Davy that I have not forgotten him, because without an epilepsy I cannot forget him; and if I wrote to him as often as I think of him, Lord have mercy on his pocket!

God bless you again and again.

S. T. COLERIDGE.

I pass this evening with Charlotte Smith at her house.

CVII. TO THE SAME.

[Postmark February 18], 1800.

MY DEAR SOUTHEY, — What do you mean by the words, "it is indeed by expectation"? speaking of your state of health. I cannot bear to think of your going to a strange country without any one who loves and understands you. But we will talk of all this. I have not a moment's time, and my head aches. I was up till five o'clock this morning. My brain is so overworked that I could doze troublously and with cold limbs, so affected was my circulation. I shall do no more for Stuart.

Read Pitt's speech [1] in the "Morning Post" of to-day (February 18, Tuesday). I reported the whole with notes so scanty, that — Mr. Pitt is much obliged to me. For, by Heaven, he never talked half as eloquently in his life-time. He is a *stupid, insipid* charlatan, that *Pitt*. Indeed, except Fox, I, you, or anybody might learn to speak better than any man in the House. For the next fortnight I expect to be so busy, that I shall go out of London a mile or so to be wholly uninterrupted. I do not understand the Beguin-nings [2] of Holland. Phillips is a good-for-nothing fellow, but what of that? He will give you sixty pounds, and advance half the money now for a book you can do in a fortnight, or three weeks at farthest. I would advise you not to give it up so hastily. Phillips eats no flesh. I observe, wittily enough, that whatever might be thought of innate ideas, there could be no doubt to a man who had seen Phillips of the existence of innate beef. Let my "Mad Ox" keep my name. "Fire and Famine" do just what you like with. I have

[1] See "Mr. Coleridge's Report of Mr. Pitt's Speech in Parliament of February 17, 1800, On the continuance of the War with France." *Morning Post*, February 18, 1800; *Essays on His Own Times*, ii. 293. See, too, Mrs. H. N. Coleridge's note, and the report of the speech in *The Times*. *Ibid.* iii. 1009–1019. The original notes, which Coleridge took in pencil, have been preserved in one of his note-books. They consist, for the most part, of skeleton sentences and fragmentary jottings. How far Coleridge may have reconstructed Pitt's speech as he went along, it is impossible to say, but the speech as reported follows pretty closely the outlines in the note-book. The remarkable description of Buonaparte as the "child and champion of Jacobinism," which is not to be found in *The Times* report, appears in the notes as "the nursling and champion of Jacobinism," and, if these were the words which Pitt used, in this instance, Coleridge altered for the worse.

[2] "The Beguines I had looked upon as a religious establishment, and the only good one of its kind. When my brother was a prisoner at Brest, the sick and wounded were attended by nurses, and these women had made themselves greatly beloved and respected." Southey to Rickman, January 9, 1800. *Life and Correspondence*, ii. 46. It is well known that Southey advocated the establishment of Protestant orders of Sisters of Mercy.

no wish either way. The "Fears in Solitude," I fear, is not my property, and I have no encouragement to think it will be given up, but if I hear otherwise I will let you know speedily; in the mean time, do not rely on it. Your review-plan[1] *cannot* answer for this reason. It could exist only as long as the ononymous anti-anonymists remained in life, health, and the humour, and no publisher would undertake a periodical publication on so gossamery a tie. Besides, it really would not be right for any man to make so many people have strange and uncomfortable feelings towards him; which must be the case, however kind the reviews might be — and what but nonsense is published? The author of "Gebir" I cannot find out. There are none of his books in town. You have made a sect of Gebirites by your review, but it was not a *fair*, though a very kind review. I have sent a letter to Mrs. Fricker, which Sara directed to you. I hope it has come safe. Let me see, are there any other questions?

So, my dear Southey, God love you, and never, never cease to believe that I am affectionately yours,

S. T. COLERIDGE.

Love to Edith.

CVIII. TO THE SAME.

No. 21 Buckingham Street [early in 1800].

MY DEAR SOUTHEY, — I will see Longman on Tuesday, at the farthest, but I pray you send me up what you have done, if you can, as I will read it to him, unless he will take my word for it. But we cannot expect that he will treat finally without seeing a considerable specimen. Send it by the coach, and be assured that it will be as

[1] In a letter from Southey to Coleridge, dated February 15, 1800 (unpublished), he proposes the establishment of a Magazine with signed articles. But a "History of the Levelling Principle," which Coleridge had suggested as a joint work, he would only publish anonymously.

safe as in your own escritoire, and I will remit it the very day Longman or any bookseller has treated for it satisfactorily. Less than two hundred pounds I would not take. Have you tried warm bathing in a high temperature? As to your travelling, your first business must, of course, be to *settle*. The Greek Islands [1] and Turkey in general are one continued Hounslow Heath, only that the highwaymen there have an awkward habit of murdering people. As to Poland and Hungary, the detestable roads and inns of them both, and the severity of the climate in the former, render travelling there little suited to your state of health. Oh! for peace and the South of France! What a detestable villainy is not the new Constitution.[2] I have written all that relates to it which has appeared in the "Morning Post;" and not without strength or elegance. But the French are children.[3] 'T is an infirmity to hope or fear concerning them. I wish they had a king again, if it were only that Sieyès and Bonaparte might be *hung*. Guillotining is too republican a death for such reptiles! You 'll write another quarter for Mr. Stuart? You will torture your-

---

[1] See Letter from Southey to Coleridge, December 27, 1799. *Life and Correspondence*, ii. 35.

[2] "Concerning the French, I wish Bonaparte had staid in Egypt and that Robespierre had guilloteened Sieyès. These cursed complex governments are good for nothing, and will ever be in the hands of intriguers: the Jacobins were the men, and one house of representatives, lodging the executive in committees, the plain and common system of government. The cause of republicanism is over, and it is now only a struggle for dominion. There wants a Lycurgus after Robespierre, a man loved for his virtue, and bold and inflexible, who should have levelled the property of France, and then would the Republic have been immortal — and the world must have been revolutionized by example." From an unpublished letter from Southey to Coleridge, dated December 23, 1799.

[3] "Alas, poor human nature! Or rather, indeed, alas, poor Gallic nature! For Γραῖοι ἀεὶ παῖδες the French are always children, and it is an infirmity of benevolence to wish, or dread, aught concerning them." S. T. C., *Morning Post*, December 31, 1797; *Essays on His Own Times*, i. 184.

self for twelve or thirteen guineas? I pray you do not
do so! You might get without the exertion, and with but
little more expenditure of time, from fifty to an hundred
pounds. Thus, for instance, bring together on your table,
or skim over successively Brücker, Lardner's "History
of Heretics," Russell's "Modern Europe," and Andrews'
"History of England," and write a history of levellers
and the levelling principle under some goodly title, neither praising or abusing them. Lacedæmon, Crete, and
the attempts at agrarian laws in Rome — all these you
have by heart. . . . Plato and Zeno are, I believe, nearly
all that relates to the purpose in Brücker. Lardner's
is a most amusing book to read. Write only a sheet
of letter paper a day, which you can easily do in an
hour, and in twelve weeks you will have produced (without any toil of brains, observing none but chronological
arrangement, and giving you little more than the trouble
of transcription) twenty - four sheets octavo. I will
gladly write a philosophical introduction that shall en-
lighten without offending, and therein state the rise of
property, etc. For this you might secure sixty or seventy
guineas, and receive half the money on producing the first
eight sheets, in a month from your first commencement of
the work. Many other works occur to me, but I mention
this because it might be doing great good, inasmuch as
boys and youths would read it with far different impressions from their fathers and godfathers, and yet the latter
find nothing alarming in the nature of the work, it being
purely historical. If I am not deceived by the *recency*
of their date, my " Ode to the Duchess " and my " Xmas
Carol " will *do* for your " Anthology." I have therefore
transcribed them for you. But I need not ask you, for
God's sake, to use your own judgment without spare.

(No signature.)

CIX. TO THE SAME.

February 28, 1800.

It goes to my heart, my dear Southey! to sit down and write to you, knowing that I can scarcely fill half a side — the postage lies on my conscience. I am translating manuscript plays of Schiller.[1] They are *poems*, full of long speeches, in very polish'd blank verse. The theatre! the theatre! my dear Southey! it will never, never, never do! If you go to Portugal, your History thereof *will* do, but, for present money, novels or translations. I do not see that a book said by you in the preface to have been written merely as a book for young persons could injure your reputation more than Milton's " Accidence " injured *his*. I *would do* it, because you can do it so easily. It is not necessary that you should say much about French or German Literature. Do it so. Poetry of savage nations — Poetry of rudely civilized — Homer and the Hebrew Poetry, etc. — Poetry of civilized nations under Republics and Polytheism, State of Poetry under the Roman and Greek Empires — Revival of it in Italy, in Spain, and England — then go steadily on with England to the end, except one chapter about German Poetry to conclude with, which I can write for you.

In the " Morning Post " was a poem of fascinating metre by Mary Robinson; 't was on Wednesday, Feb. 26, and entitled the " Haunted Beach." [2] I was so struck with it that I sent to her to desire that [it] might be preserved in the " Anthology." She was extremely flattered by the idea of its being there, as she idolizes you and your doings. So, if it be not too late, I pray you let it be in. If you should not have received that day's paper, write im-

[1] See *Poetical Works*, Appendix K, pp. 544, 545. Editor's Note, pp. 646-649.

[2] " The *winter* Moon upon the sand
A silvery Carpet made,
And mark'd the sailor reach the land —

And mark'd *his Murderer* wash his hand
Where the green billows played ! "

Annual Anthology, 1800: " The Haunted Beach," sixth stanza, p. 256.

mediately that I may transcribe it. It falls off sadly to
the last, wants tale and interest; but the images are new
and very distinct — that "silvery carpet" is so *just* that
it is unfortunate it should *seem* so bad, for it is *really*
good; but the metre, ay! that woman has an ear.   William Taylor, from whom I have received a couple of letters full of thought and information, says what astounded
me, that double rhymes in our language have always a
ludicrous association.   Mercy on the man ! where are his
ears and feelings ?   His taste cannot be *quite* right, from
this observation ; but he is a famous fellow — that is not
to be denied.

Sara is poorly still.   Hartley rampant, and emperorizes
with your pictures.   Harry is a fine boy.   Hartley told a
gentleman, " Metinks you are *like Southey*," and he *was*
not wholly unlike you — but the chick calling you simple
" Southey," so pompously !

God love you and your Edith.

S. T. COLERIDGE.

CHAPTER VI

A LAKE POET

1800–1803

CHAPTER VI

A LAKE POET

1800–1803

CX. TO THOMAS POOLE.

August 14, 1800.

MY DEAR POOLE, —Your two letters[1] I received exactly four days ago — some days they must have been lying at Ambleside before they were sent to Grasmere, and some days at Grasmere before they moved to Keswick. . . . It grieved me that you had felt so much from my silence. Believe me, I have been harassed with business, and shall remain so for the remainder of this year. Our house is a delightful residence, something less than half a mile from the lake of Keswick and something more than a furlong from the town. It commands both that lake and the lake of Bassenthwaite. Skiddaw is behind us; to the left, the right, and in front mountains of all shapes and sizes. The waterfall of Lodore is distinctly visible. In garden, etc., we are uncommonly well off, and our landlord, who resides next door in this twofold house, is already much attached to us. He is a quiet, sensible man, with as large a library as yours, — and perhaps rather larger, — well stored with encyclopædias, dictionaries, and histories, etc., all modern. The gentry of the country, titled and untitled, have all called or are about to call on me, and I shall

---

[1] These letters, under the title of "Monopolists" and "Farmers," appeared in the *Morning Post*, October 3-9, 1800. Coleridge wrote the first of the series, and the introduction to No. III. of "Farmers," "In what manner they are affected by the War." *Essays on His Own Times*, ii. 413-450; *Thomas Poole and his Friends*, ii. 15, 16.

have free access to the magnificent library of Sir Gilfrid Lawson. I wish you could come here in October after your harvesting, and stand godfather at the christening of my child. In October the country is in all its blaze of beauty.

We are well and the Wordsworths are well. The two volumes of the " Lyrical Ballads " will appear in about a fortnight or three weeks. Sara sends her best kind love to your mother. How much we rejoice in her health I need not say. Love to Ward, and to Chester, to whom I shall write as soon as I am at leisure. I was standing at the very top of Skiddaw, by a little shed of slate stones on which I had scribbled with a bit of slate my name among the other names. A lean-expression-faced man came up the hill, stood beside me a little while, then, on running over the names, exclaimed, " Coleridge! I lay my life that is the *poet Coleridge!* "

God bless you, and for God's sake never doubt that I am attached to you beyond all other men.

S. T. COLERIDGE.

CXI. TO SIR H. DAVY.

Thursday night, October 9, 1800.

MY DEAR DAVY, — I was right glad, glad with a *stagger* of the heart, to see your writing again. Many a moment have I had all my France and England curiosity suspended and lost, looking in the advertisement front column of the " Morning Post Gazeteer " for *Mr. Davy's Galvanic habitudes of charcoal.* — Upon my soul I believe there is not a letter in those words round which a world of imagery does not circumvolve; your room, the garden, the cold bath, the moonlight rocks, Barristed, Moore, and simple-looking Frere, and dreams of wonderful things attached to your name, — and Skiddaw, and Glaramara, and Eagle Crag, and you, and Wordsworth, and me, on the top of them! I pray you do write to me imme-

diately, and tell me what you mean by the possibility of your assuming a new occupation. Have you been successful to the extent of your expectations in your late chemical inquiries?

As to myself, I am doing little worthy the relation. I write for Stuart in the "Morning Post," and I am compelled by the god Pecunia — which was one name of the supreme Jupiter — to give a volume of letters from Germany, which will be a decent *lounge* book, and not an atom more. The "Christabel" was running up to 1,300 lines,[1] and was so much admired by Wordsworth, that he thought it indelicate to print two volumes with his name, in which so much of another man's was included; and, which was of more consequence, the poem was in direct opposition to the very purpose for which the lyrical ballads were published, viz., an experiment to see how far those passions which alone give any value to extraordinary incidents were capable of interesting, in and for themselves, in the incidents of common life. We mean to publish the "Christabel," therefore, with a long blank-verse poem of Wordsworth's, entitled "The Pedlar."[2] I assure you I think very differently of "Christabel." I would rather have written "Ruth," and "Nature's Lady," than a million such poems. But why do I calumniate my own spirit by saying "I would rather"? God knows it is as delightful to me that they *are* written. I *know* that at present, and I *hope* that it *will be so;* my mind has *disciplined* itself into a willing exertion of its powers, without any reference to their comparative value.

[1] It is impossible to explain this statement, which was repeated in a letter to Josiah Wedgwood, dated November 1, 1800. The printed "Christabel," even including the conclusion to Part II., makes only 677 lines, and the discarded portion, if it ever existed, has never come to light. See Mr. Dykes Campbell's valuable and exhaustive note on "Christabel," *Poetical Works*, pp. 601–607.

[2] A former title of "The Excursion."

I cannot speak favourably of W.'s health, but, indeed, he has not done common justice to Dr. Beddoes's kind prescriptions. I saw his countenance darken, and all his hopes vanish, when he saw the *prescriptions* — his *scepticism* concerning medicines! nay, it is not enough *scepticism!* Yet, now that peas and beans are over, I have hopes that he will in good earnest make a fair and full trial. I rejoice with sincere joy at Beddoes's recovery.

Wordsworth is fearful you have been much teased by the printers on his account, but you can sympathise with him. The works which I gird myself up to attack as soon as money concerns will permit me are the Life of Lessing, and the Essay on Poetry. The latter is still more at my heart than the former: its title would be an essay on the elements of poetry, — it would be in reality a disguised system of morals and politics. When you write, — and do write soon, — tell me how I can get your essay on the nitrous oxide. If you desired Johnson to have one sent to Lackington's, to be placed in Mr. Crosthwaite's monthly parcel for Keswick, I should receive it. Are your galvanic discoveries important? What do they lead to? All this is *ultra-crepidation*, but would to Heaven I had as much knowledge as I have sympathy!

My wife and children are well; the baby was dying some weeks ago, so the good people would have it baptized; his name is Derwent Coleridge,[1] so called from the

---

[1] "Sunday night, half past ten, September 14, 1800, a boy born (Bracy).

"September 27, 1800. The child being very ill was baptized by the name of Derwent. The child, hour after hour, made a noise exactly like the creaking of a door which is being shut very slowly to prevent its creaking." (*MS.*) S. T. C.

My father's life was saved by his mother's devotion. "On the occasion here recorded," he writes, "I had eleven convulsion fits. At last my father took my mother gently out of the room, and told her that she must make up her mind to lose this child. By and by she heard the nurse lulling me, and said she would try once more to give me the breast." She did so; and from that time all went well, and the child recovered.

river, for, fronting our house, the Greta runs into the Derwent. Had it been a girl the name should have been Greta. By the bye, Greta, or rather Grieta, is exactly the Cocytus of the Greeks. The word, literally rendered in modern English, is " the loud lamenter; " to griet in the Cambrian dialect, signifying to roar aloud for grief or pain, and it does *roar* with a vengeance! I will say nothing about spring — a thirsty man tries to think of anything but the stream when he knows it to be ten miles off! God bless you!

Your most affectionate S. T. COLERIDGE.

CXII. TO THE SAME.

October 18, 1800.

MY DEAR DAVY, — Our mountains northward end in the mountain Carrock, — one huge, steep, enormous bulk of stones, desolately variegated with the heath plant; at its foot runs the river Calder, and a narrow vale between it and the mountain Bowscale, so narrow, that in its greatest width it is not more than a furlong. But that narrow vale is *so* green, *so* beautiful, there are moods in which a man might weep to look at it. On this mountain Carrock, at the summit of which are the remains of a vast Druid circle of stones, I was wandering, when a thick cloud came on, and wrapped me in such darkness that I could not see ten yards before me, and with the cloud a storm of wind and hail, the like of which I had never before seen and felt. At the very summit is a cone of stones, built by the shepherds, and called the Carrock Man. Such cones are on the tops of almost all our mountains, and they are all called *men*. At the bottom of the Carrock Man I seated myself for shelter, but the wind became so fearful and tyrannous, that I was apprehensive some of the stones might topple down upon me, so I groped my way farther down and came to three rocks, placed on this wise, $\frac{1}{3}\aleph^2$, each one supported by the other like a child's house of cards, and in the hollow and screen which they made I sate for a long while sheltered, as if I had been in my own study in which I am now writing: there I sate with a total feeling worshipping the power and " eternal link " of energy.   The darkness vanished as by enchantment; far off, far, far off to the south, the mountains of Glaramara and Great Gable and their family appeared distinct, in deepest, sablest *blue*.   I rose, and behind me was a rainbow bright as the brightest.   I descended by the side of a torrent, and passed, or rather crawled (for I was forced to descend on all fours), by many a naked waterfall, till, fatigued and hungry (and with a finger almost broken, and which remains swelled to the size of two fingers), I reached the narrow vale, and the single house nestled in ash and sycamores.   I entered to claim the universal hospitality of this country; but instead of the life and comfort usual in these lonely houses, I saw dirt, and every appearance of misery — a pale woman sitting by a peat fire.   I asked her for bread and milk, and she sent a small child to fetch it, but did not rise herself.   I eat very heartily of the black, sour bread, and drank a bowl of milk, and asked her to permit me to pay her.   "Nay," says she, "we are not so scant as that — you are right welcome; but do you know any help for the rheumatics, for I have been so long ailing that I am almost fain to die?"   So I advised her to eat a great deal of mustard, having seen in an advertisement something about essence of mustard curing the most obstinate cases of rheumatism.   But do write me, and tell me some cure for the rheumatism; it is in her shoulders, and the small of her back chiefly.   I wish much to go off with some bottles of stuff to the poor creature.   I should walk the ten miles as ten yards. With love and honour, my dear Davy,

Yours,   S. T. Coleridge.

CXIII. TO THE SAME.

GRETA HALL, Tuesday night, December 2, 1800.

MY DEAR DAVY, — By an accident I did not receive your letter till this evening. I would that you had added to the account of your indisposition the probable causes of it. It has left me anxious whether or no you have not exposed yourself to unwholesome influences in your chemical pursuits. There are *few* beings both of hope and performance, but few who combine the "are" and the "will be." For God's sake, therefore, my dear fellow, do not rip open the bird that lays the golden eggs. I have not received your book. I read yesterday a sort of medical review about it. I suppose Longman will send it to me when he sends down the "Lyrical Ballads" to Wordsworth. I am solicitous to read the latter part. Did there appear to you any remote analogy between the case I translated from the German Magazine and the effects produced by your gas? Did Carlisle [1] ever communicate to you, or has he in any way published his facts concerning *pain* which he mentioned when we were with him? It is a subject which *exceedingly interests* me. I want to read something by somebody expressly on *pain*, if only to give an *arrangement* to my own thoughts, though if it were well treated I have little doubt it would revolutionize them. For the last month I have been trembling on through sands and swamps of evil and bodily grievance. My eyes have been inflamed to a degree that rendered reading and writing scarcely possible; and, strange as it seems, the act of metre composition, as I lay in bed, perceptibly affected them, and my voluntary ideas were every minute passing, more or less transformed into vivid spectra. I had leeches repeatedly applied to my temples, and a blister behind my ear — and my eyes are now my own, but in the place where the blister was,

---

[1] Afterwards Sir Anthony, the distinguished surgeon, 1768–1840.

six small but excruciating boils have appeared, and harass
me almost beyond endurance.   In the mean time my darling Hartley has been taken with a stomach illness, which
has ended in the yellow jaundice ; and this greatly alarms
me.   So much for the doleful !   Amid all these changes,
and humiliations, and fears, the sense of the Eternal
abides in me, and preserves unsubdued my cheerful faith,
that all I endure is full of blessings !

At times, indeed, I would fain be somewhat of a more
tangible utility than I am ; but so I suppose it is with all
of us — one while cheerful, stirring, feeling in resistance
nothing but a joy and a stimulus ; another while drowsy,
self-distrusting, prone to rest, loathing our own self-
promises, withering our own hopes — our hopes, the
vitality and cohesion of our being !

I purpose to have " Christabel " published by itself —
this I publish with confidence — but my travels in Germany come from me now with mortal pangs.   Nothing
but the most pressing necessity could have induced me —
and even now I hesitate and tremble.   Be so good as to
have all that is printed of " Christabel " sent to me per
post.

Wordsworth has nearly finished the concluding poem.
It is of a mild, unimposing character, but full of beauties
to those short-necked men who have their hearts sufficiently near their heads — the relative distance of which
(according to citizen Tourdes, the French translator of
Spallanzani) determines the sagacity or stupidity of all
bipeds and quadrupeds.

There is a deep blue cloud over the heavens ; the lake,
and the vale, and the mountains are all in darkness ;
only the *summits* of all the mountains in long ridges,
covered with snow, are bright to a dazzling excess.   A
glorious scene !   Hartley was in my arms the other evening, looking at the sky ; he saw the moon glide into a
large cloud.   Shortly after, at another part of the cloud,

several stars sailed in.   Says he, "Pretty creatures! they are going in to see after their mother moon."

Remember me kindly to King.   Write as often as you can; but above all things, my loved and honoured dear fellow, do not give up the idea of letting me and Skiddaw see you.   God love you!

S. T. COLERIDGE.

Tobin writes me that Thompson [1] has made some lucrative discovery.   Do you know aught about it?   Have you seen T. Wedgwood since his return?

CXIV. TO THOMAS POOLE.

GRETA HALL, KESWICK, Saturday night, December 5, 1800.

MY DEAREST FRIEND, — I have been prevented from answering your last letter entirely by the state of my eyes, and my wish to write more fully to you than their weakness would permit.   For the last month and more I have indeed been a very crazy machine. . . . *That* consequence of this long-continued ill-health which I most regret is, that it has thrown me so sadly behindhand in the performance of my engagements with the bookseller, that I almost fear I shall not be able to raise money enough by Christmas to make it prudent for me to journey southward.   I shall, however, try hard for it.   My plan was to go to London, and make a faint trial whether or no I could get a sort of dramatic romance, which I had more than half finished, upon the stage, and from London to visit Stowey and Gunville.   Dear little Hartley has been ill in a stomach complaint which ended in the yellow jaundice, and frightened me sorely, as you may well believe.   But, praise be to God, he is recovered and begins to look like himself.   He is a very extraordinary

[1] According to Dr. Davy, the editor of *Fragmentary Remains of Sir H. Davy*, London, 1858, the reference is to the late Mr. James Thompson of Clitheroe.

creature, and if he live will, I doubt not, prove a great
genius.   Derwent is a fat, pretty child, healthy and hungry.   I deliberated long whether I should not call him
Thomas Poole Coleridge, and at last gave up the idea
only because your nephew is called Thomas Poole, and
because if ever it should be my destiny once again to live
near you, I believed that such a name would give pain to
some branches of your family.   You will scarcely exact
a very severe account of what a man has been doing who
has been obliged for days and days together to keep his
bed.   Yet I have not been altogether idle, having in my
own conceit gained great light into several parts of the
human mind which have hitherto remained either wholly
unexplained or most falsely explained.   To one resolution
I am wholly made up, to wit, that as soon as I am a free-
man in the world of money I will never write a line for
the express purpose of money (but only as believing it
good and useful, in some way or other).   Although I am
certain that I have been greatly improving both in knowledge and power in these last twelve months, yet still at
times it presses upon me with a painful weight that I have
not evidenced a more tangible utility.   I have too much
trifled with my reputation.   You have conversed much
with Davy ; he is delighted with you.   What do you think
of him?   Is he not a great man, think you? . . . I and
my wife were beyond measure delighted by your account
of your mother's health.   Give our best, kindest loves to
her.   Charles Lloyd has settled at Ambleside, sixteen
miles from Keswick.   I shall not see him.   If I cannot
come, I will write you a very, very long letter, containing the most important of the many thoughts and feelings which I want to communicate to you, but hope to do
it face to face.

Give my love to Ward, and to J. Chester.   How is
poor old Mr. Rich and his wife?

God have you ever in his keeping, making life tranquil

to you.   Believe me to be what I have been ever, and am,
attached to you *one* degree more at least than to any other
living man.

S. T. COLERIDGE.

CXV. TO SIR H. DAVY.

February 3, 1801.

MY DEAR DAVY, — I can scarcely reconcile it to my
conscience to make you pay postage for another letter.
Oh, what a fine unveiling of modern politics it would be
if there were published a minute detail of all the sums
received by government from the post establishment, and
of all the outlets in which the sums so received flowed out
again! and, on the other hand, all the domestic affections
which had been stifled, all the intellectual progress that
would have been, but is not, on account of the heavy tax,
etc., etc.   The letters of a nation ought to be paid for as
an article of national expense.   Well! but I did not take
up this paper to flourish away in splenetic politics.   A
gentleman resident here, his name Calvert,[1] an idle, good-
hearted, and ingenious man, has a great desire to commence fellow-student with me and Wordsworth in chem-

---

[1] William, the elder brother of Raisley Calvert, who left Wordsworth a legacy of nine hundred pounds. In that mysterious poem, "Stanzas written in my Pocket Copy of Thomson's Castle of Indolence," it would seem that Wordsworth begins with a blended portrait of himself and Coleridge, and ends with a blended portrait of Coleridge and William Calvert. Mrs. Joshua Stanger (Mary Calvert) maintained that "the large gray eyes" and "low-hung lip" were certainly descriptive of Coleridge and could not apply to her father; but she admitted that, in other parts of the poem, Words-worth may have had her father in his mind. Of this we may be sure, that neither Coleridge nor Wordsworth had "inventions rare," or displayed beetles under a microscope. It is evident that Hartley Coleridge, who said "that his father's character and habits are here [that is, in these stanzas] preserved in a livelier way than in anything that has been written about him," regarded the first and not the second half of the poem as a description of S. T. C. "The Last of the Calverts," *Cornhill Magazine*, May, 1890, pp. 494-520.

istry.   He is an intimate friend of Wordsworth's, and he
has proposed to W. to take a house which he (Calvert)
has nearly built, called Windy Brow, in a delicious situation, scarce half a mile from Greta Hall, the residence of
S. T. Coleridge, Esq., and so for him (Calvert) to live
with them, that is, Wordsworth and his sister.   In this
case he means to build a little laboratory, etc.   Wordsworth has not quite decided, but is strongly inclined to
adopt the scheme, because he and his sister have before
lived with Calvert on the same footing, and are much
attached to him ; because my health is so precarious and
so much injured by wet, and his health, too, is like little
potatoes, no great things, and therefore Grasmere (thirteen miles from Keswick) is too great a distance for us
to enjoy each other's society without inconvenience, as
much as it would be profitable for us both ; and, likewise,
because he feels it more necessary for him to have some
intellectual pursuit less closely connected with deep passion than poetry, and is of course desirous, too, not to be so
wholly ignorant of knowledge so exceedingly important.
However, whether Wordsworth come or no, Calvert and
I have determined to begin and go on.   Calvert is a man
of sense and some originality, and is, besides, what is well
called a handy man.   He is a good practical mechanic,
etc., and is desirous to lay out any sum of money that is
necessary.   You know how long, how ardently I have
wished to initiate myself in chemical science, both for its
own sake and in no small degree likewise, my beloved
friend, that I may be able to sympathise with all that you
do and think.   Sympathise blindly with it all I do even
now, God knows! from the very middle of my heart's
heart, but I would fain sympathise with you in the light
of knowledge.   This opportunity is exceedingly precious
to me, as on my own account I could not afford the least
additional expense, having been already, by long and successive illnesses, thrown behindhand so much that for the

next four or five months I fear, let me work as hard as I
can, I shall not be able to do what my heart within me
burns to do, that is, to *concentre* my free mind to the affinities of the feelings with words and ideas under the title
of " Concerning Poetry, and the nature of the Pleasures
derived from it." I have faith that I do understand the
subject, and I am sure that if I write what I ought to
do on it, the work would supersede all the books of metaphysics, and all the books of morals too. To whom shall
a young man utter *his pride*, if not to a young man
whom he loves ?

I beg you, therefore, my dear Davy, to write me a long
letter when you are at leisure, informing me : Firstly,
What books it will be well for me and Calvert to purchase. Secondly, Directions for a convenient little laboratory. Thirdly, To what amount apparatus would run
in expense, and whether or no you would be so good as
to superintend its making at Bristol. Fourthly, Give
me your advice how to *begin*. And, fifthly, and lastly,
and mostly, do send a *drop* of hope to my parched tongue,
that you will, if you can, come and visit me in the spring.
Indeed, indeed, you ought to see this country, this beautiful country, and then the joy you would send into me !

The shape of this paper will convince you with what
eagerness I began this letter ; I really did not see that it
was not a sheet.

I have been *thinking* vigorously during my illness, so
that I cannot say that my long, long wakeful nights
have been all lost to me. The subject of my meditations
has been the relations of thoughts to things ; in the language of Hume, of ideas to impressions. I may be truly
described in the words of Descartes : I have been " res
cogitans, id est, dubitans, affirmans, negans, pauca intelli-
gens, multa ignorans, volens, nolens, imaginans etiam, et
sentiens." I please myself with believing that you will receive no small pleasure from the result of these broodings,

although I expect in you (in some points) a determined opponent, but I say of my mind in this respect: " Manet imperterritus ille hostem magnanimum opperiens, et mole suâ stat." Every poor fellow has his proud hour sometimes, and this I suppose is mine.

I am better in every respect than I was, but am still *very feeble.* The weather has been woefully against me for the last fortnight, having rained here almost incessantly. I take quantities of bark, but the effect is (to express myself with the dignity of science) $x = 0000000$, and I shall not gather strength, or that little suffusion of bloom which belongs to my healthy state, till I can walk out.

God bless you, my dear Davy! and your ever affectionate friend,

S. T. Coleridge.

P. S.   An electrical machine, and a number of little knickknacks connected with it, Mr. Calvert has. — *Write.*

CXVI. TO THOMAS POOLE.

Monday, March 16, 1801.

My dear Friend, — The interval since my last letter has been filled up by me in the most intense study.   If I do not greatly delude myself, I have not only *completely extricated the notions of time and space,* but have overthrown the doctrine of association, as taught by Hartley, and with it all the irreligious metaphysics of modern infidels — especially the doctrine of necessity.   This I have *done ;* but I trust that I am about to do more — namely, that I shall be able to evolve all the five senses, that is, to deduce them from one sense, and to state their growth and the causes of their difference, and in this evolvement to solve the process of life and consciousness. *I write this to you only, and I pray you, mention what I have written to no one.*   At Wordsworth's advice, or rather fervent entreaty, I have intermitted the pursuit.   The

intensity of thought, and the number of minute experiments with light and figure, have made me so nervous
and feverish that I cannot sleep as long as I ought and
have been used to do; and the sleep which I have is made
up of ideas so connected, and so little different from the
operations of reason, that it does not afford me the due
refreshment.   I shall therefore take a week's respite, and
make "Christabel" ready for the press; which I shall
publish by itself, in order to get rid of all my engagements
with Longman.   My German Book I have suffered to
remain suspended chiefly because the thoughts which had
employed my sleepless nights during my illness were imperious over me; and though poverty was staring me in
the face, yet I dared behold my image miniatured in the
pupil of her hollow eye, so steadily did I look her in the
face; for it seemed to me a suicide of my very soul to
divert my attention from truths so important, which came
to me almost as a revelation.   Likewise, I cannot express
to you, dear Friend of my heart! the loathing which I
once or twice felt when I attempted to write, merely for
the bookseller, without any sense of the moral utility of
what I was writing.   I shall therefore, as I said, immediately publish my "Christabel," with two essays annexed to
it, on the "Preternatural" and on "Metre."—This done, I
shall propose to Longman, instead of my Travels (which,
though nearly done, I am exceedingly anxious not to publish, because it brings me forward in a *personal* way, as
a man who relates little adventures of himself to *amuse*
people, and thereby exposes me to sarcasm and the malignity of anonymous critics, and is, besides, *beneath me*, . . .)
I shall propose to Longman to accept instead of these
Travels a work on the originality and merits of Locke,
Hobbes, and Hume, which work I mean as a *pioneer* to
my greater work, and as exhibiting a proof that I have
not formed opinions without an attentive perusal of the
works of my predecessors, from Aristotle to Kant.

I am confident that I can prove that the reputation of these three men has been wholly unmerited, and I have in what I have already written traced the whole history of the causes that effected this reputation entirely to Wordsworth's satisfaction.

You have seen, I hope, the " Lyrical Ballads."   In the divine poem called " Michael," by an infamous blunder[1] of the printer, near twenty lines are omitted in page 210, which makes it nearly unintelligible.   Wordsworth means to write to you and to send them together with a list of the numerous errata.   The character of the " Lyrical Ballads " is very great, and will increase daily.   They have extolled them in the " British Critic."   Ask Chester (to whom I shall write in a week or so concerning his German books) for Greenough's address, and be so kind as to send it immediately.   Indeed, I hope for a *long* letter from you, your opinion of the L. B., the preface, etc.   You know, I presume, that Davy is appointed Director of the Laboratory, and Professor at the Royal Institution ?   I received a very affectionate letter from him on the occasion.   Love to all.   We are all well, except, perhaps, myself.   Write !   God love you and

S. T. Coleridge.

CXVII. TO THE SAME.

Monday, March 23, 1801.

My dear Friend, — I received your kind letter of the 14th.   I was agreeably disappointed in finding that you had been interested in the letter respecting Locke.   Those which follow are abundantly more entertaining and important ; but I have no one to transcribe them.   Nay, three letters are written which have not been sent to Mr. Wedg-

---

[1] On page 210 of vol. ii. of the second edition of the *Lyrical Ballads* (1800), there is a blank space. The omitted passage, fifteen lines in all, began with the words, "Though nought was left undone." *Works of Wordsworth*, p. 134, ll. 4–18.

wood,[1] because I have no one to transcribe them for me, and I do not wish to be without copies. Of that letter which you have I have no copy. It is somewhat unpleasant to me that Mr. Wedgwood has never answered my letter requesting his opinion of the utility of such a work, nor acknowledged the receipt of the long letter containing the evidences that the whole of Locke's system, as far as it was a system, and with the exclusion of those parts only which have been given up *as absurdities* by his warmest admirers, preëxisted in the writings of Descartes, in a far more pure, elegant, and delightful form. Be not afraid that I shall join the party of the *Little-ists.* I believe that I shall delight you by the detection of their artifices. *Now Mr. Locke was the founder of this sect, himself a perfect Little-ist.*

My opinion is thus : that deep thinking is attainable only by a man of deep feeling, and that all truth is a species of

---

[1] During the preceding month Coleridge had busied himself with instituting a comparison between the philosophical systems of Locke and Descartes. Three letters of prodigious length, dated February 18, 24 (a double letter), and addressed to Josiah Wedgwood, embodied the result of his studies. They would serve, he thought, as a preliminary excursus to a larger work, and would convince the Wedgwoods that his *wanderjahr* had not been altogether misspent. Mr. Leslie Stephen, to whom this correspondence has been submitted, is good enough to allow me to print the following extract from a letter which he wrote at my request : "Coleridge writes as though he had as yet read no German philosophy. I knew that he began a serious study of Kant at Keswick ; but I fancied that he had brought back some knowledge of Kant from Germany. This letter seems to prove the contrary. There is certainly none of the transcendentalism of the Schelling kind. One point is, that he still sticks to Hartley and to the Association doctrine, which he afterwards denounced so frequently. Thus he is dissatisfied with Locke, but has not broken with the philosophy generally supposed to be on the Locke line. In short, he seems to be at the point where a study of Kant would be ready to launch him in his later direction, but is not at all conscious of the change. When he wrote the *Friend* [1809–10] he had become a Kantian. Therefore we must, I think, date his conversion later than I should have supposed, and assume that it was the study of Kant just after this letter was written which brought about the change."

revelation.   The more I understand of Sir Isaac Newton's works, the more boldly I dare utter to my own mind, and therefore to *you*, that I believe the souls of five hundred Sir Isaac Newtons would go to the making up of a Shakespeare or a Milton.   But if it please the Almighty to grant me health, hope, and a steady mind (always the three clauses of my hourly prayers), before my thirtieth year I will thoroughly understand the whole of Newton's works.   At present I must content myself with endeavouring to make myself entire master of his easier work, that on Optics. I am exceedingly delighted with the beauty and neatness of his experiments, and with the accuracy of his *immediate* deductions from them ; but the opinions founded on these deductions, and indeed his whole theory is, I am persuaded, so exceedingly superficial as without impropriety to be deemed false.   Newton was a mere materialist. *Mind*, in his system, is always *passive*, — a lazy *Looker-on* on an external world.   If the mind be not *passive*, if it be indeed made in God's Image, and that, too, in the sublimest sense, the *Image of the Creator*, there is ground for suspicion that any system built on the passiveness of the mind must be false, as a system.   I need not observe, my dear friend, how unutterably silly and contemptible these opinions would be if written to any but to another self.   I assure you, solemnly assure you, that you and Wordsworth are the only men on earth to whom I would have uttered a word on this subject.

It is a rule, by which I hope to direct all my literary efforts, to let my opinions and my proofs go together.   It is *insolent* to *differ* from the public *opinion* in *opinion*, if it be only *opinion*.   It is sticking up little *i by itself, i* against the whole alphabet.   But one *word* with *meaning* in it is worth the whole alphabet together.   Such is a sound argument, an incontrovertible fact.

Oh, for a Lodge in a land where human life was an end to which labour was only a means, instead of being,

as it is here, a mere means of carrying on labour. I am
oppressed at times with a true heart-gnawing melancholy
when I contemplate the state of my poor oppressed country. God knows, it is as much as I can do to put meat
and bread on my own table, and hourly some poor starving
wretch comes to my door to put in his claim for part of it.
It fills me with indignation to hear the *croaking* account
which the English emigrants send home of America.
" The society so bad, the manners so vulgar, the servants
so insolent!" Why, then, do they not seek out one another
and make a society? It is arrant ingratitude to talk so of
a land in which there is no poverty but as a consequence
of absolute idleness; and to talk of it, too, with abuse comparatively with England, with a place where the laborious
poor are dying with grass in their bellies. It is idle to
talk of the seasons, as if that country must not needs be
miserably governed in which an unfavourable season in-
troduces a famine. No! no! dear Poole, it is our pesti-
lent commerce, our unnatural crowding together of men
in cities, and our government by rich men, that are bringing about the manifestations of offended Deity. I am
assured that such is the depravity of the public mind, that
no literary man can find bread in England except by mis-
employing and debasing his talents; that nothing of real
excellence would be either felt or understood. The annuity which I hold, *perhaps by a very precarious tenure*, will
shortly from the decreasing value of money become less
than one half what it was when first allowed to me. If I
were allowed to retain it, I would go and settle near
Priestley, in America. I shall, no doubt, get a certain
price for the two or three works which I shall next publish, but I foresee they will not sell. The booksellers,
finding this, will treat me as an unsuccessful author, that
is, they will employ me only as an anonymous translator
at a guinea a sheet. I have no doubt that I could make
£500 a year if I liked. But then I must forego all desire

of truth and excellence. I say I would go to America if Wordsworth would go with me, and we could persuade two or three farmers of this country, who are exceedingly attached to us, to accompany us. I would go, if the difficulty of procuring sustenance in this country remain in the state and degree in which it is at present; not on any romantic scheme, but merely because society has become a matter of great indifference to me. I grow daily more and more attached to solitude; but it is a matter of the utmost importance to be removed from seeing and suffering want.

God love you, my dear friend.

S. T. COLERIDGE.

CXVIII. TO ROBERT SOUTHEY.

GRETA HALL, KESWICK, [May 6, 1801].

MY DEAR SOUTHEY, — I wrote you a very, very gloomy letter; and I have taken blame to myself for inflicting so much pain on you without any adequate motive. Not that I exaggerated anything, as far as the immediate present is concerned; but had I been in better health and a more genial state of sensation, I should assuredly have looked out upon a more cheerful future. Since I wrote you, I have had another and more severe fit of illness, which has left me weak, very weak, but with so calm a mind that I am determined to believe that this fit was *bonâ fide* the last. Whether I shall be able to pass the next winter in this country is doubtful; nor is it possible I should know till the fall of the leaf. At all events, you will (I hope and trust, and if need were, *entreat*) spend as much of the summer and autumn with us as will be in your power, and if our *healths* should permit it, I am confident there will be no other solid objection to our living together in the same house, divided. We have ample room, — room enough, and more than enough, and I am willing to believe that the blessed dreams we dreamt

some six years ago may be auguries of something really
noble which we may yet perform together.

We wait impatiently, anxiously, for a letter announcing
your arrival. Indeed, the article *Falmouth* has taken pre-
cedence of the *Leading Paragraph* with me for the last
three weeks. Our best love to Edith. Derwent is the
boast of the county; the little river god is as beautiful as
if he had been the child of Venus Anaduomene previous
to her emersion. Dear Hartley! we are at times alarmed
by the state of his health, but at present he is well. If I
were to lose him, I am afraid it would exceedingly deaden
my affection for any other children I may have.

> A little child, a limber elf
> Singing, dancing to itself ;
> A faery thing with red round cheeks
> That always *finds*, and never *seeks*,
> 5 Doth make a vision to the sight,
> Which fills a father's eyes with light!
> And pleasures flow in so thick and fast
> Upon his heart that he at last
> Must needs express his love's excess
> 10 In words of wrong and bitterness.
> Perhaps it is pretty to force together
> Thoughts so all unlike each other ;
> To mutter and mock a broken charm ;
> To dally with wrong that does no harm.
> 15 Perhaps 't is tender, too, and pretty,
> At each wild word to feel within
> A sweet recoil of love and pity ;
> And what if in a world of sin
> (Oh sorrow and shame! should this be true)
> 20 Such giddiness of heart and brain
> Comes seldom, save from rage and pain,
> So talks as it 's most used to do.[1]

[1] Nothing is known of these lines
beyond the fact that in 1816 Coleridge printed them as " Conclusion
to Part II." of " Christabel." It is
possible that they were intended to
form part of a distinct poem in the

A very metaphysical account of fathers calling their children rogues, rascals, and little varlets, etc.

God bless you, my dear Southey! I need not say, Write.   S. T. COLERIDGE.

P. S.   We shall have peas, beans, turnips (with boiled leg of mutton), cauliflowers, French beans, etc., etc., endless!   We have a noble garden.

CXIX. TO THE SAME.

Wednesday, July 22, 1801.

MY DEAR SOUTHEY, — Yesterday evening I met a boy on an ass, winding down *as picturisk a glen* as eye ever looked at, he and his beast no mean part of the picture. I had taken a liking to the little blackguard at a distance, and I could have downright hugged him when he gave me a letter in your handwriting.   Well, God be praised! I shall surely see you once more, somewhere or other.   If it be really impracticable for you to come to me, I will doubtless do anything rather than not see you, though, in simple truth, travelling in chaises, or coaches even, for one day is sure to lay me up for a week.   But do, do, for heaven's sake, come and go the shortest way, however dreary it be; for there is enough to be seen when you get to our house.   If you did but know what a flutter the old moveable at my left breast has been in since I read your letter.   I have not had such a fillip for many months. My dear Edith; how glad you were to see old Bristol again!

I am again climbing up that rock of convalescence from which I have been so often washed off and hurried

---

metre of " Christabel," or, it may be, they are the sole survival of an attempted third part of the ballad itself.   It is plain, however, that the picture is from the life, that " the little child, the limber elf," is the four-year-old Hartley, hardly as yet " fitting to unutterable thought, The breeze-like motion, and the self-born carol."

back ; but I have been so unusually well these last two days
that I should begin to look the damsel Hope full in the
face, instead of sheep's-eyeing her, were it not that the
weather has been so unusually hot, and that is my joy.
Yes, sir ! we will go to Constantinople ; but as it rains
there, which my gout loves as the devil does holy water,
the Grand Turk shall shew the exceeding attachment he
will no doubt form towards us by appointing us his vice-
roys in Egypt. I will be Supreme Bey of that shower-
less district, and you shall be my supervisor. But for
God's sake make haste and come to me, and let us talk
of the sands of Arabia while we are floating in our lazy
boat on Keswick Lake, with our eyes on massy Skiddaw,
so green and high. Perhaps Davy might accompany you.
Davy will remain unvitiated ; his deepest and most recol-
lectable delights have been in solitude, and the next to
those with one or two whom he loved. He is placed, no
doubt, in a perilous desert of good things ; but he is connected with the present race of men by a very awful tie,
that of being able to confer immediate benefit on them ;
and the cold-blooded, venom-toothed snake that winds
around him shall be only his coat of arms, as God of
Healing.

I exceedingly long to see " Thalaba," and perhaps still
more to read " Madoc " over again. I never heard of any
third edition of my poems. I think you must have confused it with the L. B. Longman could not surely be so
uncouthly ill-mannered as not to write to me to know if I
wished to make any corrections or additions. If I am
well enough, I mean to alter, with a devilish sweep of
revolution, my Tragedy, and publish it in a little volume
by itself, with a new name, as a poem. But I have no
heart for poetry. Alas ! alas ! how should I ? who have
passed nine months with giddy head, sick stomach, and
swoln knees. My dear Southey ! it is said that long sickness makes us all grow selfish, by the necessity which it

imposes of continuously thinking about ourselves. But long and sleepless nights are a fine antidote.

Oh, how I have dreamt about you! Times that *have been*, and never can return, have been with me on my bed of pain, and how I yearned towards you in those moments. I myself can know only by feeling it over again. But come " strengthen the weak hands, and confirm the feeble knees. Then shall the lame man leap as a hart, and sorrow and sighing shall flee away."

I am here, in the vicinity of Durham, for the purpose of reading from the Dean and Chapter's Library an ancient of whom you may have heard, *Duns Scotus!* I mean to set the poor old Gemman on his feet again ; and in order to wake him out of his present lethargy, I am burning Locke, Hume, and Hobbes under his nose. They stink worse than feather or assafœtida. Poor Joseph! [Cottle] he has scribbled away both head and heart. What an affecting essay I could write on that man's character! Had he gone in his quiet way on a little pony, looking about him with a sheep's-eye cast now and then at a short poem, I do verily think from many parts of the " Malvern Hill," that he would at last have become a poet better than many who have had much fame, but he would be an Epic, and so

> " Victorious o'er the Danes, I Alfred, preach,
> Of my own forces, Chaplain-General ! "

. . . Write immediately, directing Mr. Coleridge, Mr. George Hutchinson's,[1] Bishop's Middleham, Rushiford,

[1] George Hutchinson, the fourth son of John Hutchinson of Penrith, was at this time in occupation of land at Bishop's Middleham, the original home of the family. He migrated into Radnorshire in 1815, being then about the age of thirty-seven ; but between that date and his leaving Bishop's Middleham he had resided for some time in Lincolnshire, at Scrivelsby, where he was engaged probably as agent on the estate of the " Champion." His first residence after migration was at New Radnor, where he married Margaret Roberts of Curnellan, but he subsequently removed into Herefordshire, where he resided in many places, latterly at Kingston. He died at his son's house, The Vinery, Hereford, in 1866. It would seem from a letter dated July 25, 1801 (Letter

Durham, and tell me when you set off, and I will contrive and meet you at Liverpool, where, if you are jaded
with the journey, we can stay a day or two at Dr. Crompton's, and chat a bit with Roscoe and Curry,[1] whom you
will like as men far, far better than as writers. O Edith ;
how happy Sara will be, and little Hartley, who uses the
air of the breezes as skipping-ropes, and fat Derwent, so
beautiful, and so proud of his three teeth, that there's
no bearing of him !

God bless you, dear Southey, and

S. T. COLERIDGE.

P. S.   Remember me kindly to Danvers and Mrs. Danvers.

[Care of] MRS. DANVERS,
   Kingsdown Parade, Bristol.

CXX. TO THE SAME.

DURHAM, Saturday, July 25, 1801.

MY DEAR SOUTHEY, — I do loathe cities, that's certain.   I am in Durham, at an inn, — and that, too, I do
not like, and have dined with a large parcel of priests all
belonging to the cathedral, thoroughly ignorant and hard-
hearted.   I have had no small trouble in gaining permission to have a few books sent to me eight miles from the
place, which nobody has ever read in the memory of man.

CXX.), that at this time Sarah
Hutchinson kept house for her brother George, and that Mary (Mrs.
Wordsworth) and Joanna Hutchinson lived with their elder brother
Tom at Gallow Hill, in the parish of
Brompton, near Scarborough.   The
register of Brompton Church records
the marriage of William Wordsworth
and Mary Hutchinson, on October 4,
1802 ; but in the notices of marriages
in the *Gentleman's Magazine*, of October, 1802, the latter is described
as " Miss Mary Hutchinson of Wyke-
ham," an adjoining parish.

[From information kindly supplied to me by Mr. John Hutchinson,
the keeper of the Library of the Middle Temple.]

[1] The historian William Roscoe
(afterwards M. P. for Liverpool),
and the physician James Currie, the
editor and biographer of Burns,
were at this time settled at Liverpool and on terms of intimacy with
Dr. Peter Crompton of Eaton Hall.

Now you will think what follows a lie, and it is not.   I
asked a stupid haughty fool, who is the Librarian of the
Dean and Chapter's Library in this city, if it had Leibnitz.   He answered, " We have no Museum in this Library for natural curiosities ; but there is a Mathematical
Instrument setter in the town, who shews such animalcula
through a glass of great magnifying powers."   Heaven
and earth! he understood the word "*live nits.*"   Well,
I return early to-morrow to Middleham ; to a quiet good
family that love me dearly — a young farmer and his
sister, and he makes very droll verses in the northern dia-
lects and in the metre of Burns, and is a great humourist,
and the woman is so very good a woman that I have
seldom indeed seen the like of her.   Death! that everywhere there should be one or two good and excellent people like these, and that they should not have the power
given 'em . . . to whirl away the rest to Hell!

I do not approve the Palermo and Constantinople
scheme, to be secretary to a fellow that would poison you
for being a poet, while he is only a lame verse-maker.
But verily, dear Southey! it will not suit you to be under
any man's control, or biddances.   What if you were a
consul?   'T would fix you to one place, as bad as if you
were a parson.   It won't do.   Now mark my scheme!
St. Nevis is the most lovely as well as the most healthy
island in the W. Indies.   Pinney's [1] estate is there, and
he has a country-house situated in a most heavenly way,
a very large mansion.   Now between you and me I have
reason to believe that not only this house is at my service, but many advantages in a family way that would
go one half to lessen the expenses of living there, and
perhaps Pinney would appoint us sinecure negro-drivers,
at a hundred a year each, or some other snug and reputable office, and, perhaps, too, we might get some office in

---

[1] The Bristol merchant who lent the manor-house of Racedown to Wordsworth in 1795.

which there is quite nothing to do under the Governor. Now I and my family, and you and Edith, and Wordsworth and his sister might all go there, and make the Island more illustrious than Cos or Lesbos! A heavenly climate, a heavenly country, and a good house. The seashore so near us, dells and rocks and streams. Do now think of this. But say nothing about it on account of old Pinney. Wordsworth would certainly go if I went. By the living God, it is my opinion that we should not leave three such men behind us. N. B. I have every reason to believe Keswick (and Cumberland and Westmoreland in general) full as dry a climate as Bristol. Our rains fall more certainly in certain months, but we have fewer rainy days, taking the year through. As to cold, I do not believe the difference perceptible by the human body. But I feel that there is no relief for me in *any part* of England. Very hot weather brings me about in an instant, and I relapse as soon as it coldens.

You say nothing of your voyage homeward, or the circumstances that preceded it. This, however, I far rather hear from your mouth than your letters. Come! and come quickly. My love to Edith, and remember me kindly to Mary and Martha and Eliza and Mrs. Fricker. My kind respects to Charles and Mrs. Danvers. Is Davy with you? If he is, I am sure he speaks affectionately of me. God bless you! Write.

S. T. COLERIDGE.

CXXI. TO THE SAME.

SCARBOROUGH, August 1, 1801.

MY DEAR SOUTHEY, — On my return from Durham (I foolishly walked back), I was taken ill, and my left knee swelled "pregnant with agony," as Mr. Dodsley says in one of his poems. Dr. Fenwick[1] has earnestly

---

[1] In the well-known lines "On revisiting the Sea-shore," allusion is made to this "mild physician," who vainly dissuaded him from bathing

persuaded me to try horse-exercise and warm sea-bathing, and I took the opportunity of riding with Sara Hutchinson to her brother Tom, who lives near the place, where I can ride to and fro, and bathe with no other expense there than that of the bath. The fit comes on me either at nine at night, or two in the morning. In the former case it continues nine hours, in the latter five. I am often literally *sick* with pain. In the daytime, however, I am well, surprisingly so indeed, considering how very little sleep I am able to snatch. Your letter was sent after me, and arrived here this morning, and but that my letter *can* reach you on the 5th of this month, I would immediately set off again, though I arrived here only last night. But I am unwilling not to try the baths for one week. If, therefore, you have not made the immediate preparation you may stay one week longer at Bristol. But if you have, you must look at the lake, and play with my babies three or four days, though this grieves me. I do not like it. I want to be with you, and to meet you even to the very verge of the Lake Country. I would far rather that you would stay a week at Grasmere (which is on the road, fourteen miles from Keswick), with Wordsworth, than go on to Keswick, and I not there. Oh, how you will love Grasmere!

All I ever wish of you with regard to wintering at Keswick is to stay with me till you find the climate injurious. When I read that cheerful sentence, " We will climb Skiddaw this year and scale Etna the next," with a right piteous and humorous smile did I ogle my poor knee, which at this present moment is larger than the thickest part of my thigh.

A little Quaker girl (the daughter of the great Quaker

---

in the open sea. Sea-bathing was at all times an irresistible pleasure to Coleridge, and he continued the practice, greatly to his benefit, down to a late period of his life and long after he had become a confirmed invalid. *Poetical Works*, p. 159.

mathematician Slee, a friend of anti-negro-trade Clarkson, who has a house at the foot of Ulleswater, which Slee Wordsworth dined with, a pretty parenthesis !), this little girl, four years old, happened after a very hearty meal to *eructate*, while Wordsworth was there. Her mother *looked* at her, and the little creature immediately and *formally* observed : " Yan belks when yan 's fu, and when yan 's empty." That is, " One belches when one 's full and when one 's empty." Since that time this is a favourite piece of slang at Grasmere and Greta Hall, whenever we talk of poor Joey, George Dyer, and other perseverants in the noble trade of scribbleism.

Wrangham,[1] who lives near here, one of your anthology friends, has married again, a lady of a neat £700 a year. His living by the Inclosure [Act] will be something better than £600, besides what little fortune he had with his last wife, who died in the first year. His present wife's cousin observed, "Mr. W. is a *lucky* man : his present lady is very weakly and delicate." I like the idea of a man's *speculating in sickly wives.* It would be no bad character for a farce.

That letter £ was a kind-hearted, honest, well-spoken citizen. The three strokes which *did* for him were, as I

---

[1] Francis Wrangham, whom Coleridge once described as "admirer of me and a pitier of my political principles " (Letter to Cottle [April], 1796), was his senior by a few years. On failing to obtain, it is said on account of his advanced political views, a fellowship at Trinity Hall, he started taking pupils at Cobham in Surrey in partnership with Basil Montagu. The scheme was of short duration, for Montagu deserted tuition for the bar, and Wrangham, early in life, was preferred to the benefices of Hemmanby and Folkton, in the neighborhood of Scarborough. He was afterwards appointed to a Canonry of York, to the Archdeaconry of Cleveland, and finally to a prebendal stall at Chester. He published a volume of *Poems* (London, 1795), in which are included Coleridge's Translation of the "Hendecasyllabli ad Bruntonam e Grantâ exituram," and some " Verses to Miss Brunton with the preceding Translation." He died in 1842. *Poetical Works*, p. 50. See, too, Editor's Note, p. 569 ; *Reminiscences of Cambridge*, by Henry Gunning, London, 1855, ii. 12 *seq*.

take it, (1), the Ictus Cardiacus, which devitalized his
moral heart ; (2ondly) the stroke of the apoplexy in his
head ; and (thirdly) a stroke of the palsy in his right
hand, which produces a terrible shaking and impotence in
the very attempt to reach his breeches pocket.   O dear
Southey ! what incalculable blessings, worthy of thanksgiving in Heaven, do we not owe to our being and *having
been poor !*   No man's heart can wholly stand up against
property.   My love to Edith.

S. T. COLERIDGE.

CXXII. TO THOMAS POOLE.

KESWICK, September 19, 1801.

By a letter from Davy I have learnt, Poole, that your
mother is with the Blessed.   I have given her the tears
and the pang which belong to her departure, and now she
will remain to me forever, what she had long been — a
dear and venerable image, often gazed at by me in imagination, and always with affection and filial piety.   She
was the only being whom I ever *felt* in the relation of
Mother ; and she is with God !   We are all with God !

What shall I say to *you !*   I can only offer a prayer of
thanksgiving for you, that you are one who has habitually connected the act of thought with that of feeling ; and
that your natural sorrow is so mingled up with a sense
of the omnipresence of the Good Agent, that I cannot
wish it to be other than what I know it is.   The frail
and the too painful will gradually pass away from you,
and there will abide in your spirit a great and sacred
accession to those solemn Remembrances and faithful
Hopes in which, and by which, the Almighty lays deep
the foundations of our continuous Life, and distinguishes
us from the Brutes that perish.   As all things pass away,
and those habits are broken up which constituted our own
and particular Self, our nature by a moral instinct cher-
ishes the desire of an unchangeable Something, and

thereby awakens or stirs up anew the passion to promote *permanent* good, and facilitates that grand business of our existence — still further, and further still, to generalise our affections, till Existence itself is swallowed up in *Being*, and we are in Christ even as He is in the Father.

It is among the advantages of these events that they learn us to associate a keen and deep feeling with all the old good phrases, all the reverend sayings of comfort and sympathy, that belong, as it were, to the whole human race. I felt this, dear Poole! as I was about to write my old

God bless you, and love you for ever and ever!

Your affectionate friend,
S. T. COLERIDGE.

Would it not be well if you were to change the scene awhile! Come to me, Poole! No — no — no. You have none that love you so well as I. I write with tears that prevent my seeing what I am writing.

CXXIII. TO ROBERT SOUTHEY.

NETHER STOWEY, BRIDGEWATER, December 31, 1801.

DEAR SOUTHEY, — On Xmas Day I breakfasted with Davy, with the intention of dining with you; but I returned very unwell, and in very truth in so utter a dejection of spirits as both made it improper for me to go anywhither, and a most unfit man to be with you. I left London on Saturday morning, 4 o'clock, and for three hours was in such a storm as I was never before out in, for I was atop of the coach — rain, and hail, and violent wind, with vivid flashes of lightning, that seemed almost to alternate with the flash-like re-emersions of the waning moon, from the ever-shattered, ever-closing clouds. However, I was armed cap-a-pie in a complete panoply, namely, in a huge, most huge, roquelaure, which had cost the government seven guineas, and was provided for the emigrants in the Quiberon expedition, one of whom, falling sick, stayed behind and parted with his cloak to Mr. Howel,[1] who lent it me. I dipped my head down, shoved it up — and it proved a complete tent to me. I was as dry as if I had been sitting by the fire. I arrived at Bath at eleven o'clock at night, and spent the next day with Warren, who has gotten a very sweet woman to wife and a most beautiful house and situation at Whitcomb on the Hill over the bridge. On Monday afternoon I arrived at Stowey. I am a good deal better ; but my bowels are by no means de-revolutionized. So much for me. I do not know what I am to say to you of your dear mother. Life passes away from us in all modes and ways, in our friends, in ourselves. We all " die daily." Heaven knows that many and many a time I have regarded my talents and requirements as a porter's burthen, imposing on me the capital duty of going on to the end of the journey, when I would gladly lie down by the side of the road, and become the country for a mighty nation of maggots. For what is life, gangrened, as it is with me, in its very vitals, domestic tranquillity ? These things being so, I confess that I feel for you, but not for the *event*, as for the event only by an act of thought, and not by any immediate *shock* from the like feeling within myself. When I return to town I can scarcely tell. I have not yet made up my mind whether or no I shall move Devonward. My relations wish to see me, and I wish to avoid the uneasy feeling I shall have, if I remain so near them without gratifying the wish. No very brotherly mood of mind, I must confess — but it is, nine tenths of it at least, a work of their own doing. Poole desires to be remembered to you. Remember me to your wife and Mrs. Lovell.

God bless you and

S. T. COLERIDGE.

[1] " I took a first floor for him in King Street, Covent Garden, at my tailor's, Howell's, whose wife is a cheerful housewife of middle age, who I knew would nurse Coleridge as kindly as if he were her son." D. Stuart, *Gent. Mag.*, May, 1838. See, too, *Letters from the Lake Poets*, p. 7.

CXXIV. TO HIS WIFE.

King Street, Covent Garden, [February 24, 1802.]

My dear Love, — I am sure it will make you happy
to hear that both my health and spirits have greatly improved, and I have small doubts that a residence of two
years in a mild and even climate will, with God's blessing, give me a new lease in a better constitution. You
may be well assured that I shall do nothing rashly, but
our journey thither I shall defray by letters to Poole and
the Wedgwoods, or more probably addressed to Mawman,
the bookseller, who will honour my drafts in return. Of
course I shall not go till I have earned all the money
necessary for the journey that I can. The plan will be
this, unless you can think of any better. Wordsworth
will marry soon after my return, and he, Mary, and Dorothy will be our companions and neighbours. Southey
means, if it is in his power, to pass into Spain that way.
About July we shall all set sail from Liverpool to Bor-
deaux. Wordsworth has not yet settled whether he shall
be married from Gallow Hill or at Grasmere. But they
will of course make a point that either Sarah shall be
with Mary or Mary with Sarah previous to so long a
parting. If it be decided that Sarah is to come to Grasmere, I shall return by York, which will be but a few
miles out of the way, and bring her. At all events, I
shall stay a few days at Derby, — for whom, think you,
should I meet in Davy's lecture-room but Joseph Strutt?
He behaved most affectionately to me, and pressed me
with great earnestness to pass through Darley (which is
on the road to Derby) and stay a few days at his house
among my old friends. I assure you I was much affected
by his kind and affectionate invitation (though I felt a
little awkward, not knowing *whom* I might venture to
ask after). I could not bring out the word "Mrs. Evans,"
and so said, "Your sister, sir? I *hope she* is well!"

On Sunday I dined at Sir William Rush's, and on
Monday likewise, and went with them to Mrs. Billington's Benefit. 'T was the "Beggar's Opera;" it was
perfection! I seem to have acquired a new sense by
hearing her. I wished you to have been there. I assure
you I am quite a man of *fashion;* so many titled acquaintances and handsome carriages stopping at my door,
and fine cards. And then I am such an exquisite judge of
music and painting, and pass criticisms on furniture and
chandeliers, and pay such very handsome compliments to
all women of fashion, that I do verily believe that if I were
to stay three months in town and have tolerable health
and spirits, I should be a Thing in vogue, — the very *ton-
ish* poet and Jemmy-Jessamy-fine-talker in town. If you
were only to see the tender smiles that I occasionally
receive from the Honourable Mrs. Damer! you would
scratch her eyes out for jealousy! And then there's the
sweet (N. B. musky) Lady Charlotte ——! Nay, but I
won't tell you her name, — you might perhaps take it into
your head to write an anonymous letter to her, and dis-
trust our little innocent amour.

Oh that I were at Keswick with my darlings! My
Hartley and my fat Derwent! God bless you, my dear
Sarah! I shall return in love and cheerfulness, and
therefore in pleasurable convalescence, if not in health.
We shall try to get poor dear little Robert into Christ's
Hospital; that wretch of a Quaker will do nothing. The
skulking rogue! just to lay hold of the time when Mrs.
Lovell was on a visit to Southey; there was such low
cunning in the thought.

Remember me most kindly to Mr. and Mrs. Wilkinson,
and tell Mr. Jackson that I have not shaken a hand since
I quitted him with more esteem and glad feeling than I
shall soon, I trust, shake his with. God bless you, and
your affectionate and faithful husband (notwithstanding
the Honourable Mrs. D. and Lady Charlotte!),

                              S. T. Coleridge.

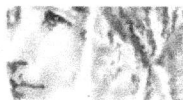

CXXV. TO W. SOTHEBY.

GRETA HALL, KESWICK, Tuesday, July 13, 1802.

MY DEAR SIR,—I had written you a letter and was about to have walked to the post with it when I received yours from Luff.[1] It gave me such lively pleasure that I threw my letter into the fire, for it related chiefly to the " Erste Schiffer " of Gesner, and I could not endure that my first letter to you should *begin* with a subject so little interesting to my heart or understanding. I trust that you are before this at the end of your journey, and that Mrs. and Miss Sotheby have so completely recovered themselves as to have almost forgotten all the fatigue except such instances of it as it may be pleasant to them to remember. Why need I say how often I have thought of you since your departure, and with what hope and pleasurable emotion? I will acknowledge to you that your very, very kind letter was not only a pleasure to me, but a relief to my mind; for, after I had left you on the road between Ambleside and Grasmere, I was dejected by the apprehension that I had been unpardonably loquacious, and had oppressed you, and still more Mrs. Sotheby, with my many words so impetuously uttered! But in simple truth, you were yourselves, in part, the innocent causes of it. For the meeting with you, the manner of the meeting, your kind attentions to me, the deep and healthful delight which every impressive and beautiful object seemed to pour out upon you ; kindred opinions, kindred pursuits, kindred feelings in persons whose habits, and, as it were, walk of life, have been so different from my own, — these and more than these, which I would but cannot say, all

[1] Captain Luff, for many years a resident at Patterdale, near Ulleswater, was held in esteem for the energy with which he procured the enrolment of large companies of volunteers. Wordsworth and Coleridge were frequent visitors at his house. For his account of the death of Charles Gough, on Helvellyn, and the fidelity of the famous spaniel, see *Coleorton Letters*, i. 97. *Letters from the Lake Poets*, p. 131.

flowed in upon me with unusually strong impulses of pleasure, — and pleasure in a body and soul such as I happen to possess "intoxicates more than strong wine." However, *I promise to be a much more subdued creature when you next meet me,* for I had but just recovered from a state of extreme dejection, brought on in part by ill health, partly by other circumstances; and solitude and solitary musings do of themselves impregnate our thoughts, perhaps, with more life and sensation than will leave the balance quite even. But you, my dear sir! looked at a brother poet with a brother's eyes. Oh that you were now in my study and saw, what is now before the window at which I am writing, — that rich mulberry-purple which a floating cloud has thrown on the lake, and that quiet boat making its way through it to the shore !

We have had little else but rain and squally weather since you left us till within the last three days. But showery weather is no evil to us; and even that most oppressive of all weathers, hot, small *drizzle,* exhibits the mountains the best of any. It produced such new combinations of ridges in the Lodore and Borrowdale mountains on Saturday morning that I declare, had I been blindfolded and so brought to the prospect, I should scarcely have known them again. It was a dream such as lovers have, — a wild and transfiguring, yet enchantingly lovely dream, of an object lying by the side of the sleeper. Wordsworth, who has walked through Switzerland, declared that he never saw anything superior, perhaps nothing equal, in the Alps.

The latter part of your letter made me truly happy. Uriel himself should not be half as welcome; and indeed he, I must admit, was never any great favourite of mine. I always thought him a bantling of zoneless Italian muses, which Milton heard cry at the door of his imagination and took in out of charity. However, come as you may, *carus mihi expectatusque venies.*[1] *De cœteris rebus si quid agendum est, et quicquid sit agendum, ut quam rectissime agantur omni meâ curâ, operâ, diligentiâ, gratiâ providebo.*[2]

On my return to Keswick, I reperused the " Erste Schiffer " with great attention, and the result was an increasing disinclination to the business of translating it; though my fancy was not a little flattered by the idea of seeing my rhymes in such a gay livery. — As poor Giordano Bruno [3] says in his strange, yet noble poem, " De Immenso et Innumerabili," —

> "Quam Garymedeo cultu, graphiceque venustus!
> Narcissis referam, peramarunt me quoque Nymphæ."

But the poem was too silly. The first conception is noble, so very good that I am spiteful enough to hope that I shall discover it not to have been original in Gesner, — he has so abominably maltreated it. First, the story is very inartificially constructed. We should have been let into the existence of the girl by her mother, through the young man, and after *his* appearance. This, however, is comparatively a trifle. But the machinery is so superlatively contemptible and commonplace; as if a young man could not dream of a tale which had deeply impressed him without Cupid, or have a fair wind all the way to an island without Æolus. Æolus himself is a god devoted and dedicated, I should have thought, to the Muse of Travestie. His speech in Gesner is not deficient in fancy, but it is a girlish fancy, and the god of the wind, exceedingly disquieted with animal love, makes a very ridiculous figure in my imagination. Besides, it was ill taste to introduce Cupid and Æolus at a time which we positively know to have been anterior to the invention

[1] *Ciceronis Epist. ad Fam.* iv. 10.
[2] *Ib.* i. 2.
[3] The lines are taken, with some alterations, from a kind of *l'envoy* or epilogue which Bruno affixed to his long philosophical poem, *Jordani Bruni Nolani de Innumerabilibus Immenso et Infigurabili; seu de Universo et Mundis libri octo.* Francofurti, 1591, p. 654.

and establishment of the Grecian Mythology; and the speech of Æolus reminds me perpetually of little engravings from the cut stones of the ancients, — seals, and whatever else they call them.   Again, the girl's yearnings and conversations with him are something between the nursery and the *Veneris volgivagæ templa, et libidinem spirat et subsusurrat, dum innocentiæ loquillam, et virginiæ cogitationis dulciter offensantis luctamina simulat.*

It is not the thought that a lonely girl could have; but exactly such as a boarding-school *miss*, whose imagination, to say no worse, had been somewhat stirred and heated by the perusal of French or German pastorals, would suppose her to say.   But this is, indeed, general in the German and French poets.   It is easy to clothe imaginary beings with our own thoughts and feelings; but to send ourselves out of ourselves, to *think* ourselves into the thoughts and feelings of beings in circumstances wholly and strangely different from our own, *hic labor hoc opus;* and who has achieved it?   Perhaps only Shakespeare. Metaphysics is a word that you, my dear sir, are no great friend to, but yet you will agree with me that a great poet must be *implicité*, if not *explicité*, a profound metaphysician.   He may not have it in logical coherence in his brain and tongue, but he must have the ear of a wild Arab listening in the silent desert, the eye of a North American Indian tracing the footsteps of an enemy upon the leaves that strew the forest, the touch of a blind man feeling the face of a darling child.   And do not think me a bigot if I say that I have read no French or German writer who appears to me to have a *heart* sufficiently pure and simple to be capable of this or anything like it.   I could say a great deal more in abuse of poor Gesner's poems, but I have said more than I fear will be creditable in your opinion to my good nature.   I must, though, tell you the malicious motto which I have written in the first part of Klopstock's " Messias : " —

> " Tale tuum carmen nobis, divine poeta !
> Quale sopor ! "

Only I would have the words *divine poeta* translated
" verse-making divine." I have read a great deal of German ; but I do dearly, dearly, dearly love my own coun-
trymen of old times, and those of my contemporaries who
write in their spirit.

William Wordsworth and his sister left me yesterday
on their way to Yorkshire. They walked yesterday to the
foot of Ulleswater, from thence they go to Penrith, and
take the coach. I accompanied them as far as the seventh
milestone. Among the last things which he said to me
was, " Do not forget to remember me to Mr. Sotheby
with whatever affectionate terms so slight an intercourse
may permit ; and how glad we shall all be to see him
again ! "

I was much pleased with your description of Wordsworth's character as it appeared to you. It is in a few
words, in half a dozen strokes, like one of Mortimer's [1]
figures, a fine portrait. The word " homogeneous " gave
me great pleasure, as most accurately and happily expressing him. I must set you right with regard to my
perfect coincidence with his poetic creed. It is most certain that the heads of our mutual conversations, etc., and
the passages, were indeed partly taken from note of mine ;
for it was at first intended that the preface should be
written by me. And it is likewise true that I warmly
accord with Wordsworth in his abhorrence of these poetic
licenses, as they are called, which are indeed mere tricks
of convenience and laziness. *Ex. gr.* Drayton has these
lines : —

> " Ouse having Ouleney past, as she were waxed mad
> From her first stayder course immediately doth gad,

---

[1] John Hamilton Mortimer, 1741–
1779. He painted *King John grant-
ing Magna Charta*, the *Battle of*
Agincourt, the *Conversion of the*
Britons, and other historical subjects.

And in meandered gyres doth whirl herself about,
That, this way, here and there, backward in and out.
And like a wanton girl oft doubling in her gait
In labyrinthian turns and twinings intricate," etc.[1]

The first poets, observing such a stream as this, would say with truth and beauty, " it *strays ;* " and now every stream shall *stray,* wherever it prattles on its *pebbled way,* instead of its bed or channel. And I have taken the instance from a poet from whom as few instances of this vile, commonplace, trashy style could be taken as from any writer [namely], from Bowles' execrable translation [2] of that lovely poem of Dean Ogle's (vol. ii. p. 27).   I am confident that Bowles good-naturedly translated it in a hurry, merely to give him an excuse for printing the admirable original.   In my opinion, every phrase, every metaphor, every personification, should have its justifying clause in some *passion*, either of the poet's mind or of the characters described by the poet.   But metre itself implies a passion, that is, a state of excitement both in the poet's mind, and is expected, in part, of the reader ; and, though I stated this to Wordsworth, and he has in some sort stated it in his preface, yet he has not done justice to it, nor has he, in my opinion, sufficiently answered it.   In my opinion, poetry justifies as poetry, independent of any other passion, some new combinations of language and

---

[1] Drayton's *Poly-Olbion*, Song 22, 1-17.

[2] The Latin Iambics, in which Dean Ogle celebrated the little Blyth, which ran through his father's park at Kirkley, near Ponteland, deserve the highest praise ; but Bowles's translation is far from being execrable. He may not have caught the peculiar tones of the Northumbrian burn which awoke the memories of the scholarly Dean, but his irregular lines are not without their own pathos and melody. Bowles was a Winchester boy, and Dr. Newton Ogle, then Dean of Winchester, was one of his earliest patrons. It was from the Dean's son, his old schoolfellow, Lieutenant Ogle, that he claimed to have gathered the particulars of Coleridge's discovery at Reading and discharge from the army. " Poems of William Lisle Bowles,"*Galignani*,1829,p.131; " The Late Mr. Coleridge a Common Soldier," *Times*, August 13, 1834.

commands the omission of many others allowable in other compositions. Now Wordsworth, *me saltem judice*, has in his system not sufficiently admitted the former, and in his practice has too frequently sinned against the latter. Indeed, we have had lately some little controversy on the subject, and we begin to suspect that there is somewhere or other a radical difference in our opinions. *Dulce est inter amicos rarissimâ dissensione condere plurimas consentiones*, saith St. Augustine, who said more good things than any saint or sinner that I ever read in Latin.

Bless me! what a letter! And I have yet to make a request to you. I have read your Georgics at a friend's house in the neighbourhood, and in sending for the book, I find that it belonged to a book-club, and has been returned. If you have a copy interleaved, or could procure one for me and will send it to me per coach, with a copy of your original poems, I will return them to you with many thanks in the autumn, and will endeavour to improve my own taste by writing on the blank leaves my feelings both of the original and your translation. Your poems I want for another purpose, of which hereafter.

Mrs. Coleridge and my children are well. She desires to be respectfully remembered to Mrs. and Miss Sotheby. Tell Miss Sotheby that I will endeavour to send her soon the completion of the "Dark Ladie," as she was good-natured enough to be pleased with the first part.

Let me hear from you soon, my dear sir! and believe me with heartfelt wishes for you and yours, in every-day phrase, but, indeed, indeed, not with every-day feeling.

Yours most sincerely,
S. T. COLERIDGE.

I long to lead Mrs. Sotheby to a scene that has the grandeur without the toil or danger of Scale Force. It is called the White Water Dash.[1]

[1] One of a series of falls made by the Dash Beck, which divides the

CXXVI. TO THE SAME.

Keswick, July 10, 1802.

My dear Sir, — I trouble you with another letter to inform you that I have finished the First Book[1] of the "Erste Schiffer." It consists of 530 lines; the Second Book will be a hundred lines less. I can transcribe both legibly in three single-sheet letters; you will only be so good as to inform me whither and whether I am to send them. If they are likely to be of any use to Tomkins he is welcome to them; if not, I shall send them to the "Morning Post." I have given a faithful translation in blank verse. To have decorated Gesner would have been, indeed, "to spice the spices;" to have lopped and pruned *somewhat* would have only produced incongruity; to have done it sufficiently would have been to have published a poem of my own, not Gesner's. I have aimed at nothing more than purity and elegance of English, a keeping and harmony in the colour of the style, a smoothness without

parishes of Caldbeck and Skiddaw Forest, and flows into Bassenthwaite Lake.

The following minute description is from an entry in a note-book dated October 10, 1800: —

"The Dash itself is by no means equal to the Churnmilk (*sic*) at Eastdale (*sic*) or the Wytheburn Fall. This I wrote standing under and seeing the whole Dash; but when I went over and descended to the bottom, then I only *saw* the real *Fall* and the curve of the steep slope, and retracted. It is, indeed, so seen, a fine thing. It falls parallel with a fine black rock thirty feet, and is more shattered, more completely atomized and white, than any I have ever seen. . . . The Fall of the Dash is in a horse-shoe basin of its own, wildly peopled with small ashes standing out of the rocks. Crossed the beck close by the white pool, and stood on the other side in a complete spray-*rain*. Here it assumes, I think, a still finer appearance. You see the vast rugged net and angular points and upright cones of the black rock; the Fall assumes a variety and complexity, parts rushing in wheels, other parts perpendicular, some in white horse-tails, while towards the right edge of the black [rock] two or three leisurely fillets have escaped out of the turmoil."

[1] I have been unable to discover any trace of the MS. of this translation.

monotony in the versification. If I have succeeded, as I
trust I have, in these respects, my translation will be just
so much better than the original as metre is better than
prose, in their judgment, at least, who prefer blank verse
to prose. I was probably too severe on the *morals* of the
poem, uncharitable perhaps. But I am a downright Englishman, and tolerate downright grossness more patiently
than this coy and distant dallying with the appetites.
" Die pflanzen entstehen aus dem saamen, gewisse thiere
gehen aus dem hervor andre so, andre anders, ich hab es
alles bemerkt, was hab ich zu thun."   Now I apprehend it
will occur to nineteen readers out of twenty, that a maiden
so *very curious*, so exceedingly *inflamed* and harassed by
a difficulty, and so *subtle* in the discovery of even comparatively *distant* analogies, would necessarily have seen
the difference of sex in her flocks and herds, and the mari-
tal as well as maternal character could not have escaped
her.   Now I avow that the grossness and vulgar plain
sense of Theocritus' shepherd lads, bad as it is, is in my
opinion less objectionable than Gesner's refinement, which
necessarily leads the imagination to ideas without *expressing them*. Shaped and clothed, the mind of a pure being
would turn away from them from natural delicacy of taste,
but in that shadowy half-being, that state of nascent existence in the twilight of imagination and just on the
vestibule of consciousness, they are far more incendiary,
stir up a more lasting commotion, and leave a deeper
stain. The suppression and obscurity arrays a simple
truth in a veil of something like guilt, that is altogether
meretricious, as opposed to the matronly majesty of our
Scripture, for instance; and the conceptions as they
recede from distinctness of *idea* approximate to the nature
of *feeling*, and gain thereby a closer and more immediate affinity with the appetites. But, independently of
this, the whole passage, consisting of precisely one fourth
of the whole poem, has not the least influence on the

action of the poem, and it is scarcely too much to say that it has nothing to do with the main subject, except indeed it be pleaded that *Love* is induced by compassion for this maiden to make a young man *dream* of her, which young man had been, without any influence of the said Cupid, deeply interested in the story, and, therefore, did not need the interference of Cupid at all ; any more than he did the assistance of Æolus for a fair wind all the way to an island that was within sight of shore.

I translated the poem, partly because I could not endure to appear *irresolute* and *capricious* to you in the first undertaking which I had connected in any way with your person ; in an undertaking which I connect with our journey from Keswick to Grasmere, the carriage in which were your son, your daughter, and your wife (all of whom may God Almighty bless! a prayer not the less fervent, my dear sir! for being a little out of place here) ; and, partly, too, because I wished to force myself out of metaphysical trains of thought, which, when I wished to write a poem, beat up game of far other kind. Instead of a covey of poetic partridges with whirring wings of music, or wild ducks *shaping* their rapid flight in forms always regular (a still better image of verse), up came a metaphysical bustard, urging its slow, heavy, laborious, earth-skimming flight over dreary and level wastes. To have done with poetical prose (which is a very vile Olio), sickness and some other and worse afflictions first forced me into downright metaphysics. For I believe that by nature I have more of the poet in me. In a poem written during that dejection, to Wordsworth, and the greater part of a private nature, I thus expressed the thought in language more forcible than harmonious : [1] —

[1] The "Ode to Dejection," of which this is the earliest version, was composed on Sunday evening, April 4, and published six months later, in the *Morning Post* of October 4, 1802. It was reprinted in the *Sibylline Leaves*, 1817. A comparison of the Ode, as sent to Sotheby, with the

> Yes, dearest poet, yes !
> There was a time when tho' my path was rough,
> The joy within me dallied with distress,
> And all misfortunes were but as the stuff
> Whence fancy made me dreams of happiness :

first printed version (*Poetical Works*, Appendix G, pp. 522–524) shows that it underwent many changes before it was permitted to see the "light of common day" in the columns of the *Morning Post*. The Ode was begun some three weeks after Coleridge returned to Keswick, after an absence of four months. He had visited Southey in London, he had been a fellow guest with Tom Wedgwood for a month at Stowey, he had returned to London and attended Davy's lectures at the Royal Institution, and on his way home he had stayed for a fortnight with his friend T. Hutchinson, Wordsworth's brother-in-law, at Gallow Hill.

He left Gallow Hill " on March 13 in a violent storm of snow, wind, and rain," and must have reached Keswick on Sunday the 14th or Monday the 15th of March. On the following Friday he walked over to Dove Cottage, and once more found himself in the presence of his friends, and, once again, their presence and companionship drove him into song. The Ode is at once a confession and a contrast, a confession that he had fled from the conflict with his soul into the fastnesses of metaphysics, and a contrast of his own hopelessness with the glad assurance of inward peace and outward happiness which attended the pure and manly spirit of his friend.

But verse was what he had been wedded to,

And his own mind did like a tempest strong
Come thus to him, and drove the weary wight along.

A MS. note-book of 1801–2, which has helped to date his movements at the time, contains, among other hints and jottings, the following almost illegible fragment: " The larches in spring push out their separate bundles of . . . into green brushes or pencils which . . . small tassels ; " — and with the note may be compared the following lines included in the version contained in the letter, but afterwards omitted : —

> In this heartless mood,
> To other thoughts by yonder throstle woo'd,
> *That pipes within the larch-tree, not unseen*
> *The larch that pushes out in tassels green*
> *Its bundled leaflts — woo'd to mild delights,*
> *By all the tender sounds and gentle sights*
> *Of this sweet primrose-month, and vainly woo'd !*
> O dearest Poet, in this heartless mood —

Another jotting in the same note-book : " A Poem on the endeavour to emancipate the mind from day-dreams, with the different attempts and the vain ones," perhaps found expression in the lines which follow " My shaping spirit of Imagination," which appeared for the first time in print in *Sibylline Leaves*, 1817, but which, as Mr. Dykes Campbell has rightly divined, belonged to the original draft of the Ode. *Poetical Works*, p. 159. Appendix G, pp. 522–524. Editor's Note, pp. 626–628.

For Hope grew round me, like the climbing vine,
And fruit, and foliage, not my own, seemed mine.
But now afflictions bow me down to earth:
Nor care I, that they rob me of my mirth,
But oh! each visitation
Suspends what nature gave me at my birth,
My shaping spirit of Imagination.
.   .   .   .
For not to think of what I needs must feel,
But to be still and patient, all I can;
And haply by abstruse research to steal
From my own nature all the natural man —
This was my sole resource, my wisest plan:
And that which suits a part infects the whole,
And now is almost grown the temper of my soul.

Thank heaven! my better mind has returned to me,
and I trust I shall go on rejoicing. As I have nothing
better to fill the blank space of this sheet with, I will
transcribe the introduction of that poem to you, that being
of a sufficiently general nature to be interesting to you.
The first lines allude to a stanza in the Ballad of Sir Patrick Spence: " Late, late yestreen I saw the new moon
with the old one in her arms, and I fear, I fear, my master
dear, there will be a deadly storm."

Letter, written Sunday evening, April 4.

Well! if the Bard was weatherwise, who made
The dear old Ballad of Sir Patrick Spence,
This night, so tranquil now, will not go hence
Unrous'd by winds, that ply a busier trade
Than that, which moulds yon clouds in lazy flakes,
Or the dull sobbing draft, that drones and rakes
Upon the strings of this Eolian lute,
Which better far were mute.
For lo! the New Moon, winter-bright!
And overspread with phantom light

(With swimming phantom light o'erspread,
But rimmed and circled with a silver thread)
I see the Old Moon in her lap foretelling
The coming on of rain and squally blast!
And O! that even now the gust were swelling,
And the slant night-shower driving loud and fast.

.   .   .   .   .   .

A grief without a pang, void, dark, and drear!
A stifling, drowsy, unimpassioned grief,
That finds no natural outlet, no relief,
In word, or sigh, or tear!
This, William, well thou know'st,
Is that sore evil which I dread the most,
And oftnest suffer.   In this heartless mood,
To other thoughts by yonder throstle woo'd,
That pipes within the larch-tree, not unseen,
The larch, that pushes out in tassels green
Its bundled leafits, woo'd to mild delights,
By all the tender sounds and gentle sights
Of this sweet primrose-month, and vainly woo'd!
O dearest Poet, in this heartless mood,
All this long eve, so balmy and serene,
Have I been gazing on the Western sky,
And its peculiar tint of yellow-green:
And still I gaze — and with how blank an eye!
And those thin clouds above, in flakes and bars,
That give away their motion to the stars;
Those stars, that glide behind them, or between,
Now sparkling, now bedimmed, but always seen;
Yon crescent moon, as fix'd as if it grew
In its own cloudless, starless lake of blue,
A boat becalm'd! thy own sweet sky-canoe![1]
I see them all, so exquisitely fair!
I see, not *feel!* how beautiful they are!

---

[1] "A lovely skye-canoe." *Morning Post.* The reference is to the Prologue to "Peter Bell." Compare stanza 22,
"My little vagrant Form of light,
My gay and beautiful Canoe."
Wordsworth's *Poetical Works*, p. 100.

My genial spirits fail ;
And what can these avail,
To lift the smoth'ring weight from off my breast ?
It were a vain endeavour,
Though I should gaze for ever
On that green light that lingers in the west ;
I may not hope from outward forms to win
The passion and the life, whose fountains are within.

.   .   .   .

O Wordsworth ! we receive but what we give,
And in our life alone does Nature live ;
Ours is her wedding garment, ours her shroud !
And would we aught behold, of higher worth,
Than that inanimate, cold world, *allow'd*
To the poor, loveless, ever-anxious crowd,
Ah ! from the soul itself must issue forth,
A light, a glory, a fair luminous cloud
     Enveloping the earth !
And from the soul itself must there be sent
A sweet and powerful voice, of its own birth,
Of all sweet sounds the life and element !
O pure of heart ! thou need'st not ask of me
What this strong music in the soul may be ?
What and wherein it doth exist,
This light, this glory, this fair luminous mist,
This beautiful and beauty-making Power.
Joy, blameless poet !   Joy that ne'er was given
Save to the pure, and in their purest hour,
Joy, William, is the spirit and the power
That wedding Nature to us gives in dower,
     A new Earth and new Heaven,
Undream'd of by the sensual and proud —
     We, we ourselves rejoice !
And thence comes all that charms or ear or sight,
All melodies an echo of that voice !
All colours a suffusion from that light !
Calm, steadfast spirit, guided from above,
O Wordsworth ! friend of my devoutest choice,
Great son of genius ! full of light and love,

> Thus, thus, dost thou rejoice.
> To thee do all things live, from pole to pole,
> Their life the eddying of thy living Soul!
> Brother and friend of my devoutest choice,
> Thus mayst thou ever, ever more rejoice!

.   .   .   .

I have selected from the poem, which was a very long one and truly written only for the solace of sweet song, all that could be interesting or even pleasing to you, except, indeed, perhaps I may annex as a fragment a few lines on the "Æolian Lute," it having been introduced in its dronings in the first stanza. I have used Yule for Christmas.

> Nay, wherefore did I let it haunt my mind,
> This dark, distressful dream?
> I turn from it and listen to the wind
> Which long has rav'd unnotic'd!   What a scream
> Of agony by torture lengthened out,
> That lute sent out!   O thou wild storm without,
> Bare crag, or Mountain Tairn, or blasted tree,
> Or pine-grove whither woodman never clomb,
> Or lonely house, long held the witches' home,
> Methinks were fitter instruments for thee
> Mad Lutanist! that, in this month of showers,
> Of dark-brown gardens, and of peeping flowers,
> Mak'st devil's Yule, with worse than wintry song,
> The blossoms, buds, and timorous leaves among!
> Thou Actor, perfect in all tragic sounds!
> Thou mighty Poet, even to frenzy bold!
>   What tell'st thou now about?
> 'T is of the rushing of an host in rout,
> With many groans from men, with smarting wounds —
> At once they groan with pain, and shudder with the cold!
> But hush! there is a pause of deeper silence!
> Again! but all that noise, as of a rushing crowd,
> With groans, and tremulous shudderings — all is over!
> And it has other sounds, less fearful and less loud —

A tale of less affright,
And tempered with delight,
As thou thyself had'st fram'd the tender lay —
'T is of a little child,
Upon a heath wild,
Not far from home, but she has lost her way —
And now moans low in utter grief and fear ;
And now screams loud, and hopes to make her mother *hear*.

. . . .

My dear sir ! ought I to make an apology for troubling you with such a long, verse-cramm'd letter ? Oh, that instead of it, I could but send to you the image now before my eyes, over Bassenthwaite. The sun is setting in a glorious, rich, brassy light, on the top of Skiddaw, and one third adown it is a huge, enormous mountain of cloud, with the outlines of a mountain. This is of a starchy grey, but floating past along it, and upon it, are various patches of sack-like clouds, bags and woolsacks, of a shade lighter than the brassy light. Of the clouds that hide the setting sun, — a fine yellow-red, somewhat more than sandy light, and these, the farthest from the sun, are suffused with the darkness of a stormy colour. Marvellous creatures ! how they pass along ! Remember me with most respectful kindness to Mrs. and Miss Sotheby, and the Captains Sotheby.   Truly yours,

S. T. COLERIDGE.

CXXVII. TO ROBERT SOUTHEY.[1]

GRETA HALL, KESWICK, July 29, 1802.

MY DEAR SOUTHEY, — Nothing has given me half the pleasure, these many, many months, as last week did Edith's heralding to us of a minor Robert ; for that it will be a boy, one always takes for granted. From the bottom of my heart I say it, I never knew a man that better

[1] For Southey's reply, dated Bristol, August 4, 1802, see *Life and Correspondence*, ii. 189–192.

deserved to be a father by right of virtues that eminently
belonged to him, than yourself ; but beside this I have
cheering hopes that Edith will be born again, and be a
healthy woman. When I said, nothing had given me
half the pleasure, I spoke truly, and yet said more than
you are perhaps aware of, for, by Lord Lonsdale's death,
there are excellent reasons for believing that the Wordsworths will gain £5,000, the share of which (and no doubt
Dorothy will have more than a mere share) will render
William Wordsworth and his sister quite independent.
They are now in Yorkshire, and he returns in about a
month *one of us*. . . . Estlin's Sermons, I fear, are mere
moral discourses. If so, there is but small chance of
their sale. But if he had published a *volume* of *sermons*,
of the same kind with those which he has published
singly, *i. e.* apologetical and ecclesiastico-historical, I *am
almost* confident, they would have a respectable circulation. To publish single sermons is almost always a foolish
thing, like single sheet quarto poems. Estlin's sermon
on the Sabbath really surprised me. It was well written
in style, I mean, and the reasoning throughout is not
only sound, but has a cast of novelty in it. A superior
sermon altogether it appeared to me. I am myself a little
theological, and if any bookseller will take the risque, I
shall in a few weeks, possibly, send to the press a small
volume under the title of " Letters to the British Critic
concerning Granville Sharp's Remarks on the uses of
the Definitive article in the Greek Text of the New
Testament, and the Revᵈ C. Wordsworth's Six Letters,
to G. Sharp Esqʳ, in confirmation of the same, together
with a Review of the Controversy between Horsley and
Priestley respecting the faith of the Primitive Christians."
This is no mere dream, like my " Hymns to the Elements," for I have written more than half the work. I
purpose afterwards to publish a book concerning Tythes
and Church Establishment, for I conceit that I can throw

great light on the subject. You are not apt to be much
surprised at any change in my mind, active as it is, but it
will perhaps please you to know that I am become very
fond of History, and that I have read much with very
great attention. I exceedingly like the job of Amadis
de Gaul. I wish you may half as well like the job, in
which I shall very shortly appear. Of its sale I have no
doubt; but of its prudence? There's the rub. "Concerning Poetry and the characteristic merits of the Poets,
our contemporaries." One volume Essays, the second
Selections. — The Essays are on Bloomfield, Burns,
Bowles, Cowper, Campbell, Darwin, Hayley, Rogers, C.
Smith, Southey, Woolcot, Wordsworth — the Selections
from every one who has written at all, any being above
the rank of mere scribblers — Pye and his Dative Case
Plural, Pybus, Cottle, etc., etc. The object is not to examine what is good in each writer, but what has *ipso facto*
pleased, and to what faculties, or passions, or habits of the
mind they may be supposed to have given pleasure. Of
course Darwin and Wordsworth having given each a
defence of their mode of poetry, and a disquisition on the
nature and essence of poetry in general, I shall necessarily be led rather deeper, and these I shall treat of
either first or last. But I will apprise you of one thing,
that although Wordsworth's Preface is half a child of my
own brain, and arose out of conversations so frequent that,
with few exceptions, we could scarcely either of us, perhaps, positively say which first started any particular
thought (I am speaking of the Preface as it stood in the
second volume), yet I am far from going all lengths with
Wordsworth. He has written lately a number of Poems
(thirty-two in all), some of them of considerable length
(the longest one hundred and sixty lines), the greater
number of these, to my feelings, very excellent compositions, but here and there a daring humbleness of language
and versification, and a strict adherence to matter of fact,

even to prolixity, that startled me. His alterations, like-wise, in "Ruth" perplexed me, and I have thought and thought again, and have not had my doubts solved by Wordsworth. On the contrary, I rather suspect that somewhere or other there is a radical difference in our theoretical opinions respecting poetry; this I shall endeav-our to go to the bottom of, and, acting the arbitrator be-tween the old school and the new school, hope to lay down some plain and perspicuous, though not superficial canons of criticism respecting poetry. What an admirable defi-nition Milton gives, quite in an "obiter" way, when he says of poetry, that it is "*simple, sensuous, passionate!*" It truly comprises the whole that can be said on the sub-ject. In the new edition of the L. Ballads there is a valu-able appendix, which I am sure you must like, and in the Preface itself considerable additions; one on the dignity and nature of the office and character of a Poet, that is very grand, and of a sort of Verulamian power and majesty, but it is, in parts (and this is the fault, *me judice*, of all the latter half of that Preface), obscure beyond any necessity, and the extreme elaboration and almost constrainedness of the diction contrasted (to my feelings) somewhat harshly with the general style of the Poems, to which the Preface is an introduction. Sara (why, dear Southey! will you write it always Sarah? Sar*a*, methinks, is associated with times that you and I cannot and do not wish ever to forget), Sara said, with some acuteness, that she wished all that part of the Pre-face to have been in blank verse, and *vice versâ*, etc. How-ever, I need not say, that any diversity of opinion on the subject between you and myself, or Wordsworth and my-self, can only be small, taken in a *practical* point of view.

I rejoice that your History marches on so victoriously. It is a noble subject, and I have the fullest confidence of your success in it. The influence of the Catholic Reli-gion — the influence of national glory on the individual

morals of a people, especially in the downfall of the
nobility of Portugal, — the strange fact (which seems to
be admitted as with one voice by all travellers) of the
vileness of the Portuguese nobles compared with the
Spanish, and of the superiority of the Portuguese com-
monalty to the same class in Spain; the effects of colo-
nization on a small and not very fruitful country; the
effects important, and too often forgotten of absolute accidents, such as the particular character of a race of Princes
on a nation — Oh what awful subjects these are ! I long
to hear you read a few chapters to me. But I conjure you
do not let " Madoc " go to sleep. Oh that without words
I could cause you to *know* all that I think, all that I feel,
all that I hope concerning that Poem ! As to myself, all
my poetic genius (if ever I really possessed any *genius*,
and it was not rather a mere general *aptitude* of talent,
and quickness in imitation) is gone, and I have been fool
enough to suffer deeply in my mind, regretting the loss,
which I attribute to my long and exceedingly severe
metaphysical investigations, and these partly to ill-health,
and partly to private afflictions which rendered any subjects, immediately connected with feeling, a source of pain
and disquiet to me.

> There was a Time when tho' my Path was rough,
>   I had a heart that dallied with distress ;
> And all misfortunes were but as the stuff
>   Whence Fancy made me dreams of Happiness ;
> For Hope grew round me like the climbing Vine,
> And Fruits and Foliage, not my own, seemed mine !
> But now afflictions bow me down to earth,
> Nor car'd I that they robb'd me of my mirth.
>   But oh ! each visitation
> Suspends what Nature gave me at my Birth,
>   My shaping Spirit of Imagination !

Here follow a dozen lines that would give you no pleasure, and then what follows : —

> For not to *think* of what I needs must feel,
>   But to be still and patient, all I can;
> And haply by abstruse Research to steal
>   From my own Nature all the Natural Man,
>   This was my sole Resource, my wisest Plan!
>   And that which suits a part, infects the whole,
>   And now is almost grown the Temper of my Soul.

Having written these lines, I rejoice for you as well as for myself, that I am able to inform you, that now for a long time there has been more love and concord in my house than I have known for years before. I had made up my mind to a very awful step, though the struggles of my mind were so violent, that my sleep became the valley of the shadows of Death and my health was in a state truly alarming. It did alarm Mrs. Coleridge. The thought of separation wounded her pride, — she was fully persuaded that deprived of the society of my children and living abroad without any friends I should pine away, and the fears of widowhood came upon her, and though these feelings were wholly selfish, yet they made her *serious*, and that was a great point gained. For Mrs. Coleridge's mind has very little that is *bad* in it; it is an innocent mind; but it is light and *unimpressible*, warm in anger, cold in sympathy, and in all disputes uniformly *projects itself forth* to recriminate, instead of turning itself inward with a silent self-questioning. Our virtues and our vices are exact antitheses. I so attentively watch my own nature that my worst self-delusion is a complete self-knowledge so mixed with intellectual complacency, that my quickness to see and readiness to acknowledge my faults is too often frustrated by the small pain which the sight of them gives me, and the consequent slowness to amend them. Mrs. C. is so stung with the very first thought of being in the wrong, because she never endures to look at her own mind in all its faulty parts, but shelters herself from painful self-inquiry by angry recrimination. Never,

I suppose, did the stern match-maker bring together two
minds so utterly contrariant in their primary and organ-
ical constitution. Alas! I have suffered more, I think,
from the amiable propensities of my nature than from
my worst faults and most erroneous habits, and I have
suffered much from both. But, as I said, Mrs. Coleridge
was made *serious*, and for the first time since our marriage she felt and acted as beseemed a wife and a mother
to a husband and the father of her children. She promised to set about an alteration in her external manners
and looks and language, and to fight against her inveterate habits of puny thwarting and unintermitting dyspa-
thy, this immediately, and to do her best endeavours to
cherish other feelings. I, on my part, promised to be
more attentive to all her feelings of pride, etc., etc., and
to try to correct my habits of impetuous censure. We
have both kept our promises, and she has found herself
so much more happy than she had been for years before,
that I have the most confident hopes that this happy
revolution in our domestic affairs will be permanent, and
that this external conformity will gradually generate a
greater inward likeness of thoughts and attachments than
has hitherto existed between us. Believe me, if you were
here, it would give you a *deep* delight to observe the difference of our minutely conduct towards each other, from
that which, I fear, could not but have disturbed your
comfort when you were here last. Enough. But I am
sure you have not felt it tedious.

So Corry[1] and you are off? I suspected it, but Edith
never mentioned an iota of the business to her sister. It
is well. It was not your destiny. Wherever you are,
God bless you! My health is weak enough, but it is so
far amended that it is far less dependent on the influences of the weather. The mountains are better friends

[1] The Right Hon. Isaac Corry, land, to whom Southey acted as
Chancellor of the Exchequer for Ire- secretary for a short time.

in this respect. Would that I could flatter myself that
the same would be the case with you. The only objection on my part is now, — God be praised ! — done away.
The services and benefits I should receive from your
society and the spur of your example would be incalculable.   The house consists — the first floor (or rather
ground floor) of a kitchen and a back kitchen, a large
parlour and two nice small parlours ; the second floor of
three bedrooms, one a large one, and one large drawing-
room ; the third floor or floors of three bedrooms — in
all twelve rooms. Besides these, Mr. Jackson offers to
make that nice outhouse or workshop either two rooms
or one noble large one for a study if I wish it. If it
suited you, you might have one kitchen, or (if Edith and
Sara thought it would answer) we might have the two
kitchens in common. You might have, I say, the whole
ground floor, consisting of two sweet wing-rooms, commanding that loveliest view of Borrowdale, and the great
parlour ; and supposing we each were forced to have two
servants, a nursemaid and a housemaid, the two house-
maids would sleep together in one of the upper rooms,
and the nursemaids have each a room to herself, and the
long room on the ground floor must be yours and
Edith's room, and if Mary be with you, the other hers.
We should have the whole second floor, consisting of the
drawing-room, which would be Mrs. Coleridge's parlour,
two bedrooms, which (as I am so often ill, and when ill
cannot rest at all, unless I have a bed to myself) is absolutely necessary for me, and one room for you if occasion should be, or any friend of yours or mine. The
highest room in the house is a very large one intended
for two, but suffered to remain one by my desire. It
would be a capital healthy nursery. The outhouse would
become my study, and I *have* a couch-bed on which I am
now sitting (in bed) and writing to you. It is now in the
study ; of course it would be removed to the outhouse

when that became my study, and would be a second spare bed. I have no doubt but that Mr. Jackson would willingly let us retain my present study, which might be your library and study room. My dear Southey, I merely state these things to you. All our lot on earth is compromise. Blessings obtained by blessings foregone, or by evils undergone. I should be glad, no doubt, if you thought that your health and happiness would find a home under the same roof with me; and I am sure you will not accuse me as indelicate or obtrusive in mentioning things as they are; but if you decline it altogether, I shall know that you have good reasons for doing so, and be perfectly satisfied, for if it detracted from your comfort it could, of course, be nothing but the contrary of all advantage to me. You would have access to four or five libraries : Sir W. Lawson's, a most magnificent one, but chiefly in Natural History, Travels, etc.; Carlton House (I am a *prodigious* favourite of Mrs. Wallis, the owner and resident, mother of the Privy Counsellor Wallis); Carlisle, Dean and Chapter; the Library at Hawkshead School, and another (of what value I know not) at St. Bees, whither I mean to walk to-morrow to spend five or six days for bathing. It is four miles from Whitehaven by the seaside. Mrs. Coleridge is but poorly, children well. Love to Edith and May, and to whom I am at all interested. God love you. If you let me hear from you, it is among my firmest resolves — God ha' mercy on 'em! — to be a regular correspondent of yours.

S. T. Coleridge.

P. S. Mrs. C. must have one room on the ground floor, but this is only putting one of your rooms on the second floor.

CXXVIII. TO THE SAME.

Monday night, August 9, 1802.

MY DEAR SOUTHEY, — Derwent can say his letters, and if you could but see his darling mouth when he shouts out Q! This is a digression.

On Sunday, August 1st,[1] after morning church, I left Greta Hall, crossed the fields to Portinscale, went through Newlands, where "Great Robinson looks down upon Marden's Bower," and drank tea at Buttermere, crossed the mountains to Ennerdale, and slept at a farm-house a little below the foot of the lake, spent the greater part of the next day mountaineering, and went in the evening through Egremont to St. Bees, and slept there; returned next day to Egremont, and slept there; went by the sea-coast as far as Gosforth, then turned off and went up Wasdale, and slept at T. Tyson's at the head of the vale. Thursday morning crossed the mountains and ascended Scafell, which is more than a hundred yards higher than either Helvellyn or Skiddaw; spent the whole day among clouds, and one of them a frightening thunder-cloud; slipped down into Eskdale, and there slept, and spent a good part of the next day; proceeded that evening to Devock Lake, and slept at Ulpha Kirk; on Saturday passed through the Dunnerdale Mountains to Broughton

---

[1] "On Sunday, August 1st, ½ after 12, I had a shirt, cravat, 2 pairs of stockings, a little paper, and half dozen pens, a German book (Voss's Poems), and a little tea and sugar, with my night cap, packed up in my natty green oil-skin, neatly squared, and put into my net knapsack, and the knapsack on my back and the besom stick in my hand, which for want of a better, and in spite of Mrs. C. and Mary, who both raised their voices against it, especially as I left the besom scattered on the kitchen floor, off I sallied over the bridge, through the hop - field, through the Prospect Bridge, at Portinscale, so on by the tall birch that grows out of the centre of the huge oak, along into Newlands." MS. Journal of tour in the Lake District, August 1–9, 1802, sent in the form of a letter to the Wordsworths and transcribed by Miss Sarah Hutchinson.

Vale, Tarver Vale, and in upon Coniston. On Sunday I surveyed the lake, etc., of Coniston, and proceeded to Bratha, and slept at Lloyd's house; this morning walked from Bratha to Grasmere, and from Grasmere to Greta Hall, where I now am, quite sweet and ablute, and have not even now read through your letter, which I will answer by the night's post, and therefore must defer all account of my very interesting tour, saying only that of all earthly things which I have beheld, the view of Seafell and from Seafell (both views from its own summit) is the most heart-exciting.

And now for business. The rent of the whole house, including taxes and the furniture we have, will not be under forty, and not above forty-two, pounds a year. You will have half the house and half the furniture, and of course your share will be either twenty pounds or twenty guineas. As to furniture, the house certainly will not be wholly, that is, completely furnished by Jackson. Two rooms we must somehow or other furnish between us, but not immediately; you may pass the winter without it, and it is hard if we cannot raise thirty pounds in the course of the winter between us. And whatever we buy may be disposed of any Saturday, to a moral certainty, at its full value, or Mr. Jackson, who is uncommonly desirous that you should come, will take it. But we can get on for the winter well enough.

Your books may come all the way from Bristol either to Whitehaven, Maryport, or Workington; sometimes directly, always by means of Liverpool. In the latter case, they must be sent to Whitehaven, from whence waggons come to Keswick twice a week. You will have twenty or thirty shillings to lay out in tin and crockery, and you must bring with you, or buy here (which you may do at eight months' credit), knives and forks, etc., and all your linen, from the diaper subvestments of the young jacobin [1]

[1] "The following month, September (1802), was marked by the birth

to diaper table clothes, sheets, napkins, etc.   But these, I suppose, you already have.

What else I have to say I cannot tell, and indeed shall be too late for the post.   But I will write soon again.   I was exceedingly amused with the Cottelism ; but I have not time to speak of this or of other parts of your letter. I believe that I can execute the criticisms with no offence to Hayley, and in a manner highly satisfactory to the admirers of the poet Bloomfield, and to the friends of the man Bloomfield.   But there are certainly other objections of great weight.

Sara is well, and the children pretty well.   Hartley is almost ill with transport at my Seafell expedition.   That child is a poet, spite of the forehead, " villainously *low*," which his mother smuggled into his face.   Derwent is more beautiful than ever, but very backward with his tongue, although he can say all his letters. — N. B. Not out of the book.   God bless you and yours!

S. T. COLERIDGE.

If you are able to determine, you will of course let me know it without waiting for a second letter from me ; as if you determine in the affirmative [1] of the scheme, it will be a great motive with Jackson, indeed, a most infallible one, to get immediately to work so as to have the whole perfectly furnished six weeks at least before your arrival. Another reason for your writing immediately is, that we may lay you in a stock of coals during the summer, which is a saving of some pounds ; when I say *determine*, of course I mean such determination as the thousand contingencies, black and white, permit a wise man to make, and which would be enough for me to act on.

of his first child, a daughter, named after her paternal grandmother, Margaret." *Southey's Life and Correspondence*, ii. 192.

[1] Southey's reply, which was not in the affirmative, has not been preserved.   The joint-residence at Greta Hall began in September, 1803.

Sara will write to Edith soon.

I have just received a letter from Poole ; but I have found so many letters that I have opened yours only.

CXXIX. TO W. SOTHEBY.

Thursday, August 26, 1802.

MY DEAR SIR, — I was absent on a little excursion when your letter arrived, and since my return I have been waiting and making every enquiry in the hopes of announcing the receipt of your " Orestes " and its companions, with my sincere thanks for your kindness. But I can hear nothing of them. Mr. Lamb,[1] however, goes to Penrith next week, and will make strict scrutiny. I am not to find the " Welsh Tour " among them ; and yet I think I am correct in referring the ode " Netley Abbey " to that collection, — a poem which I believe I can very nearly repeat by heart, though it must have been four or five years since I last read it. I well remember that, after reading your " Welsh Tour," Southey observed to me that you, I, and himself had all done ourselves harm by suffering an admiration of Bowles to bubble up too often on the surface of our poems. In perusing the second volume of Bowles, which I owe to your kindness, I met a line of my own which gave me great pleasure, from the thought what a pride and joy I should have had at the time of writing it if I had supposed it possible that Bowles would have adopted it. The line is, —

Had melancholy mus'd herself to sleep.[2]

---

[1] Charles and Mary Lamb's visit to Greta Hall, which lasted three full weeks, must have extended from (about) August 12 to September 2, 1802. *Letters of Charles Lamb*, i. 180–184.

[2] " *Here melancholy, on the pale crags laid, Might muse herself to sleep ;* or Fancy come,

Watching the mind with tender cozenage And shaping things that are not."

" Coombe-Ellen, written in Radnorshire, September, 1798." " Poems of William Lisle Bowles," *Galignani*, p. 139. For " Melancholy, a Fragment," see *Poetical Works*, p. 34.

I wrote the lines at nineteen, and published them many
years ago in the " Morning Post " as a fragment, and as
they are but twelve lines, I will transcribe them : —

> Upon a mouldering abbey's broadest wall,
> Where ruining ivies prop the ruins steep —
> Her folded arms wrapping her tatter'd pall
> Had Melancholy mused herself to sleep.
> The fern was press'd beneath her hair,
> The dark green Adder's Tongue was there ;
> And still as came the flagging sea gales weak,
> Her long lank leaf bow'd fluttering o'er her cheek.
>
> Her pallid cheek was flush'd ; her eager look
> Beam'd eloquent in slumber ! Inly wrought,
> Imperfect sounds her moving lips forsook,
> And her bent forehead work'd with troubled thought.

I met these lines yesterday by accident, and ill as they
are written there seemed to me a force and distinctness
of image in them that were buds of promise in a school-
boy performance, though I am giving them perhaps more
than their deserts in thus assuring them a reading from
you. I have finished the " First Navigator," and Mr.
Tomkins[1] may have it whenever he wishes. It would be
gratifying to me if you would look it over and alter anything you like. My whole wish and purpose is to serve
Mr. Tomkins, and you are not only much more in the
habit of writing verse than I am, but must needs have a
better tact of what will offend that class of readers into
whose hands a showy publication is likely to fall. I do
not mean, my dear sir, to impose on you ten minutes'
thought, but often *currente oculo* a better phrase or position of words will suggest itself. As to the ten pounds,
it is more than the thing is worth, either in German or
English. Mr. Tomkins will better give the true value of
it by kindly accepting what is given with kindness. Two

[1] I have not been able to verify this reference.

or three copies presented in my name, one to each of the
two or three friends of mine who are likely to be pleased
with a fine book, — this is the utmost I desire or will
receive. I shall for the ensuing quarter send occasional
verses, etc., to the "Morning Post," under the signature
Ἐστησε, and I mention this to you because I have some
intention of translating Voss's " Idylls " in English hexameter, with a little prefatory essay on modern hexameters. I have discovered that the poetical parts of the
Bible and the best parts of Ossian are little more than
slovenly hexameters, and the rhythmical prose of Gesner
is still more so, and reads exactly like that metre in Boe-
thius' and Seneca's tragedies, which consists of the latter
half of the hexameter. The thing is worth an experiment, and I wish it to be considered merely as an experiment. I need not say that the greater number of the
verses signed Ἐστησε will be such as were never meant
for anything else but the *peritura charta* of the " Morning Post."

I had written thus far when your letter of the 16th
arrived, franked on the 23d from Weymouth, with a polite apology from Mr. Bedingfell (if I have rightly deci-
phered the name) for its detention. I am vexed I did not
write immediately on my return home, but I waited, day
after day, in hopes of the " Orestes," etc. It is an old
proverb that "extremes meet," and I have often regretted
that I had not noted down as they incurred the interesting instances in which the proverb is verified. The
newest subject, though brought from the planets (or as-
teroids) Ceres and Pallas, could not excite my curiosity
more than " Orestes." I will write immediately to Mr.
Clarkson, who resides at the foot of Ulleswater, and beg
him to walk into Penrith, and ask at all the inns if any
parcel have arrived ; if not, I will myself write to Mr.
Faulder and inform him of the failure. There is a subject of great merit in the ancient mythology hitherto un-

touched — I believe so, at least.   But for the *mode* of the
death, which mingles the ludicrous and terrible, but which
might be easily altered, it is one of the finest subjects for
tragedy that I am acquainted with.   Medea, after the
murder of her children [having] fled to the court of the
old King Pelias, was regarded with superstitious horror,
and shunned or insulted by the daughters of Pelias, till,
hearing of her miraculous restoration of Æson, they conceived the idea of recalling by her means the youth of their
own father.   She avails herself of their credulity, and so
works them up by pretended magical rites that they
consent to kill their father in his sleep and throw him
into the magic cauldron.   Which done, Medea leaves them
with bitter taunts of triumph.   The daughters are called
Asteropæa, Autonoe, and Alcestis.   Ovid alludes briefly
to this story in the couplet, —

> " Quid referam Peliæ natas pietate nocentes,
>   Cæsaque virgineâ membra paterna manu ? "
>   Ovid, Epist. XII. 129, 130.

What a thing to have seen a tragedy raised on this fable
by Milton, in rivalry of the " Macbeth " of Shakespeare !
The character of Medea, wandering and fierce, and in-
vested with impunity by the strangeness and excess of her
guilt, and truly an injured woman on the other hand and
possessed of supernatural powers !   The same story is told
in a very different way by some authors, and out of their
narrations matter might be culled that would very well
coincide with and fill up the main incidents — her imposing the sacred image of Diana on the priesthood of Iolcus,
and persuading them to join with her in inducing the
daughters of Pelias to kill their father; the daughters
under the persuasion that their father's youth would be
restored, the priests under the faith that the goddess required the death of the old king, and that the safety of
the country depended on it.   In this way Medea might be
suffered to escape under the direct protection of the priest-

hood, who may afterwards discover the delusion. The moral of the piece would be a very fine one.

Wordsworth wrote a very animated account of his difficulties and his joyous meeting with you, which he calls the happy rencontre or fortunate rainstorm. Oh! that you had been with me during a thunder-storm [1] on Thursday, August the 3d! I was sheltered (in the phrase of the country, *lownded*) in a sort of natural porch on the summit of Sea Fell, the central mountain of our Giants, said to be higher than Skiddaw or Helvellyn, and in chasm, naked crag, bursting springs, and waterfall the most interesting, without a rival. When the cloud passed away, to my right and left, and behind me, stood a great national convention of mountains which our ancestors most descriptively called Copland, that is, the Land of Heads. Before me the mountains died away down to the sea in eleven parallel ridges; close under my feet, as it

---

[1] "O my God! what enormous mountains there are close by me, and yet below the hill I stand on. . . . And here I am, *lounded* [i. e., sheltered], — so fully lounded, — that though the wind is strong and the clouds are hastening hither from the sea, and the whole air seaward has a lurid look, and we shall certainly have thunder, — yet here (but that I am hungered and provisionless), *here* I could be warm and wait, methinks, for to-morrow's sun — and on a nice stone table am I now at this moment writing to you — between 2 and 3 o'clock, as I guess. Surely the first letter ever written from the top of Sea Fell."

"After the thunder-storm I shouted out all your names in the sheep-fold — where echo came upon echo, and then Hartley and Derwent, and then I laughed and shouted Joanna. It leaves all the echoes I ever heard far, far behind, in number, distinctness and humanness of voice; and then, not to forget an old friend, I made them all say Dr. Dodd etc." *MS. Journal,* August 6, 1802. Compare Lamb's Latin letter of October 9, 1802: —

"Ista tua Carmina Chamouniana satis grandia esse mihi constat; sed hoc mihi nonnihil displicet, quod in iis illæ montium Grisosonum inter se responsiones totidem reboant anglicé, *God, God*, haud aliter atque temet audivi tuas [sic] montes Cumbrianas [sic] resonare docentes, *Tod, Tod*, nempe Doctorem infelicem: vocem certe haud Deum sonantem." *Letters of Charles Lamb,* i. 185. See, too, Canon Ainger's translation and note, *ibid.* p. 331. See, also, Southey's Letter to Grosvenor Bedford, January 9, 1804. *Life and Correspondence,* ii. 248.

were, were three vales: Wastdale, with its lake; Miter-
dale and Eskdale, with the rivers Irt, Mite, and Esk seen
from their very fountains to their fall into the sea at Ra-
venglass Bay, which, with these rivers, form to the eye
a perfect trident.

Turning round, I looked through Borrowdale out upon
the Derwentwater and the Vale of Keswick, even to my
own house, where my own children were. Indeed, I had
altogether a most interesting walk through Newlands to
Buttermere, over the fells to Ennerdale, to St. Bees; up
Wastdale to Sea Fell, down Eskdale to Devock Lake,
Ulpha Kirk, Broughton Mills, Tarver, Coniston, Winder-
mere, Grasmere, Keswick. If it would entertain you, I
would transcribe my notes and send them you by the first
opportunity. I have scarce left room for my best wishes
to Mrs. and Miss Sotheby, and affectionate wishes for
your happiness and all who constitute it.

With unfeigned esteem, dear sir,

   Yours, etc.,   S. T. COLERIDGE.

P. S. I am ashamed to send you a scrawl so like in
form to a servant wench's first letter. You will see that
the first half was written before I received your last letter.

CXXX. TO THE SAME.

GRETA HALL, KESWICK, September 10, 1802.

MY DEAR SIR, — The books have not yet arrived, and
I am wholly unable to account for the delay. I suspect
that the cause of it may be Mr. Faulder's mistake in sending them by the Carlisle waggon. A person is going to
Carlisle on Monday from this place, and will make diligent inquiry, and, if he succeed, still I cannot have them
in less than a week, as they must return to Penrith and
there wait for the next Tuesday's carrier. I ought, perhaps, to be ashamed of my weakness, but I must confess I
have been downright vexed by the business. Every cart,

every return-chaise from Penrith has renewed my hopes,
till I began to play tricks with my own impatience, and say,
" Well, I take it for granted that I shan't get them for
these seven days," etc., — with other of those half-lies that
fear begets on hope. You have imposed a pleasing task
on me in requesting the minutiæ of my opinions concerning your "Orestes." Whatever these opinions may be,
the disclosure of them will be a sort of *map* of my mind,
as a poet and reasoner, and my curiosity is strongly excited. I feel you a man of genius in the choice of the
subject. It is my faith that the *genus irritabile* is a
phrase applicable only to bad poets. Men of great genius
have, indeed, as an essential of their composition, great
sensibility, but they have likewise great confidence in their
own powers, and fear must always precede anger in the
human mind. I can with truth say that, from those I
love, mere general praise of anything I have written is as
far from giving me pleasure as mere general censure ; in
anything, I mean, to which I have devoted much time or
effort. " Be minute, and assign your reasons often, and
your first impressions always, and then blame or praise.
I care not which, I shall be gratified." These are *my*
sentiments, and I assuredly believe that they are the sentiments of all who have indeed felt a *true call* to the ministry of *song*. Of course, I, too, will act on the golden rule
of doing to others what I wish others to do unto me. But,
while I think of it, let me say that I should be much concerned if you applied this to the " First Navigator." It
would absolutely mortify me if you did more than look
over it, and when a correction suggested itself to you, take
your pen and make it, and let the copy go to Tomkins.
What they have been, I shall know when I see the thing
in print ; for it must please the present times if it please
any, and you have been far more in the fashionable world
than I, and must needs have a finer and surer tact of that
which will offend or disgust in the higher circles of life.

Yet it is not what I should have advised Tomkins to do,
and that is one reason why I cannot and will not accept
more than a brace of copies from him. I do not like to
be associated in a man's mind with his losses. If he have
the translation gratis, he must take it on his own judgment; but when a man pays for a thing, and he loses by
it, the idea will creep in, spite of himself, that the failure
was in part owing to the badness of the translation.
While I was translating the "Wallenstein," I told Longman it would never answer; when I had finished it I
wrote to him and foretold that it would be waste paper
on his shelves, and the dullness charitably laid upon my
shoulders. Longman lost two hundred and fifty pounds
by the work, fifty pounds of which had been paid to me,
— poor pay, Heaven knows! for a thick octavo volume of
blank verse; and yet I am sure that Longman never
thinks of me but "Wallenstein" and the ghosts of his
departed guineas dance an ugly waltz round my idea.
This would not disturb me a tittle, if I thought well of
the work myself. I should feel a confidence that it would
win its way at last; but this is not the case with Gesner's
"Der erste Schiffer." It may as well lie here till Tomkins wants it. Let him only give me a week's notice, and
I will transmit it to you with a large margin. Bowles's
stanzas on "Navigation"[1] are among the best in that second volume, but the whole volume is wofully inferior to
its predecessor. There reigns through all the blank verse
poems such a perpetual trick of moralizing everything,
which is very well, occasionally, but never to see or describe any interesting appearance in nature without connecting it, by dim analogies, with the moral world proves
faintness of impression. Nature has her proper interest,
and he will know what it is who believes and feels that
everything has a life of its own, and that we are all *One*

[1] "The Spirit of Navigation and Discovery." "Bowles's Poetical
Works," *Galignani*, p. 142.

Life. A poet's heart and intellect should be *combined*, intimately combined and unified with the great appearances of nature, and not merely held in solution and loose mixture with them, in the shape of formal similes. I do not mean to exclude these formal similes; there are moods of mind in which they are natural, pleasing moods of mind, and such as a poet will often have, and sometimes express; but they are not his highest and most appropriate moods. They are " sermoni propriora," which I once translated " properer for a sermon." The truth is, Bowles has indeed the *sensibility* of a poet, but he has not the *passion* of a great poet. His latter writings all want *native* passion. Milton here and there supplies him with an appearance of it, but he has no native passion because he is not a thinker, and has probably weakened his intellect by the haunting fear of becoming extravagant. Young, somewhere in one of his prose works, remarks that there is as profound a logic in the most daring and dithyrambic parts of Pindar as in the " Organon " of Aristotle. The remark is a valuable one.

> Poetic feelings, like the flexuous boughs
> Of mighty oaks! yield homage to the gale,
> Toss in the strong winds, drive before the gust,
> Themselves one giddy storm of fluttering leaves;
> Yet, all the while, self-limited, remain
> Equally near the fix'd and parent trunk
> Of truth in nature — in the howling blast,
> As in the calm that stills the aspen grove.[1]

That this is deep in our nature, I felt when I was on Scafell. I involuntarily poured forth a hymn[2] in the man-

---

[1] These lines form part of the poem addressed " To Matilda Betham. From a Stranger." The date of composition was September 9, 1802, the day before they were quoted in the letter to Sotheby. *Poetical Works*, p. 168.

[2] The " Hymn before Sunrise in the Vale of Chamouni " was first printed in the *Morning Post*, September 11, 1802. It was reprinted in the original issue of *The Friend*, No. xi. (October 16, 1809, pp. 174-176), and again in *Sibylline Leaves*, 1817.

ner of the Psalms, though afterwards I thought the ideas, etc., disproportionate to our humble mountains. . . . You will soon see it in the " Morning Post," and I should be glad to know whether and how far it pleased you. It has struck me with great force lately that the Psalms afford a most complete answer to those who state the Jehovah of the Jews, as a personal and national God, and the Jews as differing from the Greeks only in calling the minor Gods Cherubim and Seraphim, and confining the word " God " only to their Jupiter. It must occur to every reader that the Greeks in their religious poems address always the Numina Loci, the Genii, the Dryads, the Naiads, etc., etc. All natural objects were *dead*, mere hollow statues, but there was a Godkin or Goddessling *included* in each. In the Hebrew poetry you find nothing of this poor stuff, as poor in genuine imagination as it is mean in intellect. At best, it is but fancy, or the aggregating faculty of the mind, not imagination or the *modifying* and coadunating faculty. This the Hebrew poets appear to me to have possessed beyond all others, and

As De Quincey was the first to point out, Coleridge was indebted to the Swiss poetess, Frederica Brun, for the framework of the poem and for many admirable lines and images, but it was his solitary walk on Scafell, and the consequent uplifting of spirit, which enabled him " to create the dry bones of the German outline into the fulness of life."

Coleridge will never lose his title of a *Lake Poet*, but of the ten years during which he was nominally resident in the Lake District, he was absent at least half the time. Of his greater poems there are but four, the second part of " Christabel," the " Dejection : an Ode," the " Picture," and the " Hymn before Sunrise," which take their colouring from the scenery of Westmoreland and Cumberland.

He was but twenty-six when he visited Ottery for the last time. It was in his thirty-fifth year that he bade farewell to Stowey and the Quantocks, and after he was turned forty he never saw Grasmere or Keswick again. Ill health and the *res angusta domi* are stern gaolers, but, if he had been so minded, he would have found a way to revisit the pleasant places in which he had passed his youth and early manhood. In truth, he was well content to be a dweller in " the depths of the huge city " or its outskirts, and, like Lamb, he " could not *live* in Skiddaw." *Poetical Works*, p. 165, and Editor's Note, pp. 629, 630.

next to them the English. In the Hebrew poets each
thing has a life of its own, and yet they are all our life.
In God they move and live and *have* their being; not *had*,
as the cold system of Newtonian Theology represents, but
have. Great pleasure indeed, my dear sir, did I receive
from the latter part of your letter. If there be any two
subjects which have in the very depths of my nature
interested me, it has been the Hebrew and Christian
Theology, and the Theology of Plato. Last winter I
read the Parmenides and the Timæus with great care, and
oh, that you were here — even in this howling rainstorm
that dashes itself against my windows — on the other
side of my blazing fire, in that great armchair there! I
guess we should encroach on the morning ere we parted.
How little the commentators of Milton have availed
themselves of the writings of Plato, Milton's darling!
But alas, commentators only hunt out verbal parallelisms
— *numen abest*. I was much impressed with this in all
the many notes on that beautiful passage in "Comus"
from l. 629 to 641. All the puzzle is to find out what
plant Hæmony is; which they discover to be the English
spleenwort, and decked out as a mere play and licence of
poetic fancy with all the strange properties suited to the
purpose of the drama. They thought little of Milton's
platonizing spirit, who wrote nothing without an interior
meaning. "Where more is meant than meets the ear,"
is true of himself beyond all writers. He was so great a
man that he seems to have considered fiction as profane
unless where it is consecrated by being emblematic of
some truth. What an unthinking and ignorant man we
must have supposed Milton to be, if, without any hidden
meaning, he had described it as growing in such abundance that the dull swain treads on it daily, and yet as
never *flowering*. Such blunders Milton of all others was
least likely to commit. Do look at the passage. Apply
it as an allegory of Christianity, or, to speak more pre-

cisely, of the Redemption by the Cross, every syllable is
full of light!   "*A small unsightly root.*" — "To the
Greeks folly, to the Jews a stumbling-block " — "*The leaf
was darkish and had prickles on it* " — "If in this life
only we have hope, we are of all men the most miserable,"
and a score of other texts.   "*But in another country, as
he said, Bore a bright golden flower* " — "The exceeding
weight of glory prepared for us hereafter " — "*But not in
this soil ; Unknown and like esteemed and the dull swain
Treads on it daily with his clouted shoon* " — The promises of Redemption offered daily and hourly, and to all,
but accepted scarcely by any — "*He called it Hæmony.*"
Now what is Hæmony ? αἷμα οἶνος, Blood-wine.   "And
he took the wine and blessed it and said, 'This is my
Blood,' " — the great symbol of the Death on the Cross.
There is a general ridicule cast on all allegorising of
poets.   Read Milton's prose works, and observe whether
he was one of those who joined in this ridicule.   There is
a very curious passage in Josephus [De Bello Jud. 6, 7,
cap. 25 (vi. § 3)] which is, in its literal meaning, more
wild and fantastically absurd than the passage in Milton ;
so much so, that Lardner quotes it in exultation and says
triumphantly, "Can any man who reads it think it any
disparagement to the Christian Religion that it was not
embraced by a man who would believe such stuff as this?
God forbid that it should affect Christianity, that it is not
believed by the learned of this world ! "   But the passage
in Josephus, I have no doubt, is wholly allegorical.

'Εστησε signifies "He hath stood,"[1] which, in these

---

[1] Coleridge must have presumed
on the ignorance of Sotheby and of
his friends generally.   He could
hardly have passed out of Boyer's
hands without having learned that
'Εστησε signifies, "He hath placed,"
not "He hath stood."   But, like
most people who have changed their
opinions, he took an especial pride
in proclaiming his unswerving alle-
giance to fixed principles.   The in-
itials S. T. C.; Grecised and mis-
translated, expressed this pleasing
delusion, and the Greek, "Punic
[sc. punnic] Greek," as he elsewhere
calls it, might run the risk of detection.

times of apostasy from the principles of freedom or of
religion in this country, and from both by the same persons in France, is no unmeaning signature, if subscribed
with humility, and in the remembrance of " Let him that
stands take heed lest he fall! " However, it is, in truth,
no more than S. T. C. written in Greek — Es tee see.

Pocklington will not sell his house, but he is ill, and
perhaps it may be to be sold, but it is sunless all winter.

God bless you, and   S. T. COLERIDGE.

CXXXI. TO THE SAME.

GRETA HALL, KESWICK, Tuesday, September 27, 1802.

MY DEAR SIR, — The river is full, and Lodore is full,
and silver-fillets come out of clouds and glitter in every
ravine of all the mountains; and the hail lies like snow,
upon their tops, and the impetuous gusts from Borrowdale snatch the water up high, and continually at the
bottom of the lake it is not distinguishable from snow
slanting before the wind — and under this seeming snow-
drift the sunshine *gleams*, and over all the nether half of
the Lake it is *bright* and *dazzles*, a cauldron of melted
silver boiling! It is in very truth a sunny, misty, cloudy,
dazzling, howling, omniform day, and I have been looking at as pretty a sight as a father's eyes could well see —
Hartley and little Derwent running in the green where
the gusts blow most madly, both with their hair floating
and tossing, a miniature of the agitated trees, below
which they were playing, inebriate both with the pleasure — Hartley whirling round for joy, Derwent eddying,
half-willingly, half by the force of the gust, — driven
backward, struggling forward, and shouting his little
hymn of joy. I can write thus to you, my dear sir, with
a confident spirit; for when I received your letter on the
22nd, and had read the " family history," I laid down
the sheet upon my desk, and sate for half an hour thinking of you, dreaming of you, till the tear grown cold

upon my cheek awoke me from my reverie. May you
live long, long, thus blessed in your family, and often,
often may you all sit around one fireside.   Oh happy
should I be now and then to sit among you — your pilot
and guide in some of your summer walks !

> " Frigidus nt sylvis Aquilo si increverit, aut si
>   Hiberni pluviis dependent nubibus imbres,
>   Nos habeat domus, et multo Lar luceat igne.
>   Ante focum mihi parvus erit, qui ludat, Iulus,
>   Blanditias ferat, et nondum constantia verba;
>   Ipse legam magni tecum monumenta Platonis ! "

Or, what would be still better, I could talk to you (and, if
if you were here now, to an accompaniment of winds that
would well suit the subject) instead of writing to you concerning your "Orestes."   When we talk we are our own
living commentary, and there are so many *running notes*
of look, tone, and gesture, that there is small danger of
being misunderstood, and less danger of being imperfectly
understood — in writing ; but no ! it is foolish to abuse a
good substitute because it is not all that the original is, —
so I will do my best and, believe me, I consider this letter
which I am about to write as merely an exercise of my
own judgment — a something that may make you better
acquainted, perhaps, with the architecture and furniture of
my mind, though it will probably convey to you little or
nothing that had not occurred to you before respecting
your own tragedy.   One thing I beg solicitously of you,
that, if anywhere I appear to speak positively, you will
acquit me of any correspondent feeling.   I hope that it is
not a frequent feeling with me in any case, and, that if it
appear so, I am belied by my own warmth of manner.
In the present instance it is impossible.   I have been too
deeply impressed by the work, and I am now about to
give you, not criticisms nor decisions, but a history of my
impressions, and, for the greater part, of my first impressions, and if anywhere there seem anything like a tone

of warmth or dogmatism, do, my dear sir, be kind enough
to regard it as no more than a way of conveying to you
the *whole* of my meaning; or, for I am writing too seriously, as the dexterous *toss*, necessary to turn an idea out
of its pudding-bag, round and *unbroken*.

[No signature.]

Several pages of minute criticisms on Sotheby's
"Orestes" form part of the original transcript of the
letter.

CXXXII. TO HIS WIFE.

St. Clear, Caermarthen, Tuesday, November 16, 1802.

My dear Love, — I write to you from the New
Passage, Saturday morning, November 13. We had a favourable passage, dined on the other side, and proceeded
in a post-chaise to Usk, and from thence to Abergavenny,
where we supped and slept and breakfasted — a vile
supper, vile beds, and vile breakfast. From Abergavenny
to Brecon, through the vale of Usk, I believe, nineteen miles of most delightful country. It is not indeed
comparable with the meanest part of our Lake Country,
but hills, vale, and river, cottages and woods are nobly
blended, and, thank Heaven, I seldom permit my past
greater pleasures to lessen my enjoyment of present
charms. Of the things which this nineteen miles has in
common with our whole vale of Keswick (which is about
nineteen miles long), I may say that the two vales and
the two rivers are equal to each other, that the Keswick
vale beats the Welsh one all hollow in cottages, but is as
much surpassed by it in woods and timber trees. I am
persuaded that every tree in the south of England has
three times the number of *leaves* that a tree of the same
sort and size has in Cumberland or Westmoreland, and
there is an incomparably larger number of very large
trees. Even the Scotch firs luxuriate into beauty and
pluminess, and the larches are magnificent creatures in-

deed, in S. Wales. I must not deceive you, however,
with all the advantages. S. Wales, if you came into it
with the very pictures of Keswick, Ulleswater, Grasmere,
etc., in your fancy, and were determined to hold them,
and S. Wales together with all its richer fields, woods,
and ancient trees, would needs appear flat and tame as
ditchwater. I have no firmer persuasion than this, that
there is no place in our island (and, saving Switzerland, none in Europe perhaps), which really equals the
vale of Keswick, including Borrowdale, Newlands, and
Bassenthwaite. O Heaven! that it had but a more
genial climate! It is now going on for the eighteenth
week since they have had any rain here, more than a few
casual refreshing showers, and we have monopolized the
rain of the whole kingdom. From Brecon to Trecastle —
a churchyard, two or three miles from Brecon, is belted
by a circle of the largest and noblest yews I ever saw —
in a belt, to wit; they are not so large as the yew in
Borrowdale or that in Lorton, but so many, so large and
noble, I never saw before — and quite *glowing* with those
heavenly - coloured, silky - pink - scarlet berries. From
Trecastle to Llandovery, where we found a nice inn, an
excellent supper, and good beds. From Llandovery to
Llandilo — from Llandilo to Caermarthen, a large town all
whitewashed — the roofs of the houses all whitewashed!
a great town in a confectioner's shop, on Twelfth-cake-
Day, or a huge snowpiece at a distance. It is nobly
situated along a hill among hills, at the head of a very
extensive vale. From Caermarthen after dinner to St.
Clear, a little hamlet nine miles from Caermarthen, three
miles from the sea (the nearest seaport being Llangan,
pronounced *Larne*, on Caermarthen Bay — look in the
map), and not quite a hundred miles from Bristol. The
country immediately round is exceedingly bleak and
dreary — just the sort of country that there is around
Shurton, etc. But the inn, the *Blue Boar*, is the most

comfortable little public-house I was ever in.   Miss S.
Wedgwood left us this morning (we arrived here at half
past four yesterday evening) for Crescelly, Mr. *Allen's*
seat (the Mrs. Wedgwood's father), fifteen miles from
this place, and T. Wedgwood is gone out cock-shooting,
in high glee and spirits.   He is very much better than I
expected to have found him — he says, the thought of my
coming, and my really coming so immediately, has sent a
new life into him.   He will be out all the mornings.
The evenings we chat, discuss, or I read to him.   To me
he is a delightful and instructive companion.   He possesses the *finest*, the *subtlest* mind and taste I have ever
yet met with.   His mind resembles that miniature in my
" Three Graves : " [1] —

> A small blue sun! and it has got
> A perfect glory too!
> Ten thousand hairs of colour'd light,
> Make up a glory gay and bright,
> Round that small orb so blue!

I continue in excellent health, compared with my state
at Keswick. . . . I have now left off beer too, and will
persevere in it.   I take no tea; in the morning coffee,
with a teaspoonful of ginger in the last cup; in the afternoon a large cup of ginger-tea, and I take ginger at twelve
o'clock at noon, and a glass after supper.   I find not the
least inconvenience from any quantity, however large.   I
dare say I take a large table-spoonful in the course of the
twenty-four hours, and once in the twenty-four hours (but
not always at the same time) I take half a grain of puri-

[1] Parts III. and IV. of the " Three Graves " were first published in *The Friend*, No. vi. Sept. 21, 1809. Parts I. and II. were published for the first time in *The Poetical Works of Samuel Taylor Coleridge*, Macmillan, 1893. The final version of this stanza (ll. 509–513) differs from that in the text. " A small blue sun " became " A tiny sun," and for " Ten thousand hairs of colour'd light " Coleridge sub-stituted " Ten thousand hairs and threads of light."   See *Poetical Works*, p. 92, and Editor's Note, pp. 589–591.

fied opium, equal to twelve drops of laudanum, which is
not more than an eighth part of what I took at Keswick,
exclusively of beer, brandy, and tea, which last is undoubtedly a pernicious thing — all which I have left off,
and will give this regimen a *fair, complete* trial of one
month, with no other deviation than that I shall sometimes lessen the opiate, and sometimes miss a day.   But
I am fully convinced, and so is T. Wedgwood, that to
a person with such a stomach and bowels as mine, if any
stimulus is needful, opium in the small quantities I now
take it is incomparably better in every respect than beer,
wine, spirits, or any *fermented* liquor, nay, far less pernicious than even tea.   It *is my particular wish that
Hartley and Derwent should have as little tea as possible, and always very weak, with more than half milk.*
Read this sentence to Mary, and to Mrs. Wilson.   I
should think that ginger-tea, with a good deal of milk
in it, would be an excellent thing for Hartley.   A teaspoonful piled up of ginger would make a potful of tea,
that would serve him for two days.   And let him drink
it half milk.   I dare say that he would like it very well,
for it is pleasant with sugar, and tell him that his dear
father takes it instead of tea, and believes that it will
make his dear Hartley grow.   The whole kingdom is
getting ginger-mad.   My dear love!   I have said nothing
of Italy, for I am as much in the dark as when I left
Keswick, indeed much more.   For I now doubt very
much whether we shall go or no.   Against our going you
must place T. W.'s improved state of health, and his exceeding dislike to continental travelling, and horror of
the sea, and his exceeding attachment to his family; for
our going, you must place his past experience, the tran-
siency of his enjoyments, the craving after change, and
the effect of a cold winter, especially if it should come on
wet or *sleety*.   His determinations are made so rapidly,
that two or three days of wet weather with a raw cold air

might have such an effect on his spirits, that he might
go off immediately to Naples, or perhaps for Teneriffe,
which latter place he is always talking about. Look out
for it in the Encyclopædia. Again, these latter causes
make it not impossible that the pleasure he has in me as
a companion may languish. I must subscribe myself in
haste,

      Your dear husband,   S. T. COLERIDGE.
The mail is waiting.

CXXXIII. TO THE REV. J. P. ESTLIN.

CRESCELLY, near Narbarth, Pembrokeshire,
December 7, 1802.

MY DEAR FRIEND, — I took the liberty of desiring
Mrs. Coleridge to direct a letter for me to you, fully
expecting to have seen you ; but I passed rapidly through
Bristol, and left it with Mr. Wedgwood immediately —
I literally had *no time* to see any one. I hope, however,
to see you on my return, for I wish very much to have
some hours' conversation with you on a subject that will
not cease to interest either of us while we *live* at least,
and I trust that is a synonym of "for ever!" . . . Have
you seen my different essays in the "Morning Post"?[1] —
the comparison of Imperial Rome and France, the "Once
a Jacobin, always a Jacobin," and the two letters to Mr.
Fox? Are my politics yours?

Have you heard lately from America? A gentleman
informed me that the progress of religious Deism in the
middle Provinces is exceedingly rapid, that there are
numerous congregations of Deists, etc., etc. Would to
Heaven this were the case in France! Surely, religious
Deism is infinitely nearer the religion of our Saviour than
the *gross* idolatry of Popery, or the more decorous, but
not less genuine, idolatry of a vast majority of Protest-

[1] The six essays to which he calls Estlin's attention are reprinted in *Essays on His Own Times*, ii. 478–585.

ants. If there be meaning in words, it appears to me
that the Quakers and Unitarians are the only Christians,
altogether pure from Idolatry, and even of these I am
sometimes jealous, that some of the Unitarians make too
much an *Idol* of their *one* God. Even the worship of
one God becomes *Idolatry* in my convictions, when, instead of the Eternal and Omnipresent, in whom we live
and move and *have* our Being, we set up a distinct Jehovah, tricked out in the *anthropomorphic* attributes of
Time and *successive* Thoughts, and think of him as a
Person, from whom we *had* our Being. The tendency
to *Idolatry* seems to me to lie at the root of all our
human vices — it is our original Sin. When we dismiss
three Persons in the Deity, only by subtracting *two*, we
talk more intelligibly, but, I fear, do not feel more reli-
giously — for God is a Spirit, and must be worshipped in
spirit.

O my dear sir! it is long since we have seen each
other — believe me, my esteem and grateful affection for
you and Mrs. Estlin has suffered no abatement or intermission — nor can I persuade myself that my opinions,
fully stated and fully understood, would appear to you
to differ *essentially* from your own. My creed is very
simple — my confession of Faith very brief. I approve
altogether and embrace entirely the *Religion* of the
Quakers, but exceedingly dislike the *sect*, and their own
notions of their own Religion. By Quakerism I understand the opinions of George Fox rather than those of
Barclay — who was the St. Paul of Quakerism. — I pray
for you and yours!

S. T. COLERIDGE.

CXXXIV. TO ROBERT SOUTHEY.

Christmas Day, 1802.

MY DEAR SOUTHEY, — I arrived at Keswick with T.
Wedgwood on Friday afternoon, that is to say, yester-

day, and had the comfort to find that Sara was safely brought to bed, the morning before, that is on Thursday, half-past six, of a healthy GIRL. I had never thought of a girl as a possible event; the words child and man-child were perfect synonyms in my feelings. However, I bore the sex with great fortitude, and she shall be called Sara. Both Mrs. Coleridge and the Coleridgiella are as well as can be. I left the little one sucking at a great rate. Derwent and Hartley are both well.

I was at Cote[1] in the beginning of November, and of course had calculated on seeing you, and, above all, on seeing little Edith's physiognomy, among the certain things of my expedition, but I had no sooner arrived at Cote than I was forced to quit it, T. Wedgwood having engaged to go into Wales with his sister. I arrived at Cote in the afternoon, and till late evening did not know or conjecture that we were to go off early in the next morn-ing. I do not say this for you, — you must know how earnestly I yearn to see you, — but for Mr. Estlin, who expressed himself wounded by the circumstance. When you see him, therefore, be so good as to mention this to him. I was much affected by Mrs. Coleridge's account of your health and eyes. God have mercy on us! We are all sick, all mad, all slaves! It is a theory of mine that virtue and genius are diseases of the hypochondriacal and scrofulous genera, and exist in a peculiar state of the nerves and diseased digestion, analogous to the beautiful diseases that colour and variegate certain trees. How-ever, I add, by way of comfort, that it is my faith that the virtue and genius produce the disease, not the disease the virtue, etc., though when present it fosters them. Heaven knows, there are fellows who have more vices than scabs, and scabs countless, with fewer ideas than plaisters. As to my own health it is very indifferent. I am exceedingly temperate in everything, abstain wholly

[1] The residence of Josiah Wedgwood.

from wine, spirits, or fermented liquors, almost wholly from tea, abjure all fermentable and vegetable food, bread excepted, and use *that* sparingly; live almost entirely on eggs, fish, flesh, and fowl, and thus contrive not to be *ill*. But well I am not, and in this climate never shall be. A deeply ingrained though mild scrofula is diffused through me, and is a very Proteus. I am fully determined to *try* Teneriffe or Gran Canaria, influenced to prefer them to Madeira solely by the superior cheapness of living. The climate and country are heavenly, the inhabitants Papishes, all of whom I would burn with fire and faggot, for what did n't they do to us Christians under bloody Queen Mary? Oh the Devil sulphur-roast them! I would have no mercy on them, unless they drowned all their priests, and then, spite of the itch (which they have in an inveterate degree, rich and poor, gentle and simple, old and young, male and female), would shake hands with them ungloved.

By way of *one* impudent half line in this meek and mild letter — will you go with me? " I " and " you " mean mine and yours, of course. Remember you are to give me Thomas Aquinas and Scotus Erigena.

God bless you and   S. T. COLERIDGE.

I can have the best letters and recommendation. My love and their sisters to Mary and Edith, and if you see Mrs. Fricker, be so good as to tell her that she will hear from me or Sara in the course of ten days.

CXXXV. TO THOMAS WEDGWOOD.

[The text of this letter, which was first published in Cottle's " Reminiscences," 1849, p. 450, has been collated with that of the original.]

KESWICK, January 9, 1803.

MY DEAR WEDGWOOD, — I send you two letters, one from your dear sister, the second from Sharp, by

which you will see at what short notice I must be off, if I
go to the Canaries. If your last plan continue in full
force in your mind, of course I have not even the phantom
of a wish thitherward struggling, but if aught have happened to you, in the things without, or in the world within,
to induce you to change the plan in itself, or the plan
relatively to me, I think I could raise the money, at all
events, and go and see. But I would a thousand-fold
rather go with you whithersoever you go. I shall be
anxious to hear how you have gone on since I left you.
Should you decide in favour of a better climate somewhere or other, the best scheme I can think of is that in
some part of Italy or Sicily which we both liked. I
would look out for two houses. Wordsworth and his
family would take the one, and I the other, and then you
might have a home either with me, or, if you thought of
Mr. and Mrs. Luff, under this modification, one of your
own; and in either case you would have neighbours, and
so return to England when the homesickness pressed
heavy upon you, and back to Italy when it was abated,
and the climate of England began to poison your comforts. So you would have abroad, in a genial climate, certain comforts of society among simple and enlightened
men and women; and I should be an alleviation of the
pang which you will necessarily feel, always, as often as
you quit your own family.

I know no better plan: for travelling in search of
objects is, at best, a dreary business, and whatever excitement it might have had, you must have exhausted it.
God bless you, my dear friend. I write with dim eyes,
for indeed, indeed, my heart is very full of affectionate
sorrowful thoughts toward you.

I found Mrs. Coleridge not so well as I expected, but
she is better to-day — and I, myself, write with difficulty,
with all the fingers but one of my right hand very much
swollen. Before I was half up *Kirkstone* the storm had

wetted me through and through, and before I reached the
top it was so wild and outrageous, that it would have been
unmanly to have suffered the poor woman (guide) to continue pushing on, up against such a torrent of wind and
rain; so I dismounted and sent her home with the storm
to her back. I am no novice in mountain mischiefs, but
such a storm as this was I never witnessed, combining the
intensity of the cold with the violence of the wind and
rain. The rain-drops were pelted or, rather, slung against
my face by the gusts, just like splinters of flint, and I felt
as if every drop *cut* my flesh. My hands were all shrivelled
up like a washerwoman's, and so benumbed that I was
obliged to carry my stick under my arm. Oh, it was a wild
business! Such hurry-skurry of clouds, such volleys of
sound! In spite of the wet and the cold, I should have
had some pleasure in it but for two vexations: first, an
almost intolerable pain came into my right eye, a *smart-
ing* and *burning* pain; and secondly, in consequence of
riding with such cold water under my seat, extremely uneasy and burthensome feelings attacked my groin, so that,
what with the pain from the one, and the alarm from the
other, I had *no enjoyment at all!*

Just at the brow of the hill I met a man dismounted,
who could not sit on horseback. He seemed quite
scared by the uproar, and said to me, with much feeling,
"Oh, sir, it is a perilous buffeting, but it is worse for you
than for me, for I have it at my back." However I got
safely over, and, immediately, all was calm and breath-
less, as if it was some mighty fountain just on the summit
of Kirkstone, that shot forth its volcano of air, and precipitated huge streams of invisible lava down the road to
Patterdale.

I went on to Grasmere. I was not at all unwell when
I arrived there, though wet of course to the skin. My
right eye had nothing the matter with it, either to the sight
of others, or to my own feelings, but I had a bad night,

with distressful dreams, chiefly about my eye ; and awaking
often in the dark I thought it was the effect of mere recollection, but it appeared in the morning that my right eye
was bloodshot, and the lid swollen. That morning, however, I walked home, and before I reached Keswick my
eye was quite well, but *I felt unwell all over.* Yesterday
I continued unusually unwell all over me till eight o'clock
in the evening. I took no *laudanum or opium*, but at
eight o'clock, unable to bear the stomach uneasiness and
aching of my limbs, I took two large teaspoonsfull of
ether in a wine-glass of camphorated gum water, and a
third teaspoonfull at ten o'clock, and I received complete
relief, — my body calmed, my sleep placid, — but when I
awoke in the morning my right hand, with three of the
fingers, was swollen and inflamed. . . . This has been a
very rough attack, but though I am much weakened by
it, and look sickly and haggard, yet I am not out of heart.
Such a *bout*, such a " perilous buffeting," was enough to
have hurt the health of a strong man. Few constitutions
can bear to be long wet through in intense cold. I fear
it will tire you to death to read this prolix scrawled
story, but my health, I know, interests you. Do continue
to send me a few lines by the market people on Friday —
I shall receive it on Tuesday morning.

   Affectionately, dear friend, yours ever,

       S. T. COLERIDGE.

[Addressed " T. Wedgwood, Esq., C. Luff's Esq., Glenridding,
Ulleswater.]

CXXXVI. TO HIS WIFE.

       [LONDON], Monday, April 4, 1803.

MY DEAR SARA, — I have taken my place for Wednesday night, and, barring accidents, shall arrive at Penrith
on Friday noon. If Friday be a fine morning, that is,
if it do not rain, you will get Mr. Jackson to send a lad
with a horse or pony to Penruddock. The boy ought to

be at Penruddock by twelve o'clock that his horse may bait and have a feed of corn. But if it be rain, there is no choice but that I must take a chaise. At all events, if it please God, I shall be with you by Friday, five o'clock, at the latest. You had better dine early. I shall take an egg or two at Penrith and drink tea at home. For more than a fortnight we have had burning July weather. The effect on my health was manifest, but Lamb objected, very sensibly, "How do you know what part may not be owing to the excitement of bustle and company?" On Friday night I was unwell and restless, and uneasy in limbs and stomach, though I had been extremely regular. I told Lamb on Saturday morning that I guessed the weather had changed. But there was no mark of it; it was hotter than ever. On Saturday evening my right knee and both my ankles swelled and were very painful; and within an hour after there came a storm of wind and rain. It continued raining the whole night. Yesterday it was a fine day, but cold; to-day the same, but I am a great deal better, and the swelling in my ankle is gone down and that in my right knee much decreased. Lamb observed that he was glad he had seen all this with his own eyes; he now *knew* that my illness was truly linked with the weather, and no whim or restlessness of disposition in me. It is curious, but I have found that the weather-glass changed on Friday night, the very hour that I found myself unwell. I will try to bring down something for Hartley, though toys are so outrageously dear, and I so short of money, that I shall be puzzled.

To-day I dine again with Sotheby. He had informed me that ten gentlemen who have met me at his house desired him to solicit me to finish the "Christabel," and to permit them to publish it for me; and they engaged that it should be in paper, printing, and decorations the most magnificent thing that had hitherto appeared. Of course I declined it. The lovely lady shan't come to that pass! Many times rather would I have it printed at Soulby's on the true ballad paper. However, it was civil, and Sotheby is very civil to me.

I had purposed not to speak of Mary Lamb, but I had better write it than tell it. The Thursday before last she met at Rickman's a Mr. Babb, an old friend and admirer of her mother. The next day she *smiled* in an ominous way; on Sunday she told her brother that she was getting bad, with great agony. On Tuesday morning she laid hold of me with violent agitation and talked wildly about George Dyer. I told Charles there was not a moment to lose; and I did not lose a moment, but went for a hackney-coach and took her to the private madhouse at Hugsden. She was quite calm, and said it was the best to do so. But she wept bitterly two or three times, yet all in a calm way. Charles is cut to the heart. You will send this note to Grasmere or the contents of it, though, if I have time, I shall probably write myself to them to-day or to-morrow.

Yours affectionately,   S. T. COLERIDGE.

CXXXVII. TO ROBERT SOUTHEY.

KESWICK, Wednesday, July 2, 1803.

MY DEAR SOUTHEY, — You have had much illness as well as I, but I thank God for you, you have never been equally diseased in voluntary power with me. I knew a lady who was seized with a sort of asthma which she knew would be instantly relieved by a dose of ether. She had the full use of her limbs, and was not an arm's-length from the bell, yet could not command voluntary power sufficient to pull it, and might have died but for the accidental coming in of her daughter. From such as these the doctrines of materialism and mechanical necessity have been deduced; and it is some small argument against the truth of these doctrines that I have perhaps had a more various experience, a more intuitive knowledge of such facts than most men, and yet I do not believe these doctrines. My health is *middling*. If this hot weather continue, I hope to go on endurably, and oh, for peace! for I forbode a miserable winter in this country. Indeed, I am rather induced to determine on wintering in Madeira, rather than staying at home. I have enclosed ten pounds for Mrs. Fricker. Tell her I wish it were in my power to increase this poor half year's mite; but ill health keeps me poor. Bella is with us, and seems likely to recover. I have not seen the "Edinburgh Review." The truth is that Edinburgh is a place of literary gossip, and even *I* have had my portion of puff there, and of course my portion of hatred and envy. One man puffs me up — he has seen and talked with me; another hears him, goes and reads my poems, written when almost a boy, and candidly and logically hates me, because he does not admire my poems, in the proportion in which one of his acquaintance had admired me. It is difficult to say whether these reviewers do you harm or good.

You read me at Bristol a very interesting piece of casuistry from Father Somebody, the author, I believe, of the "Theatre Critic," respecting a double infant. If you do not immediately want it, or if my using it in a book of logic, with proper acknowledgment, will not interfere with your use of it, I should be extremely obliged to you if you would send it me without delay. I rejoice to hear of the progress of your History. The only thing I dread is the division of the European and Colonial History. In style you have only to beware of short, biblical, and pointed periods. Your general style is delightfully natural and yet striking.

You may expect certain explosions in the "Morning Post," Coleridge *versus* Fox, in about a week. It grieved me to hear (for I have a sort of affection for the man) from Sharp, that Fox had not read my two letters, but had heard of them, and that they were mine, and had expressed himself more wounded by the circumstance than anything that had happened since Burke's business. Sharp told this to Wordsworth, and told Wordsworth that he had been so affected by Fox's manner, that he himself had declined reading the two letters. Yet Sharp himself thinks my opinions right and true; but Fox is not to be attacked, and why? Because he is an amiable man; and not by me, because he had thought highly of me, etc., etc. O Christ! this is a pretty age in the article *morality!* When I cease to love Truth best of all things, and Liberty the next best, may I cease to live: nay, it is my creed that I should thereby cease to live, for as far as anything can be called probable in a subject so dark, it seems to me most probable that our immortality is to be a work of our own hands.

All the children are well, and love to hear Bella talk of Margaret. Love to Edith and to Mary and

S. T. COLERIDGE.

I have received great delight and instruction from *Scotus Erigena.* He is clearly the modern founder of the school of Pantheism; indeed he expressly defines the divine nature as *quæ fit et facit, et creat et creatur;* and repeatedly declares creation to be *manifestation*, the epiphany of philosophers. The eloquence with which he writes astonished me, but he had read more Greek than Latin, and was a Platonist rather than an Aristotelian. There is a good deal of *omne meus oculus* in the notion of the dark ages, etc., taken intensively; in extension it might be true. They had *wells:* we are flooded ankle high: and what comes of it but grass rank or rotten? Our age eats from that poison-tree of knowledge yclept "Too-Much and Too-Little." Have you read Paley's last book?[1] Have you it to review? I could make a dashing review of it.

[1] Paley's last work, "*Natural Theology;* or, Evidences of the Existence

CXXXVIII. TO THE SAME.

KESWICK, July, 1803.

MY DEAR SOUTHEY, — . . . I write now to propose a scheme,[1] or rather a rude outline of a scheme, of your grand work. What harm can a proposal do? If it be no pain to you to reject it, it will be none to me to have it rejected. I would have the work entitled Bibliotheca Britannica, or an History of British Literature, bibliographical, biographical, and critical. The two *last* volumes I would have to be a chronological catalogue of all noticeable or extant books; the others, be the number six or eight, to consist entirely of separate treatises, each giving a critical biblio-biographical history of some one subject. I will, with great pleasure, join you in learning Welsh and Erse; and you, I, Turner, and Owen,[2] might dedicate ourselves for the first half-year to a complete history of all Welsh, Saxon, and Erse books that are not translations that are the native growth of Britain. If the Spanish neutrality continues, I will go in October or November to Biscay, and throw light on the Basque.

Let the next volume contain the history of *English* poetry and poets, in which I would include all prose truly poetical. The first half of the second volume should be dedicated to great single names, Chaucer and Spenser, Shakespeare, Milton and Taylor, Dryden and Pope; the poetry of witty logic, — Swift, Fielding, Richardson, Sterne; I write *par hasard*, but I mean to say all great names as have either formed epochs in our taste, or such, at least, as are representative; and the great object to be

and Attributes of A Deity, collected from the Appearances of Nature," was published in 1802.

[1] For Southey's well known rejoinder to this "ebullience of schematism," see *Life and Correspondence*, ii. 220–223.

[2] Southey's correspondence contains numerous references to the historian Sharon Turner [1768–1847], and to William Owen, the translator of the *Mabinogion* and author of the *Welsh Paradise Lost*.

in each instance to determine, first, the true merits and demerits of the *books ;* secondly, what of these belong to the age — what to the author *quasi peculium.* The second half of the second volume should be a history of poetry and romances, everywhere interspersed with biography, but more flowing, more consecutive, more bibliographical, chronological, and complete. The third volume I would have dedicated to English prose, considered as to style, as to eloquence, as to general impressiveness; a history of styles and manners, their causes, their birth-places and parentage, their analysis. . . .

These three volumes would be so generally interesting, so exceedingly entertaining, that you might bid fair for a sale of the work at large. Then let the fourth volume take up the history of metaphysics, theology, medicine, alchemy, common canon, and Roman law, from Alfred to Henry VII.; in other words, a history of the dark ages in Great Britain : the fifth volume — carry on metaphysics and ethics to the present day in the first half; the second half, comprise the theology of all the reformers. In the fourth volume there would be a grand article on the philosophy of the theology of the Roman Catholic religion; in this (fifth volume), under different names, — Hooker, Baxter, Biddle, and Fox, — the spirit of the theology of all the other parts of Christianity. The sixth and seventh volumes must comprise all the articles you can get, on all the separate arts and sciences that have been treated of in books since the Reformation; and, by this time, the book, if it answered at all, would have gained so high a reputation that you need not fear having whom you liked to write the different articles — medicine, surgery, chemistry, etc., etc., navigation, travellers, voyagers, etc., etc. If I go into Scotland, shall I engage Walter Scott to write the history of Scottish poets? Tell me, however, what you think of the plan. It would have one prodigious advantage : whatever accident stopped the work, would only prevent the future good, not mar the past ; each volume would be a great and valuable work *per se.* Then each volume would awaken a new interest, a new set of readers, who would buy the past volumes of course ; then it would allow you ample time and opportunities for the slavery of the catalogue volumes, which should be at the same time an index to the work, which would be in very truth a pandect of knowledge, alive and swarming with human life, feeling, incident. By the bye, what a strange abuse has been made of the word encyclopædia ! It signifies properly, grammar, logic, rhetoric, and ethics, and metaphysics, which last, explaining the ultimate principle of grammar — log. — rhet., and eth. — formed a circle of knowledge. . . . To call a huge unconnected miscellany of the *omne scibile,* in an arrangement determined by the accident of initial letters, an encyclopædia is the impudent ignorance of your Presbyterian book-makers. Good night !

God bless you !   S. T. C.

CXXXIX. TO THE SAME.

Keswick, Sunday, August 7, 1803.

(Read the last lines first ; I send you this letter merely to show you how anxious I have been about your work.)

MY DEAR SOUTHEY, — The last three days I have been fighting up against a restless wish to write to you. I am afraid lest I should infect you with my fears rather than furnish you with any new arguments, give you impulses rather than motives, and prick you with *spurs* that had been dipped in the vaccine matter of my own cowardliness. While I wrote that last sentence, I had a vivid recollection, indeed an ocular spectrum, of our room in College Street, a curious instance of association. You remember how incessantly in that room I used to be compounding these half-verbal, half-visual metaphors. It argues, I am persuaded, a particular state of general feeling, and I

hold that association depends in a much greater degree on
the recurrence of resembling states of feeling than on
trains of ideas, that the recollection of early childhood in
latest old age depends on and is explicable by this, and if
this be true, Hartley's system totters.   If I were asked
how it is that very old people remember *visually* only the
events of early childhood, and remember the intervening
spaces either not at all or only verbally, I should think it
a perfectly philosophical answer that old age remembers
childhood by becoming " a second childhood ! "   This
explanation will derive some additional value if you would
look into Hartley's solution of the phenomena — how flat,
how wretched!   Believe me, Southey! a metaphysical solution, that does not instantly *tell* you something in the
heart is grievously to be suspected as apocryphal.   I almost think that ideas *never* recall ideas, as far as they are
ideas, any more than leaves in a forest create each other's
motion.   The breeze it is that runs through them — it is
the soul, the state of feeling.   If I had said no *one*
idea ever recalls another, I am confident that I could support the assertion.   And this is a digression. — My dear
Southey, again and again I say, that whatever your plan
may be, I will contrive to work for you with equal zeal
if not with equal pleasure.   But the arguments against
your plan weigh upon me the more heavily, the more I
reflect; and it could not be otherwise than that I should
feel a confirmation of them from Wordsworth's complete
coincidence — I having requested his deliberate opinion
without having communicated an iota of my own.   You
seem to me, dear friend, to hold the dearness of a scarce
work for a proof that the work would have a general sale,
if not scarce.   Nothing can be more fallacious than this.
Burton's Anatomy used to sell for a guinea to two guineas.
It was republished.   Has it paid the expense of reprint-
ing?   Scarcely.   Literary history informs us that most
of those great continental bibliographies, etc., were pub-

lished by the munificence of princes, or nobles, or great
monasteries. A book from having had little or no sale,
except among great libraries, may become so scarce that
the number of competitors for it, though few, may be
proportionally very great. I have observed that great
works are nowadays bought, not for curiosity or the
amor proprius, but under the notion that they contain all
the *knowledge* a man may ever want, and if he has it on
his *shelf* why there it is, as snug as if it were in his *brain*.
This has carried off the encyclopædia, and will continue
to do so. I have weighed most patiently what you said
respecting the persons and classes likely to purchase a
catalogue of all British books. I have endeavoured to
make some rude calculation of their numbers according
to your own numeration table, and it falls very short of
an adequate number. Your scheme appears to be in
short faulty, (1) because, everywhere, the generally unin-
teresting, the catalogue part will overlay the interesting
parts; (2) because the first volume will have nothing in
it tempting or deeply valuable, for there is not time or
room for it; (3) because it is impossible that any one of
the volumes can be executed as well as they would otherwise be from the to-and-fro, now here, now there motion
of the mind, and employment of the industry. Oh how I
wish to be talking, not writing, for my mind is so full
that my thoughts stifle and jam each other. And I have
presented them as shapeless jellies, so that I am ashamed
of what I have written — it so imperfectly expresses what
I meant to have said. My advice certainly would be,
that at all events you should make *some classification*.
Let all the law books form a catalogue *per se*, and so
forth; otherwise it is not a book of reference, without an
index half as large as the work itself. I see no well-
founded objection to the plan which I first sent. The
two main advantages are that, stop where you will, you
are in harbour, you sail in an archipelago so thickly

clustered, (that) at each island you take in a completely
new cargo, and the former cargo is in safe housage ; and
(2dly) that each labourer working by the *piece*, and not
by the *day*, can give an undivided attention in some instances for three or four years, and bring to the work the
whole weight of his interest and reputation. . . . An
encyclopædia appears to me a worthless monster.   What
surgeon, or physician, professed student of pure or mixed
mathematics, what chemist or architect, would go to an
encyclopædia for *his* books?   If valuable treatises exist
on these subjects in an encyclopædia, they are out of their
place — an equal hardship on the general reader, who pays
for whole volumes which he *cannot* read, and on the professed student of that particular subject, who must buy a
great work which he does not want in order to possess a
valuable treatise, which he might otherwise have had for
six or seven shillings.   You omit those things only from
your encyclopædia which are excrescences — each volume
will *set up* the reader, give him at once connected trains of
thought and facts, and a delightful miscellany for lounge-
reading.   Your treatises will be long in exact proportion
to their general interest.   Think what a strange confusion
it will make, if you speak of each book, according to its
date, passing from an Epic Poem to a treatise on the
treatment of sore legs?   Nobody can become an enthu-
siast in favour of the work. . . . A great change of weather
has come on, heavy rain and wind, and I have been *very*
ill, and still I am in uncomfortable restless health.   I am
not even certain whether I shall not be forced to put off
my Scotch tour ; but if I go, I go on Tuesday.   I shall
not send off this letter till this is decided.

    God bless you and   S. T. C.

CXL. TO HIS WIFE.

Friday afternoon, 4 o'clock, Sept. (1), [1803].

MY DEAR SARA, — I write from the Ferry of Ballater.
. . . This is the first post since the day I left Glasgow.
We went thence to Dumbarton (look at Stoddart's tour,
where there is a very good view of Dumbarton Rock and
Tower), thence to Loch Lomond, and a single house called
Luss — horrible inhospitality and a fiend of a landlady!
Thence eight miles up the Lake to E. Tarbet, where the
lake is so like Ulleswäter that I could scarcely see the
difference; crossed over the lake and by a desolate moor-
land walked to another lake, Loch Katrine, up to a place
called Trossachs, the Borrowdale of Scotland, and the
only thing which really beats us. You must conceive the
Lake of Keswick pushing itself up a mile or two into
Borrowdale, winding round Castle Crag, and in and out
among all the nooks and promontories, and you must imagine all the mountains more *detachedly* built up, a general dislocation; every rock its own precipice, with trees
young and old. This will give you some faint idea of the
place, of which the character is extreme intricacy of effect
produced by very simple means. One rocky, high island,
four or five promontories, and a Castle Crag, just like that
in the gorge of Borrowdale, but not so large. It rained all
the way, all the long, long day. We slept in a hay-loft, —
that is, Wordsworth, I, and a young man who came in at
the Trossachs and joined us. Dorothy had a bed in the
hovel, which was varnished *so rich* with peat smoke an
apartment of highly polished [oak] would have been poor
to it — it would have wanted the metallic lustre of the
smoke-varnished rafters. This was [the pleasantest]
evening I had spent since my tour; for Wordsworth's
hypochondriacal feelings keep him silent and self-centred.
The next day it still was rain and rain; the ferry-boat
was out for the preaching, and we stayed all day in the

ferry wet to the skin.   Oh, such a wretched hovel!   But
two Highland lassies,[1] who kept house in the absence of
the ferryman and his wife, were very kind, and one of
them was beautiful as a vision, and put both Dorothy and
me in mind of the Highland girl in William's "Peter
Bell."[2]   We returned to E. Tarbet, I with the rheumatism
in my head.   And now William proposed to me to leave
them and make my way on foot to Loch Katrine, the
Trossachs, whence it is only twenty miles to Stirling,
where the coach runs through to Edinburgh.   He and
Dorothy resolved to fight it out.   I eagerly caught at the
proposal; for the *sitting* in an open carriage in the rain
is death to me, and somehow or other I had not been quite
comfortable.   So on Monday I accompanied them to Arrochar, on purpose to see the *Cobbler* which had impressed

[1] It may be interesting to compare the following unpublished note
from Coleridge's Scotch Journal
with the well known passage in
Dorothy Wordsworth's Journal of
her tour in the Highlands (*Memoir of
Wordsworth*, i. 235): "Next morning we went in the boat to the end of
the lake, and so on by the old path
to the Garrison to the Ferry House
by Loch Lomond, where now the Fall
was in all its fury, and formed with
the Ferry cottage, and the sweet
Highland lass, a nice picture.   The
boat gone to the preaching we stayed
all day in the comfortless hovel,
comfortless, but the two little lassies
did everything with such sweetness,
and one of them, 14, with such native elegance.   Oh! she was a divine
creature!   The sight of the boat,
full of Highland men and women
and children from the preaching, exquisitely fine.   We soon reached E.
Tarbet — all the while rain.   Never,
never let me forget that small herd-
boy in his tartan-plaid, dim-seen on

the hilly field, and long heard ere
seen, a melancholy voice calling to
his cattle! nor the beautiful harmony of the heath, and the dancing
fern, and the ever-moving birches.
That of itself enough to make Scotland visitable, its fields of heather
giving a sort of shot silk finery in
the apotheosis of finery.   On Monday we went to Arrochar.   Here I
left W. and D. and returned myself
to E. Tarbet, slept there, and now,
Tuesday, Aug. 30, 1803, am to make
my own way to Edinburgh."

Many years after he added the
words: "O Esteese, that thou hadst
from thy 22nd year indeed made thy
own way and *alone!*"

[2] A sweet and playful Highland girl,
    As light and beauteous as a squirrel,
    As beauteous and as wild!

    Her dwelling was a lonely house,
    A cottage in a heathy dell;
    And she put on her gown of green
    And left her mother at sixteen,
    And followed Peter Bell.
            Peter Bell, Part III.

me so much in Mr. Wilkinson's drawings; and there I
parted with them, having previously sent on all my things
to Edinburgh by a Glasgow carrier who happened to be
at E. Tarbet. The worst thing was the money. They
took twenty-nine guineas, and I six — all our remaining
cash. I returned to E. Tarbet; slept there that night;
the next day walked to the very head of Loch Lomond to
Glen Falloch, where I slept at a cottage-inn, two degrees
below John Stanley's (but the good people were very
kind), — meaning from hence to go over the mountains to
the head of Loch Katrine again; but hearing from the
gude man of the house that it was 40 miles to Glencoe
(of which I had formed an idea from Wilkinson's drawings), and having found myself so happy alone (such
blessing is there in perfect liberty!) I walked off. I have
walked forty-five miles since then, and, except during the
last mile, I am sure I may say I have not met with ten
houses. For eighteen miles there are but two habitations!
and all that way I met no sheep, no cattle, only one goat!
All through moorlands with huge mountains, some craggy
and bare, but the most green, with deep pinky channels
worn by torrents. Glencoe interested me, but rather disappointed me. There was no *superincumbency* of crag,
and the crags not so bare or precipitous as I had expected.
I am now going to cross the ferry for Fort William, for I
have resolved to eke out my cash by all sorts of self-denial,
and to walk along the *whole line of the Forts*. I am unfortunately shoeless; there is no town where I can get a
pair, and I have no money to spare to buy them, so I expect to enter Perth barefooted. I burnt my shoes in drying
them at the boatman's hovel on Loch Katrine, and I have
by this means hurt my heel. Likewise my left leg is a
little inflamed, and the rheumatism in the right of my
head afflicts me sorely when I begin to grow warm in my
bed, chiefly my right eye, ear, cheek, and the three teeth;
but, nevertheless, I am enjoying myself, having Nature

with solitude and liberty — the liberty natural and solitary, the solitude natural and free! But you must contrive somehow or other to borrow ten pounds, or, if that cannot be, five pounds, for me, and send it without delay, directed to me at the Post Office, Perth. I guess I shall be there in seven days or eight at the furthest; and your letter will be two days getting thither (counting the day you put it into the office at Keswick as nothing); so you must calculate, and if this letter does not reach you in time, that is, within five days from the date hereof, you must then direct to Edinburgh. I will make five pounds do (you must borrow of Mr. Jackson), and I must *beg* my way for the last three or four days! It is useless repining, but if I had set off myself in the Mail for Glasgow or Stirling, and so gone by foot, as I am now doing, I should have saved twenty-five pounds; but then Wordsworth would have lost it.

I have said nothing of you or my dear children. God bless us all! I have but one untried misery to go through, the loss of Hartley or Derwent, ay, or dear little Sara! In my health I am middling. While I can walk twenty-four miles a day, with the excitement of new objects, I can *support* myself; but still my sleep and dreams are distressful, and I am hopeless. I take no opiates . . . nor have I any temptation; for since my disorder has taken this asthmatic turn opiates produce none but positively unpl[easant effects].

[No signature.]

Mrs. Coleridge,
       Greta Hall, Keswick, Cumberland, S. Britain.

CXLI. TO ROBERT SOUTHEY.

[Edinburgh], Sunday night, 9 o'clock, September 10, 1803.

My dearest Southey, — I arrived here half an hour ago, and have only read your letters — scarce read them. — O dear friend! it is idle to talk of what I feel — I am

stunned at present by this beginning to write, making a
beginning of living feeling within me. Whatever comfort I can be to you I will — I have no aversions, no
dislikes that interfere with you — whatever is necessary
or proper for you becomes *ipso facto* agreeable to me.
I will not stay a day in Edinburgh — or only one to hunt
out my clothes. I cannot chitchat with Scotchmen while
you are at Keswick, childless![1] Bless you, my dear
Southey! I will knit myself far closer to you than I
have hitherto done, and my children shall be yours till
it please God to send you another.

I have been a wild journey, taken up for a spy and
clapped into Fort Augustus, and I am afraid they may
[have] frightened poor Sara by sending her off a scrap
of a letter I was writing to her. I have walked 263 miles
in eight days, so I must have strength somewhere, but my
spirits are dreadful, owing entirely to the horrors of every
night — I truly dread to sleep. It is no shadow with
me, but substantial misery foot-thick, that makes me
sit by my bedside of a morning and cry. — I have abandoned all opiates, except ether be one . . . And when
you see me drink a glass of spirit-and-water, except by
prescription of a physician, you shall despise me, — but
still I cannot get quiet rest.

> When on my bed my limbs I lay,
> It hath not been my use to pray
> With moving lips or bended knees;
> But silently, by slow degrees,
> 5 My spirit I to Love compose,
> In humble trust my eyelids close,
> With reverential resignation,
> No wish conceiv'd, no thought exprest,
> Only a *Sense* of supplication,
> 10 A *Sense* o'er all my soul imprest

---

[1] Margaret Southey, who was born in September, 1802, died in the latter
part of August, 1803.

That I am weak, yet not unblest,
Since round me, in me, everywhere
Eternal strength and Goodness are ! —

But yester-night I pray'd aloud
15 In anguish and in agony,
Awaking from the fiendish crowd
Of shapes and thoughts that tortur'd me !
Desire with loathing strangely mixt,
On wild or hateful objects fixt.
20 Sense of revenge, the powerless will,
Still baffled and consuming still ;
Sense of intolerable wrong,
And men whom I despis'd made strong !
Vain glorious threats, unmanly vaunting,
25 Bad men my boasts and fury taunting ;
Rage, sensual passion, mad'ning Brawl,
And shame and terror over all !
Deeds to be hid that were not hid,
Which all confus'd I might not know,
30 Whether I suffer'd or I did :
For all was Horror, Guilt, and Woe,
My own or others still the same,
Life-stifling Fear, soul-stifling Shame !

Thus two nights pass'd : the night's dismay
35 Sadden'd and stunn'd the boding day.
I fear'd to sleep : Sleep seemed to be
Disease's worst malignity.
The third night, when my own loud scream
Had freed me from the fiendish dream,
40 O'ercome by sufferings dark and wild,
I wept as I had been a child ;
And having thus by Tears subdued
My Trouble to a milder mood,
Such punishments, I thought, were due
45 To Natures, deepliest stain'd with Sin ;
Still to be stirring up anew
The self-created Hell within,

The Horror of the crimes to view,
To know and loathe, yet wish to do!
50 With such let fiends make mockery —
But I — Oh, wherefore this *on me?*
Frail is my soul, yea, strengthless wholly,
Unequal, restless, melancholy;
But free from Hate and sensual Folly!
55 To live belov'd is all I need,
And whom I love, I love indeed,
And etc., etc., etc., etc.[1]

I do not know how I came to scribble down these verses to you — my heart was aching, my head all confused — but they are, doggerel as they may be, a true portrait of my nights. What to do, I am at a loss; for it is hard thus to be withered, having the faculties and attainments which I have. We will soon meet, and I will do all I can to console poor Edith. — O dear, dear Southey! my head is sadly confused. After a rapid walk of thirty-three miles your letters have had the effect of perfect intoxication in my head and eyes. Change! change! change! O God of Eternity! When shall we be at rest in thee?

S. T. COLERIDGE.

CXLII. TO THE SAME.

EDINBURGH, Tuesday morning, September 13, 1803.

MY DEAR SOUTHEY, — I wrote you a strange letter, I fear. But, in truth, yours affected my wretched stomach, and my head, in such a way that I wrote mechanically in the *wake* of the first vivid idea. No conveyance left or leaves this place for Carlisle earlier than to-morrow morn-

[1] The "Pains of Sleep" was published for the first time, together with "Christabel" and "Kubla Khan," in 1816. With the exception of the insertion of the remarkable lines 52-54, the first draft of the poem does not materially differ from the published version. A transcript of the same poem was sent to Poole in a letter dated October 3, 1803. *Poetical Works*, p. 170, and Editor's Note, pp. 631, 632.

ing, for which I have taken my place. If the coachman
do not turn Panaceist, and cure all my ills by breaking my
neck, I shall be at Carlisle on Wednesday, midnight, and
whether I shall go on in the coach to Penrith, and walk
from thence, or walk off from Carlisle at once, depends on
two circumstances, first, whether the coach goes on with
no other than a common bait to Penrith, and secondly,
whether, if it should not do so, I can trust my clothes,
etc., to the coachman safely, to be left at Penrith. There
is but eight miles difference in the walk, and eight or nine
shillings difference in the expense. At all events, I trust
that I shall be with you on Thursday by dinner time, if you
dine at half-past two or three o'clock. God bless you! I will
go and call on Elmsley.[1] What a wonderful city Edinburgh[2] is! What alternation of height and depth! A
city looked at in the polish'd back of a Brobdingnag spoon
held lengthways, so enormously *stretched-up* are the houses!
When I first looked down on it, as the coach drove up on
the higher street, I cannot express what I felt — such a
section of wasps' nests striking you with a sort of bastard
sublimity from the enormity and infinity of its littleness —
the infinity swelling out the mind, the enormity striking
it with wonder. I think I have seen an old plate of Mont-
serrat that struck me with the same feeling, and I am sure
I have seen huge quarries of lime and free stone in which
the shafts or strata stood perpendicularly instead of hori-

[1] The Rev. Peter Elmsley, the
well known scholar, who had been
a school and college friend of
Southey's, was at this time resident
at Edinburgh. The *Edinburgh Review* had been founded the year before, and Elmsley was among the
earliest contributors. His name frequently recurs in Southey's correspondence.

[2] Compare Southey's first impressions of Edinburgh, contained in a
letter to Wynn, dated October 20,
1805: "You cross a valley (once a
loch) by a high bridge, and the back
of the old city appears on the edge
of this depth — so vast, so irregular
— with such an outline of roofs and
chimneys, that it looks like the ruins
of a giant's palace. I never saw anything so impressive as the first sight
of this; there was a wild red sunset
slanting along it." *Selections from
the Letters of R. Southey*, i. 342.

zontally with the same high thin slices and corresponding interstices. I climbed last night to the crags just below Arthur's Seat — itself a rude triangle-shaped-base cliff, and looked down on the whole city and firth — the sun then setting behind the magnificent rock, crested by the castle. The firth was full of ships, and I counted fifty-four heads of mountains, of which at least forty-four were cones or pyramids. The smoke was rising from ten thousand houses, each smoke from some one family. It was an affecting sight to me! I stood gazing at the setting sun, so tranquil to a passing look, and so restless and vibrating to one who looked stedfast; and then, all at once, turning my eyes down upon the city, it and all its smokes and figures became all at once dipped in the brightest blue-purple : such a sight that I almost grieved when my eyes recovered their natural tone! Meantime, Arthur's Crag, close behind me, was in dark blood-like crimson, and the sharp-shooters were behind exercising minutely, and had chosen that place on account of the fine thunder echo which, indeed, it would be scarcely possible for the ear to distinguish from thunder. The passing a day or two, quite unknown, in a strange city, does a man's heart good. He rises " a sadder and a wiser man."

I had not read that part in your second requesting me to call on Elmsley, else perhaps I should have been talking instead of learning and feeling.

Walter Scott is at Lasswade, five or six miles from Edinburgh. His house in Edinburgh is divinely situated. It looks up a street, a new magnificent street, full upon the rock and the castle, with its zigzag walls like painters' lightning — the other way down upon cultivated fields, a fine expanse of water, either a lake or not to be distinguished from one, and low pleasing hills beyond — the country well wooded and cheerful. " I' faith," I exclaimed, " the monks formerly, but the poets now, know where to fix their habitations." There are about four things worth going into Scotland for,[1] to one who has been in Cumberland and Westmoreland: First, the views of all the islands at the foot of Loch Lomond from the top of the highest island called Inch devanna (*sic*); secondly, the Trossachs at the foot of Loch Katrine; third, the chamber and ante-chamber of the Falls of Foyers (the fall itself is very fine, and so, after rain, is White-Water Dash, seven miles below Keswick and very like it); and how little difference a height makes, you know as well as I. No fall of itself, perhaps, can be worth giving a long journey to see, to him who has seen any fall of water, but the pool and whole rent of the mountain is truly magnificent. Fourthly and lastly; the City of Edinburgh. Perhaps I might add Glencoe. It is at all events a good makeweight and very well worth going to see, if a man be a Tory and hate the memory of William the Third, which I am very willing to do; for the more of these fellows dead and living one hates, the less spleen and gall there remains for those with whom one is likely to have anything to do in real life. . . .

I am tolerably well, meaning the day. My last night was not such a noisy night of horrors as three nights out of four are with me.[2] O God! when a man blesses the loud screams of agony that awake him night after night, night after night, and when a man's repeated night screams have made him a nuisance in his own house, it is better to die than to live. I have a joy in life that passeth all understanding; but it is not in its present Epiphany and Incarnation. Bodily torture! All who have been with me can bear witness that I can bear it like an Indian. It is constitutional with me to sit still, and look earnestly upon it and ask it what it is? Yea, often and often, the

---

[1] Compare *Table Talk*, for September 26, 1830, where a similar statement is made in almost the same words.

[2] The same sentence occurs in a letter to Sir G. Beaumont, dated September 22, 1803. *Coleorton Letters*, i. 6.

seeds of Rabelaisism germinating in me, I have laughed aloud at my own poor metaphysical soul. But these burrs by day of the will and the reason, these total eclipses by night! Oh, it is hard to bear them. I am complaining bitterly to others, I should be administrating comfort; but even this is one way of comfort. There are states of mind in which even distraction is still a diversion; we must none of us *brood;* we are not made to be brooders.

God bless you, dear friend, and

S. T. COLERIDGE.

Mrs. C. will get clean flannels ready for me.

CXLIII. TO MATTHEW COATES.[1]

GRETA HALL, KESWICK, December 5, 1803.

DEAR SIR, — After a time of sufferings, great as mere bodily sufferings can well be conceived to be, and which the horrors of my sleep and night screams (so loud and so frequent as to make me almost a nuisance in my own house) seemed to carry beyond mere *body,* counterfeiting as it were the tortures of guilt, and what we are told of the punishment of a spiritual world, I am at length a convalescent, but dreading such another bout as much as I dare dread a thing which has no immediate connection with my conscience. My left hand is swollen and inflamed, and the least attempt to bend the fingers very painful, though not half as much so as I could wish; for if I could but fix this Jack-o'-lanthorn of a disease in my hand or foot, I should expect complete recovery in a year or two! But though I have no hope of this, I have a persuasion strong as fate, that from twelve to eighteen months' residence in a genial climate would send me back to dear old England a sample of the first resurrection. Mr. Wordsworth, who has seen me in all my illnesses for

---

[1] The MS. of this letter was given to my father by the Rev. Dr. Wreford. I know nothing of the person to whom it was addressed, except that he was "Matthew Coates, Esq., of Bristol."

nearly four years, and noticed this strange dependence
on the state of my moral feelings and the state of the
atmosphere conjointly, is decidedly of the same opinion.
Accordingly, after many sore struggles of mind from
reluctance to quit my children for so long a time, I have
arranged my affairs fully and finally, and hope to set sail
for Madeira in the first vessel that clears out from Liverpool for that place.   Robert Southey, who lives with us,
informed me that Mrs. Matthew Coates had a near relative
(a brother, I believe) in that island, the Dr. Adams[1] who
wrote a very nice little pamphlet on Madeira, relative to
the different sorts of consumption, and which I have now
on my desk.   I need not say that it would be a great
comfort to me to be introduced to him by a letter from
you or Mrs. Coates, entreating him to put me in a way of
living as cheaply as possible.   I have no appetites, passions, or vanities which lead to expense ; it is now absolute
habit to me, indeed, to consider my eating and drinking
as a course of medicine.   In books only am I intemperate
— they have been both bane and blessing to me.   For
the last three years I have not read less than eight hours
a day whenever I have been well enough to be out of bed,
or even to sit up in it.   Quiet, therefore, a comfortable
bed and bedroom, and still better than that, the comfort
of kind faces, English tongues, and English hearts now
and then, — this is the sum total of my wants, as it is a
thing which I *need*.   I am far too contented with solitude.
The same fullness of mind, the same crowding of thoughts
and constitutional vivacity of feeling which makes me
sometimes the first fiddle, and too often a watchman's
rattle in society, renders me likewise independent of its
excitements.   However, I am wondrously calmed down
since you saw me — perhaps through this unremitting
disease, affliction, and self-discipline.

[1] Dr. Joseph Adams, the biographer of Hunter, who in 1810 recommended Coleridge to the care of
Mr. James Gillman.

Mrs. Coleridge desires me to remember her with respectful regards to Mrs. Coates, and to enquire into the history of your little family. I have three children, *Hartley*, seven years old, *Derwent*, three years, and *Sara*, one year on the 23d of this month. *Hartley* is considered a genius by Wordsworth and Southey; indeed by every one who has seen much of him. But what is of much more consequence and much less doubtful, he has the sweetest temper and most awakened moral feelings of any child I ever saw. He is very backward in his book-learning, cannot write at all, and a very lame reader. We have never been anxious about it, taking it for granted that loving me, and seeing how I love books, he would come to it of his own accord, and so it has proved, for in the last month he has made more progress than in all his former life. Having learnt everything almost from the mouths of people whom he loves, he has connected with his words and notions a passion and a feeling which would appear strange to those who had seen no children but such as had been taught almost everything in books. *Derwent* is a large, fat, beautiful child, quite the *pride* of the village, as Hartley is the *darling*. Southey says wickedly that " all Hartley's guts are in his brains, and all Derwent's brains are in his guts." Verily the constitutional differences in the children are great indeed. From earliest infancy Hartley was absent, a mere dreamer at his meals, put the food into his mouth by one effort, and made a second effort to remember it was there and swallow it. With little Derwent it is a time of rapture and jubilee, and any story that has not *pie* or *cake* in it comes very flat to him. Yet he is but a baby. Our girl is a darling little thing, with large blue eyes, a quiet creature that, as I have often said, seems to bask in a sunshine as mild as moonlight, of her own happiness. Oh! bless them! Next to the Bible, Shakespeare, and Milton, *they* are the three books from which I

have learned the most, and the most important and with
the greatest delight.

I have been thus prolix about me and mine purposely,
to induce you to tell me something of yourself and yours.

Believe me, I have never ceased to think of you with
respect and a sort of yearning. You were the first man
from whom I heard that article of my faith enunciated
which is the nearest to my heart, — the pure fountain of
all my moral and religious feelings and comforts, — I
mean the absolute Impersonality of the Deity.

I remain, my dear sir, with unfeigned esteem and with
good wishes, ever yours,

S. T. COLERIDGE.

www.ingramcontent.com/pod-product-compliance
Lightning Source LLC
Chambersburg PA
CBHW031811270326
41932CB00008B/384